GETTING STARTED

WELCOME

Congratulations on taking the first step toward becoming an **AWS Certified CloudOps Engineer Associate!** By choosing this resource, you've gained access to top-quality practice tests designed to thoroughly prepare you for your exam.

This book includes 4 full-length practice exams, each with 65 questions, covering all domains of the latest **SOA-C03** exam. These 260 practice questions mirror the format and difficulty of the real AWS exam, ensuring you're fully prepared to pass on your first attempt.

To maximize your chances for success, we recommend re-taking these practice tests until you consistently score 80% or higher - that's when you're ready to sit the exam and achieve a great score!

If you're looking for easy-to-pass questions, then these Practice Tests are <u>not</u> for you! Our students love these high-quality practice tests because they match the level of difficulty and pattern of the actual exam and help them understand the AWS concepts. Students who have recently passed the **SOA-C03** exam confirm that these questions are the closest to the real thing.

Over 1,000,000 students have trusted our resources to achieve their AWS certifications. With dedicated effort and the help of these practice tests, you'll be perfectly positioned to succeed in your **AWS Certified CloudOps Engineer Associate** exam and accelerate your cloud career.

Wishing you all the best on your cloud journey!

Neal Davis

Neal Davis
Founder of Digital Cloud Training

WHAT DO OTHER STUDENTS SAY?

Check out the excellent reviews from our many students who successfully passed their AWS exam:

*****

These practice questions are very similar to the ones in the actual exam, and actually explain both the right answers AND the wrong answers, Would definitely recommend.

*****

Neal practice tests are the best and top-notch! The questions and material is framed well and meet AWS testing standards

*****

I passed my exam recently. Many thanks for these practice exams - they surely helped.

*****

A must have. Very useful for training and to learn. I don't know how to do whithout it.

*****

I've been using this book to evaluate my knowlege as I prepare to certifiy. I've already worked through the AWS training, but the questions in the book force me to think about how to apply the knowlege. If I don't guess the correct answer, the explanations help me understand the answer, so I can further tune my understanding. I would highly recommend this.

ABOUT THE AWS CERTIFIED CLOUDOPS ENGINEER ASSOCIATE

In 2025, AWS renamed the AWS Certified SysOps Administrator Associate to the AWS Certified CloudOps Engineer Associate. The change reflects modern operations roles while keeping the same core purpose: proving you can run, monitor, automate, and troubleshoot workloads on AWS.

The exam code moved from SOA-C02 to SOA-C03 to signal the update.

The exam remains associate level with 65 questions over 130 minutes. The passing score is 720 out of 1000. Registration costs USD $150, and you can test online with a proctor or at a test center.

The hands-on labs that were removed in March 2023 remain retired, so the format is multiple-choice and multiple-response throughout.

HOW TO BEST USE THIS RESOURCE

The practice questions are organized into 4 sets, with each set provided twice: once without answers and explanations and once with them. This structure allows you to choose from two methods of preparation:

1. Exam simulation

To simulate the real exam, use the "PRACTICE QUESTIONS ONLY" sets. Grab a pen and paper to record your answers for all 65 questions. After completing each set, check your responses using the "PRACTICE QUESTIONS, ANSWERS & EXPLANATIONS" section.

To calculate your total score, count the number of correct answers and multiply them by 1.54 (weighting out of 100%) to get your percentage score. For example, if you answered 50 questions correctly, your score would be 50 x 1.54 = 77%. The pass mark for the official AWS exam is 72% (scaled scoring).

2: Training Mode

To use the practice questions as a learning tool, work directly with the "PRACTICE QUESTIONS, ANSWERS & EXPLANATIONS" sets. Read the in-depth explanations as you move through the questions, to deepen your understanding of AWS concepts.

KEY TRAINING ADVICE

AIM FOR A MINIMUM SCORE OF 80%: While the official AWS exam has a pass mark of 72%, we recommend repeatedly retaking our AWS practice exams until you consistently score 80% or higher. Dedicate time to carefully study the explanations for each question in detail. Once you achieve the recommended score in the practice tests - you are ready to sit the exam and achieve a great score!

FAMILIARIZE YOURSELF WITH THE QUESTION STYLE: Our AWS practice exams mimic the format and structure of the latest SAA-C03 exam. By practicing with these tests, you'll become familiar with the question styles and structure, ensuring you are fully prepared for the real AWS certification exam experience.

DEEPEN YOUR KNOWLEDGE: While our AWS practice exams closely match the exam pattern, they are NOT brain dumps. Memorizing answers alone does not guarantee success. Instead, use these tests to build a deeper understanding of the AWS concepts. This approach ensures you're fully prepared to answer any question that may appear on the actual AWS exam.

YOUR PATHWAY TO SUCCESS

1: **BUILD FOUNDATIONAL KNOWLEDGE**
2: **ASSESS YOUR EXAM READINESS**
3: **REVIEW KEY FACTS**
4: **ACE YOUR EXAM**

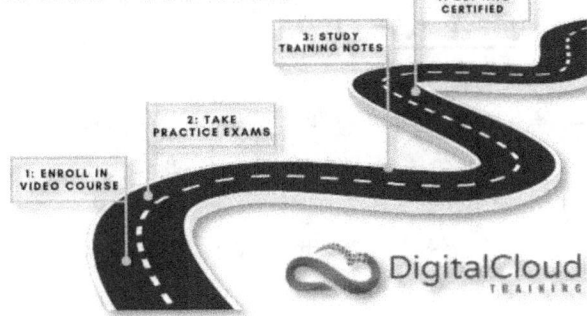

On-demand Video Course

We recommend starting with the **AWS Certified CloudOps Engineer Associate** video course from Digital Cloud Training. This comprehensive course will help you build a strong foundation in AWS and familiarize yourself with the platform before assessing your exam readiness with these practice exams.

Training Notes

The Training Notes for the **AWS Certified CloudOps Engineer Associate** by Digital Cloud Training provide an in-depth understanding of AWS services. Deep dive into the **SOA-C03** exam objectives with detailed facts, tables and diagrams to shortcut your time to success. To learn more about our training resources, visit: https://digitalcloud.training/aws-certified-cloudops-engineer-associate

Cloud Mastery Bootcamp

Did you know that Digital Cloud Training offers remote live training to help you achieve your cloud career goals? The Cloud Mastery Bootcamp is designed to fast-track your cloud career through structured, hands-on training, and comprehensive support.

The Cloud Mastery Bootcamp offers direct access to expert instructors, personalized career guidance, and real-world projects - everything you need to develop job-ready skills for your next-level cloud role. Explore the Cloud Mastery Bootcamp to see if it's the right fit for your career goals:

https://digitalcloud.training/cloud-mastery-bootcamp/

LIMITED TIME BONUS OFFER

As a special bonus, we're excited to offer **FREE Access** to the Online Exam Simulator on the Digital Cloud Training website! The exam simulator has the same format, style, time limit and passing score as the real AWS exam. You get to evaluate your progress and identify your strengths and weaknesses. Simply the best way to assess your exam readiness.

Navigate to the BONUS OFFER section at end of this book for instructions on how to claim your bonus.

CONTACT & FEEDBACK

We aim to provide you with a 5-star learning experience and ensure you get the most value from these training resources. If for any reason you are not 100% satisfied, please contact us at support@digitalcloud.training. We promise to address all questions and concerns, typically within 24 hours.

The AWS platform is evolving quickly, and the exam tracks these changes with a typical lag of around 6 months. Your feedback plays a crucial role in helping us keep our resources aligned with the latest exam content. If you encounter topics on your exam that weren't covered in our materials, please share your feedback: https://digitalcloud.training/student-feedback/. We appreciate your input that will help us further improve our AWS training resources.

REVIEWS REALLY MATTER

If you enjoy reading reviews, please consider paying it forward. Reviews guide students and allow us to continually improve our courses. We value every honest review and truly appreciate your feedback. We'd be thrilled if you could leave us a rating at amazon.com/ryp or your local amazon store (e.g. amazon.co.uk/ryp).

JOIN THE AWS COMMUNITY

Connect with fellow learners and AWS professionals by joining our private LinkedIn group 'AWS Certification & Training' - a great space to ask questions, share knowledge, and exchange exam tips with the AWS community. To join the discussion about all things related to AWS on Slack, visit: http://digitalcloud.training/slack for instructions.

CONNECT WITH US ON SOCIAL MEDIA

Stay updated and engage with us on your favorite platforms.

All Links available on https://digitalcloud.training/about-neal-davis-and-digital-cloud-training/

  digitalcloud.training   youtube.com/c/digitalcloudtraining

  facebook.com/digitalcloudtraining   Twitter / X @digitalcloudt

  linkedin.com/company/digitalcloudtraining   Instagram @digitalcloudtraining

TABLE OF CONTENTS

GETTING STARTED 1
    Welcome 1
    What do other Students say? 1
    About the AWS Certified CloudOps Engineer Associate 2
    How to best use this Resource 2
    Key Training Advice 2
    Your Pathway to Success 3
    Limited Time Bonus Offer 3
    Contact & Feedback 3
    Reviews Really Matter 3
    Join the AWS Community 4
    Connect with us on Social Media 4

TABLE OF CONTENTS 5
SET 1: PRACTICE QUESTIONS ONLY 6
SET 1: PRACTICE QUESTIONS AND ANSWERS 23
SET 2: PRACTICE QUESTIONS ONLY 75
SET 2: PRACTICE QUESTIONS AND ANSWERS 92
SET 3: PRACTICE QUESTIONS ONLY 142
SET 3: PRACTICE QUESTIONS AND ANSWERS 157
SET 4: PRACTICE QUESTIONS ONLY 200
SET 4: PRACTICE QUESTIONS AND ANSWERS 217

CONCLUSION 266
    Reach out and Connect 266
    Bonus: FREE Access to Online Exam Simulator 266

LIVE BOOTCAMPS AND ON-DEMAND TRAINING 267
    Cloud Mastery Bootcamp (Virtual Classroom) 267
    On-demand / Self-Paced AWS Training 267

ABOUT THE AUTHOR 268
    Connect with us on Social Media 268

SET 1: PRACTICE QUESTIONS ONLY

For training purposes, go directly to Set 1: Practice Questions, Answers & Explanations

QUESTION 1

Change control procedures at a company mandate that all production changes in the infrastructure must be carefully reviewed before deploying updates to their AWS CloudFormation stacks.

Which action will allow an Administrator to understand the impact of these changes before implementation?

1. Implement a blue/green strategy using AWS Elastic Beanstalk.
2. Perform a canary deployment using Application Load Balancers and target groups.
3. Create a change set for the running stack.
4. Submit the update using the UpdateStack API call.

QUESTION 2

A CloudOps Administrator needs to restrict access to a bucket to users connecting from the company IP address range. The company address range is: 51.210.100.0/24 and the Administrator has created the following policy:

```
{
        "Version": "2008-10-17",
        "Id": "S3BucketPolicyId",
        "Statement": [
                {
                        "Sid": "S3Allow",
                        "Effect": "Allow",
                        "Principal": "*",
                        "Action": "s3:*",
                        "Resource": [
                                "arn:aws:53:::examples3bucket",
                                "arn:aws:s3:::examples3bucket/*"
                        ]
                },
                {
                        "Sid": "IPAllow",
                        "Effect": "Allow",
                        "Principal": "*",
                        "Action": "s3:*",
                        "Resource": [
                                "arn:aws:s3:::examples3bucket",
                                "arn:aws:s3: : :examples3bucket/*"
                        ],
                        "Condition": {
                                "NotIpAddress": {
                                        "aws: SourceIP": "51.210.100.0/24"
```

                }
            }
        }
    ]
}

During testing it has been identified that users can connect from IP addresses outside the company IP address range.

How can the Administrator address this issue?

1. Modify the Condition operator to include both NotIpAddress and IpAddress to prevent unauthorized access to the S3 bucket.
2. Modify the Condition element from the IAM policy to aws:StringEquals instead of aws:SourceIp.
3. Modify the IAM policy instead of the bucket policy to restrict users from accessing the bucket based on their source IP addresses.
4. Change Effect from Allow to Deny in the second statement of the policy to deny requests not from the source IP range.

QUESTION 3

A CloudOps Administrator needs to add SSL/TLS encryption for a website that uses an internet-facing Application Load Balancer (ALB). The Administrator is attempting to create a certificate using AWS Certificate Manager (ACM). After the request was submitted using the ALB fully qualified domain name (FQDN) it failed with the error "Domain Not Allowed."

How can the administrator fix this issue?

1. Submit a new request in ACM with the correct domain name rather than the ALB FQDN.
2. Use email validation and confirm ownership of the domain through the root account email address.
3. Use DNS validation and follow the instructions to add a CNAME record to the hosted zone in Amazon Route 53.
4. Contact AWS Support and verify the request by answering security challenge questions.

QUESTION 4

A CloudOps Administrator has been tasked with deploying a web application on two Amazon EC2 instances behind an Application Load Balancer (ALB). The database layer will also run on two EC2 instances. The deployment must include high availability across Availability Zones (AZs) and public access must be limited as much as possible.

How should this be achieved within an Amazon VPC?

1. Create a public subnet in each AZ for the ALB, a private subnet in each AZ for the web servers, and a private subnet in each AZ for the database servers.
2. Create a public subnet in each AZ for the ALB, a public subnet in each AZ for the web servers, and a public subnet in each AZ for the database servers.
3. Create a public subnet in each AZ for the ALB, a private subnet in each AZ for the web servers, and a public subnet in each AZ for the database servers.
4. Create a public subnet in each AZ for the ALB, a public subnet in each AZ for the web servers, and a private subnet in each AZ for the database servers.

QUESTION 5

A company runs a data center in their office location. The company needs to provide low-latency local access to image files for users in the office. A synchronized backup of the images must be maintained in an offsite location.

Which AWS storage solution would allow access to the image data for local users while also providing for disaster recovery?

1. Create an AWS Storage Gateway volume gateway configured as a stored volume. Mount it from clients using Internet Small Computer System Interface (iSCSI).
2. Mount an Amazon EFS volume on a local server. Share this volume with employees who need access to the images.
3. Store the images in Amazon S3 and use AWS Server Migration Service to enable synchronization of S3 data to the local server.
4. Use Amazon S3 for file storage and enable S3 Transfer Acceleration to maintain a cache for frequently used files to increase local performance.

QUESTION 6

A CloudOps Administrator needs to audit requests to AWS Organizations for creating new AWS accounts. The company users authenticate to AWS through federation.

What should the Administrator review to determine who made the request?

1. AWS CloudTrail for the federated identity user name.
2. AWS IAM Access Analyzer for the federated user name.
3. AWS X-Ray traces for the federated identity user name.
4. Federated identity provider logs for the user name.

QUESTION 7

Employees in an IT department have been using individual AWS accounts that are not under the control of the company. The security department has requested that these accounts be linked to the central organization in AWS Organizations.

Which action should a CloudOps Administrator take to accomplish this?

1. Add each existing account to the central organization using AWS IAM.
2. Create a new organization in each account and join them to the central organization.
3. Log in to each existing account and add them to the central organization.
4. Send each existing account an invitation from the central organization.

QUESTION 8

A CloudOps Administrator accidentally deleted a folder containing important data from an Amazon EBS volume. A recent snapshot of the volume is available.

What should the Administrator do to restore the user's file from the snapshot?

1. Launch a new Amazon EC2 instance in the same Availability Zone and copy the deleted folder over the network.
2. Use the Amazon EC2 console to browse the contents of the snapshot, locate the folder, and then copy it to the EBS volume.
3. Create a new EBS volume from the snapshot, attach the volume to an Amazon EC2 instance, and copy the deleted file.
4. Restore the file from the snapshot onto the EC2 instance using the Amazon EC2 console.

QUESTION 9

A website runs on Amazon EC2 instances and uses an Amazon RDS database with the MySQL engine. A caching layer based on Amazon ElastiCache for Redis (cluster mode enabled) is used to improve read performance.

A new product launch is expected to result in a significant traffic increase over the first few days, potentially doubling the load on the website.

What can a CloudOps Administrator do to ensure improved read times for users during the event?

1. Add shards to the existing Redis cluster.
2. Offload static data to Amazon S3.
3. Use a message queue to cache data.
4. Use Amazon RDS Multi-AZ.

QUESTION 10

A CloudOps Administrator needs to control access to a small group of Amazon EC2 instances. Specific tags have been added to the EC2 instances.

Which additional actions should the Administrator take to control access? (Select TWO.)

1. Attach an IAM policy to the users or groups that require access.
2. Attach an IAM role to the Amazon EC2 instances.
3. Create an Auto Scaling group for the EC2 instances and add a specific tag.
4. Create an IAM policy that grants access to the instances based on the Principal element.
5. Create an IAM policy that grants access to the instances with the specific tag using the Condition element.

QUESTION 11

A CloudOps Administrator has deployed an infrastructure stack for a company using AWS CloudFormation. The company made some manual changes to the infrastructure.

The Administrator needs to capture the changes and update the CloudFormation template. How can the Administrator determine what changes were made?

1. Create a new CloudFormation stack based on the changes that were made. Delete the old stack and deploy the new stack.
2. Update the CloudFormation stack using a change set. Review the changes and update the stack.
3. Update the CloudFormation stack by modifying the selected parameters in the template to match what was changed.
4. Use drift detection on the CloudFormation stack. Use the output to update the CloudFormation template and redeploy the stack.

QUESTION 12

A company wishes to restrict the ability to launch specific instance types to specific teams. The company has separate AWS accounts for its development and production teams and uses federated login with single sign-on (SSO). The AWS accounts are both under one organization in AWS Organizations.

How can a CloudOps Administrator restrict users in the development team's account so they can only launch T2 instances in the us-east-1 Region? (Select TWO.)

1. Create a developer IAM group inside the development team account with an IAM policy to allow EC2 T2 instances.
2. Create a developer IAM group inside the production team account and attach an IAM policy to allow EC2 T2 instances.
3. Create a developer IAM role inside the development team account with an IAM policy to allow EC2 T2 instances.
4. Create a service control policy (SCP) to deny instance launches unless the instance type is T2 and apply it to the developer organizational unit (OU).
5. Create a service control policy (SCP) to deny instance launches unless the instance type is T2 and apply it to the root.

QUESTION 13

A company runs a fleet of Amazon EC2 instances in a private subnet. The instances must send data to peers over the internet. A recent bill shows that the NAT gateway charges have increased significantly.

How can a CloudOps Administrator identify which instances are creating the most network traffic?
1. Enable flow logs on the NAT gateway elastic network interface and use Amazon CloudWatch insights to filter data based on the source IP addresses.
2. Run an AWS Cost and Usage report and group the findings by instance ID.
3. Use an Elastic IP on each instance, monitor the metrics generated in Amazon CloudWatch, and filter by instance ID.
4. View the Amazon CloudTrail logs and look for the API actions to use the NAT gateway.

QUESTION 14

A company manage an application that is deployed on Amazon EC2 instances within a private subnet. The EC2 instances must be restricted from the internet for security and compliance reasons. The CloudOps team must be able to manage the instances from the corporate office using the SSH protocol.

Which combination of actions should be taken to permit SSH access to the EC2 instances while meeting the security and compliance requirements? (Select TWO.)

1. Attach a NAT gateway to the VPC and configure routing.
2. Attach a virtual private gateway to the VPC and configure routing.
3. Attach an internet gateway to the VPC and configure routing.
4. Configure a VPN connection back to the corporate office.
5. Configure a Network Load Balancer in front of the EC2 instances.

QUESTION 15

A CloudOps Administrator has stored the login credentials for a database as secure string parameters in AWS Systems Manager Parameter Store. An application running on an Amazon EC2 instance must use the credentials to access the database.

What is the MOST secure way to grant the application access to the credentials?

1. Create an IAM role for the EC2 instances and grant the role permission to read the Systems Manager parameters.
2. Create an IAM group for the application and grant the group permission to read the Systems Manager parameters.
3. Create an IAM policy for the application and grant the policy permission to read the Systems Manager parameters.
4. Create an IAM user for the application and grant the user permission to read the Systems Manager parameters.

QUESTION 16

An application runs across two Amazon EC2 instances behind an Application Load Balancer (ALB) across two Availability Zones. An Amazon DynamoDB table is used by the application. Amazon Route 53 record sets are used to route requests for dynamic content to the ALB and requests for static content to an Amazon S3 bucket. Users of the application have reported poor performance with long loading times.

Which actions should be taken to improve the performance of the website? (Select TWO.)

1. Add Amazon CloudFront caching for static content.
2. Move the dynamic content from the web servers to Amazon S3.
3. Enable Amazon Route 53 latency-based routing.
4. Implement Amazon EC2 Auto Scaling for the web servers.
5. Move the static content from Amazon S3 to the web servers.

QUESTION 17

A web application runs on two Amazon EC2 instances behind an Application Load Balancer (ALB). There have been reports from users of poor performance and HTTP 503 and 504 errors. A CloudOps Administrator has reviewed Amazon CloudWatch metrics and discovered that the CPU utilization on the instances is extremely high.

Which action should the Administrator take to resolve these issues?

1. Place the EC2 instances into an Amazon EC2 Auto Scaling group.
2. Configure the load balancer to use a TCP listener instead of HTTPS.
3. Enable sticky sessions on the Application Load Balancer.
4. Enable cross-zone load balancing on the Application Load Balancer.

QUESTION 18

An application server running on an Amazon EC2 instance recently failed due to an Amazon EBS volume running out of space. The failure caused an outage of a critical application.

Which steps should a CloudOps Administrator take to prevent this from happening again?

1. Configure Amazon CloudWatch Events to monitor Amazon EC2 status checks for the status of the EBS volumes. Post a notification to an Amazon SNS topic to notify the if the disk is impaired.
2. Create an AWS Lambda function that monitors the disk space metrics using the Amazon EBS API. Post a notification to an Amazon SNS topic when disk space is running low.
3. Enable detailed monitoring for the EC2 instances. Create an Amazon CloudWatch alarm to notify the Administrator when disk space is running low.
4. Install the Amazon CloudWatch agent on the EC2 instance to collect disk metrics. Create a CloudWatch alarm to notify the Administrator when disk space is running low.

QUESTION 19

A CloudOps Administrator deployed an application using AWS CloudFormation. The application runs on Amazon EC2 instances in an Auto Scaling group behind an Application Load Balancer (ALB). A new version of the application must be deployed. The update must avoid DNS changes and support rollback

Which solution should the Administrator use to meet the deployment requirements for application update?

1. Configure the Auto Scaling group to use lifecycle hooks. Deploy new instances with the new application version. Complete the lifecycle hook action once healthy.
2. Create a new Amazon Machine Image (AMI) containing the updated code. Create a launch configuration with the AMI. Update the Auto Scaling group to use the new launch configuration.
3. Deploy a second CloudFormation stack. Wait for the application to be available. Cut over to the new Application Load Balancer.
4. Modify the CloudFormation template to use an AutoScalingReplacingUpdate policy. Update the stack. Perform a second update with the new release.

QUESTION 20

A company is using an AWS Storage Gateway volume gateway configuration running on a virtual machine. Usage of the Storage Gateway has recently increased, and users have reported that performance of the iSCSI drives has degraded. A CloudOps Administrator checked the Amazon CloudWatch metrics and noticed the CacheHitPercent metric is below 55% and the CachePercentUsed metric is above 95%.

What steps are MOST likely to resolve the performance issues?

1. Optimize the iSCSI settings on the Storage Gateway's iSCSI initiator to achieve higher I/O performance.
2. Create a larger disk for the cached volume. In the AWS Management Console, edit the local disks, then select the new disk as the cached volume.
3. Ensure that the physical disks for the Storage Gateway are in a RAID 1 configuration to allow higher throughput.
4. Create a recovery snapshot from the volume, then deploy and activate a new volume gateway from the snapshot.

QUESTION 21

A company plans to use AWS CloudFormation to deploy their infrastructure using templates. The deployments will include several environments across multiple AWS Regions. A CloudOps Administrator plans to write a single template that can be reused for each environment deployment.

What is the recommended way to use AWS CloudFormation to meet this requirement?

1. Use parameters to provision the resources.
2. Use nested stacks to provision the resources.
3. Use change sets to provision additional environments.
4. Use cross-stack references to provision the resources.

QUESTION 22

A CloudOps Administrator has installed the CloudWatch agent on several Amazon EC2 instances. The agent has been configured to send custom metrics to Amazon CloudWatch. The Administrator needs to create a CloudWatch dashboard to display these metrics.

What steps should the Administrator take to complete this task?

1. Select the AWS Namespace, filter by metric name, then add to the dashboard.
2. Select the appropriate widget and metrics from the custom namespace, then add to the dashboard.
3. Open the CloudWatch Logs console, create metric filters, and select the custom metrics.
4. Open the CloudWatch console, then from CloudWatch Events, add all custom metrics.

QUESTION 23

A manager has requested that all Amazon S3 buckets must have logging enabled due to compliance requirements. A CloudOps Administrator needs to ensure that the compliance requirements are met whilst allowing teams to continue to create S3 buckets.

How can this be achieved for both existing and new S3 buckets?

1. Create a CloudWatch Alarm that notifies the Administrator when a bucket is created without logging enabled.
2. Create an IAM policy that restricts the ability to create new buckets to specific teams.
3. Auto remediate any non-compliant S3 buckets with the AWS Config managed rule S3_BUCKET_LOGGING_ENABLED.
4. Create an AWS Lambda function to automatically delete any Amazon S3 buckets if logging is not enabled.

QUESTION 24

A CloudOps Administrator is responsible for a large fleet of Amazon EC2 instances. There is an important event planned and the Administrator needs to understand if any instances will be affected by upcoming hardware maintenance.

Which option would provide this information with the LEAST administrative overhead?

1. Deploy the CloudWatch agent on all instances and monitor availability.
2. View any planned maintenance in the AWS Service Health Dashboard.
3. Monitor AWS CloudTrail for any StopInstances API calls that are issued.
4. Review the Personal Health Dashboard for any scheduled maintenance.

QUESTION 25

A company experienced a security incident and has decided to block public access to HTTP (TCP port 80). All incoming web traffic must use HTTPS (TCP port 443). A CloudOps Administrator must provide real-time compliance reporting on security groups in the Amazon VPC.

How can the Administrator provide near real-time compliance reporting?

1. Enable AWS Trusted Advisor create a CloudWatch alarm that triggers on Red alerts for the unrestricted ports check.
2. Schedule an AWS Lambda function to run hourly to scan and evaluate all security groups and send a report.
3. Use AWS Config to enable the restricted-common-ports rule and add port 80 to the parameters.
4. Use Amazon Inspector to evaluate the security groups during scans and send the completed reports.

QUESTION 26

A company uses an Amazon ElastiCache Memcached cluster for a popular website. The CloudOps Administrator received reports of performance issues. The Administrator checked the CloudWatch metrics and noticed high CPU utilization.

Which remediation steps should be taken to resolve this issue? (Select TWO.)

1. Add a larger Amazon EBS volume to the ElastiCache cluster nodes.
2. Add a load balancer to route traffic to the ElastiCache cluster.
3. Add additional nodes to the existing ElastiCache cluster.
4. Create an Auto Scaling group for the ElastiCache cluster.
5. Vertically scale the ElastiCache cluster by changing the node type.

QUESTION 27

A company uses AWS Service Catalog to manage approved services. A new AWS account has been created and a CloudOps Administrator needs to create a replica of the company's existing AWS infrastructure in the new AWS account. Currently, an AWS Service Catalog portfolio is used to create and manage resources.

What is the MOST efficient way to accomplish this?

1. Create an AWS CloudFormation template to redeploy the AWS Service Catalog portfolio in the new AWS account.
2. Manually create an AWS Service Catalog portfolio in the new AWS account and recreate the original portfolio.
3. Run an AWS Lambda function to create a new AWS Service Catalog portfolio based on the output of the DescribePortfolio API operation.
4. Share the AWS Service Catalog portfolio with the other AWS account and import the portfolio into the AWS account.

QUESTION 28

A company is creating a new application that will run in a hybrid environment. The application processes data that must be secured and the developers require encryption in-transit across shared networks and encryption at rest.

Which combination of actions should a CloudOps Administrator take to meet these requirements? (Select TWO.)

1. Configure an AWS VPN between the on-premises data center and AWS.
2. Use AWS Certificate Manager to create TLS/SSL certificates.
3. Use AWS CloudHSM to encrypt the data using a CMK.
4. Use AWS KMS to create TLS/SSL certificates.
5. Use AWS KMS to manage the encryption keys used for data encryption.

QUESTION 29

A company plans to use Amazon Route 53 to enable high availability for a website running on-premises. The website consists of an active and passive server. Route 53 must be configured to route traffic to the primary active server if the associated health returns a 2xx status code. All other traffic should be directed to the secondary passive server.

A CloudOps Administrator needs to configure the record type and health check. Which options should the Administrator choose?

1. An A record for each server with an Amazon Route 53 HTTP health check.
2. An A record for each server with an Amazon Route 53 TCP health check.
3. An alias record with evaluate health set to yes and associated with a Route 53 HTTP health check.
4. An alias record with evaluate health set to yes and associated with a Route 53 TCP health check.

QUESTION 30

A network administrator made a change to the networking configuration of an Amazon VPC. After the change, an application server running on Amazon EC2 is unable to connect to an Amazon RDS MySQL database. A CloudOps Administrator must identify the root cause.

What should the CloudOps Administrator analyze?

1. VPC Flow Logs.
2. Amazon Elastic Load Balancing logs.
3. Amazon Auto Scaling logs.
4. Amazon RDS MySQL error logs.

QUESTION 31

A CloudOps Administrator manages an application that is used by several front-end servers in different regions. An AWS Web Application Firewall (WAF) is used to protect the application. Each request contains a header that includes the ID of the front-end server making the request. The CloudOps Administrator wants to identify and count the requests from each front-end server.

Which condition should be added to the web ACL of the AWS WAF to accomplish this?

1. Size constraint
2. ID match
3. IP match
4. String match

QUESTION 32

A CloudOps Administrator manages and application that uses an Application Load Balancer (ALB) in front of six Amazon EC2 instances in a single security group. The Administrator notices that the CloudWatch metric for HealthyHostCount has dropped from 6 to 2.

What is MOST likely causing this issue?

1. The security groups of the instances are not allowing the ALB health checks to succeed.
2. The route tables are not updated to allow traffic to flow between the ALB and the EC2 instances.
3. The ALB health checks have failed, and the ALB has taken EC2 instances out of service.
4. The Amazon Route 53 health checks have failed, and the ALB has taken EC2 instances out of service.

QUESTION 33

A company runs an Amazon RDS multi-AZ deployment for an eCommerce website. An automated failover occurred, and a CloudOps Administrator needs to determine the root cause.

Which of the following are possible conditions that may cause the database to failover? (Select TWO.)

1. Read contention on the secondary database.
2. A storage failure on the primary database.
3. Write contention on the primary database.

4. Database corruption errors.
5. The database instance type was changed.

QUESTION 34

A web application runs on several Amazon EC2 instances in an Auto Scaling group across all Availability Zones in the Region. A CloudOps Administrator notices that the ASG does not launch new instances during busy periods. The maximum capacity of the ASG has not been reached.

What should the Administrator do to identify the cause of the issue? (Select TWO.)

1. Use AWS Trusted Advisor to check if service limits have been reached.
2. Check the AWS Personal Health Dashboard for outage events.
3. Monitor limits in AWS Systems Manager.
4. Use Amazon Inspector to view performance information.
5. Use AWS CloudTrail to check the result of RunInstances requests.

QUESTION 35

A CloudOps Administrator must choose an EBS volume type that will be attached to an Amazon EC2 instance. The volume will be used by a big data application and the application data will be accessed infrequently and stored sequentially.

What EBS volume type will be the MOST cost-effective solution?

1. Provisioned IOPS SSD (io1)
2. Throughput Optimized HDD (st1)
3. Cold HDD (sc1)
4. General Purpose SSD (gp2)

QUESTION 36

An application runs on several Amazon EC2 instances behind an Application Load Balancer (ALB). The instances run in an Auto Scaling group that is configured to determine the health status of EC2 instances using both EC2 status checks and ALB health checks. An application fault has been detected and it is necessary to analyze unhealthy instances before they are terminated.

What should a CloudOps Administrator do to accomplish this?

1. Configure the Auto Scaling group to only use ALB health checks so instances are taken out of service but are not terminated.
2. Create an AWS Lambda function that takes a snapshot of the instances before they are terminated.
3. Implement Amazon CloudWatch Events to capture lifecycle events and trigger an AWS Lambda function for remediation.
4. Use an Amazon EC2 Auto Scaling lifecycle hook to pause instance termination after the instance has been removed from service.

QUESTION 37

A company has created an Amazon CloudFront distribution in front of an application. The application uses the domain name www.mywebapp.com which is managed using Amazon Route 53. A CloudOps Administrator has been asked to configure the application to be accessed using www.mywebapp.com through CloudFront.

What is the MOST cost-effective way to achieve this?

1. Create a CNAME record in Amazon Route 53 that points to the CloudFront distribution URL.
2. Create an Alias record in Amazon Route 53 that points to the CloudFront distribution URL.
3. Create an A record in Amazon Route 53 that points to the public IP address of the web application.

4. Create an SRV record in Amazon Route 53 that points to the custom domain name A record.

QUESTION 38

A company has several AWS accounts in a single organization in AWS Organizations. The company requires that no Amazon S3 buckets can be deleted its production account.

What is the SIMPLEST approach to ensuring that the S3 buckets in the production account cannot be deleted?

1. Set up MFA Delete on all the S3 buckets in the production account to prevent the buckets from being deleted.
2. Use a service control policy to deny the s3:DeleteBucket API action in the production account.
3. Create an IAM group that has an IAM policy to deny the s3:DeleteBucket action on all buckets in the production account.
4. Create an IAM role that restricts the API actions that can be used for Amazon S3 and assign it to EC2 instances.

QUESTION 39

A company runs an application on Amazon EC2 instances in a VPC private subnet. The instances must upload objects to an Amazon S3 bucket. The company requires access to the bucket to be restricted to the EC2 instances in the private network and data must not traverse the public network.

What actions should the CloudOps Administrator take to meet these requirements?

1. Create a VPC endpoint for the S3 bucket and create an IAM policy that conditionally limits all S3 actions on the bucket to the VPC endpoint as the source.
2. Create a VPC endpoint for the S3 bucket and create a S3 bucket policy that conditionally limits all S3 actions on the bucket to the VPC endpoint as the source.
3. Create an AWS VPN tunnel between the VPC private subnet and the Amazon S3 public endpoint.
4. Create a NAT gateway in the VPC and modify the private subnet route table to route all traffic destined for S3 through the NAT gateway.

QUESTION 40

A company uses AWS Organizations to manage several AWS accounts. A department in the company requires a new AWS account. A CloudOps Administrator must create the new account and configure user-defined cost allocation tags.

What should the Administrator do to enable user-defined cost allocation tags?

1. Use the Billing and Cost Management console in the new account to create the new user-defined cost allocation tags.
2. Use the Billing and Cost Management console in the payer account to create the new user-defined cost allocation tags.
3. Use the Tag Editor in the new account to create the new user-defined tags, then use the Billing and Cost Management console in the new account to mark the tags as cost allocation tags.
4. Use the Tag Editor in the new account to create the new user-defined tags, then use the Billing and Cost Management console in the payer account to mark the tags as cost allocation tags.

QUESTION 41

A company runs an application behind an Application Load Balancer (ALB). The CloudOps Administrator has noticed a large number of suspicious HTTP requests hitting the ALB. The requests originate from various IP addresses.

How can the Administrator block this traffic with the LEAST effort?

1. Create an Amazon CloudFront distribution to cache content and automatically block access to the suspicious source IP addresses.

2. Use Amazon GuardDuty to analyze network activity, detect anomalies, and trigger a Lambda function to prevent access.
3. Use AWS Lambda to analyze a VPC Flow Log, detect the suspicious traffic, and block the IP address in the security groups.
4. Create an AWS WAF rate-based rule to block this traffic when it exceeds a defined threshold.

QUESTION 42

A CloudOps Administrator manages an application running on an Auto Scaling group of Amazon EC2 instances behind an Application Load Balancer (ALB). The database layer uses Amazon RDS MySQL with an Amazon ElastiCache for Memcached cluster as a caching layer. The CloudOps Administrator must perform all system patching at 10pm on a Wednesday.

Which resources require the configuration of a maintenance window? (Select TWO.)

1. Elastic Load Balancer
2. Amazon EC2 instances
3. Amazon RDS instance
4. Amazon ElastiCache cluster
5. Amazon EC2 Auto Scaling

QUESTION 43

A fleet of Amazon EC2 instances run in an Amazon VPC. The instances must regularly upload log data to a third-party service using the internet. The third-party service has recently implemented IP whitelisting and requires all uploads to come from a single IP address.

What change should the CloudOps Administrator make to the configuration to enable all instances to continue to upload their log files?

1. Move all of the EC2 instances behind a NAT gateway and provide the gateway IP address to the service.
2. Move all of the EC2 instances behind an internet gateway and provide the gateway IP address to the service.
3. Move all of the EC2 instances into a single subnet and provide the subnet CIDR block to the service.
4. Create a single Elastic Network Interface for the EC2 instances and provide the ENI Elastic IP to the service.

QUESTION 44

A CloudOps Administrator has configured a static website on Amazon S3. The bucket name is "mystaticsite". The Administrator plans to use Amazon Route 53 to route traffic to the website and has configured an A record for www.mystaticsite.com. However, users are unable to connect to www.mystaticsite.com using their browsers.

Which of the following is the cause of this issue?

1. An Amazon CloudFront distribution must be configured for the S3 bucket.
2. The Route 53 record set requires a certificate to be configured.
3. The Route 53 record set must be in the same region as the S3 bucket.
4. The S3 bucket name must match the record set name in Route 53.

QUESTION 45

An Amazon EBS volume attached to an Amazon EC2 instance running a database and is encrypted using AWS KMS customer-managed customer master keys (CMKs). A CloudOps Administrator wants to rotate the AWS KMS keys using automatic key rotation and needs to ensure that the EBS volume encrypted with the current key remains readable.

What should be done to accomplish this?
1. Back up the current KMS data key and enable automatic key rotation.
2. Create a new data key in KMS and assign the key to Amazon EBS.
3. Enable automatic key rotation of the customer master key in KMS.
4. Create a new customer master key in KMS and enable rotation.

QUESTION 46

A CloudOps Administrator has been asked to monitor the costs incurred by each user in an AWS account.

How can a CloudOps Administrator collect this information? (Select TWO.)
1. Activate the createdBy tag in the account.
2. Create user metrics in Amazon CloudWatch.
3. Analyze the usage with Cost Explorer.
4. Use Amazon Inspector to advise on resource costs.
5. Create a billing alarm in AWS Budgets.

QUESTION 47

A company security and compliance policy mandates that specific AMIs are approved for usage in the company's AWS accounts. A CloudOps Administrator needs to review existing Amazon EC2 instances to ensure they are in compliance with this policy.

Which action should a CloudOps Administrator take?
1. Create a custom report using AWS Systems Manager Inventory to identify unapproved AMIs.
2. Create an AWS Lambda function that checks that approved AMI Is have been used.
3. Create an AWS Config rule to check that approved AMI IDs have been used.
4. Use AWS Trusted Advisor to identify EC2 workloads using unapproved AMIs.

QUESTION 48

A company has several departments and needs to ensure that each department operates within their own isolated environment. They should also only be able to use AWS services that have been pre-approved.

How can these requirements be met?
1. Use an AWS Organization to create accounts for each department and apply service control policies (SCPs) to control access to pre-approved services.
2. Create IAM policies for each department that grant access to specific services and attach them to the user accounts.
3. Create a catalog of services that are approved for use by each department in AWS Service Catalog.
4. Create separate Amazon VPCs for each department and restrict access to approved services using IAM roles.

QUESTION 49

An application runs on Amazon EC2 instances behind an Application Load Balancer (ALB). One of the EC2 instances in the target group has exceeded the UnhealthyThresholdCount for consecutive health check failures.

What actions will be taken next? (Select TWO.)
1. The load balancer will continue to perform the health check on the EC2 instance.
2. The EC2 instance will be terminated based on the health check failure.
3. The EC2 instance will be rebooted by Amazon EC2 Auto Scaling.
4. The load balancer will take the EC2 instance out of service.
5. A new EC2 instance will be deployed to replace the unhealthy instance.

QUESTION 50

A company uses a NAT instance to enable Amazon EC2 instances in private subnets to download software and updates from the internet. Latency on the NAT instance has increased as more EC2 instances have been deployed into the private subnets. A CloudOps Administrator needs to reduce latency cost-efficiently and ensure the solution can scale with increasing demand.

Which action should be taken to accomplish this?

1. Add Auto Scaling for the NAT instance.
2. Change the instance type to use a larger instance type.
3. Replace the NAT instance with a NAT gateway.
4. Replace the NAT instance with a virtual private gateway.

QUESTION 51

A CloudOps Administrator checked the AWS Personal Health Dashboard and noticed that scheduled maintenance is going to affect a critical EBS-backed Amazon EC2 instance. The instance must be available during business hours and an interruption in service is unacceptable.

What can the Administrator do to ensure that the scheduled maintenance does not cause an outage?

1. Configure an Amazon CloudWatch Events rule to restart the instance if it is stopped.
2. Create an Amazon Machine Image (AMI) of the instance and use the AMI to launch a new instance after the current instance is shut down.
3. Use the EC2 Management Console to move the instance onto different host hardware.
4. Stop and start the EC2 instance during a maintenance window outside of normal business hours.

QUESTION 52

A CloudOps Administrator manages a fleet of Amazon EC2 instances running a distribution of Linux. The operating systems are patched on a schedule using AWS Systems Manager Patch Manager. Users of the application have complained about poor response times when the systems are being patched.

What can be done to ensure patches are deployed automatically with MINIMAL customer impact?

1. Use separate patch groups and update the groups at different times to spread the updates out.
2. Update the instances one at a time using a snapshot of a patched Amazon Machine Image (AMI).
3. Configure the maintenance window to patch 10% of the instances in the patch group at a time.
4. Create a patched Amazon Machine Image (AMI). Configure the maintenance window option to deploy the patched AMI on only 10% of the fleet at a time.

QUESTION 53

A team of Analysts require a specialized Amazon EC2 configuration. The team need to able to launch and terminate instances across the company's AWS accounts but do not wish to configure EC2 settings on their own. The specialized EC2 configuration contains licensed software and must be available for use only by the Analysts.

Which solution should a CloudOps Administrator use to allow the Analysts to deploy their workloads with MINIMAL effort?

1. Create an Amazon Machine Image (AMI) encrypted with an AWS KMS key. Share the encrypted AMI with authorized accounts. Allow the Analysts access to use the KMS key.
2. Create an AWS CloudFormation template and configure launch permissions on the AMI used by the template to add the authorized accounts. Share the template in an Amazon S3 bucket.
3. Create an AWS Elastic Beanstalk environment. Share the environment across accounts and use IAM policies to enable access for the team of Analysts.
4. Create an AWS CloudFormation template and use it to create a portfolio in AWS Service Catalog. Grant the Analysts permissions to launch products from the portfolio.

QUESTION 54

A company has a web application that uses an Amazon CloudFront web distribution, an Application Load Balancer (ALB) and Amazon EC2 instances with a shared Amazon EFS filesystem. Where applicable, all services have logging enabled. There have been some connection issues reported and the CloudOps Administrator needs to check HTTP layer 7 status codes to determine the root cause.

Which log files should the Administrator check? (Select TWO.)

1. VPC Flow Logs
2. Amazon CloudWatch Logs
3. ALB access logs
4. CloudFront access logs
5. Amazon EFS logs

QUESTION 55

A CloudOps Administrator manages a fleet of Amazon EC2 instances that use a custom Linux Amazon Machine Image (AMI). The Administrator is attempting to use AWS Systems Manager Session Manager to initiate an SSH session with one of the instances. The Administrator cannot find the target instance in the Session Manager console.

Which combination of actions will solve this issue? (Select TWO.)

1. Add permissions for Session Manager to the instance profile.
2. Add access keys to the instance that grant access to Session Manager.
3. Install the Systems Manager agent (SSM Agent) on the instances.
4. Modify the instance security group to allow inbound traffic on SSH port 22.
5. Run Systems Manager Inventory to refresh the instance data.

QUESTION 56

An application runs on Amazon EC2 instances in multiple Availability Zones (AZs) behind an internet-facing Application Load Balancer (ALB). A CloudOps Administrator needs to track the originating IP address of each application request and the EC2 instance that processes it.

What should the Administrator use to access this information?

1. Amazon CloudWatch
2. The ALB access logs
3. AWS CloudTrail
4. VPC Flow Logs

QUESTION 57

A CloudOps Administrator successfully launched an Amazon EC2 instance in the us-east-1 Region using an AWS CloudFormation template. The Administrator then attempted to use the same template to launch an EC2 instance in the eu-west-1 Region, but the Stack creation failed.

What is the MOST likely cause of this failure?

1. Resource tags defined in the CloudFormation template are specific to the eu-west-1 Region.
2. The user account being used does not have permissions to launch instances in the eu-west-1 Region.
3. The Amazon Machine Image (AMI) ID referenced in the CloudFormation template could not be found in the eu-west-1 Region.
4. The Availability Zone in the eu-west-1 Region has insufficient capacity to handle the request.

QUESTION 58

A CloudOps Administrator has been asked to identify potential cost savings through downsizing underutilized Amazon EC2 instances.

How can this be done with MINIMAL effort?

1. Use AWS Cost Explorer to generate resource optimization recommendations.
2. Use AWS Budgets to generate alerts for underutilized EC2 instances.
3. Run an AWS Lambda function that checks for utilization of EC2 instances.
4. Use Amazon CloudWatch metrics to identify EC2 instances with low utilization.

QUESTION 59

A distributed application runs across many Amazon EC2 instances and processes large quantities of data. The application is designed to handle processing interruptions without causing issues. A CloudOps Administrator needs to determine the MOST cost-effective pricing model for this use case.

Which EC2 pricing model should the Administrator use?

1. Dedicated Hosts
2. On-Demand Instances
3. Reserved Instances
4. Spot Instances

QUESTION 60

An application uses an Amazon RDS Multi-AZ DB instance. Due to new security compliance requirements a CloudOps Administrator needs to encrypt the database.

Which approach can the Administrator take to encrypt the database?

1. Use the RDS management console to enable encryption for the database.
2. Create an encrypted read replica and promote the replica to master.
3. Encrypt the standby replica in the secondary Availability Zone and promote it to the primary instance.
4. Take a snapshot of the RDS instance, copy and encrypt the snapshot, and then restore to the new RDS instance.

QUESTION 61

A company launched a static website using Amazon S3 which is being used by thousands of users from around the world. Soon after launch the website users started reporting 503 service unavailable errors.

What is the most likely cause of these errors?

1. The request rate to Amazon S3 is too high.
2. There is an issue with the S3 Transfer Acceleration service.
3. The pre-signed URL has expired and no longer exists.
4. The users do not have the correct permissions to access the website.

QUESTION 62

A company runs an application across two public and two private subnets in two availability zones (AZs). They use a single internet gateway and a single NAT gateway. Amazon CloudFront is used to cache static and dynamic content.

What would potentially cause applications in the VPC to fail during a brief AZ outage?

1. Amazon CloudFront, as it cannot use origins in multiple subnets.
2. A single internet gateway, because it is not redundant across multiple AZs.
3. A single NAT gateway, because it is not redundant across multiple AZs.
4. The main route table, as it cannot be associated with multiple subnets.

QUESTION 63

An eCommerce application consists of Amazon EC2 instances in an Auto Scaling group. The ASG scales based on CPU utilization. Users report the application response time is slow at the beginning of each business day

What action will address this issue?

1. Create a scheduled scaling action to scale up in anticipation of the traffic.
2. Change the Auto Scaling group to scale up and down based on memory utilization.
3. Change the launch configuration to launch larger EC2 instance types.
4. Modify the scaling policy to deploy more EC2 instances when scaling up.

QUESTION 64

An application runs on Amazon EC2 instances in an Auto Scaling group behind an Application Load Balancer (ALB). A CloudOps Administrator needs to set an Amazon CloudWatch alarm for when all target instances behind the ALB are unhealthy.

How should the Administrator configure the alarm?

1. In the AWS/ApplicationELB namespace, alarm when the HealthyHostCount metric is >=1
2. In the AWS/ApplicationELB namespace, alarm when the HealthyHostCount metric is <=0
3. In the AWS/EC2 namespace, alarm when the StatusCheckFailed_Instance metric is >=1
4. In the AWS/EC2 namespace, alarm when the StatusCheckFailed_System metric is <=0

QUESTION 65

A company run an application on a single Amazon EC2 instance in a single Availability Zone (AZ). The company requires that the application is made highly available. A CloudOps Administrator has created an Application Load Balancer (ALB) and a launch configuration from the running instance. The Administrator needs to create an Auto Scaling group for the launch configuration.

How should the Auto Scaling group be configured to make the application highly available?

1. Use at least 2 Availability Zones with a minimum size of 1, desired capacity of 1, and a maximum size of 1.
2. Use at least 3 Availability Zones with a minimum size of 2, desired capacity of 2, and a maximum of 2.
3. Use at least 2 regions with a minimum size of 1, desired capacity of 1, and a maximum size of 1.
4. Use at least 3 regions with a minimum size of 2, desired capacity of 2, and a maximum size of 2.

SET 1: PRACTICE QUESTIONS AND ANSWERS

QUESTION 1

Change control procedures at a company mandate that all production changes in the infrastructure must be carefully reviewed before deploying updates to their AWS CloudFormation stacks.

Which action will allow an Administrator to understand the impact of these changes before implementation?

1. Implement a blue/green strategy using AWS Elastic Beanstalk.
2. Perform a canary deployment using Application Load Balancers and target groups.
3. Create a change set for the running stack.
4. Submit the update using the UpdateStack API call.

Answer: 3

Explanation:

Change sets allow you to preview how proposed changes to a stack might impact your running resources. For example, you can check whether your changes will delete or replace any critical resources.

AWS CloudFormation makes the changes to your stack only when you decide to execute the change set, allowing you to decide whether to proceed with your proposed changes or explore other changes by creating another change set. You can create and manage change sets using the AWS CloudFormation console, AWS CLI, or AWS CloudFormation API.

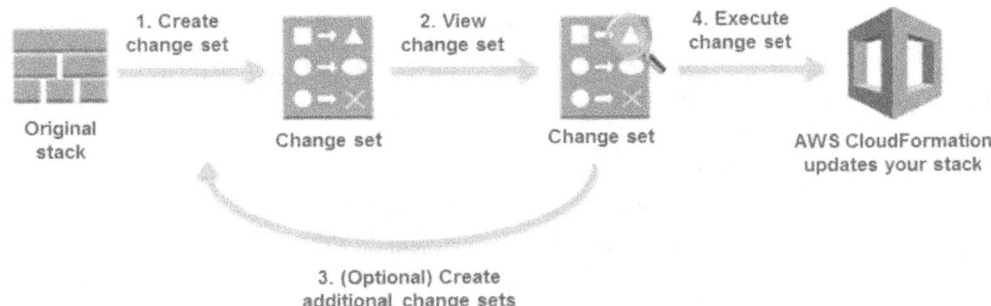

CORRECT: "Create a change set for the running stack" is the correct answer.

INCORRECT: "Implement a blue/green strategy using AWS Elastic Beanstalk" is incorrect. In this case Elastic Beanstalk is not being used, the Administrator needs to review changes directly to an AWS CloudFormation infrastructure stack. If you use Elastic Beanstalk you would make change in the EB console, not in the CloudFormation stack.

INCORRECT: "Perform a canary deployment using Application Load Balancers and target groups" is incorrect. You cannot perform canary deployments of CloudFormation updates using ALBs and target groups. This is a strategy you might use with AWS CodeDeploy.

INCORRECT: "Submit the update using the UpdateStack API call" is incorrect. This API action will immediately start the update. The correct API action would be "create-change-set".

References:

https://docs.aws.amazon.com/AWSCloudFormation/latest/UserGuide/using-cfn-updating-stacks-changesets.html

Save time with our exam-specific cheat sheets:

https://digitalcloud.training/certification-training/aws-certified-sysops-administrator-associate/aws-cloudformation/

QUESTION 2

A CloudOps Administrator needs to restrict access to a bucket to users connecting from the company IP address range. The company address range is: 51.210.100.0/24 and the Administrator has created the following policy:

```
{
        "Version": "2008-10-17",
        "Id": "S3BucketPolicyId",
        "Statement": [
                {
                        "Sid": "S3Allow",
                        "Effect": "Allow",
                        "Principal": "*",
                        "Action": "s3:*",
                        "Resource": [
                                "arn:aws:53:::examples3bucket",
                                "arn:aws:s3:::examples3bucket/*"
                        ]
                },
                {
                        "Sid": "IPAllow",
                        "Effect": "Allow",
                        "Principal": "*",
                        "Action": "s3:*",
                        "Resource": [
                                "arn:aws:s3:::examples3bucket",
                                "arn:aws:s3: : :examples3bucket/*"
                        ],
                        "Condition": {
                                "NotIpAddress": {
                                        "aws: SourceIP": "51.210.100.0/24"
                                }
                        }
                }
        ]
}
```

During testing it has been identified that users can connect from IP addresses outside the company IP address range.

How can the Administrator address this issue?

1. Modify the Condition operator to include both NotIpAddress and IpAddress to prevent unauthorized access to the S3 bucket.
2. Modify the Condition element from the IAM policy to aws:StringEquals instead of aws:SourceIp.

3. Modify the IAM policy instead of the bucket policy to restrict users from accessing the bucket based on their source IP addresses.
4. Change Effect from Allow to Deny in the second statement of the policy to deny requests not from the source IP range.

Answer: 4

Explanation:

As it is currently written the statement is actually having the opposite effect from the desired outcome. Let's break down the statement.

The "Effect": "Allow" statement will allow any principal (*), to perform any action (s3:*), on the specific resources:

"arn:aws:s3:::examples3bucket", - provides bucket-level access.

"arn:aws:s3: : :examples3bucket/*" – provides object-level access within the bucket.

The allow takes effect only if the source IP address is NOT (NotIpAddress) within the company address space (aws: SourceIP": "51.210.100.0/24).

Therefore, the resolution is to change the "Effect": "Allow" to "Effect": "Deny". This will mean that all connections are denied if they come from IP addresses that are not within the company address space.

CORRECT: "Change Effect from Allow to Deny in the second statement of the policy to deny requests not from the source IP range" is the correct answer.

INCORRECT: "Modify the Condition operator to include both NotIpAddress and IpAddress to prevent unauthorized access to the S3 bucket" is incorrect. Simply changing the effect from allow to deny has the desired result.

INCORRECT: "Modify the Condition element from the IAM policy to aws:StringEquals instead of aws:SourceIp" is incorrect. This will not assist as the issue is that the statement is set to allow addresses from outside the company IP range rather than excluding them.

INCORRECT: "Modify the IAM policy instead of the bucket policy to restrict users from accessing the bucket based on their source IP addresses" is incorrect. For this use case a bucket policy should be used instead of an IAM policy.

References:

https://aws.amazon.com/premiumsupport/knowledge-center/block-s3-traffic-vpc-ip/

Save time with our exam-specific cheat sheets:

https://digitalcloud.training/certification-training/aws-certified-sysops-administrator-associate/amazon-s3/

QUESTION 3

A CloudOps Administrator needs to add SSL/TLS encryption for a website that uses an internet-facing Application Load Balancer (ALB). The Administrator is attempting to create a certificate using AWS Certificate Manager (ACM). After the request was submitted using the ALB fully qualified domain name (FQDN) it failed with the error "Domain Not Allowed."

How can the administrator fix this issue?

1. Submit a new request in ACM with the correct domain name rather than the ALB FQDN.
2. Use email validation and confirm ownership of the domain through the root account email address.
3. Use DNS validation and follow the instructions to add a CNAME record to the hosted zone in Amazon Route 53.
4. Contact AWS Support and verify the request by answering security challenge questions.

Answer: 1

Explanation:

You must own the domain name that you register your certificate for. Also, users will not be entering the ALB FQDN in their browsers, they will be entering the domain name for the website. The Administrator must therefore submit a request to ACM using the domain name of the website. Validation can be via email or DNS. In Route 53 an Alias record can be created that maps the domain name to the ALB.

CORRECT: "Submit a new request in ACM with the correct domain name rather than the ALB FQDN" is the correct answer.

INCORRECT: "Use email validation and confirm ownership of the domain through the root account email address" is incorrect. You cannot confirm ownership for the FQDN of the ALB as this is owned by AWS.

INCORRECT: "Use DNS validation and follow the instructions to add a CNAME record to the hosted zone in Amazon Route 53" is incorrect. You cannot confirm ownership for the FQDN of the ALB as this is owned by AWS.

INCORRECT: "Contact AWS Support and verify the request by answering security challenge questions" is incorrect. This is not going to work, the Administrator needs to submit a request for the correct domain name, not the ALB FQDN.

References:

https://docs.aws.amazon.com/acm/latest/userguide/gs-acm-request-public.html

https://aws.amazon.com/premiumsupport/knowledge-center/associate-acm-certificate-alb-nlb/

QUESTION 4

A CloudOps Administrator has been tasked with deploying a web application on two Amazon EC2 instances behind an Application Load Balancer (ALB). The database layer will also run on two EC2 instances. The deployment must include high availability across Availability Zones (AZs) and public access must be limited as much as possible.

How should this be achieved within an Amazon VPC?

1. Create a public subnet in each AZ for the ALB, a private subnet in each AZ for the web servers, and a private subnet in each AZ for the database servers.
2. Create a public subnet in each AZ for the ALB, a public subnet in each AZ for the web servers, and a public subnet in each AZ for the database servers.
3. Create a public subnet in each AZ for the ALB, a private subnet in each AZ for the web servers, and a public subnet in each AZ for the database servers.
4. Create a public subnet in each AZ for the ALB, a public subnet in each AZ for the web servers, and a private subnet in each AZ for the database servers.

Answer: 1

Explanation:

The key to answering this question correctly is understanding whether to use public or private subnets for each layer of the infrastructure. A public subnet must be used for the ALB as it is Internet facing and will receive incoming traffic. The other layers should be private as the requirement is to limit public access as much as possible.

You can use a public ALB with a target group of EC2 instances in a private subnet. You must create public subnets in the same Availability Zones as the private subnets that are used by your private instances. Then associate these public subnets to the internet-facing load balancer. For more information on how to achieve this configuration see the AWS article referenced below.

CORRECT: "Create a public subnet in each AZ for the ALB, a private subnet in each AZ for the web servers, and a private subnet in each AZ for the database servers" is the correct answer.

INCORRECT: "Create a public subnet in each AZ for the ALB, a public subnet in each AZ for the web servers, and a public subnet in each AZ for the database servers" is incorrect as a private subnet should be used for the web servers and database servers.

INCORRECT: "Create a public subnet in each AZ for the ALB, a private subnet in each AZ for the web servers, and a public subnet in each AZ for the database servers" is incorrect as a private subnet should be used for the database servers.

INCORRECT: "Create a public subnet in each AZ for the ALB, a public subnet in each AZ for the web servers, and a private subnet in each AZ for the database servers" is incorrect as a private subnet should be used for the web servers.

References:

https://aws.amazon.com/premiumsupport/knowledge-center/public-load-balancer-private-ec2/

Save time with our exam-specific cheat sheets:

https://digitalcloud.training/certification-training/aws-certified-sysops-administrator-associate/elastic-load-balancing/

QUESTION 5

A company runs a data center in their office location. The company needs to provide low-latency local access to image files for users in the office. A synchronized backup of the images must be maintained in an offsite location.

Which AWS storage solution would allow access to the image data for local users while also providing for disaster recovery?

1. Create an AWS Storage Gateway volume gateway configured as a stored volume. Mount it from clients using Internet Small Computer System Interface (iSCSI).
2. Mount an Amazon EFS volume on a local server. Share this volume with employees who need access to the images.
3. Store the images in Amazon S3 and use AWS Server Migration Service to enable synchronization of S3 data to the local server.
4. Use Amazon S3 for file storage and enable S3 Transfer Acceleration to maintain a cache for frequently used files to increase local performance.

Answer: 1

Explanation:

You can run Volume Gateway in two modes: Cached and stored. With cached volumes, the Storage Gateway service stores the full volume in its Amazon S3 service bucket, and a portion of the volume—your recently accessed data—is retained in the gateway's local cache for low-latency access.

With stored volumes, your entire data volume is available locally in the gateway, for fast read access. At the same time, Volume Gateway maintains an asynchronous copy of your stored volume in the service's Amazon S3 bucket.

This a good solution for the requirements in this scenario. The data will be served at low-latency from the local AWS Storage Gateway virtual machine / appliance and will be backed up to S3 as snapshots which can be used for DR.

CORRECT: "Create an AWS Storage Gateway volume gateway configured as a stored volume. Mount it from clients using Internet Small Computer System Interface (iSCSI)" is the correct answer.

INCORRECT: "Mount an Amazon EFS volume on a local server. Share this volume with employees who need access to the images" is incorrect. This would not provide low-latency local access as the filesystem would be at AWS. Also, there is no DR copy of the data.

INCORRECT: "Store the images in Amazon S3 and use AWS Server Migration Service to enable synchronization of S3 data to the local server" is incorrect. You cannot use AWS SMS to synchronize data from S3 to a local server. AWS SMS is used for migrating servers.

INCORRECT: "Use Amazon S3 for file storage and enable S3 Transfer Acceleration to maintain a cache for frequently used files to increase local performance" is incorrect. Amazon S3 is not a local service and transfer acceleration is used for improving the speed of uploads to S3 (not for caching data locally).

References:

https://aws.amazon.com/storagegateway/volume/

Save time with our exam-specific cheat sheets:

https://digitalcloud.training/certification-training/aws-certified-sysops-administrator-associate/aws-storage-gateway/

QUESTION 6

A CloudOps Administrator needs to audit requests to AWS Organizations for creating new AWS accounts. The company users authenticate to AWS through federation.

What should the Administrator review to determine who made the request?

1. AWS CloudTrail for the federated identity user name.
2. AWS IAM Access Analyzer for the federated user name.
3. AWS X-Ray traces for the federated identity user name.
4. Federated identity provider logs for the user name.

Answer: 1

Explanation:

AWS CloudTrail can be used to track the activity of federated users. To capture the activity of these federated users, CloudTrail records the following AWS Security Token Service (AWS STS) API calls: AssumeRoleWithWebIdentity and AssumeRoleWithSAML.

In this case, AWS CloudTrail will record the attempt to create a new AWS account using AWS Organizations.

CORRECT: "AWS CloudTrail for the federated identity user name" is the correct answer.

INCORRECT: "AWS IAM Access Analyzer for the federated user name" is incorrect. This service helps you identify the resources in your organization and accounts, such as Amazon S3 buckets or IAM roles, that are shared with an external entity.

INCORRECT: "AWS X-Ray traces for the federated identity user name" is incorrect. This service is used for analyzing and debugging production, distributed applications. It is not used for auditing account activity.

INCORRECT: "Federated identity provider logs for the user name" is incorrect. The request to AWS Organizations will be recorded by CloudTrail and the federated identity user name will be recorded in the log entry.

References:

https://docs.aws.amazon.com/organizations/latest/userguide/services-that-can-integrate-ct.html

https://aws.amazon.com/blogs/security/how-to-easily-identify-your-federated-users-by-using-aws-cloudtrail/

Save time with our exam-specific cheat sheets:

https://digitalcloud.training/certification-training/aws-certified-sysops-administrator-associate/aws-cloudtrail/

QUESTION 7

Employees in an IT department have been using individual AWS accounts that are not under the control of the company. The security department has requested that these accounts be linked to the central organization in AWS Organizations.

Which action should a CloudOps Administrator take to accomplish this?

1. Add each existing account to the central organization using AWS IAM.
2. Create a new organization in each account and join them to the central organization.
3. Log in to each existing account and add them to the central organization.
4. Send each existing account an invitation from the central organization.

Answer: 4

Explanation:

The easiest way to achieve this objective is for the CloudOps Administrator to simply send an invitation from the central organization to each individual AWS account.

When you invite an account, AWS Organizations sends an invitation to the account owner, who decides whether to accept or decline the invitation. If you are the administrator of an AWS account, you can then accept or decline the invitation from the organization.

If you accept the invitation, your account becomes a member of that organization. The account is then subject to the controls of the central organization which is what the security team requires.

CORRECT: "Send each existing account an invitation from the central organization" is the correct answer.

INCORRECT: "Add each existing account to the central organization using AWS IAM" is incorrect. This is not the correct procedure; an invitation should be sent through AWS Organizations.

INCORRECT: "Create a new organization in each account and join them to the central organization" is incorrect. The accounts should be joined to the central organization, more organizations are not required.

INCORRECT: "Log in to each existing account and add them to the central organization" is incorrect. An invitation should be sent from the central organization and then in each existing account the current administrator should accept the invitation.

References:

https://docs.aws.amazon.com/organizations/latest/userguide/orgs_manage_accounts_invites.html

Save time with our exam-specific cheat sheets:

https://digitalcloud.training/certification-training/aws-certified-sysops-administrator-associate/aws-organizations/

QUESTION 8

A CloudOps Administrator accidentally deleted a folder containing important data from an Amazon EBS volume. A recent snapshot of the volume is available.

What should the Administrator do to restore the user's file from the snapshot?

1. Launch a new Amazon EC2 instance in the same Availability Zone and copy the deleted folder over the network.
2. Use the Amazon EC2 console to browse the contents of the snapshot, locate the folder, and then copy it to the EBS volume.
3. Create a new EBS volume from the snapshot, attach the volume to an Amazon EC2 instance, and copy the deleted file.
4. Restore the file from the snapshot onto the EC2 instance using the Amazon EC2 console.

Answer: 3

Explanation:

The resolution to this issue is to use the snapshot to create a new EBS volume. The volume should be created in the same AZ as the Amazon EC2 instance. The CloudOps Administrator can then attach the volume to the EC2 instance and copy the folder from the new EBS volume to the original location.

CORRECT: "Create a new EBS volume from the snapshot, attach the volume to an Amazon EC2 instance, and copy the deleted file" is the correct answer.

INCORRECT: "Launch a new Amazon EC2 instance in the same Availability Zone and copy the deleted folder over the network" is incorrect. This solution does not mention how the data is restored. It is also unnecessary to copy the data over the network when you can attach an additional volume directly to the instance.

INCORRECT: "Use the Amazon EC2 console to browse the contents of the snapshot, locate the folder, and then copy it to the EBS volume" is incorrect. You cannot browse the contents of a snapshot of copy data out of a snapshot using the EC2 console.

INCORRECT: "Restore the file from the snapshot onto the EC2 instance using the Amazon EC2 console" is incorrect. You cannot restore files from the EC2 console.

References:

https://docs.aws.amazon.com/AWSEC2/latest/UserGuide/ebs-restoring-volume.html

Save time with our exam-specific cheat sheets:

https://digitalcloud.training/certification-training/aws-certified-sysops-administrator-associate/amazon-ebs/

QUESTION 9

A website runs on Amazon EC2 instances and uses an Amazon RDS database with the MySQL engine. A caching layer based on Amazon ElastiCache for Redis (cluster mode enabled) is used to improve read performance.

A new product launch is expected to result in a significant traffic increase over the first few days, potentially doubling the load on the website.

What can a CloudOps Administrator do to ensure improved read times for users during the event?

1. Add shards to the existing Redis cluster.
2. Offload static data to Amazon S3.
3. Use a message queue to cache data.
4. Use Amazon RDS Multi-AZ.

Answer: 1

Explanation:

As demand on Amazon ElastiCache clusters changes, you might decide to improve performance or reduce costs by changing the number of shards in your Redis (cluster mode enabled) cluster. AWS recommend using online horizontal scaling to do so, because it allows your cluster to continue serving requests during the scaling process.

Horizontal scaling allows you to change the number of node groups (shards) in the replication group by adding or removing node groups (shards). The online resharding process allows scaling in/out while the cluster continues serving incoming requests.

For this scenario, adding shards to the Redis cluster using online horizontal scaling will ensure improved performance during the product launch.

CORRECT: "Add shards to the existing Redis cluster" is the correct answer.

INCORRECT: "Offload static data to Amazon S3" is incorrect. Though this may reduce cost it may not improve performance as Redis provides in-memory performance. This solution may also add further complexity to application design.

INCORRECT: "Use a message queue to cache data" is incorrect. Message queues are used for storing data for later processing. This will reduce performance for the end users of the website.

INCORRECT: "Use Amazon RDS Multi-AZ" is incorrect. Multi-AZ is used for disaster recovery with Amazon RDS, it does not improve performance.

References:

https://docs.aws.amazon.com/AmazonElastiCache/latest/red-ug/scaling-redis-cluster-mode-enabled.html

Save time with our exam-specific cheat sheets:

https://digitalcloud.training/certification-training/aws-certified-sysops-administrator-associate/amazon-elasticache/

QUESTION 10

A CloudOps Administrator needs to control access to a small group of Amazon EC2 instances. Specific tags have been added to the EC2 instances.

Which additional actions should the Administrator take to control access? (Select TWO.)

1. Attach an IAM policy to the users or groups that require access.
2. Attach an IAM role to the Amazon EC2 instances.
3. Create an Auto Scaling group for the EC2 instances and add a specific tag.
4. Create an IAM policy that grants access to the instances based on the Principal element.
5. Create an IAM policy that grants access to the instances with the specific tag using the Condition element.

Answer: 1, 5

Explanation:

The condition element of an IAM policy can be used to identify the EC2 instances to which access should be granted. The IAM policy can be attached to the users or groups that require access. The best practice is to add the users to a group and attach the policy to the group.

CORRECT: "Attach an IAM policy to the users or groups that require access" is the correct answer.

CORRECT: "Create an IAM policy that grants access to the instances with the specific tag using the Condition element" is also the correct answer.

INCORRECT: "Attach an IAM role to the Amazon EC2 instances" is incorrect. The policy should be attached to the users or groups for whom you wish to grant access.

INCORRECT: "Create an Auto Scaling group for the EC2 instances and add a specific tag" is incorrect. An ASG will not assist with granting access, tags have already been added to the instances for identification in the IAM policy.

INCORRECT: "Create an IAM policy that grants access to the instances based on the Principal element" is incorrect. The policy should be added to the users or groups for whom you wish to grant access. Therefore, there is no need to identify the users through the Principal element, the Condition element should be used to identify the specific EC2 instances.

References:

https://docs.aws.amazon.com/IAM/latest/UserGuide/list_amazonec2.html#amazonec2-policy-keys

Save time with our exam-specific cheat sheets:

https://digitalcloud.training/certification-training/aws-certified-sysops-administrator-associate/aws-iam/

QUESTION 11

A CloudOps Administrator has deployed an infrastructure stack for a company using AWS CloudFormation. The company made some manual changes to the infrastructure.

The Administrator needs to capture the changes and update the CloudFormation template. How can the Administrator determine what changes were made?

1. Create a new CloudFormation stack based on the changes that were made. Delete the old stack and deploy the new stack.
2. Update the CloudFormation stack using a change set. Review the changes and update the stack.
3. Update the CloudFormation stack by modifying the selected parameters in the template to match what was changed.
5. Use drift detection on the CloudFormation stack. Use the output to update the CloudFormation template and redeploy the stack.

Answer: 4

Explanation:

Drift detection enables you to detect whether a stack's actual configuration differs, or has *drifted*, from its expected configuration. Use AWS CloudFormation to detect drift on an entire stack, or on individual resources within the stack. A resource is considered to have drifted if any of its actual property values differ from the expected property values.

AWS CloudFormation generates detailed information on each resource in the stack that has drifted. The Administrator can use this information to update the stack.

CORRECT: "Use drift detection on the CloudFormation stack. Use the output to update the CloudFormation template and redeploy the stack" is the correct answer.

INCORRECT: "Create a new CloudFormation stack based on the changes that were made. Delete the old stack and deploy the new stack" is incorrect. The Administrator does not know what changes were made; the changes must be detected.

INCORRECT: "Update the CloudFormation stack using a change set. Review the changes and update the stack" is incorrect. You cannot update a stack using a change set unless you have an updated template. The Administrator first needs to determine the changes and update the template.

INCORRECT: "Update the CloudFormation stack by modifying the selected parameters in the template to match what was changed" is incorrect. This does need to be done. However, the Administrator needs to first determine what the changes are, so the template can be updated.

References:

https://docs.aws.amazon.com/AWSCloudFormation/latest/UserGuide/using-cfn-stack-drift.html

Save time with our exam-specific cheat sheets:

https://digitalcloud.training/certification-training/aws-certified-sysops-administrator-associate/aws-cloudformation/

QUESTION 12

A company wishes to restrict the ability to launch specific instance types to specific teams. The company has separate AWS accounts for its development and production teams and uses federated login with single sign-on (SSO). The AWS accounts are both under one organization in AWS Organizations.

How can a CloudOps Administrator restrict users in the development team's account so they can only launch T2 instances in the us-east-1 Region? (Select TWO.)

1. Create a developer IAM group inside the development team account with an IAM policy to allow EC2 T2 instances.
2. Create a developer IAM group inside the production team account and attach an IAM policy to allow EC2 T2 instances.
3. Create a developer IAM role inside the development team account with an IAM policy to allow EC2 T2 instances.
4. Create a service control policy (SCP) to deny instance launches unless the instance type is T2 and apply it to the developer organizational unit (OU).
5. Create a service control policy (SCP) to deny instance launches unless the instance type is T2 and apply it to the root.

Answer: 3, 4

Explanation:

AWS SSO seamlessly leverages IAM permissions and policies for federated users and roles to help you manage federated access centrally across all AWS accounts in your AWS Organization.

There are two elements to implementing this restriction. Firstly, you can restrict the ability to launch only T2 instances using a service control policy (SCP) in AWS Organizations. The SCP is applied to an OU.

With the example SCP below, any instance launches not using the t2.micro instance type are denied.

```json
{
  "Version": "2012-10-17",
  "Statement": [
    {
      "Sid": "RequireMicroInstanceType",
      "Effect": "Deny",
      "Action": "ec2:RunInstances",
      "Resource": "arn:aws:ec2:*:*:instance/*",
      "Condition": {
        "StringNotEquals":{
          "ec2:InstanceType":"t2.micro"
        }
      }
    }
  ]
}
```

The next step is to provide the permissions required. The company is using federated login with AWS SSO. In this setup, the process results in using the AssumeRole* API actions to assume an IAM role that has a permissions policy attached granting the necessary permissions.

CORRECT: "Create a developer IAM role inside the development team account with an IAM policy to allow EC2 T2 instances" is correct.

CORRECT: "Create a service control policy (SCP) to deny instance launches unless the instance type is T2 and apply it to the developer organizational unit (OU)" is also a correct answer.

INCORRECT: "Create a developer IAM group inside the production team account and attach an IAM policy to allow EC2 T2 instances" is incorrect. This does not provide the permissions the development team need within the developer account.

INCORRECT: "Create a developer IAM group inside the development team account with an IAM policy to allow EC2 T2 instances" is incorrect. An IAM role should be used as the identities are coming from a federated source and will use AssumeRole* API actions.

INCORRECT: "Create a service control policy (SCP) to deny instance launches unless the instance type is T2 and apply it to the root" is incorrect. This would restrict the ability to launch only T2 instance types to the entire AWS Organization. The SCP should be applied to the relevant OU instead.

References:

https://docs.aws.amazon.com/organizations/latest/userguide/orgs_getting-started_concepts.html

https://docs.aws.amazon.com/organizations/latest/userguide/orgs_manage_policies_example-scps.html#example-ec2-instances

Save time with our exam-specific cheat sheets:

https://digitalcloud.training/certification-training/aws-certified-sysops-administrator-associate/aws-organizations/

QUESTION 13

A company runs a fleet of Amazon EC2 instances in a private subnet. The instances must send data to peers over the internet. A recent bill shows that the NAT gateway charges have increased significantly.

How can a CloudOps Administrator identify which instances are creating the most network traffic?

1. Enable flow logs on the NAT gateway elastic network interface and use Amazon CloudWatch insights to filter data based on the source IP addresses.
2. Run an AWS Cost and Usage report and group the findings by instance ID.
3. Use an Elastic IP on each instance, monitor the metrics generated in Amazon CloudWatch, and filter by instance ID.
4. View the Amazon CloudTrail logs and look for the API actions to use the NAT gateway.

Answer: 1

Explanation:

VPC flow logs can be enabled on either the NAT gateway elastic network interface or the VPC. Amazon CloudWatch Insights can then be used to filter the data based on the source IP addresses.

For example, to find which instances are sending the most traffic through your NAT gateway, run the following query:

```
filter (dstAddr like 'x.x.x.x' and srcAddr like 'y.y.')
| stats sum(bytes) as bytesTransferred by srcAddr, dstAddr
| sort bytesTransferred desc
| limit 10
```

Note: you don't need to know the specifics of how to define a filter; the above is purely to illustrate how you might do this if you're interested (also see article linked below).

CORRECT: "Enable flow logs on the NAT gateway elastic network interface and use Amazon CloudWatch insights to filter data based on the source IP addresses" is the correct answer.

INCORRECT: "Run an AWS Cost and Usage report and group the findings by instance ID" is incorrect. You cannot find this information in the cost and usage report.

INCORRECT: "Use an Elastic IP on each instance, monitor the metrics generated in Amazon CloudWatch, and filter by instance ID" is incorrect. There is no need to add an EIP to each instance and you will not find this information in CloudWatch (it has performance metrics, not flow logs).

INCORRECT: "View the Amazon CloudTrail logs and look for the API actions to use the NAT gateway" is incorrect. CloudTrail monitors API actions and there are no API actions issued to send data through a NAT gateway.

References:

https://aws.amazon.com/premiumsupport/knowledge-center/vpc-find-traffic-sources-nat-gateway/

Save time with our exam-specific cheat sheets:

https://digitalcloud.training/certification-training/aws-certified-sysops-administrator-associate/amazon-virtual-private-cloud-vpc/

QUESTION 14

A company manage an application that is deployed on Amazon EC2 instances within a private subnet. The EC2 instances must be restricted from the internet for security and compliance reasons. The CloudOps team must be able to manage the instances from the corporate office using the SSH protocol.

Which combination of actions should be taken to permit SSH access to the EC2 instances while meeting the security and compliance requirements? (Select TWO.)

1. Attach a NAT gateway to the VPC and configure routing.

2. Attach a virtual private gateway to the VPC and configure routing.
3. Attach an internet gateway to the VPC and configure routing.
4. Configure a VPN connection back to the corporate office.
5. Configure a Network Load Balancer in front of the EC2 instances.

Answer: 2, 4

Explanation:

The best solution for this requirement is to configure an AWS site-to-site virtual private network (VPN). To do this you must add a virtual private gateway to the VPC, update the route table, and configure the customer gateway to connect the VPN to the corporate office.

The following diagram shows the key components of the configuration for this scenario.

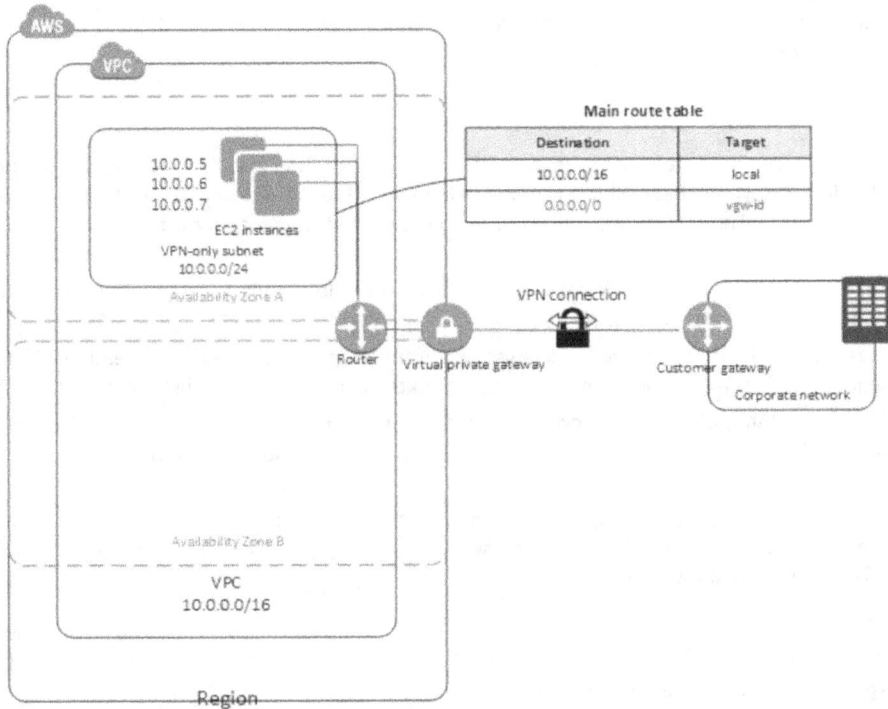

CORRECT: "Attach a virtual private gateway to the VPC and configure routing" is the correct answer.

CORRECT: "Configure a VPN connection back to the corporate office" is the correct answer.

INCORRECT: "Attach a NAT gateway to the VPC and configure routing" is incorrect. NAT gateways are used to enable internet connectivity for instances in private subnets. In this case internet connectivity should be restricted.

INCORRECT: "Attach an internet gateway to the VPC and configure routing" is incorrect. An internet gateway is used for internet connectivity which should be restricted in this case. An internet gateway is not required for a VPN connection.

INCORRECT: "Configure a Network Load Balancer in front of the EC2 instances" is incorrect. This does not enable secure access to the corporate network that avoids the internet.

References:

https://docs.aws.amazon.com/vpc/latest/userguide/VPC_Scenario4.html

Save time with our exam-specific cheat sheets:

https://digitalcloud.training/certification-training/aws-certified-sysops-administrator-associate/amazon-virtual-private-cloud-vpc/

QUESTION 15

A CloudOps Administrator has stored the login credentials for a database as secure string parameters in AWS Systems Manager Parameter Store. An application running on an Amazon EC2 instance must use the credentials to access the database.

What is the MOST secure way to grant the application access to the credentials?

1. Create an IAM role for the EC2 instances and grant the role permission to read the Systems Manager parameters.
2. Create an IAM group for the application and grant the group permission to read the Systems Manager parameters.
3. Create an IAM policy for the application and grant the policy permission to read the Systems Manager parameters.
4. Create an IAM user for the application and grant the user permission to read the Systems Manager parameters.

Answer: 1

Explanation:

Systems Manager supports only identity-based policies. Therefore, you can grant access based on users, groups and roles. In this case the best solution is to create an IAM role and attach the role the EC2 instance's instance profile. The role should have permissions assigned to grant access to read the Systems Manager parameters.

CORRECT: "Create an IAM role for the EC2 instances and grant the role permission to read the Systems Manager parameters" is the correct answer.

INCORRECT: "Create an IAM group for the application and grant the group permission to read the Systems Manager parameters" is incorrect. You cannot assign a group to an instance; you must use a role.

INCORRECT: "Create an IAM policy for the application and grant the policy permission to read the Systems Manager parameters" is incorrect. You must apply the policy to the EC2 instance and therefore an IAM role is required.

INCORRECT: "Create an IAM user for the application and grant the user permission to read the Systems Manager parameters" is incorrect. A role should be used instead of a user so delegation can be used to grant the access to the EC2 instance.

References:

https://docs.aws.amazon.com/systems-manager/latest/userguide/security_iam_service-with-iam.html

Save time with our exam-specific cheat sheets:

https://digitalcloud.training/certification-training/aws-certified-sysops-administrator-associate/aws-systems-manager/

QUESTION 16

An application runs across two Amazon EC2 instances behind an Application Load Balancer (ALB) across two Availability Zones. An Amazon DynamoDB table is used by the application. Amazon Route 53 record sets are used to route requests for dynamic content to the ALB and requests for static content to an Amazon S3 bucket. Users of the application have reported poor performance with long loading times.

Which actions should be taken to improve the performance of the website? (Select TWO.)

1. Add Amazon CloudFront caching for static content.
2. Move the dynamic content from the web servers to Amazon S3.
3. Enable Amazon Route 53 latency-based routing.
4. Implement Amazon EC2 Auto Scaling for the web servers.
5. Move the static content from Amazon S3 to the web servers.

Answer: 1,4

Explanation:

Amazon CloudFront can be used to cache the static content from the Amazon S3 bucket. This will help to improve the performance for delivery of the static content. Adding an Auto Scaling group to the solution will enable the web servers to scale based on demand and this will ensure performance is maintained in busy periods.

CORRECT: "Add Amazon CloudFront caching for static content" is the correct answer.

CORRECT: "Implement Amazon EC2 Auto Scaling for the web servers" is also a correct answer.

INCORRECT: "Move the dynamic content from the web servers to Amazon S3" is incorrect. You cannot host dynamic content on an Amazon S3 bucket configured as a website.

INCORRECT: "Enable Amazon Route 53 latency-based routing" is incorrect. Latency-based routing directs traffic to the records the correspond to the closest deployment of an application. In this case the application is deployed in a single region and single S3 bucket. Therefore, latency-based routing will not assist.

INCORRECT: "Move the static content from Amazon S3 to the web servers" is incorrect. This is not going to improve the performance of the application. Using CloudFront will provide better performance.

References:

https://aws.amazon.com/cloudfront/

https://aws.amazon.com/ec2/autoscaling/

Save time with our exam-specific cheat sheets:

https://digitalcloud.training/certification-training/aws-certified-sysops-administrator-associate/amazon-cloudfront/

https://digitalcloud.training/certification-training/aws-certified-sysops-administrator-associate/amazon-ec2-auto-scaling/

QUESTION 17

A web application runs on two Amazon EC2 instances behind an Application Load Balancer (ALB). There have been reports from users of poor performance and HTTP 503 and 504 errors. A CloudOps Administrator has reviewed Amazon CloudWatch metrics and discovered that the CPU utilization on the instances is extremely high.

Which action should the Administrator take to resolve these issues?

1. Place the EC2 instances into an Amazon EC2 Auto Scaling group.
2. Configure the load balancer to use a TCP listener instead of HTTPS.
3. Enable sticky sessions on the Application Load Balancer.
4. Enable cross-zone load balancing on the Application Load Balancer.

Answer: 1

Explanation:

The simplest solution to this issue is to implement Auto Scaling for the application. With Amazon EC2 Auto Scaling the number of instances serving the application can be modified automatically based on the actual load placed on the application by users.

Existing EC2 instances can be attached to an Auto Scaling group. After the instances are attached, they become a part of the Auto Scaling group.

CORRECT: "Place the EC2 instances into an Amazon EC2 Auto Scaling group" is the correct answer.

INCORRECT: "Configure the load balancer to use a TCP listener instead of HTTPS" is incorrect. The ALB does not support TCP listeners, and this would not improve performance anyway.

INCORRECT: "Enable sticky sessions on the Application Load Balancer" is incorrect. Sticky sessions results in connections being sent to the same back-end instance for the life of the session. This would not reduce load on the instances and lower their CPU utilization.

INCORRECT: "Enable cross-zone load balancing on the Application Load Balancer" is incorrect. Cross-zone load balancing helps to distributed traffic evenly between instances in different Availability Zones, especially when running an odd number of instances. In this scenario this would not assist as there are an even number of instances.

References:

https://docs.aws.amazon.com/autoscaling/ec2/userguide/attach-instance-asg.html

Save time with our exam-specific cheat sheets:

https://digitalcloud.training/certification-training/aws-certified-sysops-administrator-associate/amazon-ec2-auto-scaling/

QUESTION 18

An application server running on an Amazon EC2 instance recently failed due to an Amazon EBS volume running out of space. The failure caused an outage of a critical application.

Which steps should a CloudOps Administrator take to prevent this from happening again?

1. Configure Amazon CloudWatch Events to monitor Amazon EC2 status checks for the status of the EBS volumes. Post a notification to an Amazon SNS topic to notify the if the disk is impaired.
2. Create an AWS Lambda function that monitors the disk space metrics using the Amazon EBS API. Post a notification to an Amazon SNS topic when disk space is running low.
3. Enable detailed monitoring for the EC2 instances. Create an Amazon CloudWatch alarm to notify the Administrator when disk space is running low.
4. Install the Amazon CloudWatch agent on the EC2 instance to collect disk metrics. Create a CloudWatch alarm to notify the Administrator when disk space is running low.

Answer: 4

Explanation:

CORRECT: "Install the Amazon CloudWatch agent on the EC2 instance to collect disk metrics. Create a CloudWatch alarm to notify the Administrator when disk space is running low" is the correct answer.

INCORRECT: "Configure Amazon CloudWatch Events to monitor Amazon EC2 status checks for the status of the EBS volumes. Post a notification to an Amazon SNS topic to notify the if the disk is impaired" is incorrect. EC2 status checks do not tell you the status of an Amazon EBS volume.

INCORRECT: "Create an AWS Lambda function that monitors the disk space metrics using the Amazon EBS API. Post a notification to an Amazon SNS topic when disk space is running low" is incorrect. You cannot monitor disk utilization of an individual EBS volume using the EBS API.

INCORRECT: "Enable detailed monitoring for the EC2 instances. Create an Amazon CloudWatch alarm to notify the Administrator when disk space is running low" is incorrect. Detailed monitoring changes the frequency of metric reporting but it does not enable monitoring of disk utilization. You must use the CloudWatch agent.

References:

https://docs.aws.amazon.com/AmazonCloudWatch/latest/monitoring/Install-CloudWatch-Agent.html

Save time with our exam-specific cheat sheets:

https://digitalcloud.training/certification-training/aws-certified-sysops-administrator-associate/amazon-cloudwatch/

QUESTION 19

A CloudOps Administrator deployed an application using AWS CloudFormation. The application runs on Amazon EC2 instances in an Auto Scaling group behind an Application Load Balancer (ALB). A new version of the application must be deployed. The update must avoid DNS changes and support rollback

Which solution should the Administrator use to meet the deployment requirements for application update?

1. Configure the Auto Scaling group to use lifecycle hooks. Deploy new instances with the new application version. Complete the lifecycle hook action once healthy.
2. Create a new Amazon Machine Image (AMI) containing the updated code. Create a launch configuration with the AMI. Update the Auto Scaling group to use the new launch configuration.

3. Deploy a second CloudFormation stack. Wait for the application to be available. Cut over to the new Application Load Balancer.
4. Modify the CloudFormation template to use an AutoScalingReplacingUpdate policy. Update the stack. Perform a second update with the new release.

Answer: 4

Explanation:

You should always try and update the resources that were deployed through AWS CloudFormation by updating the stack rather than updating the resources directly.

You can use the AutoScalingRollingUpdate policy to control how AWS CloudFormation handles rolling updates for an Auto Scaling group. This common approach keeps the same Auto Scaling group, and then replaces the old instances based on the parameters that you set.

CloudFormation offers the ability to rollback the configuration in the event of any issues by simply redeploying the older version of the template. No DNS changes are required in this instance as the ALB is not replaced.

CORRECT: "Modify the CloudFormation template to use an AutoScalingReplacingUpdate policy. Update the stack. Perform a second update with the new release" is the correct answer.

INCORRECT: "Configure the Auto Scaling group to use lifecycle hooks. Deploy new instances with the new application version. Complete the lifecycle hook action once healthy" is incorrect. You should use AWS CloudFormation to update the stack rather than updating the resources directly.

INCORRECT: "Deploy a second CloudFormation stack. Wait for the application to be available. Cut over to the new Application Load Balancer" is incorrect. This method would require a DNS update. It hasn't been mentioned in the question but presumably there would be an Amazon Route 53 Alias record or similar pointing to the existing ALB. This would need to be updated to point to the new ALB.

INCORRECT: "Create a new Amazon Machine Image (AMI) containing the updated code. Create a launch configuration with the AMI. Update the Auto Scaling group to use the new launch configuration" is incorrect. This method means you would cause issues with stack drift as you are updating the resources directly rather than through CloudFormation.

References:

https://aws.amazon.com/premiumsupport/knowledge-center/auto-scaling-group-rolling-updates/

Save time with our exam-specific cheat sheets:

https://digitalcloud.training/certification-training/aws-certified-sysops-administrator-associate/aws-cloudformation/

QUESTION 20

A company is using an AWS Storage Gateway volume gateway configuration running on a virtual machine. Usage of the Storage Gateway has recently increased, and users have reported that performance of the iSCSI drives has degraded. A CloudOps Administrator checked the Amazon CloudWatch metrics and noticed the CacheHitPercent metric is below 55% and the CachePercentUsed metric is above 95%.

What steps are MOST likely to resolve the performance issues?

1. Optimize the iSCSI settings on the Storage Gateway's iSCSI initiator to achieve higher I/O performance.
2. Create a larger disk for the cached volume. In the AWS Management Console, edit the local disks, then select the new disk as the cached volume.
3. Ensure that the physical disks for the Storage Gateway are in a RAID 1 configuration to allow higher throughput.
4. Create a recovery snapshot from the volume, then deploy and activate a new volume gateway from the snapshot.

Answer: 2

Explanation:

A volume gateway deployment where you are storing data on S3 and have a local cache is known as a cached volume configuration. The Amazon CloudWatch metrics indicate that the cache has insufficient capacity to service the requests it is receiving.

The CacheHitPercent should be higher to indicate that more requests are being served from the cache and the CachePercentUsed metric should be lower, indicating that there is space available in the cache. The resolution to this is to create a larger cache so more requests can be served from the iSCSI disks and don't result in data being retrieved from S3.

CORRECT: "Create a larger disk for the cached volume. In the AWS Management Console, edit the local disks, then select the new disk as the cached volume" is the correct answer.

INCORRECT: "Optimize the iSCSI settings on the Storage Gateway's iSCSI initiator to achieve higher I/O performance" is incorrect. The CloudWatch metrics indicate that the cache size is the primary issue here and therefore increasing the cache size is most likely to resolve the issues.

INCORRECT: "Ensure that the physical disks for the Storage Gateway are in a RAID 1 configuration to allow higher throughput" is incorrect. RAID 1 is mirroring and does not offer any performance improvements.

INCORRECT: "Create a recovery snapshot from the volume, then deploy and activate a new volume gateway from the snapshot" is incorrect. The volume has not failed so there is no need to perform a recovery. In this case the cache size must be increased to improve performance.

References:

https://docs.aws.amazon.com/storagegateway/latest/userguide/WhatIsStorageGateway.html

https://docs.aws.amazon.com/storagegateway/latest/userguide/ManagingLocalStorage-common.html

Save time with our exam-specific cheat sheets:

https://digitalcloud.training/certification-training/aws-certified-sysops-administrator-associate/aws-storage-gateway/

QUESTION 21

A company plans to use AWS CloudFormation to deploy their infrastructure using templates. The deployments will include several environments across multiple AWS Regions. A CloudOps Administrator plans to write a single template that can be reused for each environment deployment.

What is the recommended way to use AWS CloudFormation to meet this requirement?

1. Use parameters to provision the resources.
2. Use nested stacks to provision the resources.
3. Use change sets to provision additional environments.
4. Use cross-stack references to provision the resources.

Answer: 1

Explanation:

You can use the optional Parameters section to customize your templates. Parameters enable you to input custom values to your template each time you create or update a stack. You use the Ref intrinsic function to reference a parameter, and AWS CloudFormation uses the parameter's value to provision the stack. You can reference parameters from the Resources and Outputs sections of the same template.

To make templates reusable, parameters can be used with mappings, and conditions sections so that you can customize your stacks when you create them. For example, for your development environments, you can specify a lower-cost instance type compared to your production environment, but all other configurations and settings remain the same.

CORRECT: "Use parameters to provision the resources" is the correct answer.

INCORRECT: "Use nested stacks to provision the resources" is incorrect. Nested stacks are good for defining common patterns for reuse in separate templates. However, to use a single template, use parameters, mappings, and conditions.

INCORRECT: "Use change sets to provision additional environments" is incorrect. A change set helps to identify and view the changes that will happen before you actually update your stack.

INCORRECT: "Use cross-stack references to provision the resources" is incorrect. This is simply a way of referencing to export resources from a stack so that other stacks can use them.

References:

https://docs.aws.amazon.com/AWSCloudFormation/latest/UserGuide/best-practices.html#reuse

https://docs.aws.amazon.com/AWSCloudFormation/latest/UserGuide/parameters-section-structure.html

Save time with our exam-specific cheat sheets:

https://digitalcloud.training/certification-training/aws-certified-sysops-administrator-associate/aws-cloudformation/

QUESTION 22

A CloudOps Administrator has installed the CloudWatch agent on several Amazon EC2 instances. The agent has been configured to send custom metrics to Amazon CloudWatch. The Administrator needs to create a CloudWatch dashboard to display these metrics.

What steps should the Administrator take to complete this task?

1. Select the AWS Namespace, filter by metric name, then add to the dashboard.
2. Select the appropriate widget and metrics from the custom namespace, then add to the dashboard.
3. Open the CloudWatch Logs console, create metric filters, and select the custom metrics.
4. Open the CloudWatch console, then from CloudWatch Events, add all custom metrics.

Answer: 2

Explanation:

You can create a dashboard in CloudWatch to display custom metrics. To do this you simply create a dashboard, add a widget, and choose the metrics from the custom namespace. In this case the Administrator would choose the EC2 metrics.

For more information on the process for creating this dashboard see the AWS article linked below.

CORRECT: "Select the appropriate widget and metrics from the custom namespace, then add to the dashboard" is the correct answer.

INCORRECT: "Select the AWS Namespace, filter by metric name, then add to the dashboard" is incorrect. The custom namespace must be selected.

INCORRECT: "Open the CloudWatch Logs console, create metric filters, and select the custom metrics" is incorrect. The custom metrics will be available in CloudWatch and a dashboard should be created to view them. This question is not related to CloudWatch Logs.

INCORRECT: "Open the CloudWatch console, then from CloudWatch Events, add all custom metrics" is incorrect. The custom metrics can be viewed by creating a dashboard in CloudWatch, not by finding the metrics in CloudWatch events.

References:

https://aws.amazon.com/blogs/aws/cloudwatch-dashboards-create-use-customized-metrics-views/

Save time with our exam-specific cheat sheets:

https://digitalcloud.training/certification-training/aws-certified-sysops-administrator-associate/amazon-cloudwatch/

QUESTION 23

A manager has requested that all Amazon S3 buckets must have logging enabled due to compliance requirements. A CloudOps Administrator needs to ensure that the compliance requirements are met whilst allowing teams to continue to create S3 buckets.

How can this be achieved for both existing and new S3 buckets?

1. Create a CloudWatch Alarm that notifies the Administrator when a bucket is created without logging enabled.
2. Create an IAM policy that restricts the ability to create new buckets to specific teams.
3. Auto remediate any non-compliant S3 buckets with the AWS Config managed rule S3_BUCKET_LOGGING_ENABLED.
4. Create an AWS Lambda function to automatically delete any Amazon S3 buckets if logging is not enabled.

Answer: 3

Explanation:

The easiest way to achieve this outcome is to use the AWS Config managed rule. This will check that logging is enabled and auto remediate any non-compliant buckets.

CORRECT: "Auto remediate any non-compliant S3 buckets with the AWS Config managed rule S3_BUCKET_LOGGING_ENABLED" is the correct answer.

INCORRECT: "Create a CloudWatch Alarm that notifies the Administrator when a bucket is created without logging enabled" is incorrect. You cannot configure CloudWatch to notify based on a creation event with a certain configuration.

INCORRECT: "Create an IAM policy that restricts the ability to create new buckets to specific teams" is incorrect. This would limit the teams from being able to create buckets which is not desired.

INCORRECT: "Create an AWS Lambda function to automatically delete any Amazon S3 buckets if logging is not enabled" is incorrect. There needs to be a method of identification or a trigger such as an event source mapping from the bucket (not mentioned). This may be troublesome as you would have buckets being deleted which may cause issues for teams. The better solution is to enforce the compliance requirements through AWS Config.

References:

https://aws.amazon.com/blogs/mt/aws-config-auto-remediation-s3-compliance/

Save time with our exam-specific cheat sheets:

https://digitalcloud.training/certification-training/aws-certified-sysops-administrator-associate/aws-config/

QUESTION 24

A CloudOps Administrator is responsible for a large fleet of Amazon EC2 instances. There is an important event planned and the Administrator needs to understand if any instances will be affected by upcoming hardware maintenance.

Which option would provide this information with the LEAST administrative overhead?

1. Deploy the CloudWatch agent on all instances and monitor availability.
2. View any planned maintenance in the AWS Service Health Dashboard.
3. Monitor AWS CloudTrail for any StopInstances API calls that are issued.
4. Review the Personal Health Dashboard for any scheduled maintenance.

Answer: 4

Explanation:

AWS Personal Health Dashboard provides alerts and remediation guidance when AWS is experiencing events that may impact you. While the Service Health Dashboard displays the general status of AWS services, Personal Health Dashboard gives you a personalized view into the performance and availability of the AWS services underlying your AWS resources.

The dashboard displays relevant and timely information to help you manage events in progress and provides proactive notification to help you plan for scheduled activities. With Personal Health Dashboard, alerts are triggered by changes in the health of AWS resources, giving you event visibility, and guidance to help quickly diagnose and resolve issues.

CORRECT: "Review the Personal Health Dashboard for any scheduled maintenance" is the correct answer.

INCORRECT: "Deploy the CloudWatch agent on all instances and monitor availability" is incorrect. The

CloudWatch agent cannot be used to determine what upcoming maintenance will be performed on hardware.

INCORRECT: "View any planned maintenance in the AWS Service Health Dashboard" is incorrect. The service health dashboard only shows current information, not planned maintenance activities.

INCORRECT: "Monitor AWS CloudTrail for any StopInstances API calls that are issued" is incorrect. This would only tell you when resources are shut down, it would not assist with planning for upcoming outages.

References:

https://aws.amazon.com/premiumsupport/technology/personal-health-dashboard/

QUESTION 25

A company experienced a security incident and has decided to block public access to HTTP (TCP port 80). All incoming web traffic must use HTTPS (TCP port 443). A CloudOps Administrator must provide real-time compliance reporting on security groups in the Amazon VPC.

How can the Administrator provide near real-time compliance reporting?

1. Enable AWS Trusted Advisor create a CloudWatch alarm that triggers on Red alerts for the unrestricted ports check.
2. Schedule an AWS Lambda function to run hourly to scan and evaluate all security groups and send a report.
3. Use AWS Config to enable the restricted-common-ports rule and add port 80 to the parameters.
4. Use Amazon Inspector to evaluate the security groups during scans and send the completed reports.

Answer: 3

Explanation:

The AWS Config restricted-common-ports check is used to check whether the security groups in use do not allow unrestricted incoming TCP traffic to the specified ports. The rule is COMPLIANT when the IP addresses for inbound TCP connections are restricted to the specified ports. This rule applies only to IPv4.

You can specify the ports you want to check for and it will evaluate your security groups for compliance. In the example rule below port 80 has been added to the list:

Description	Checks whether security groups that are in use disallow unrestricted incoming TCP traffic to the specified ports.
Trigger type	Configuration changes
Scope of changes	Resources
Resource types	EC2 SecurityGroup
Auto remediation	Off
Config rule ARN	arn:aws:config:us-east-1:515148227241:config-rule/config-rule-cqobrx
Parameters	blockedPort1: 20 blockedPort2: 21 blockedPort3: 3389 blockedPort4: 3306 blockedPort5: 80
Overall rule status	Last successful invocation on August 3, 2020 at 10:05:56 AM Last successful evaluation on August 3, 2020 at 10:05:56 AM

CORRECT: "Use AWS Config to enable the restricted-common-ports rule and add port 80 to the parameters" is the correct answer.

INCORRECT: "Enable AWS Trusted Advisor create a CloudWatch alarm that triggers on Red alerts for the unrestricted ports check" is incorrect. The alert criteria for this rule has port 80 in the Green category, not the Red category.

INCORRECT: "Schedule an AWS Lambda function to run hourly to scan and evaluate all security groups and send a report" is incorrect. This is not near real-time.

INCORRECT: "Use Amazon Inspector to evaluate the security groups during scans and send the completed reports" is incorrect. The scans will not run in near real-time, so this is not a good solution.

References:

https://docs.aws.amazon.com/config/latest/developerguide/restricted-common-ports.html

Save time with our exam-specific cheat sheets:

https://digitalcloud.training/certification-training/aws-certified-sysops-administrator-associate/aws-config/

QUESTION 26

A company uses an Amazon ElastiCache Memcached cluster for a popular website. The CloudOps Administrator received reports of performance issues. The Administrator checked the CloudWatch metrics and noticed high CPU utilization.

Which remediation steps should be taken to resolve this issue? (Select TWO.)

1. Add a larger Amazon EBS volume to the ElastiCache cluster nodes.
2. Add a load balancer to route traffic to the ElastiCache cluster.
3. Add additional nodes to the existing ElastiCache cluster.
4. Create an Auto Scaling group for the ElastiCache cluster.
5. Vertically scale the ElastiCache cluster by changing the node type.

Answer: 3, 5

Explanation:

You can scale ElastiCache Memcached clusters either horizontally or vertically.

Scaling Memcached Horizontally: The Memcached engine supports partitioning your data across multiple nodes. Because of this, Memcached clusters scale horizontally easily. A Memcached cluster can have from 1 to 20 nodes. To horizontally scale your Memcached cluster, merely add or remove nodes.

Scaling Memcached Vertically: Scale vertically by using a different node type. When you scale your Memcached cluster up or down, you must create a new cluster. Memcached clusters always start out empty unless your application populates it.

CORRECT: "Add additional nodes to the existing ElastiCache cluster" is the correct answer.

CORRECT: "Vertically scale the ElastiCache cluster by changing the node type" is also a correct answer.

INCORRECT: "Add a larger Amazon EBS volume to the ElastiCache cluster nodes" is incorrect. This will not resolve CPU issues for the nodes.

INCORRECT: "Add a load balancer to route traffic to the ElastiCache cluster" is incorrect. You cannot use a load balancer to distribute traffic to ElastiCache nodes, you must map the key space in your application.

INCORRECT: "Create an Auto Scaling group for the ElastiCache cluster" is incorrect. You cannot use Auto Scaling for ElastiCache nodes.

References:

https://docs.aws.amazon.com/AmazonElastiCache/latest/mem-ug/Scaling.html

Save time with our exam-specific cheat sheets:

https://digitalcloud.training/certification-training/aws-certified-sysops-administrator-associate/amazon-elasticache/

QUESTION 27

A company uses AWS Service Catalog to manage approved services. A new AWS account has been created and a CloudOps Administrator needs to create a replica of the company's existing AWS infrastructure in the new AWS account. Currently, an AWS Service Catalog portfolio is used to create and manage resources.

What is the MOST efficient way to accomplish this?

1. Create an AWS CloudFormation template to redeploy the AWS Service Catalog portfolio in the new AWS account.
2. Manually create an AWS Service Catalog portfolio in the new AWS account and recreate the original portfolio.
3. Run an AWS Lambda function to create a new AWS Service Catalog portfolio based on the output of the DescribePortfolio API operation.

4. Share the AWS Service Catalog portfolio with the other AWS account and import the portfolio into the AWS account.

Answer: 4

Explanation:

To enable an AWS Service Catalog administrator for another AWS account to distribute your products to end users, share your AWS Service Catalog portfolio with them using either account-to-account sharing or AWS Organizations.

When you share a portfolio using account-to-account sharing or Organizations, you are sharing a *reference* of that portfolio. The products and constraints in the imported portfolio stay in sync with changes that you make to the *shared portfolio*, the original portfolio that you shared. The recipient cannot change the products or constraints, but can add AWS Identity and Access Management (IAM) access for end users.

CORRECT: "Share the AWS Service Catalog portfolio with the other AWS account and import the portfolio into the AWS account" is the correct answer.

INCORRECT: "Create an AWS CloudFormation template to redeploy the AWS Service Catalog portfolio in the new AWS account" is incorrect. This would not be the most efficient method as you must create the AWS CloudFormation template.

INCORRECT: "Manually create an AWS Service Catalog portfolio in the new AWS account and recreate the original portfolio" is incorrect. This would not be the most efficient method as there would be lots of manual work.

INCORRECT: "Run an AWS Lambda function to create a new AWS Service Catalog portfolio based on the output of the DescribePortfolio API operation" is incorrect. This does not represent the most efficient method, it's easier to simply share the portfolio across accounts or organizations.

References:

https://docs.aws.amazon.com/servicecatalog/latest/adminguide/catalogs_portfolios_sharing.html

QUESTION 28

A company is creating a new application that will run in a hybrid environment. The application processes data that must be secured and the developers require encryption in-transit across shared networks and encryption at rest.

Which combination of actions should a CloudOps Administrator take to meet these requirements? (Select TWO.)

1. Configure an AWS VPN between the on-premises data center and AWS.
2. Use AWS Certificate Manager to create TLS/SSL certificates.
3. Use AWS CloudHSM to encrypt the data using a CMK.
4. Use AWS KMS to create TLS/SSL certificates.
5. Use AWS KMS to manage the encryption keys used for data encryption.

Answer: 1, 5

Explanation:

An AWS virtual private network (VPN) connection can be configured to encrypt data over the shared, hybrid network connection. This ensures encryption in-transit and if you don't have a certificate you can create a pre-shared key.

AWS KMS can be used to manage encryption keys that can be used for data encryption. In this case the keys would then be used outside of KMS to actually encrypt the data.

CORRECT: "Configure an AWS VPN between the on-premises data center and AWS" is the correct answer.

CORRECT: "Use AWS KMS to manage the encryption keys used for data encryption" is the correct answer.

INCORRECT: "Use AWS Certificate Manager to create TLS/SSL certificates" is incorrect. The answer does not mention how these certificates will be used. They could be useful for end-to-end encryption but this is dependent on application design so it's unclear if this is a suitable option.

INCORRECT: "Use AWS CloudHSM to encrypt the data using a CMK" is incorrect. You do not use CloudHSM to actually encrypt data. CloudHSM manages the encryption keys and you must then encrypt your data outside of CloudHSM.

INCORRECT: "Use AWS KMS to create TLS/SSL certificates" is incorrect. You cannot create TLS/SSL certificates using AWS KMS, you must use AWS Certificate Manager.

References:

https://docs.aws.amazon.com/kms/latest/developerguide/concepts.html#data-keys

Save time with our exam-specific cheat sheets:

https://digitalcloud.training/certification-training/aws-certified-sysops-administrator-associate/amazon-virtual-private-cloud-vpc/

https://digitalcloud.training/certification-training/aws-certified-sysops-administrator-associate/aws-kms-and-aws-cloudhsm/

QUESTION 29

A company plans to use Amazon Route 53 to enable high availability for a website running on-premises. The website consists of an active and passive server. Route 53 must be configured to route traffic to the primary active server if the associated health returns a 2xx status code. All other traffic should be directed to the secondary passive server.

A CloudOps Administrator needs to configure the record type and health check. Which options should the Administrator choose?

1. An A record for each server with an Amazon Route 53 HTTP health check.
2. An A record for each server with an Amazon Route 53 TCP health check.
3. An alias record with evaluate health set to yes and associated with a Route 53 HTTP health check.
4. An alias record with evaluate health set to yes and associated with a Route 53 TCP health check.

Answer: 1

Explanation:

The website runs on-premises and therefore an Alias record cannot be used as this would only be used for AWS resources. Therefore, an A record should be used for each server. The health check must return HTTP status codes and therefore the only option is to use a HTTP health check.

CORRECT: "An A record for each server with an Amazon Route 53 HTTP health check" is the correct answer.

INCORRECT: "An A record for each server with an Amazon Route 53 TCP health check" is incorrect. A TCP health check will not return the HTTP status codes.

INCORRECT: "An alias record with evaluate health set to yes and associated with a Route 53 HTTP health check" is incorrect. You cannot create an alias record for an on-premises website.

INCORRECT: "An alias record with evaluate health set to yes and associated with a Route 53 TCP health check" is incorrect. You cannot create an alias record for an on-premises website.

References:

https://docs.aws.amazon.com/Route53/latest/DeveloperGuide/dns-failover-types.html

Save time with our exam-specific cheat sheets:

https://digitalcloud.training/certification-training/aws-certified-sysops-administrator-associate/amazon-route-53/

QUESTION 30

A network administrator made a change to the networking configuration of an Amazon VPC. After the change, an application server running on Amazon EC2 is unable to connect to an Amazon RDS MySQL database. A CloudOps Administrator must identify the root cause.

What should the CloudOps Administrator analyze?

1. VPC Flow Logs.
2. Amazon Elastic Load Balancing logs.
3. Amazon Auto Scaling logs.
4. Amazon RDS MySQL error logs.

Answer: 1

Explanation:

A change was made to the network and this is the most likely cause of the issue. Therefore, the investigation should focus on the checking the network layer.

VPC Flow Logs is a feature that enables you to capture information about the IP traffic going to and from network interfaces in your VPC. Flow logs can help you with a number of tasks, such as:

- Diagnosing overly restrictive security group rules.
- Monitoring the traffic that is reaching your instances.
- Determining the direction of the traffic to and from the network interfaces.

CORRECT: "VPC Flow Logs" is the correct answer.

INCORRECT: "Amazon Elastic Load Balancing logs" is incorrect as an ELB is not placed between an application server and an RDS database.

INCORRECT: "Amazon Auto Scaling logs" is incorrect. Auto Scaling is unlikely to be the root cause of this issue, the network layer should be investigated.

INCORRECT: "Amazon RDS MySQL error logs" is incorrect. It is unlikely that there will be anything particularly useful in the RDS MySQL error logs to diagnose the issue if it has been caused by a network change.

References:

https://docs.aws.amazon.com/vpc/latest/userguide/flow-logs.html

Save time with our exam-specific cheat sheets:

https://digitalcloud.training/certification-training/aws-certified-sysops-administrator-associate/amazon-virtual-private-cloud-vpc/

QUESTION 31

A CloudOps Administrator manages an application that is used by several front-end servers in different regions. An AWS Web Application Firewall (WAF) is used to protect the application. Each request contains a header that includes the ID of the front-end server making the request. The CloudOps Administrator wants to identify and count the requests from each front-end server.

Which condition should be added to the web ACL of the AWS WAF to accomplish this?

1. Size constraint
2. ID match
3. IP match
4. String match

Answer: 4

Explanation:

A string match statement indicates the string that you want AWS WAF to search for in a request, where in the request to search, and how. For example, you can look for a specific string at the start of any query string in the request or as an exact match for the request's User-agent header.

A string match would be the best way to find the ID of the front-end server. This can then be used to count connection requests from the different front-end servers.

CORRECT: "String match" is the correct answer.

INCORRECT: "Size constraint" is incorrect. A size constraint will simply enforce a size limit.

INCORRECT: "ID match" is incorrect. This is not a valid type of match constraint.

INCORRECT: "IP match" is incorrect. In this case the ID would be a string, not an IP address.

References:

https://docs.aws.amazon.com/en_us/waf/latest/developerguide/waf-rule-statement-type-string-match.html

Save time with our exam-specific cheat sheets:

https://digitalcloud.training/certification-training/aws-certified-sysops-administrator-associate/aws-waf-and-shield/

QUESTION 32

A CloudOps Administrator manages and application that uses an Application Load Balancer (ALB) in front of six Amazon EC2 instances in a single security group. The Administrator notices that the CloudWatch metric for HealthyHostCount has dropped from 6 to 2.

What is MOST likely causing this issue?

1. The security groups of the instances are not allowing the ALB health checks to succeed.
2. The route tables are not updated to allow traffic to flow between the ALB and the EC2 instances.
3. The ALB health checks have failed, and the ALB has taken EC2 instances out of service.
4. The Amazon Route 53 health checks have failed, and the ALB has taken EC2 instances out of service.

Answer: 3

Explanation:

Though it is unclear what caused 4 instances to fail their health checks and the other 2 to remain operational, this is the most likely cause. None of the other options make sense as they would either apply to all instances or none at all.

CORRECT: "The ALB health checks have failed, and the ALB has taken EC2 instances out of service" is the correct answer.

INCORRECT: "The security groups of the instances are not allowing the ALB health checks to succeed" is incorrect. The instances are attached to a single security group so if it is misconfigured then all health checks would fail, and all instances would be removed from service.

INCORRECT: "The route tables are not updated to allow traffic to flow between the ALB and the EC2 instances" is incorrect. If the route tables are not configured correctly then none of the instances will be operational.

INCORRECT: "The Amazon Route 53 health checks have failed, and the ALB has taken EC2 instances out of service" is incorrect. Amazon ALB does not take instances out of service based on Amazon Route 53 health checks. It will only remove instances from service if they fail the ALB health checks.

References:

https://docs.aws.amazon.com/elasticloadbalancing/latest/application/load-balancer-cloudwatch-metrics.html

Save time with our exam-specific cheat sheets:

https://digitalcloud.training/certification-training/aws-certified-sysops-administrator-associate/elastic-load-balancing/

QUESTION 33

A company runs an Amazon RDS multi-AZ deployment for an eCommerce website. An automated failover occurred, and a CloudOps Administrator needs to determine the root cause.

Which of the following are possible conditions that may cause the database to failover? (Select TWO.)

1. Read contention on the secondary database.
2. A storage failure on the primary database.
3. Write contention on the primary database.
4. Database corruption errors.

    5. The database instance type was changed.

Answer: 2, 5

Explanation:

Amazon RDS handles failovers automatically so you can resume database operations as quickly as possible without administrative intervention. The primary DB instance switches over automatically to the standby replica if any of the following conditions occur:

- An Availability Zone outage.
- The primary DB instance fails.
- The DB instance's server type is changed.
- The operating system of the DB instance is undergoing software patching.
- A manual failover of the DB instance was initiated using **Reboot with failover.**

Therefore, a storage failure on the primary database and the DB instance type being changed are both conditions that would cause a failover event to occur.

CORRECT: "A storage failure on the primary database" is the correct answer.

CORRECT: "The database instance type was changed" is the correct answer.

INCORRECT: "Read contention on the secondary database" is incorrect. This is not an event that would cause the primary to failover to the secondary.

INCORRECT: "Write contention on the primary database" is incorrect. RDS does not failover based on performance.

INCORRECT: "Database corruption errors" is incorrect. RDS does not detect and failover when corruption occurs within the database.

References:

https://docs.aws.amazon.com/AmazonRDS/latest/UserGuide/Concepts.MultiAZ.html

Save time with our exam-specific cheat sheets:

https://digitalcloud.training/certification-training/aws-certified-sysops-administrator-associate/amazon-rds/

QUESTION 34

A web application runs on several Amazon EC2 instances in an Auto Scaling group across all Availability Zones in the Region. A CloudOps Administrator notices that the ASG does not launch new instances during busy periods. The maximum capacity of the ASG has not been reached.

What should the Administrator do to identify the cause of the issue? (Select TWO.)

1. Use AWS Trusted Advisor to check if service limits have been reached.
2. Check the AWS Personal Health Dashboard for outage events.
3. Monitor limits in AWS Systems Manager.
4. Use Amazon Inspector to view performance information.
5. Use AWS CloudTrail to check the result of RunInstances requests.

Answer: 1, 5

Explanation:

You can use AWS Trusted Advisor's Service Limit Dashboard to determine whether the service limits for EC2 instances have been reached. This is one possible cause of the issue. Additionally, the Administrator can check CloudTrail logs to view the results of the RunInstances requests. If a permissions issue exists this will be identified.

CORRECT: "Use AWS Trusted Advisor to check if service limits have been reached" is the correct answer.

CORRECT: "Use AWS CloudTrail to check the result of RunInstances requests" is also a correct answer.

INCORRECT: "Check the AWS Personal Health Dashboard for outage events" is incorrect. It is unlikely that an outage will prevent new instances from running on any AZ. This particular ASG is set to use all AZs so an outage is less likely to be the cause.

INCORRECT: "Monitor limits in AWS Systems Manager" is incorrect. You cannot monitor AWS service limits using AWS Systems Manager.

INCORRECT: "Use Amazon Inspector to view performance information" is incorrect. Amazon Inspector is used for security and compliance, not for performance monitoring.

References:

https://aws.amazon.com/premiumsupport/technology/trusted-advisor/best-practice-checklist/

Save time with our exam-specific cheat sheets:

https://digitalcloud.training/certification-training/aws-certified-sysops-administrator-associate/aws-cloudtrail/

QUESTION 35

A CloudOps Administrator must choose an EBS volume type that will be attached to an Amazon EC2 instance. The volume will be used by a big data application and the application data will be accessed infrequently and stored sequentially.

What EBS volume type will be the MOST cost-effective solution?

1. Provisioned IOPS SSD (io1)
2. Throughput Optimized HDD (st1)
3. Cold HDD (sc1)
4. General Purpose SSD (gp2)

Answer: 3

Explanation:

The Cold HDD (sc1) volume type is the most cost-effective storage solution that is suitable for throughput-oriented storage for large volumes of data that are infrequently accessed.

	Solid State Drives (SSD)		Hard Disk Drives (HDD)	
Volume Type	General Purpose SSD (gp2)	Provisioned IOPS SSD (io1)	Throughput Optimized (st1)	Cold HDD (sc1)
Description	Balance of price to performance	High performance SSD	Low cost HDD	Lowest cost HDD
Use Cases	• Most workloads • System boot volumes • Virtual desktops	• Critical business apps that require sustained IOPS performance • Apps that require more than 10,000 IOPS or 160 MiB/s • Large database workloads	• Streaming workloads with fast throughput • Low price • Big data • Data warehouses	• Throughput oriented storage for large volumes of infrequently accessed data • Lowest cost • Cannot be a boot volume
Volume Size	1 GiB – 16 TiB	4 GiB – 16 TiB	500 GiB – 16 TiB	500 GiB – 16 TiB
Max IOPS Per Volume	10,000	32,000	500	250
Max Throughput Per Volume	160 MiB/s	500 MiB/s	500 MiB/s	250 MiB/s

CORRECT: "Cold HDD (sc1)" is the correct answer.

INCORRECT: "Throughput Optimized HDD (st1)" is incorrect. This is not the most cost-effective storage volume for this use case. It is better suited to throughput-oriented storage that requires frequent access.

INCORRECT: "Provisioned IOPS SSD (io1)" is incorrect. This is a much more expensive storage volume type for IOPS intensive workloads.

INCORRECT: "General Purpose SSD (gp2)" is incorrect. This is a more expensive storage volume type that uses SSD and is suitable for use as a boot volume.

References:

https://docs.aws.amazon.com/AWSEC2/latest/UserGuide/ebs-volume-types.html

Save time with our exam-specific cheat sheets:

https://digitalcloud.training/certification-training/aws-certified-sysops-administrator-associate/amazon-ebs/

QUESTION 36

An application runs on several Amazon EC2 instances behind an Application Load Balancer (ALB). The instances run in an Auto Scaling group that is configured to determine the health status of EC2 instances using both EC2 status checks and ALB health checks. An application fault has been detected and it is necessary to analyze unhealthy instances before they are terminated.

What should a CloudOps Administrator do to accomplish this?

1. Configure the Auto Scaling group to only use ALB health checks so instances are taken out of service but are not terminated.
2. Create an AWS Lambda function that takes a snapshot of the instances before they are terminated.
3. Implement Amazon CloudWatch Events to capture lifecycle events and trigger an AWS Lambda function for remediation.
4. Use an Amazon EC2 Auto Scaling lifecycle hook to pause instance termination after the instance has been removed from service.

Answer: 4

Explanation:

Lifecycle hooks enable you to perform custom actions by *pausing* instances as an Auto Scaling group launches or terminates them. When an instance is paused, it remains in a wait state either until you complete the lifecycle action using the **complete-lifecycle-action** command or the CompleteLifecycleAction operation, or until the timeout period ends (one hour by default).

For example, when a scale-in event occurs, the terminating instance is first deregistered from the load balancer. Then, a lifecycle hook pauses the instance before it is terminated. While the instance is in the wait state, you can, for example, connect to the instance and download logs or other data before the instance is fully terminated.

This is a good way to ensure that the instances are not terminated until the analysis has been completed.

CORRECT: "Use an Amazon EC2 Auto Scaling lifecycle hook to pause instance termination after the instance has been removed from service" is the correct answer.

INCORRECT: "Implement Amazon CloudWatch Events to capture lifecycle events and trigger an AWS Lambda function for remediation" is incorrect. The CloudWatch lifecycle events would only trigger upon instance termination, which is too late. In this case the trigger needs to be when the instance is taken out of service after failing a health check and for this lifecycle hooks should be used.

INCORRECT: "Configure the Auto Scaling group to only use ALB health checks so instances are taken out of service but are not terminated" is incorrect. You cannot configure an Auto Scaling group to use only ALB health checks, they are always in addition to the EC2 status checks.

INCORRECT: "Create an AWS Lambda function that takes a snapshot of the instances before they are terminated" is incorrect. The Lambda function would require a trigger and this must be when the instance is taken out of service after failing a health check, not when it is terminated. Therefore, there is no clear way to trigger the function at the correct stage for this scenario.

References:

https://docs.aws.amazon.com/autoscaling/ec2/userguide/lifecycle-hooks.html

Save time with our exam-specific cheat sheets:

https://digitalcloud.training/certification-training/aws-certified-sysops-administrator-associate/amazon-ec2-auto-scaling/

QUESTION 37

A company has created an Amazon CloudFront distribution in front of an application. The application uses the domain name www.mywebapp.com which is managed using Amazon Route 53. A CloudOps Administrator has been asked to configure the application to be accessed using www.mywebapp.com through CloudFront.

What is the MOST cost-effective way to achieve this?

1. Create a CNAME record in Amazon Route 53 that points to the CloudFront distribution URL.
2. Create an Alias record in Amazon Route 53 that points to the CloudFront distribution URL.

3. Create an A record in Amazon Route 53 that points to the public IP address of the web application.
4. Create an SRV record in Amazon Route 53 that points to the custom domain name A record.

Answer: 2

Explanation:

The most cost-effective record type to use is an alias record. Route 53 doesn't charge for alias queries to AWS resources and this includes to Amazon CloudFront distributions. You can create an alias record that uses the www.mywebapp.com domain name and points to the Amazon CloudFront distribution. This will enable users to access the distribution using the custom domain name.

CORRECT: "Create an Alias record in Amazon Route 53 that points to the CloudFront distribution URL" is the correct answer.

INCORRECT: "Create a CNAME record in Amazon Route 53 that points to the CloudFront distribution URL" is incorrect. Route 53 charges for CNAME queries. If you create a CNAME record that redirects to the name of another record in a Route 53 hosted zone (the same hosted zone or another hosted zone), each DNS query is charged as two queries.

INCORRECT: "Create an A record in Amazon Route 53 that points to the public IP address of the web application" is incorrect. You cannot use the public IP of CloudFront, you are only provided the DNS name of the CloudFront distribution.

INCORRECT: "Create an SRV record in Amazon Route 53 that points to the custom domain name A record" is incorrect. A service locator record is not the correct record type to use for this use case.

References:

https://docs.aws.amazon.com/Route53/latest/DeveloperGuide/resource-record-sets-choosing-alias-non-alias.html

Save time with our exam-specific cheat sheets:

https://digitalcloud.training/certification-training/aws-certified-sysops-administrator-associate/amazon-route-53/

QUESTION 38

A company has several AWS accounts in a single organization in AWS Organizations. The company requires that no Amazon S3 buckets can be deleted its production account.

What is the SIMPLEST approach to ensuring that the S3 buckets in the production account cannot be deleted?

1. Set up MFA Delete on all the S3 buckets in the production account to prevent the buckets from being deleted.
2. Use a service control policy to deny the s3:DeleteBucket API action in the production account.
3. Create an IAM group that has an IAM policy to deny the s3:DeleteBucket action on all buckets in the production account.
4. Create an IAM role that restricts the API actions that can be used for Amazon S3 and assign it to EC2 instances.

Answer: 2

Explanation:

Service control policies (SCPs) are a type of organization policy that you can use to manage permissions in your organization. SCPs offer central control over the maximum available permissions for all accounts in your organization.

For this scenario, an SCP can be used to restrict the s3:DeleteBucket API action on the production account. This will ensure that no user will be able to delete a bucket in this account as API action is restricted. This will apply even to users who have the necessary IAM permissions to delete the bucket.

CORRECT: "Use a service control policy to deny the s3:DeleteBucket API action in the production account" is the correct answer.

INCORRECT: "Set up MFA Delete on all the S3 buckets in the production account to prevent the buckets from being deleted" is incorrect. MFA delete does not prevent deletion; it just adds a layer of protection to reduce the likelihood of accidental deletion.

INCORRECT: "Create an IAM group that has an IAM policy to deny the s3:DeleteBucket action on all buckets in the production account" is incorrect. This will only apply to users that are added to the group which means ongoing administrative challenges in ensuring that all users are added to the group so that no one has the ability to delete a bucket.

INCORRECT: "Create an IAM role that restricts the API actions that can be used for Amazon S3 and assign it to EC2 instances" is incorrect. You restrict permissions but not API actions when using IAM policies. Also, it doesn't make sense to just apply the policy to EC2 instances, this must apply to everyone.

References:

https://docs.aws.amazon.com/organizations/latest/userguide/orgs_manage_policies_type-auth.html

Save time with our exam-specific cheat sheets:

https://digitalcloud.training/certification-training/aws-certified-sysops-administrator-associate/aws-organizations/

QUESTION 39

A company runs an application on Amazon EC2 instances in a VPC private subnet. The instances must upload objects to an Amazon S3 bucket. The company requires access to the bucket to be restricted to the EC2 instances in the private network and data must not traverse the public network.

What actions should the CloudOps Administrator take to meet these requirements?

1. Create a VPC endpoint for the S3 bucket and create an IAM policy that conditionally limits all S3 actions on the bucket to the VPC endpoint as the source.
2. Create a VPC endpoint for the S3 bucket and create a S3 bucket policy that conditionally limits all S3 actions on the bucket to the VPC endpoint as the source.
3. Create an AWS VPN tunnel between the VPC private subnet and the Amazon S3 public endpoint.
4. Create a NAT gateway in the VPC and modify the private subnet route table to route all traffic destined for S3 through the NAT gateway.

Answer: 2

Explanation:

You can use a bucket policy to specify which VPC endpoints can access the S3 bucket. For example, the following bucket policy blocks traffic to the bucket unless the request is from specified VPC endpoints (aws:sourceVpce):

```
{
    "Version": "2012-10-17",
    "Id": "Policy1415115909152",
    "Statement": [
      {
        "Sid": "Access-to-specific-VPCE-only",
        "Principal": "*",
        "Action": "s3:*",
        "Effect": "Deny",
        "Resource": ["arn:aws:s3:::awsexamplebucket1",
                     "arn:aws:s3:::awsexamplebucket1/*"],
        "Condition": {
          "StringNotEquals": {
            "aws:SourceVpce": "vpce-1a2b3c4d"
          }
        }
      }
    ]
}
```

This policy will ensure that only traffic coming from the specific VPC endpoint will be allowed. The traffic over the VPC endpoint will be private traffic that does not traverse the public network.

CORRECT: "Create a VPC endpoint for the S3 bucket and create a S3 bucket policy that conditionally limits all S3 actions on the bucket to the VPC endpoint as the source" is the correct answer.

INCORRECT: "Create a VPC endpoint for the S3 bucket and create an IAM policy that conditionally limits all S3 actions on the bucket to the VPC endpoint as the source" is incorrect. The IAM policy needs to be applied somewhere to be affected. In this case we actually need the policy to be applied to the bucket, so a bucket policy is more suitable

INCORRECT: "Create an AWS VPN tunnel between the VPC private subnet and the Amazon S3 public endpoint" is incorrect. You cannot create a VPN tunnel from a private subnet to Amazon S3.

INCORRECT: "Create a NAT gateway in the VPC and modify the private subnet route table to route all traffic destined for S3 through the NAT gateway" is incorrect. A NAT gateway is used to enable instances in private subnets to access the public internet. In this case the traffic would go via the public internet and reach the public endpoint of S3 which is not desired.

References:

https://aws.amazon.com/premiumsupport/knowledge-center/block-s3-traffic-vpc-ip/

Save time with our exam-specific cheat sheets:

https://digitalcloud.training/certification-training/aws-certified-sysops-administrator-associate/amazon-virtual-private-cloud-vpc/

QUESTION 40

A company uses AWS Organizations to manage several AWS accounts. A department in the company requires a new AWS account. A CloudOps Administrator must create the new account and configure user-defined cost allocation tags.

What should the Administrator do to enable user-defined cost allocation tags?

1. Use the Billing and Cost Management console in the new account to create the new user-defined cost allocation tags.
2. Use the Billing and Cost Management console in the payer account to create the new user-defined cost allocation tags.

3. Use the Tag Editor in the new account to create the new user-defined tags, then use the Billing and Cost Management console in the new account to mark the tags as cost allocation tags.
4. Use the Tag Editor in the new account to create the new user-defined tags, then use the Billing and Cost Management console in the payer account to mark the tags as cost allocation tags.

Answer: 4

Explanation:

User-defined tags are tags that you define, create, and apply to resources. After you have created and applied the user-defined tags, you can activate by using the Billing and Cost Management console for cost allocation tracking. Cost Allocation Tags appear on the console after you've enabled Cost Explorer, Budgets, AWS Cost and Usage reports, or legacy reports.

When using AWS Organizations, you must use the Billing and Cost Management console in the payer account to mark the tags as cost allocation tags. You can use the Cost Allocation Tags manager to do this.

CORRECT: "Use the Tag Editor in the new account to create the new user-defined tags, then use the Billing and Cost Management console in the payer account to mark the tags as cost allocation tags" is the correct answer.

INCORRECT: "Use the Tag Editor in the new account to create the new user-defined tags, then use the Billing and Cost Management console in the new account to mark the tags as cost allocation tags" is incorrect. You must use the billing console in the payer (master) account.

INCORRECT: "Use the Billing and Cost Management console in the new account to create the new user-defined cost allocation tags" is incorrect. You must use the Tag Editor in the new account and then the billing console in the payer (master) account.

INCORRECT: "Use the Billing and Cost Management console in the payer account to create the new user-defined cost allocation tags" is incorrect. You must use the Tag Editor in the new account and then the billing console in the payer (master) account.

References:

https://docs.aws.amazon.com/awsaccountbilling/latest/aboutv2/custom-tags.html

QUESTION 41

A company runs an application behind an Application Load Balancer (ALB). The CloudOps Administrator has noticed a large number of suspicious HTTP requests hitting the ALB. The requests originate from various IP addresses.

How can the Administrator block this traffic with the LEAST effort?

1. Create an Amazon CloudFront distribution to cache content and automatically block access to the suspicious source IP addresses.
2. Use Amazon GuardDuty to analyze network activity, detect anomalies, and trigger a Lambda function to prevent access.
3. Use AWS Lambda to analyze a VPC Flow Log, detect the suspicious traffic, and block the IP address in the security groups.
4. Create an AWS WAF rate-based rule to block this traffic when it exceeds a defined threshold.

Answer: 4

Explanation:

AWS WAF is a web application firewall that helps protect web applications from attacks by allowing you to configure rules that allow, block, or monitor (count) web requests based on conditions that you define. These conditions include IP addresses, HTTP headers, HTTP body, URI strings, SQL injection and cross-site scripting.

Rate-based Rules are a new type of Rule that can be configured in AWS WAF. This feature allows you to specify the number of web requests that are allowed by a client IP in a trailing, continuously updated, 5-minute period. If an IP address breaches the configured limit, new requests will be blocked until the request rate falls below the configured threshold.

CORRECT: "Create an AWS WAF rate-based rule to block this traffic when it exceeds a defined threshold" is the correct answer.

INCORRECT: "Create an Amazon CloudFront distribution to cache content and automatically block access to the suspicious source IP addresses" is incorrect. CloudFront cannot automatically detect malicious traffic and block access to the source IP addresses.

INCORRECT: "Use Amazon GuardDuty to analyze network activity, detect anomalies, and trigger a Lambda function to prevent access" is incorrect. GuardDuty can analyze logs and network flows and trigger a function to perform remediation. However, this does not represent the option that requires the least effort as you would need to write the Lambda function.

INCORRECT: "Use AWS Lambda to analyze a VPC Flow Log, detect the suspicious traffic, and block the IP address in the security groups" is incorrect. This is not the option that requires the least effort (must write a Lambda function) and you cannot block IP addresses in security groups (they do not support deny rules).

References:

https://aws.amazon.com/waf/faq/

Save time with our exam-specific cheat sheets:

https://digitalcloud.training/certification-training/aws-certified-sysops-administrator-associate/amazon-virtual-private-cloud-vpc/

QUESTION 42

A CloudOps Administrator manages an application running on an Auto Scaling group of Amazon EC2 instances behind an Application Load Balancer (ALB). The database layer uses Amazon RDS MySQL with an Amazon ElastiCache for Memcached cluster as a caching layer. The CloudOps Administrator must perform all system patching at 10pm on a Wednesday.

Which resources require the configuration of a maintenance window? (Select TWO.)

1. Elastic Load Balancer
2. Amazon EC2 instances
3. Amazon RDS instance
4. Amazon ElastiCache cluster
5. Amazon EC2 Auto Scaling

Answer: 3, 4

Explanation:

Both Amazon RDS and Amazon ElastiCache offer maintenance windows. For both of these services a default maintenance window is provided. However, you can configure your own custom maintenance window that suits your system update schedule.

CORRECT: "Amazon RDS instance" is the correct answer.

CORRECT: "Amazon ElastiCache cluster" is also a correct answer.

INCORRECT: "Elastic Load Balancer" is incorrect. You do not configure maintenance windows for ELBs.

INCORRECT: "Amazon EC2 instances" is incorrect. You do not configure maintenance windows for EC2 instances.

INCORRECT: "Amazon EC2 Auto Scaling" is incorrect. You do not configure maintenance windows for Auto Scaling groups.

References:

https://docs.aws.amazon.com/AmazonElastiCache/latest/mem-ug/maintenance-window.html

https://docs.aws.amazon.com/AmazonRDS/latest/UserGuide/USER_UpgradeDBInstance.Maintenance.html

QUESTION 43

A fleet of Amazon EC2 instances run in an Amazon VPC. The instances must regularly upload log data to a third-party service using the internet. The third-party service has recently implemented IP whitelisting and requires all uploads to come from a single IP address.

What change should the CloudOps Administrator make to the configuration to enable all instances to continue to upload their log files?

1. Move all of the EC2 instances behind a NAT gateway and provide the gateway IP address to the service.
2. Move all of the EC2 instances behind an internet gateway and provide the gateway IP address to the service.
3. Move all of the EC2 instances into a single subnet and provide the subnet CIDR block to the service.
4. Create a single Elastic Network Interface for the EC2 instances and provide the ENI Elastic IP to the service.

Answer: 1

Explanation:

A NAT gateway provides internet connectivity to instances in private subnets. It performs network address translation (NAT) so that the source private IP addresses are translated to an internet-routable public IP address.

The simplest way to solve this problem is to move all of the Amazon EC2 instances behind a NAT gateway which will ensure that all source IP addresses for internet traffic come from a single IP address.

CORRECT: "Move all of the EC2 instances behind a NAT gateway and provide the gateway IP address to the service" is the correct answer.

INCORRECT: "Move all of the EC2 instances behind an internet gateway and provide the gateway IP address to the service" is incorrect. An internet gateway does not perform NAT so all source IP addresses will be the individual public IP addresses of the instances in public subnets that are able to directly use the IGW.

INCORRECT: "Move all of the EC2 instances into a single subnet and provide the subnet CIDR block to the service" is incorrect. A CIDR block is a private IP range, it will not help to provide a single public IP source address for configuration in the service.

INCORRECT: "Create a single Elastic Network Interface for the EC2 instances and provide the ENI Elastic IP to the service" is incorrect. You cannot attach multiple EC2 instances to a single ENI.

References:

https://docs.aws.amazon.com/vpc/latest/userguide/vpc-nat-gateway.html

Save time with our exam-specific cheat sheets:

https://digitalcloud.training/certification-training/aws-certified-sysops-administrator-associate/amazon-virtual-private-cloud-vpc/

QUESTION 44

A CloudOps Administrator has configured a static website on Amazon S3. The bucket name is "mystaticsite". The Administrator plans to use Amazon Route 53 to route traffic to the website and has configured an A record for www.mystaticsite.com. However, users are unable to connect to www.mystaticsite.com using their browsers.

Which of the following is the cause of this issue?

1. An Amazon CloudFront distribution must be configured for the S3 bucket.
2. The Route 53 record set requires a certificate to be configured.
3. The Route 53 record set must be in the same region as the S3 bucket.
4. The S3 bucket name must match the record set name in Route 53.

Answer: 4

Explanation:

When you use static website hosting on Amazon S3 with a custom domain name the name of the bucket must match the website DNS name. To support requests from both the root domain and subdomain, you create two buckets.

- **Domain bucket** - mystaticsite.com
- **Subdomain bucket** - www.mystaticsite.com

In this case the Administrator has not configured the correct S3 bucket name so the configuration will not work.

CORRECT: "The S3 bucket name must match the record set name in Route 53" is the correct answer.

INCORRECT: "An Amazon CloudFront distribution must be configured for the S3 bucket" is incorrect. You don't need an Amazon CloudFront distribution to make this work though you can use one if desired.

INCORRECT: "The Route 53 record set requires a certificate to be configured" is incorrect. This is not required; certificates are not associated with record sets.

INCORRECT: "The Route 53 record set must be in the same region as the S3 bucket" is incorrect. Amazon Route 53 is a global service, you do not create record sets within Regions.

References:

https://docs.aws.amazon.com/AmazonS3/latest/dev/website-hosting-custom-domain-walkthrough.html

Save time with our exam-specific cheat sheets:

https://digitalcloud.training/certification-training/aws-certified-sysops-administrator-associate/amazon-route-53/

QUESTION 45

An Amazon EBS volume attached to an Amazon EC2 instance running a database and is encrypted using AWS KMS customer-managed customer master keys (CMKs). A CloudOps Administrator wants to rotate the AWS KMS keys using automatic key rotation and needs to ensure that the EBS volume encrypted with the current key remains readable.

What should be done to accomplish this?

1. Back up the current KMS data key and enable automatic key rotation.
2. Create a new data key in KMS and assign the key to Amazon EBS.
3. Enable automatic key rotation of the customer master key in KMS.
4. Create a new customer master key in KMS and enable rotation.

Answer: 3

Explanation:

Automatic key rotation is disabled by default on customer managed CMKs. When you enable (or re-enable) key rotation, AWS KMS automatically rotates the CMK 365 days after the enable date and every 365 days thereafter.

When you enable *automatic key rotation* for a customer managed CMK, AWS KMS generates new cryptographic material for the CMK every year. AWS KMS also saves the CMK's older cryptographic material in perpetuity so it can be used to decrypt data that it encrypted. AWS KMS does not delete any rotated key material until you delete the CMK.

Key rotation changes only the CMK's *backing key*, which is the cryptographic material that is used in encryption operations. The CMK is the same logical resource, regardless of whether or how many times its backing key changes. The properties of the CMK do not change, as shown in the following image.

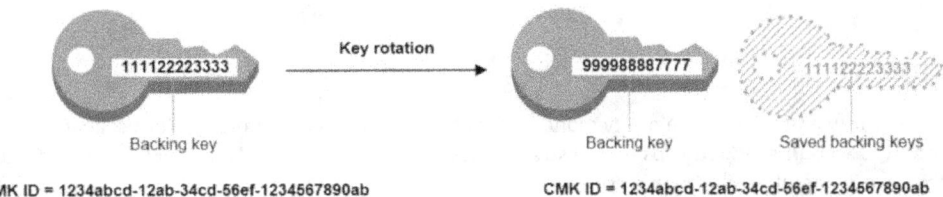

CORRECT: "Enable automatic key rotation of the customer master key in KMS" is the correct answer.

INCORRECT: "Back up the current KMS data key and enable automatic key rotation" is incorrect. The data key should not be changed, the backing key for the CMK should be rotated. This ensures that the date is still readable.

INCORRECT: "Create a new data key in KMS and assign the key to Amazon EBS" is incorrect. The data key should not be changed, the backing key for the CMK should be rotated. This ensures that the date is still readable.

INCORRECT: "Create a new customer master key in KMS and enable rotation" is incorrect. There is no need to create a new CMK, simply enable key rotation for the existing CMK.

References:

https://docs.aws.amazon.com/kms/latest/developerguide/rotate-keys.html

Save time with our exam-specific cheat sheets:

https://digitalcloud.training/certification-training/aws-certified-sysops-administrator-associate/aws-kms-and-aws-cloudhsm/

QUESTION 46

A CloudOps Administrator has been asked to monitor the costs incurred by each user in an AWS account.

How can a CloudOps Administrator collect this information? (Select TWO.)

1. Activate the createdBy tag in the account.
2. Create user metrics in Amazon CloudWatch.
3. Analyze the usage with Cost Explorer.
4. Use Amazon Inspector to advise on resource costs.
5. Create a billing alarm in AWS Budgets.

Answer: 1, 3

Explanation:

The AWS generated tags createdBy is a tag that AWS defines and applies to supported AWS resources for cost allocation purposes. After the tag is activated, AWS starts applying the tag to resources that are created after the AWS generated tags was activated.

The AWS generated tags is available only in the Billing and Cost Management console and reports, and doesn't appear anywhere else in the AWS console, including the AWS Tag Editor. The createdBy tag does not count towards your tags per resource limit.

CORRECT: "Activate the createdBy tag in the account" is the correct answer.

CORRECT: "Analyze the usage with Cost Explorer" is the correct answer.

INCORRECT: "Create user metrics in Amazon CloudWatch" is incorrect. Users do not report metrics to CloudWatch, only AWS resources report metrics.

INCORRECT: "Use Amazon Inspector to advise on resource costs" is incorrect. Inspector does not advise on costs; it is an automated security assessment service.

INCORRECT: "Create a billing alarm in AWS Budgets" is incorrect. A billing alarm will not assist with reporting on costs incurred by individual users.

References:

https://docs.aws.amazon.com/awsaccountbilling/latest/aboutv2/aws-tags.html

QUESTION 47

A company security and compliance policy mandates that specific AMIs are approved for usage in the company's AWS accounts. A CloudOps Administrator needs to review existing Amazon EC2 instances to ensure they are in compliance with this policy.

Which action should a CloudOps Administrator take?

1. Create a custom report using AWS Systems Manager Inventory to identify unapproved AMIs.
2. Create an AWS Lambda function that checks that approved AMI Is have been used.
3. Create an AWS Config rule to check that approved AMI IDs have been used.
4. Use AWS Trusted Advisor to identify EC2 workloads using unapproved AMIs.

Answer: 3

Explanation:

AWS Config enables AWS resource inventory and change management as well as Config Rules to confirm that resources are configured in compliance with policies that you define.

AWS Config rules can check that running instances are using approved Amazon Machine Images, or AMIs. You can specify a list of approved AMI by ID or provide a tag to specify the list of AMI Ids.

CORRECT: "Create an AWS Config rule to check that approved AMI IDs have been used" is the correct answer.

INCORRECT: "Create a custom report using AWS Systems Manager Inventory to identify unapproved AMIs" is incorrect. AWS Config provides this information and should be used for compliance reporting.

INCORRECT: "Create an AWS Lambda function that checks that approved AMI Is have been used" is incorrect. This is more complex and unnecessary when AWS Config provides this data.

INCORRECT: "Use AWS Trusted Advisor to identify EC2 workloads using unapproved AMIs" is incorrect. This is not a function of trusted advisor.

References:

https://aws.amazon.com/blogs/devops/aws-config-checking-for-compliance-with-new-managed-rule-options/

Save time with our exam-specific cheat sheets:

https://digitalcloud.training/certification-training/aws-certified-sysops-administrator-associate/aws-config/

QUESTION 48

A company has several departments and needs to ensure that each department operates within their own isolated environment. They should also only be able to use AWS services that have been pre-approved.

How can these requirements be met?

1. Use an AWS Organization to create accounts for each department and apply service control policies (SCPs) to control access to pre-approved services.
2. Create IAM policies for each department that grant access to specific services and attach them to the user accounts.
3. Create a catalog of services that are approved for use by each department in AWS Service Catalog.
4. Create separate Amazon VPCs for each department and restrict access to approved services using IAM roles.

Answer: 1

Explanation:

AWS Organizations can be used to create new accounts programmatically using the Organizations API. This will create an isolated environment for each department. Service Control Policies (SCPs) can then be used to limit the AWS services that the users can use in that account. This enables a pre-approved set of services to be accessible whilst denying access to all others.

CORRECT: "Use an AWS Organization to create accounts for each department and apply service control policies (SCPs) to control access to pre-approved services" is the correct answer.

INCORRECT: "Create IAM policies for each department that grant access to specific services and attach them to the user accounts" is incorrect. This is administratively extremely challenging. It also does not offer an isolated environment for the departments to run in.

INCORRECT: "Create a catalog of services that are approved for use by each department in AWS Service Catalog" is incorrect. This option does not provide an isolated environment for each department to run in.

INCORRECT: "Create separate Amazon VPCs for each department and restrict access to approved services using IAM roles" is incorrect. Separate VPCs will isolate some resources however using IAM roles will not limit access to services unless the role is assumed.

References:

https://docs.aws.amazon.com/organizations/latest/userguide/orgs_manage_policies_type-auth.html

Save time with our exam-specific cheat sheets:

https://digitalcloud.training/certification-training/aws-certified-sysops-administrator-associate/aws-organizations/

QUESTION 49

An application runs on Amazon EC2 instances behind an Application Load Balancer (ALB). One of the EC2 instances in the target group has exceeded the UnhealthyThresholdCount for consecutive health check failures.

What actions will be taken next? (Select TWO.)

1. The load balancer will continue to perform the health check on the EC2 instance.
2. The EC2 instance will be terminated based on the health check failure.
3. The EC2 instance will be rebooted by Amazon EC2 Auto Scaling.
4. The load balancer will take the EC2 instance out of service.
5. A new EC2 instance will be deployed to replace the unhealthy instance.

Answer: 1, 4

Explanation:

If the health checks exceed **UnhealthyThresholdCount** consecutive failures, the load balancer takes the target out of service. The load balancer continues to send health checks. When the health checks exceed **HealthyThresholdCount** consecutive successes, the load balancer puts the target back in service.

CORRECT: "The load balancer will continue to perform the health check on the EC2 instance" is the correct answer.

CORRECT: "The load balancer will take the EC2 instance out of service" is also a correct answer.

INCORRECT: "The EC2 instance will be terminated based on the health check failure" is incorrect. Amazon ELB does not terminate instances based on health check failures. You need an Auto Scaling group for that.

INCORRECT: "The EC2 instance will be rebooted by Amazon EC2 Auto Scaling" is incorrect. There is no mention of using Auto Scaling and it does not reboot unhealthy instances anyway (it will terminate them).

INCORRECT: "A new EC2 instance will be deployed to replace the unhealthy instance" is incorrect. This is something an Auto Scaling group will do if configured with the ELB health checks. However, there is no mention of there being an Auto Scaling group in this scenario.

References:

https://docs.aws.amazon.com/elasticloadbalancing/latest/application/target-group-health-checks.html#check-target-health

Save time with our exam-specific cheat sheets:

https://digitalcloud.training/certification-training/aws-certified-sysops-administrator-associate/elastic-load-balancing/

QUESTION 50

A company uses a NAT instance to enable Amazon EC2 instances in private subnets to download software and updates from the internet. Latency on the NAT instance has increased as more EC2 instances have been deployed into the private subnets. A CloudOps Administrator needs to reduce latency cost-efficiently and ensure the solution can scale with increasing demand.

Which action should be taken to accomplish this?

1. Add Auto Scaling for the NAT instance.

2. Change the instance type to use a larger instance type.
3. Replace the NAT instance with a NAT gateway.
4. Replace the NAT instance with a virtual private gateway.

Answer: 3

Explanation:

The solution to this issue is to use a NAT gateway instead of a NAT instance. A NAT gateway scales automatically up to 45 Gbps so it will provide plenty of room for increasing demand. You are charged for creating and using a NAT gateway in your account. NAT gateway hourly usage and data processing rates apply. Amazon EC2 charges for data transfer also apply.

CORRECT: "Replace the NAT instance with a NAT gateway" is the correct answer.

INCORRECT: "Add Auto Scaling for the NAT instance" is incorrect. This is not a supported solution and does not work well.

INCORRECT: "Change the instance type to use a larger instance type" is incorrect. This is not the best solution as it does not scale well for future demand.

INCORRECT: "Replace the NAT instance with a virtual private gateway" is incorrect. A VPG is associated with an AWS VPN. It is not related to a NAT instance or NAT gateway.

References:

https://docs.aws.amazon.com/vpc/latest/userguide/vpc-nat-gateway.html

Save time with our exam-specific cheat sheets:

https://digitalcloud.training/certification-training/aws-certified-sysops-administrator-associate/amazon-virtual-private-cloud-vpc/

QUESTION 51

A CloudOps Administrator checked the AWS Personal Health Dashboard and noticed that scheduled maintenance is going to affect a critical EBS-backed Amazon EC2 instance. The instance must be available during business hours and an interruption in service is unacceptable.

What can the Administrator do to ensure that the scheduled maintenance does not cause an outage?

1. Configure an Amazon CloudWatch Events rule to restart the instance if it is stopped.
2. Create an Amazon Machine Image (AMI) of the instance and use the AMI to launch a new instance after the current instance is shut down.
3. Use the EC2 Management Console to move the instance onto different host hardware.
4. Stop and start the EC2 instance during a maintenance window outside of normal business hours.

Answer: 4

Explanation:

When you stop and start an Amazon EC2 instance it is usually launched on a different underlying host computer. This can be performed outside of business hours to ensure the service is not interrupted during the working day. By moving the instance onto different host hardware, the instance will then not be affected by the AWS scheduled maintenance.

CORRECT: "Stop and start the EC2 instance during a maintenance window outside of normal business hours" is the correct answer.

INCORRECT: "Configure an Amazon CloudWatch Events rule to restart the instance if it is stopped" is incorrect. This will not prevent an interruption of service during business hours as the instance will still be affected by the scheduled maintenance.

INCORRECT: "Create an Amazon Machine Image (AMI) of the instance and use the AMI to launch a new instance after the current instance is shut down" is incorrect. This will not prevent an interruption of service during business hours as the instance will still be affected by the scheduled maintenance.

INCORRECT: "Use the EC2 Management Console to move the instance onto different host hardware" is incorrect. You cannot move instances onto different host hardware through the EC2 management console.

References:

https://docs.aws.amazon.com/AWSEC2/latest/UserGuide/Stop_Start.html

Save time with our exam-specific cheat sheets:

https://digitalcloud.training/certification-training/aws-certified-sysops-administrator-associate/amazon-ec2/

QUESTION 52

A CloudOps Administrator manages a fleet of Amazon EC2 instances running a distribution of Linux. The operating systems are patched on a schedule using AWS Systems Manager Patch Manager. Users of the application have complained about poor response times when the systems are being patched.

What can be done to ensure patches are deployed automatically with MINIMAL customer impact?

1. Use separate patch groups and update the groups at different times to spread the updates out.
2. Update the instances one at a time using a snapshot of a patched Amazon Machine Image (AMI).
3. Configure the maintenance window to patch 10% of the instances in the patch group at a time.
4. Create a patched Amazon Machine Image (AMI). Configure the maintenance window option to deploy the patched AMI on only 10% of the fleet at a time.

Answer: 3

Explanation:

CORRECT: "Configure the maintenance window to patch 10% of the instances in the patch group at a time" is the correct answer.

INCORRECT: "Use separate patch groups and update the groups at different times to spread the updates out" is incorrect. This may not reduce the impact enough unless the rate control is set to lower the number of instances that are patched at the same time.

INCORRECT: "Update the instances one at a time using a snapshot of a patched Amazon Machine Image (AMI)" is incorrect. This is not an automated approach and would only be possible if the applications are stateless or store state on separate volumes to the OS (unknown).

INCORRECT: "Create a patched Amazon Machine Image (AMI). Configure the maintenance window option to deploy the patched AMI on only 10% of the fleet at a time" is incorrect. Patch Manager deploys updates to EC2 instances, it does not replace the AMIs.

References:

https://aws.amazon.com/blogs/mt/patching-your-windows-ec2-instances-using-aws-systems-manager-patch-manager/

Save time with our exam-specific cheat sheets:

https://digitalcloud.training/certification-training/aws-certified-sysops-administrator-associate/aws-systems-manager/

QUESTION 53

A team of Analysts require a specialized Amazon EC2 configuration. The team need to able to launch and terminate instances across the company's AWS accounts but do not wish to configure EC2 settings on their own. The specialized EC2 configuration contains licensed software and must be available for use only by the Analysts.

Which solution should a CloudOps Administrator use to allow the Analysts to deploy their workloads with MINIMAL effort?

1. Create an Amazon Machine Image (AMI) encrypted with an AWS KMS key. Share the encrypted AMI with authorized accounts. Allow the Analysts access to use the KMS key.
2. Create an AWS CloudFormation template and configure launch permissions on the AMI used by the template to add the authorized accounts. Share the template in an Amazon S3 bucket.

3. Create an AWS Elastic Beanstalk environment. Share the environment across accounts and use IAM policies to enable access for the team of Analysts.
4. Create an AWS CloudFormation template and use it to create a portfolio in AWS Service Catalog. Grant the Analysts permissions to launch products from the portfolio.

Answer: 4

Explanation:

In AWS Service Catalog a *product* is an IT service that you want to make available for deployment on AWS. A *portfolio* is a collection of *products*, together with configuration information. Portfolios help manage who can use specific products and how they can use them.

Granting a user access to a portfolio enables that user to browse the portfolio and launch the products in it. You apply AWS Identity and Access Management (IAM) permissions to control who can view and modify your catalog.

This solution ensures that the Analysts can launch the specialized EC2 instances without needing to configure any settings in EC2 as the instances will be launched using AWS CloudFormation. The permissions are also configured so only the Analysts can launch the specialized instances.

CORRECT: "Create an AWS CloudFormation template and use it to create a portfolio in AWS Service Catalog. Grant the Analysts permissions to launch products from the portfolio" is the correct answer.

INCORRECT: "Create an Amazon Machine Image (AMI) encrypted with an AWS KMS key. Share the encrypted AMI with authorized accounts. Allow the Analysts access to use the KMS key" is incorrect. Though you can share encrypted AMIs across accounts, this does not solve the issue of ensuring that the Analysts do not need to configure EC2 settings.

INCORRECT: "Create an AWS CloudFormation template and configure launch permissions on the AMI used by the template to add the authorized accounts. Share the template in an Amazon S3 bucket" is incorrect. This does not limit the usage of the AMI to only the Analysts as it will be available for launch within each authorized account.

INCORRECT: "Create an AWS Elastic Beanstalk environment. Share the environment across accounts and use IAM policies to enable access for the team of Analysts" is incorrect. You cannot share an Elastic Beanstalk environment across accounts.

References:

https://docs.aws.amazon.com/servicecatalog/latest/adminguide/what-is_concepts.html

Save time with our exam-specific cheat sheets:

https://digitalcloud.training/certification-training/aws-certified-sysops-administrator-associate/aws-cloudformation/

QUESTION 54

A company has a web application that uses an Amazon CloudFront web distribution, an Application Load Balancer (ALB) and Amazon EC2 instances with a shared Amazon EFS filesystem. Where applicable, all services have logging enabled. There have been some connection issues reported and the CloudOps Administrator needs to check HTTP layer 7 status codes to determine the root cause.

Which log files should the Administrator check? (Select TWO.)

1. VPC Flow Logs
2. Amazon CloudWatch Logs
3. ALB access logs
4. CloudFront access logs
5. Amazon EFS logs

Answer: 3, 4

Explanation:

Both ALB access logs and Amazon CloudFront access logs contain layer 7 information including the HTTP status codes. These logs would be the best place to find the HTTP status codes and investigate any issues that are occurring.

CORRECT: "ALB access logs" is the correct answer.

CORRECT: "CloudFront access logs" is also a correct answer.

INCORRECT: "VPC Flow Logs" is incorrect. VPC Flow Logs do not contain HTTP status codes. They show layer 3/4 data and information about the subnets, interfaces, and instances involved in the communication.

INCORRECT: "Amazon CloudWatch Logs" is incorrect. You cannot find HTTP status codes in CloudWatch Logs.

INCORRECT: "Amazon EFS logs" is incorrect. There are no log files in Amazon EFS, you must use Amazon CloudWatch Logs (will not store HTTP status codes).

References:

https://docs.aws.amazon.com/AmazonCloudFront/latest/DeveloperGuide/AccessLogs.html

QUESTION 55

A CloudOps Administrator manages a fleet of Amazon EC2 instances that use a custom Linux Amazon Machine Image (AMI). The Administrator is attempting to use AWS Systems Manager Session Manager to initiate an SSH session with one of the instances. The Administrator cannot find the target instance in the Session Manager console.

Which combination of actions will solve this issue? (Select TWO.)

1. Add permissions for Session Manager to the instance profile.
2. Add access keys to the instance that grant access to Session Manager.
3. Install the Systems Manager agent (SSM Agent) on the instances.
4. Modify the instance security group to allow inbound traffic on SSH port 22.
5. Run Systems Manager Inventory to refresh the instance data.

Answer: 1, 3

Explanation:

The SSM Agent must be installed on the instances you want to connect to through sessions. In this case the custom AMI will not have the SSM Agent installed so the Administrator must install it.

By default, AWS Systems Manager doesn't have permission to perform actions on your instances. You must grant access by using an IAM instance profile. An instance profile is a container that passes IAM role information to an EC2 instance at launch. This requirement applies to permissions for all AWS Systems Manager capabilities, not only those specific to Session Manager.

CORRECT: "Add permissions for Session Manager to the instance profile" is the correct answer.

CORRECT: "Install the Systems Manager agent (SSM Agent) on the instances" is also a correct answer.

INCORRECT: "Add access keys to the instance that grant access to Session Manager" is incorrect. You must use an IAM instance profile and attach an IAM policy to add permissions to Session Manager.

INCORRECT: "Modify the instance security group to allow inbound traffic on SSH port 22" is incorrect. With Session Manager you do not need to open port 22 to enable sessions with EC2 instances. This is one of the advantages of using Session Manager instead of traditional SSH.

INCORRECT: "Run Systems Manager Inventory to refresh the instance data" is incorrect. You do not need to run an inventory, and this will not work until you install the SSM Agent and provide the necessary permissions anyway.

References:

https://docs.aws.amazon.com/systems-manager/latest/userguide/session-manager-getting-started.html

Save time with our exam-specific cheat sheets:

https://digitalcloud.training/certification-training/aws-certified-sysops-administrator-associate/aws-systems-manager/

QUESTION 56

An application runs on Amazon EC2 instances in multiple Availability Zones (AZs) behind an internet-facing Application Load Balancer (ALB). A CloudOps Administrator needs to track the originating IP address of each application request and the EC2 instance that processes it.

What should the Administrator use to access this information?

1. Amazon CloudWatch
2. The ALB access logs
3. AWS CloudTrail
4. VPC Flow Logs

Answer: 2

Explanation:

Elastic Load Balancing provides access logs that capture detailed information about requests sent to your load balancer. The entries include the **client:port** which shows the the IP address and port of the requesting client and the **target:port** which includes the IP address and port of the target that processed this request.

CORRECT: "The ALB access logs" is the correct answer.

INCORRECT: "Amazon CloudWatch" is incorrect. CloudWatch monitors performance metrics, it does not show connectivity information.

INCORRECT: "AWS CloudTrail" is incorrect. CloudTrail tracks API actions for auditing.

INCORRECT: "VPC Flow Logs" is incorrect. VPC Flow Logs will not see the source IP of the originating client because that traffic flow it outside the VPC and is terminated at the ALB. The connectivity within the VPC will be between the ALB and the target so the originating source address is not present.

References:

https://docs.aws.amazon.com/elasticloadbalancing/latest/application/load-balancer-access-logs.html

Save time with our exam-specific cheat sheets:

https://digitalcloud.training/certification-training/aws-certified-sysops-administrator-associate/elastic-load-balancing/

QUESTION 57

A CloudOps Administrator successfully launched an Amazon EC2 instance in the us-east-1 Region using an AWS CloudFormation template. The Administrator then attempted to use the same template to launch an EC2 instance in the eu-west-1 Region, but the Stack creation failed.

What is the MOST likely cause of this failure?

1. Resource tags defined in the CloudFormation template are specific to the eu-west-1 Region.
2. The user account being used does not have permissions to launch instances in the eu-west-1 Region.
3. The Amazon Machine Image (AMI) ID referenced in the CloudFormation template could not be found in the eu-west-1 Region.
4. The Availability Zone in the eu-west-1 Region has insufficient capacity to handle the request.

Answer: 3

Explanation:

AMI IDs are specific to an AWS Region and therefore you must ensure you specify the correct AMI IDs for the Region into which you are launching Amazon EC2 instances. You can use mappings with the AWS::Region pseudo parameter (which resolves the region into which you're deploying the stack) to return different AMI IDs depending on where the stack is deployed.

The following code would solve the issue in this scenario:

```
    Parameters:
      KeyName:
        Description: Name of an existing EC2 KeyPair to enable SSH access to the instance
        Type: String
      Mappings:
        RegionMap:
          us-east-1:
            AMI: ami-76f0061f
          us-west-1:
            AMI: ami-655a0a20
          eu-west-1:
            AMI: ami-7fd4e10b
          ap-southeast-1:
            AMI: ami-72621c20
          ap-northeast-1:
            AMI: ami-8e08a38f
      Resources:
        Ec2Instance:
          Type: 'AWS::EC2::Instance'
          Properties:
            KeyName: !Ref KeyName
            ImageId: !FindInMap
              - RegionMap
              - !Ref 'AWS::Region'
              - AMI
            UserData: !Base64 '80'
```

CORRECT: "The Amazon Machine Image (AMI) ID referenced in the CloudFormation template could not be found in the eu-west-1 Region" is the correct answer.

INCORRECT: "Resource tags defined in the CloudFormation template are specific to the eu-west-1 Region" is incorrect. Resource tags apply metadata to your resources for identification and categorization and are unlikely to have prevented stack creation.

INCORRECT: "The user account being used does not have permissions to launch instances in the eu-west-1 Region" is incorrect. You can limit permissions to launch stacks in regions using conditions but would need to manually add in this code so it's not likely to happen accidentally.

INCORRECT: "The Availability Zone in the eu-west-1 Region has insufficient capacity to handle the request" is incorrect. This is a possible issue but is highly unlikely when launching a single EC2 instance.

References:

https://docs.aws.amazon.com/AWSCloudFormation/latest/UserGuide/gettingstarted.templatebasics.html#gettingstarted.templatebasics.mappings

Save time with our exam-specific cheat sheets:

https://digitalcloud.training/certification-training/aws-certified-sysops-administrator-associate/aws-cloudformation/

QUESTION 58

A CloudOps Administrator has been asked to identify potential cost savings through downsizing underutilized Amazon EC2 instances.

How can this be done with MINIMAL effort?

1. Use AWS Cost Explorer to generate resource optimization recommendations.
2. Use AWS Budgets to generate alerts for underutilized EC2 instances.
3. Run an AWS Lambda function that checks for utilization of EC2 instances.
4. Use Amazon CloudWatch metrics to identify EC2 instances with low utilization.

Answer: 1

Explanation:

You can use AWS Cost Explorer with to generate Amazon EC2 resource optimization recommendations. These recommendations identify idle and underutilized instances across your accounts and regions. To generate these recommendations, AWS analyzes your historical EC2 resource usage, your Amazon CloudWatch metrics, and your existing reservation footprint to identify opportunities for cost savings (e.g., by terminating idle instances or downsizing active instances to lower-cost options).

This option requires the least administrative effort.

CORRECT: "Use AWS Cost Explorer to generate resource optimization recommendations" is the correct answer.

INCORRECT: "Use AWS Budgets to generate alerts for underutilized EC2 instances" is incorrect. AWS Budgets alerts you when you reach certain billing thresholds, it does not report on underutilization of resources.

INCORRECT: "Run an AWS Lambda function that checks for utilization of EC2 instances" is incorrect. This would require more effort than using the AWS Cost Explorer recommendations.

INCORRECT: "Use Amazon CloudWatch metrics to identify EC2 instances with low utilization" is incorrect. This would require more effort than using the AWS Cost Explorer recommendations.

References:

https://aws.amazon.com/about-aws/whats-new/2019/07/introducing-amazon-ec2-resource-optimization-recommendations/

QUESTION 59

A distributed application runs across many Amazon EC2 instances and processes large quantities of data. The application is designed to handle processing interruptions without causing issues. A CloudOps Administrator needs to determine the MOST cost-effective pricing model for this use case.

Which EC2 pricing model should the Administrator use?

1. Dedicated Hosts
2. On-Demand Instances
3. Reserved Instances
4. Spot Instances

Answer: 4

Explanation:

The most cost-effective pricing model for this use case is to use Spot instances. With Spot instances you need to be able to handle the termination of resources when AWS need the capacity back. Therefore, it should only be used with applications that can accept processing interruptions. In this case this distributed application can handle the processing interruptions so the best way to lower costs is to use Spot instances.

CORRECT: "Spot Instances" is the correct answer.

INCORRECT: "Dedicated Hosts" is incorrect. This is a more expensive option and there are no requirements for the use of dedicated hosts.

INCORRECT: "On-Demand Instances" is incorrect. There are no cost savings to be gained by using on-demand instances.

INCORRECT: "Reserved Instances" is incorrect. This would be a good pricing model for longer term (1 or 3 years) use cases for steady-state workloads. For this particular scenario, Spot instances are better to further lower costs.

References:

https://docs.aws.amazon.com/AWSEC2/latest/UserGuide/using-spot-instances.html

Save time with our exam-specific cheat sheets:

https://digitalcloud.training/certification-training/aws-certified-sysops-administrator-associate/amazon-ec2/

QUESTION 60

An application uses an Amazon RDS Multi-AZ DB instance. Due to new security compliance requirements a CloudOps Administrator needs to encrypt the database.

Which approach can the Administrator take to encrypt the database?

1. Use the RDS management console to enable encryption for the database.
2. Create an encrypted read replica and promote the replica to master.
3. Encrypt the standby replica in the secondary Availability Zone and promote it to the primary instance.
4. Take a snapshot of the RDS instance, copy and encrypt the snapshot, and then restore to the new RDS instance.

Answer: 4

Explanation:

You can only enable encryption for an Amazon RDS DB instance when you create it, not after the DB instance is created. However, because you can encrypt a copy of an unencrypted DB snapshot, you can effectively add encryption to an unencrypted DB instance.

To do this you create a snapshot of your DB instance, and then create an encrypted copy of that snapshot. You can then restore a DB instance from the encrypted snapshot, and thus you have an encrypted copy of your original DB instance.

CORRECT: "Take a snapshot of the RDS instance, copy and encrypt the snapshot, and then restore to the new RDS instance" is the correct answer.

INCORRECT: "Encrypt the standby replica in the secondary Availability Zone and promote it to the primary instance" is incorrect. You cannot create an encrypted standby from an unencrypted primary instance.

INCORRECT: "Create an encrypted read replica and promote the replica to master" is incorrect. You cannot create an encrypted read replica from an unencrypted master.

INCORRECT: "Use the RDS management console to enable encryption for the database" is incorrect. You cannot add encryption to an existing instance using the RDS management console.

References:

https://docs.aws.amazon.com/AmazonRDS/latest/UserGuide/Overview.Encryption.html

Save time with our exam-specific cheat sheets:

https://digitalcloud.training/certification-training/aws-certified-sysops-administrator-associate/amazon-rds/

QUESTION 61

A company launched a static website using Amazon S3 which is being used by thousands of users from around the world. Soon after launch the website users started reporting 503 service unavailable errors.

What is the most likely cause of these errors?

1. The request rate to Amazon S3 is too high.
2. There is an issue with the S3 Transfer Acceleration service.
3. The pre-signed URL has expired and no longer exists.
4. The users do not have the correct permissions to access the website.

Answer: 1

Explanation:

A 503 service unavailable error is most likely caused by too many requests coming in within a very short period of time. This can be an issue with Amazon S3 for extremely high request rates.

CORRECT: "The request rate to Amazon S3 is too high" is the correct answer.

INCORRECT: "There is an issue with the S3 Transfer Acceleration service" is incorrect. Transfer acceleration is used for uploading data to S3 so it is not related to static websites.

INCORRECT: "The pre-signed URL has expired and no longer exists" is incorrect. This would not give a 503 service unavailable error as the page would not exist.

INCORRECT: "The users do not have the correct permissions to access the website" is incorrect. A permissions error would not be a 503 service unavailable, you would get an access denied error instead.

References:

https://aws.amazon.com/premiumsupport/knowledge-center/http-5xx-errors-s3/

Save time with our exam-specific cheat sheets:

https://digitalcloud.training/certification-training/aws-certified-sysops-administrator-associate/amazon-s3/

QUESTION 62

A company runs an application across two public and two private subnets in two availability zones (AZs). They use a single internet gateway and a single NAT gateway. Amazon CloudFront is used to cache static and dynamic content.

What would potentially cause applications in the VPC to fail during a brief AZ outage?

1. Amazon CloudFront, as it cannot use origins in multiple subnets.
2. A single internet gateway, because it is not redundant across multiple AZs.
3. A single NAT gateway, because it is not redundant across multiple AZs.
4. The main route table, as it cannot be associated with multiple subnets.

Answer: 3

Explanation:

Each NAT gateway is created in a specific Availability Zone and implemented with redundancy in that zone. Therefore, if you only have a single NAT gateway you could lose it in the event of an AZ outage.

CORRECT: "A single NAT gateway, because it is not redundant across multiple AZs" is the correct answer.

INCORRECT: "A single internet gateway, because it is not redundant across multiple AZs" is incorrect. Internet gateways are redundant across multiple AZs as they are highly available and attached at the VPC level.

INCORRECT: "Amazon CloudFront, as it cannot use origins in multiple subnets" is incorrect. You can use CloudFront with multiple origins or the origin could be an ELB with multiple targets. In a brief outage it should not matter as the content will be cached.

INCORRECT: "The main route table, as it cannot be associated with multiple subnets" is incorrect. You can associate any route table with multiple subnets and those subnets can be created within different AZs.

References:

https://docs.aws.amazon.com/vpc/latest/userguide/vpc-nat-gateway.html

Save time with our exam-specific cheat sheets:

https://digitalcloud.training/certification-training/aws-certified-sysops-administrator-associate/amazon-virtual-private-cloud-vpc/

QUESTION 63

An eCommerce application consists of Amazon EC2 instances in an Auto Scaling group. The ASG scales based on CPU utilization. Users report the application response time is slow at the beginning of each business day

What action will address this issue?

1. Create a scheduled scaling action to scale up in anticipation of the traffic.
2. Change the Auto Scaling group to scale up and down based on memory utilization.
3. Change the launch configuration to launch larger EC2 instance types.
4. Modify the scaling policy to deploy more EC2 instances when scaling up.

Answer: 1

Explanation:

In this scenario the application is not scaling fast enough for the amount of traffic that is being received at the beginning of the business day. The best way to ensure that there's always enough capacity available at a specific time is to configure a scheduled scaling action.

To configure your Auto Scaling group to scale based on a schedule, you create a scheduled action. The scheduled action tells Amazon EC2 Auto Scaling to perform a scaling action at specified times.

To create a scheduled scaling action, you specify the start time when the scaling action should take effect, and the new minimum, maximum, and desired sizes for the scaling action.

At the specified time, Amazon EC2 Auto Scaling updates the group with the values for minimum, maximum, and desired size that are specified by the scaling action.

CORRECT: "Create a scheduled scaling action to scale up in anticipation of the traffic" is the correct answer.

INCORRECT: "Change the Auto Scaling group to scale up and down based on memory utilization" is incorrect. You cannot configure Auto Scaling to scale based on memory as this is not a metric reported to CloudWatch.

INCORRECT: "Change the launch configuration to launch larger EC2 instance types" is incorrect. This would cost more and still may not adequately resolve the spike in usage at the beginning of the day. It is better to use scheduled scaling to provide additional capacity only when it's needed.

INCORRECT: "Modify the scaling policy to deploy more EC2 instances when scaling up" is incorrect. The with this option is that it still takes time to deploy and bring up the instances and have them available to service requests. During this time users are experiencing issues. The best resolution is to have the instances ready ahead of peak usage by using scheduled scaling.

References:

https://docs.aws.amazon.com/autoscaling/ec2/userguide/schedule_time.html

Save time with our exam-specific cheat sheets:

https://digitalcloud.training/certification-training/aws-certified-sysops-administrator-associate/amazon-ec2-auto-scaling/

QUESTION 64

An application runs on Amazon EC2 instances in an Auto Scaling group behind an Application Load Balancer (ALB). A CloudOps Administrator needs to set an Amazon CloudWatch alarm for when all target instances behind the ALB are unhealthy.

How should the Administrator configure the alarm?

1. In the AWS/ApplicationELB namespace, alarm when the HealthyHostCount metric is >=1
2. In the AWS/ApplicationELB namespace, alarm when the HealthyHostCount metric is <=0
3. In the AWS/EC2 namespace, alarm when the StatusCheckFailed_Instance metric is >=1
4. In the AWS/EC2 namespace, alarm when the StatusCheckFailed_System metric is <=0

Answer: 2

Explanation:

The alarm should go off when all target instances associated with the ALB are unhealthy. Therefore the AWS/ApplicationELB namespace should be used and the HealthyHostCount metric should alarm when there are less than or equal to 0 healthy instances (<=0).

In the Amazon CloudWatch console the alarm should look like the following image:

Metric

Edit

Graph
This alarm will trigger when the blue line goes below the red line for 1 datapoints within 5 minutes.

[Graph showing UnHealthyHostCount from 17:00 to 20:00, flat at 1]

Namespace
AWS/ApplicationELB

Metric name
UnHealthyHostCount

TargetGroup
targetgroup/TG2/137443c57f78ca10

LoadBalancer
app/MyALB/8f06321a4ba59bf9

Statistic
Average

Period
5 minutes

Conditions

Threshold type

○ Static
Use a value as a threshold

○ Anomaly detection
Use a band as a threshold

Whenever UnHealthyHostCount is...
Define the alarm condition.

○ Greater
\> threshold

○ Greater/Equal
\>= threshold

● Lower/Equal
<= threshold

○ Lower
< threshold

than...
Define the threshold value.

1

Must be a number

CORRECT: "In the AWS/ApplicationELB namespace, alarm when the HealthyHostCount metric is <=0" is the correct answer.

INCORRECT: "In the AWS/ApplicationELB namespace, alarm when the HealthyHostCount metric is >=1" is incorrect. This configuration would alarm when there are 1 or more healthy instances.

INCORRECT: "In the AWS/EC2 namespace, alarm when the StatusCheckFailed_Instance metric is >=1" is incorrect. The AWS/EC2 namespace is not related to the ALB, this alarm would trigger based on .Amazon EC2 status checks.

INCORRECT: "In the AWS/EC2 namespace, alarm when the StatusCheckFailed_System metric is <=0" is incorrect. The AWS/EC2 namespace is not related to the ALB, this alarm would trigger based on .Amazon EC2 status checks.

References:

https://docs.aws.amazon.com/elasticloadbalancing/latest/application/load-balancer-cloudwatch-metrics.html

Save time with our exam-specific cheat sheets:

https://digitalcloud.training/certification-training/aws-certified-sysops-administrator-associate/amazon-cloudwatch/

QUESTION 65

A company run an application on a single Amazon EC2 instance in a single Availability Zone (AZ). The company requires that the application is made highly available. A CloudOps Administrator has created an Application Load Balancer (ALB) and a launch configuration from the running instance. The Administrator needs to create an Auto Scaling group for the launch configuration.

How should the Auto Scaling group be configured to make the application highly available?

1. Use at least 2 Availability Zones with a minimum size of 1, desired capacity of 1, and a maximum size of 1.
2. Use at least 3 Availability Zones with a minimum size of 2, desired capacity of 2, and a maximum of 2.
3. Use at least 2 regions with a minimum size of 1, desired capacity of 1, and a maximum size of 1.
4. Use at least 3 regions with a minimum size of 2, desired capacity of 2, and a maximum size of 2.

Answer: 2

Explanation:

For high availability the Auto Scaling group should launch at least 2 instances in at least 2 AZs. Therefore, the minimum size of the ASG should be 2, the desired capacity should be 2, and the maximum should be 2.

CORRECT: "Use at least 3 Availability Zones with a minimum size of 2, desired capacity of 2, and a maximum of 2" is the correct answer.

INCORRECT: "Use at least 2 Availability Zones with a minimum size of 1, desired capacity of 1, and a maximum size of 1" is incorrect. This would result in an outage if the AZ with the 1 running instance fails.

INCORRECT: "Use at least 2 regions with a minimum size of 1, desired capacity of 1, and a maximum size of 1" is incorrect. You cannot select multiple regions in an ASG.

INCORRECT: "Use at least 3 regions with a minimum size of 2, desired capacity of 2, and a maximum size of 2" is incorrect. You cannot select multiple regions in an ASG.

References:

https://docs.aws.amazon.com/autoscaling/ec2/userguide/as-add-availability-zone.html

Save time with our exam-specific cheat sheets:

https://digitalcloud.training/certification-training/aws-certified-sysops-administrator-associate/amazon-ec2-auto-scaling/

SET 2: PRACTICE QUESTIONS ONLY

For training purposes, go directly to Set 2: Practice Questions, Answers & Explanations

QUESTION 1

A company is testing a new application which is expected to receive a large amount of traffic. The application runs on Amazon EC2 instances in an Auto Scaling group and uses an Amazon RDS Multi-AZ database. Static content is hosted in an Amazon S3 bucket. During performance testing the application response time increased significantly.

How can a CloudOps Administrator increase the performance and scalability of the application?

1. Serve the static content from the EC2 instances backed by an Amazon EFS filesystem.
2. Move the database from Amazon RDS to Amazon ElastiCache for Memcached.
3. Use Amazon CloudFront to cache the static content.
4. Use Amazon Route 53 with geolocation routing.

QUESTION 2

A CloudOps Administrator created an AWS CloudFormation template and attempted to use it for the first time to create a new stack. The stack creation failed with a status of ROLLBACK_COMPLETE. The issues in the template have been resolved and the administrator wishes to continue with the stack deployment.

How can the administrator continue?

1. Relaunch the template to create a new stack.
2. Run the execute-change-set command.
3. Perform an **update-stack** action on the failed stack.
4. Run a **validate-template** command.

QUESTION 3

A CloudOps Administrator has started to use Amazon Inspector to assess Amazon EC2 instances for security and compliance. The Administrator noticed that some security findings are missing for some instances.

Which action should the Administrator take to attempt to resolve this issue?

1. Generate the missing security findings list manually by logging in to the affected EC2 instances and running CLI commands.
2. Verify that the unified agent for Amazon CloudWatch is installed on the instances and collecting the necessary metrics.
3. Move the instances to a public subnet and attach an Elastic IP address to ensure connectivity to the Amazon Inspector service.
4. Verify that the Amazon Inspector agent is installed and running on the affected instances and then restart the agent.

QUESTION 4

A team of Data Analysts launched an Amazon RedShift Spectrum cluster. When the team attempts to use the query editor to query data, they received an "[Amazon](500310) Invalid operation: AwsClientException: Failed connect to datacatalog.us-west-2.amazonaws.com:443" error.

How can this issue be resolved?

1. Enhanced VPC Routing is enabled and must be disabled when using the query editor.
2. There is insufficient capacity in the cluster, use Elastic resize to adjust capacity.
3. The cluster login credentials are incorrect; specify the correct credentials and try again.

4. The cluster nodes are running in multiple Availability Zones, launch nodes in a single AZ only.

QUESTION 5

A group of systems administrators use IAM access keys to manage Amazon EC2 instances using the AWS CLI. The company policy mandates that access keys are automatically disabled after 60 days.

Which solution can be used to automate this process?

1. Create an Amazon CloudWatch alarm to trigger an AWS Lambda function that disables keys older than 60 days.
2. Use an AWS Config rule to identify noncompliant keys. Create a custom AWS Systems Manager Automation document for remediation.
3. Configure Amazon Inspector to provide security best practice recommendations and automatically disable the keys.
4. Create a script that checks the key age and disables keys older than 60 days. Use a cron job on an Amazon EC2 instance to execute the script.

QUESTION 6

An application is deployed on three separate environments using AWS CloudFormation. The environments, development, test, and production, each require unique credentials to access external services.

Which option provides a secure means for providing the required credentials with a MINIMUM of operational overhead?

1. Use parameters to pass the credentials to the CloudFormation template. Use the user data script to insert the parameterized credentials into the EC2 instances.
2. Use AWS Systems Manager Parameter Store to store the credentials as secure strings. Pass an environment tag as a parameter to the CloudFormation template. Use the user data script to insert the environment tag in the EC2 instances.
3. Use a separate CloudFormation template for each environment. In the Resources section, include a user data script for each EC2 instance. Use the user data script to insert the proper credentials for the environment into the EC2 instances.
4. Use separate Amazon Machine Images (AMIs) for each environment with the required credentials. Pass the environment tag as a parameter to the CloudFormation template and us mappings to map the environment tag to the proper AMI.

QUESTION 7

A group of Developer have been given access to a separate AWS account to work on a new project. The Developers require full administrative access to create IAM policies and roles in the account, but corporate policies require that they are blocked from using a few specific AWS services.

What is the BEST way to grant the Developers privileges in the new account while still ensuring compliance with corporate policies?

1. Create a service control policy in AWS Organizations and apply it to the new account.
2. Create a customer managed policy in IAM and apply it to all users within the new account.
3. Create a job-specific policy in IAM and apply it to all users within the new account.
4. Create an IAM group for the Developers and apply a policy restricting access to the specific services.

QUESTION 8

The performance of an Amazon RDS MySQL database has been suffering during a recent busy period. A CloudOps Administrator noticed that database queries were running more slowly than is acceptable. Amazon CloudWatch metrics show that the CPU utilization was reaching close to 100%.

Which action should the Administrator take to resolve this issue?

1. Configure Amazon CloudFront to cache database queries and reduce load on RDS.
2. Scale horizontally by adding additional RDS MySQL nodes to offload write requests.
3. Enable the Multi-AZ feature for the RDS instance to enable extra capacity.
4. Modify the RDS MySQL instance so it is a larger instance type.

QUESTION 9

A CloudOps Administrator has an AWS CloudFormation template created from an infrastructure stack deployed in us-east-1. The Administrator attempts to use the template to launch a stack in us-west-1. The stack partially deploys but then errors and rolls back.

What are the most likely reasons for the failure of the stack deployment? (Select TWO.)

1. The template referenced an IAM user that is not available in us-west-1.
2. The template referenced an Amazon Machine Image (AMI) that is not available in us-west-1.
3. The template did not have the proper level of permissions to deploy the resources in us-west-1.
4. The template referenced services that do not exist in us-west-1.
5. CloudFormation templates can be used only to deploy stacks in a single Region.

QUESTION 10

A CloudOps Administrator is preparing for the release of a new application running on a fleet of Amazon EC2 instances. The Administrator needs to test an Amazon CloudWatch alarm that is configured to send an SNS notification when the CPU hits 70% utilization to ensure the notification is delivered successfully.

How should the Administrator test that the alarm triggers the notification?

1. Use the set-alarm-state command in AWS CloudTrail to invoke the Amazon SNS notification.
2. Send custom metrics reporting that the CPU is running at 80% utilization to AWS CloudTrail.
3. Manually configure the CPU to 80% utilization using the EC2 Management Console.
4. Use the set-alarm-state command in the AWS CLI for CloudWatch.

QUESTION 11

A company is connected to an Amazon VPC from an on-premises data center with a VPN connection. A CloudOps Administrator attempted to ping an Amazon EC2 instance in a private subnet with the IP 172.31.10.10 and did not receive a response. The ping command was issued from a computer in the data center with the IP address 3.104.75.244. VPC Flow Logs were enabled and showed the following entries:

2 123456789010 eni-1234abcd 3.104.75.244 172.31.10.10 0 0 1 4 336 1432917027 1432917142 ACCEPT OK

2 123456789010 eni-1234abcd 172.31.10.10 3.104.75.244 0 0 1 4 336 1432917094 1432917142 REJECT OK

What is the most likely cause of the issue?

1. The EC2 security group rules need to be modified to allow inbound traffic from the on-premises computer.
2. The EC2 security group rules need to be modified to allow outbound traffic to the on-premises computer.
3. The network ACL rules need to be modified to allow inbound traffic from the on-premises computer.
4. The network ACL rules need to be modified to allow outbound traffic to the on-premises computer.

QUESTION 12

A CloudOps Administrator needs to know the number of objects in an Amazon S3 bucket and noticed a discrepancy between an Amazon CloudWatch report and the output of the AWS CLI.

Which S3 feature can the Administrator use to get a definitive answer?
1. Amazon S3 analytics
2. Amazon S3 inventory
3. AWS Management Console
4. Object tags

QUESTION 13

A company is preparing for an audit to become accredited. To be compliant, encryption keys must be rotated a minimum of once every 365 days.

Which action should be taken to meet this requirement with the LEAST amount of operational overhead?
1. Import key material into customer master keys (CMKs) in AWS KMS. Create an AWS Lambda function to rotate the keys.
2. Use AWS-managed customer master keys (CMKs) and enable automatic key rotation.
3. Use customer-managed customer master keys (CMKs) in AWS KMS and enable automatic key rotation.
4. Use customer-managed customer master keys (CMKs) in AWS KMS and enforce key rotation with AWS Trusted Advisor.

QUESTION 14

A CloudOps Administrator has received a request from the security department to enforce server-side encryption on all new objects uploaded to the digitalcloud-encrypted bucket.

How can the Administrator enforce encryption on all objects uploaded to the bucket?
1. Add the following policy statement to the bucket:
```
{
  "Version": "2012-10-17",
  "Id": "PutObjPolicy",
  "Statement": [
    {
      "Sid": "DenyUnEncryptedObjectUploads",
      "Effect": "Deny",
      "Principal": "*",
      "Action": "s3:PutObject",
      "Resource": "arn:aws:s3:::digitalcloud-encrypted/*",
      "Condition": {
        "Null": {
          "s3:x-amz-server-side-encryption": "true"
        }
      }
    }
  ]
}
```
2. Add the following policy statement to the IAM user permissions policy:
```
{
  "Version": "2012-10-17",
  "Id": "PutObjPolicy",
```

```
        "Statement": [
          {
            "Sid": "DenyUnEncryptedObjectUploads",
            "Effect": "Deny",
            "Principal": "*",
            "Action": "s3:PutObject",
            "Resource": "arn:aws:s3:::digitalcloud-encrypted/",
            "Condition": {
              "Null": {
                "s3:x-amz-server-side-encryption": "true"
              }
            }
          }
        ]
      }
```
3. Enable Amazon S3 default encryption on the objects.
4. Generate a presigned URL for the Amazon S3 PUT operation with server-side encryption flag set and send the URL to the user.

QUESTION 15

A company needs a way to share Amazon RDS database snapshots of an encrypted database across different AWS accounts they own. The database must be encrypted at rest in the destination accounts.

How can the Administrator share the snapshots?

1. Take an unencrypted snapshot of the RDS database. Share the snapshot with the AWS accounts and then launch an encrypted database from the snapshot.
2. Update the key policy to grant access to the target accounts. Copy the snapshot using the CMK and then share the snapshot with the target accounts.
3. Take an encrypted snapshot of the RDS database. Share the snapshot with the AWS accounts and then then launch an encrypted database from the snapshot.
4. Create a new unencrypted RDS instance from the encrypted snapshot, copy the database contents to a file and then share the file with the AWS accounts.

QUESTION 16

Users in a company have reported issues connecting to an application server running on an Amazon EC2 instance using it's DNS hostname and a custom port (8121). The DNS name resolves to a private IP address within the Amazon VPC.

Which log type will confirm whether users are trying to connect to the correct port?

1. AWS CloudTrail logs
2. Elastic Load Balancer access logs
3. Amazon S3 access logs
4. VPC Flow Logs

QUESTION 17

A CloudOps Administrator needs to verify that security best practices are being followed with the AWS account root user.

How can the Administrator check?

1. Change the root user password by using the AWS CLI regularly.
2. Periodically use the AWS CLI to rotate access keys and secret keys for the root user.
3. Use AWS Trusted Advisor security checks to review the configuration of the root user.
4. Periodically run reports using AWS Artifact that verify that security standards are being met.

QUESTION 18

A serverless application uses an AWS Lambda function that is expected to receive a large increase in traffic during a promotional event. A CloudOps Administrator needs to configure the Lambda function to scale and handle the increase in traffic.

How can the Administrator accomplish this?

1. Create additional Lambda functions and configure them as targets for a Network Load Balancer (NLB).
2. Configure AWS Application Auto Scaling to scale concurrent executions.
3. Ensure the concurrency limit for the Lambda function is higher than the expected simultaneous function executions.
4. Increase the amount of memory available to the Lambda function.

QUESTION 19

A company runs a critical production application that uses an Amazon RDS MySQL database. The CloudOps Administrator needs to ensure that downtime is kept to a minimum in the event o fa database failure. Any changes that are required must not impact the customer experience during business hours.

Which action will make the database MORE highly available?

1. Modify the instance type to one with redundant Elastic Network Interfaces (ENIs).
2. Create an Amazon RDS DB cluster. Migrate all data to the new cluster.
3. Create a read replica from the existing database outside of business hours.
4. Modify the DB instance outside of business hours to be a Multi-AZ deployment.

QUESTION 20

An application records highly sensitive customer data to several Amazon S3 buckets. The S3 buckets are secured with bucket policies. There have been reports of attempts at unauthorized access and the security team have requested that information about which buckets are being targeted and by whom is gathered.

Which steps should a CloudOps Administrator gather the requested information? (Select TWO.)

1. Configure Amazon S3 Server Access Logging on all of the affected S3 buckets and store the logs in a separate, dedicated bucket.
2. Configure Amazon S3 Analytics on all of the affected S3 buckets and generate a report showing the unauthorized access attempts.
3. Use Amazon Athena to query the S3 Server Access Logs for HTTP 403 errors, and determine the IAM user or role making the requests.
4. Use Amazon Athena to query the S3 Server Access Logs for HTTP 503 errors and determine the IAM user or role making the requests.
5. Use Amazon Athena to query S3 Analytics reports for HTTP 403 errors and determine the IAM user or role making the requests.

QUESTION 21

A CloudOps Administrator manages an Auto Scaling group of Amazon EC2 instances in an Amazon VPC. The EC2 instances use a NAT instance to access the internet.

Based on the shared responsibility model, AWS is responsible for managing which element of this deployment?

1. Configuring the route table with the NAT instance ID.

2. Managing scaling policies for the Auto Scaling group.
3. Managing the health of the underlying EC2 hosts.
4. Ensuring high availability of the NAT instance.

QUESTION 22

A CloudOps Administrator manages a group of Amazon EC2 Linux instances that use an Amazon RDS database. The EC2 instances use a NAT gateway to access the internet.

Based on the shared responsibility model, AWS is responsible for managing which element of this deployment?

1. Configuring the route table with the NAT gateway ID.
2. Configuring encryption settings for RDS database data.
3. Ensuring high availability of the NAT gateway.
4. Managing the health of the Linux operating systems.

QUESTION 23

An application is being deployed that hosts highly sensitive data that must not be leaked outside of the company. A security team has asked a CloudOps Administrator to configure the environment to address this concern.

How can the Administrator ensure that the servers in the VPC cannot send traffic to the internet?

1. Ensure that the servers do not have Elastic IP addresses.
2. Create a blackhole NAT gateway that prevents outbound access.
3. Use instance stores to ensure there is no persistent data.
4. Launch the EC2 instances in private subnets.

QUESTION 24

A CloudOps Administrator made some changes to a production AWS CloudFormation stack and the update failed and then returned the error UPDATE_ROLLBACK_FAILED. The Administrator needs to return the CloudFormation stack back to its previous working state without the loss of existing resources.

How can this be accomplished?

1. Correct the error that caused the failure, then select the Continue Update Rollback action in the console.
2. Delete the stack, then recreate the stack with the original working template.
3. Select the Update Stack action with a working template in the console.
4. Use the AWS CLI to manually change the stack status to UPDATE_COMPLETE, then continue updating the stack with a working template.

QUESTION 25

A CloudOps Administrator has created a new Amazon VPC in the us-east-1 Region. A development site will be deployed running on Amazon EC2 instances. The application requires both incoming and outgoing connectivity to the internet.

Which combination of steps are required to provide internet connectivity to the EC2 instances? (Select TWO.)

1. Add a NAT gateway to a public subnet.
2. Add a NAT gateway to a private subnet.
3. Attach an Elastic IP address to the internet gateway.
4. Add an entry to the route table for the subnet that points to the internet gateway.
5. Create an internet gateway and attach it to the VPC.

QUESTION 26

An application generates data that must be archived for at least 7 years. Amazon Glacier will be used for archiving the data. What configuration option should be used to meet the compliance requirement?

1. A Glacier data retrieval policy.
2. A Glacier vault lock policy.
3. A Glacier vault access policy.
4. A Glacier vault notification.

QUESTION 27

A company has deployed an application on Amazon EC2 instances behind an Application Load Balancer (ALB). There have been reports of errors from users who have attempted to use the application. The CloudOps Administrator noticed an increase in the HTTPCode_ELB_5XX_Count Amazon CloudWatch metric for the load balancer.

What is a possible cause for this increase?

1. The ALB is associated with private subnets within the VPC.
2. The service limits for ALBs in the VPC has been exceeded.
3. The ALB security group does not allow inbound traffic from the users.
4. The target group of the ALB does not contain healthy EC2 instances.

QUESTION 28

A company uses AWS Organizations with consolidated billing for several AWS accounts. The CEO is concerned about rising costs and has asked a CloudOps Administrator to determine what is causing the increase.

What is the MOST comprehensive tool that will accomplish this task?

1. AWS Trusted Advisor
2. Cost allocation tags
3. AWS Cost Explorer
4. Resource groups

QUESTION 29

A CloudOps Administrator manages a web application that is deployed in an on-premises data center and on Amazon EC2 instances. There have been crashes reported across on-premises servers and EC2 instances and the Administrator suspects a memory leak.

What is the SIMPLEST way to track both the EC2 memory utilization and on-premises server memory utilization over time?

1. Write a script or use a third-party application to report memory utilization for both EC2 instances and on-premises servers.
2. Use the Amazon CloudWatch agent for EC2 instances to report MemoryUtilization metrics to CloudWatch. Use third-party software for the on-premises servers.
3. Create an Auto Scaling group for both on-premises servers and EC2 instances and monitor the memory utilization metrics reported by the ASG.
4. Use the Amazon CloudWatch agent for both EC2 instances and on-premises servers to report MemoryUtilization metrics to CloudWatch.

QUESTION 30

A CloudOps Administrator needs to provide internet access for several Amazon EC2 instances in a private subnet. The Administrator has deployed a NAT instance using an amzn-ami-vpc-nat AMI, updated security groups, and configured the appropriate route within the route table. The instances still cannot access the internet.

What should be done to resolve the issue?

1. Configure a VPN and route via the company proxy server.
2. Delete the NAT instance and replace it with an internet gateway.
3. Start/stop the NAT instance so it is launched on a different host.
4. Disable source/destination checks on the NAT instance.

QUESTION 31

A company run an application on Amazon EC2 instances in an Auto Scaling group. The Auto Scaling group is configured to terminate EC2 instances on scale-in events. A CloudOps Administrator needs to retain the application logs from the instances that have been terminated.

Which action should the Administrator take to achieve this objective?

1. Configure the unified CloudWatch agent to stream the logs to Amazon CloudWatch Logs.
2. Configure a script to capture application logs and run the script once every hour using cron.
3. Configure an Amazon CloudWatch Events rule to transfer the logs to Amazon S3 when the EC2 state changes to terminated.
4. Configure VPC Flow Logs for the subnet hosting the EC2 instance and publish the data to Amazon S3.

QUESTION 32

An application uses Amazon EC2 instances to process messages from an Amazon Simple Queue Service (SQS) queue. Amazon EC2 Auto Scaling scales in and out based on CPU utilization. A CloudOps Administrator notices that the number of messages in the SQS queue are increasing significantly.

Which action will remediate the issue?

1. Deploy an Elastic Load Balancer (ELB) to balance the load more evenly across the EC2 instances.
2. Change the scaling policy to scale based upon the number of messages in the Amazon SQS queue.
3. Change the scaling policy to scale based upon the memory utilization of the EC2 instances.
4. Increase the retention period of the Amazon SQS queue so messages are not lost.

QUESTION 33

A web application for a popular online store is using Amazon ElastiCache with Memcached for frequently used data. Performance has been poor for a couple of weeks and complaints about the user experience have been reported. The metric data for the Amazon EC2 instances and the Amazon RDS instance appear normal, but the eviction count metrics are high.

What can a CloudOps Administrator do to address this issue and resolve the performance issues?

1. Scale the Memcached cluster by adding read replicas.
2. Scale the Memcached cluster by increasing CPU capacity.
3. Scale the RDS instance by changing instance types.
4. Scale the Memcached cluster by adding additional nodes.

QUESTION 34

A CloudOps Administrator creating a system that will run analytics on financial data for several hours a night, 5 days a week. The analysis is expected to run for the same duration and cannot be interrupted once it is started. The system will be required for a minimum of 1 year.

What should the CloudOps Administrator configure to ensure the EC2 instances are available when they are needed?

1. Savings Plans
2. On-Demand Instances

3. Regional Reserved Instances
4. On-Demand Capacity Reservations

QUESTION 35

An application encrypts data using an AWS KMS customer master key (CMK) with imported key material. The CMK is referenced by an alias in the application code. Company policy mandates that the CMK must be rotated every 6 months

What is the process to rotate the key?

1. Import new key material into a new CMK, update the key alias to point to the new CMK.
2. Enable automatic key rotation for the CMK and specify a period of 6 months.
3. Delete the current key material and import new material into the existing CMK.
4. Use an AWS managed CMK with automatic rotation every 6 months. Update the alias.

QUESTION 36

A university is using a distributed computing application to run complex calculations on a fleet of Amazon EC2 instances. The calculations will be running for at least 1 year. The application uses 2 control nodes and between 8 and 24 worker nodes as required. The control nodes run continuously while the worker nodes run for 8 hours a day and are launched when required.

What is the MOST cost-effective pricing model for the application? (Select TWO.)

1. Use Reserved Instances for the control nodes.
2. Use Dedicated Hosts for the control nodes.
3. Use Reserved Instances for the worker nodes.
4. Use Spot Instances for the worker nodes and On-Demand Instances if there is no Spot availability.
5. Use Spot Instances for the control nodes and On-Demand Instances if there is no Spot availability.

QUESTION 37

A company's website has been running slowly during busy periods. The website runs on Amazon EC2 instances and uses and Amazon RDS database. The CloudOps Administrator suspects the issue is related to high CPU usage on a component of this application.

How should the CloudOps Administrator investigate which component is causing the performance bottleneck?

1. Use AWS CloudTrail to review the API usage metrics for each component.
2. Use Amazon Inspector to view the detailed resource usage for each component.
3. Use Amazon CloudWatch Logs and Amazon Athena to search for utilization data.
4. Use Amazon CloudWatch metrics to examine the resource usage of each component.

QUESTION 38

A CloudOps Administrator manages a website for an online store that uses an Application Load Balancer (ALB). The Administrator detected many 404 errors occurring from a single source IP address every few seconds and suspects a bot is scraping data from the website.

Which service should the Administrator use to block the suspected malicious activity?

1. AWS CloudTrail
2. AWS WAF
3. Amazon Inspector
4. AWS Shield Standard

QUESTION 39

A critical Amazon EC2 instance has stopped responding. The CloudOps Administrator checked the EC2 management console and noticed that the system status checks are impaired

What first step should the CloudOps Administrator take to resolve this issue?

1. Reboot the EC2 instance so it can be launched on a new host.
2. Terminate the EC2 instance and launch a replacement in another AZ.
3. Stop and then start the EC2 instance so that it can be launched on a new host.
4. Take a snapshot, create an AMI, and launch a new instance from the AMI.

QUESTION 40

A CloudOps Administrator plans to use a single AWS CloudFormation template to create and manage stacks across multiple AWS accounts and regions with a single operation.

What feature of AWS CloudFormation will help the Administrator to accomplish this?

1. StackSets
2. Change sets
3. Nested stacks
4. Stack policies

QUESTION 41

A consulting company deploy applications for many customers in a single AWS account and AWS Region. The consultants use a base AWS CloudFormation template that configures a new VPC for each application. When a consultant attempted to deploy an application for a new customer, it failed to deploy. A CloudOps Administrator has been asked to determine the cause of the failure.

What is most likely to be the problem?

1. The account has reached the default limit for VPCs allowed.
2. The Amazon Machine Image used is not available in that region.
3. The AWS CloudFormation template needs to be updated to the latest version.
4. Scheduled maintenance is occurring on the region and it is temporarily unavailable.

QUESTION 42

A CloudOps Administrator created an Amazon Route 53 health check using a String Matching condition. The String Matching condition is searching for /html at the end of the page to ensure it fully loads. After enabling the health check, the administrator received an alert stating that the health check failed. However, the page loads successfully when navigating directly to it.

What is the MOST likely cause of the health check failure?

1. The search string is not in the first 5120 bytes of the response body.
2. The search string is not HTML-encoded.
3. The search string should not include the forward slash (/).
4. The search string must be longer than 4 characters.

QUESTION 43

The owner of an AWS Service Catalog portfolio shared the portfolio with a second AWS account. The second AWS account is managed by a different CloudOps Administrator.

Which action will the Administrator of the second account be able to perform?

1. Add a product from the imported portfolio to a local portfolio.
2. Add new products to the imported portfolio.
3. Change the launch role for the products contained in the imported portfolio.
4. Remove products from the imported portfolio.

QUESTION 44

A company manages a fleet of Amazon EC2 instances in a VPC and wishes to remove their public IP addresses to protect them from internet-based threats. Some applications still require access to Amazon S3 buckets. A CloudOps Administrator has been tasked with providing continued access to the S3 buckets.

Which solutions can the Administrator recommend? (Select TWO.)

1. Deploy a NAT gateway in a public subnet and configure the route tables in the VPC appropriately.
2. Configure the internet gateway to route connections to S3 using private IP addresses.
3. Add an outbound rule in the security groups of the EC2 instances for Amazon S3 using private IP addresses.
4. Set up AWS Direct Connect and configure a virtual interface between the EC2 instances and the S3 buckets.
5. Create a VPC endpoint in the VPC and configure the route tables appropriately.

QUESTION 45

A developer is receiving access denied errors when attempting to list the objects in an Amazon S3 bucket. The developer us using the IAM user account "arn:aws:iam::513259117252:user/paul". The following S3 bucket policy has been applied to the bucket:

```
{
  "Id": "Policy1597781793102",
  "Version": "2012-10-17",
  "Statement": [
    {
      "Sid": "Stmt1597781787330",
      "Action": [
        "s3:List*"
      ],
      "Effect": "Allow",
      "Resource": "arn:aws:s3:::dcttestbucket/*",
      "Principal": {
        "AWS": [
          "arn:aws:iam::513259117252:user/paul"
        ]
      }
    }
  ]
}
```

How can a CloudOps Administrator modify the S3 bucket policy to fix the issue?

1. Change the "Resource" from "arn:aws:s3:::dcttestbucket/*" to "arn:aws:s3:::dcttestbucket".
2. Change the "Principal" from "arn:aws:iam::513259117252:user/paul" to "arn:aws:iam::513259117252:role/paul".

3. Change the "Action" from "s3:List*" to "s3:ListBucket".
4. Change the "Effect" from "Allow" to "Deny".

QUESTION 46

A manager in a company needs to see a breakdown of costs in an AWS account on a project by project basis. The manager would like to view this information in AWS Cost Explorer.

Which combination of configuration updates should be applied? (Select TWO.)

1. Activate cost allocation tags.
2. Enable server access logging.
3. Activate consolidated billing.
4. Create and apply resource tags.
5. Enable AWS Budgets.

QUESTION 47

A company's CloudOps Administrator received a notification from AWS that an Amazon EC2 instance is on a degraded host that is scheduled for retirement. The scheduled retirement occurs during business-critical hours.

What can be done to MINIMIZE disruption?

1. Restart the EC2 instance as immediately to ensure the application is not taken offline when the host is retired.
2. Write an AWS Lambda function to migrate the EC2 instance between hosts. Run the function prior to the scheduled retirement and outside of business hours.
3. Restart the instance outside business hours to perform the system maintenance before the scheduled retirement.
4. Stop/start the instance outside business hours to move to a new host before the scheduled retirement.

QUESTION 48

An application has been deployed that stores configuration files in an Amazon S3 bucket. A history of revisions of the configuration files must be maintained in case a rollback is required.

How can a CloudOps Administrator configure the S3 bucket to meet these requirements?

1. Enable versioning on the S3 bucket.
2. Enable a lifecycle policy on the S3 bucket.
3. Enable cross-origin resource sharing on the S3 bucket.
4. Enable object tagging on the S3 bucket.

QUESTION 49

Each IT staff member in a company uses a unique IAM user account. Permissions are applied to users using IAM policies and IAM groups. The security team has requested that staff members should log in with their on-premises Active Directory user accounts instead of their IAM user accounts when accessing the AWS Management Console.

Which solution can a CloudOps Administrator implement to the requirements of the security team?

1. Implement a VPN tunnel and configure an Active Directory connector.
2. Use the IAM connector to synchronize the on-premises Active Directory.
3. Enable an Active Directory federation in an Amazon Route 53 private zone.
4. Implement a two-way trust relationship between AWS IAM and Active Directory.

QUESTION 50

A security team has identified some malicious connection requests from an IP address. They have requested that the IP address should be explicitly denied for both ingress and egress requests for all services in an Amazon VPC immediately.

How can this be quickly achieved?

1. Install a host-based firewall on each Amazon EC2 instance and block the IP address.
2. Remove the Internet Gateway from the VPC and use a NAT gateway instead.
3. Add a rule to the Security Groups attached to the instances in the affected subnets.
4. Add a rule to the Network Access Control Lists for all subnets in the VPC.

QUESTION 51

A CloudOps Administrator created a script that generates custom Amazon CloudWatch metrics. The EC2 instance on which the script was run had a misconfigured clock resulting in timestamps on the logs that were set to 30 minutes in the past.

What will be the result of this situation?

1. Amazon CloudWatch will not capture the data because it is in the past.
2. Amazon CloudWatch will correct the time when recording the timestamp.
3. Amazon CloudWatch will accept the custom metric data and record it.
4. Amazon CloudWatch creates its own timestamps and ignores metric timestamps.

QUESTION 52

A company recently performed a security audit of its AWS cloud-based applications. An application that uses an Amazon SQS queue was flagged for review as the IAM policy attached the queue allowed more access than required.

Who is responsible for correcting the issue?

1. AWS Premium Support
2. The Amazon SQS team
3. The AWS IAM team
4. The CloudOps Administrator

QUESTION 53

For security reasons the connectivity to an Amazon S3 bucket must remain within the AWS network using private IP addresses. A VPC endpoint has been created and an endpoint policy with the correct permissions has been set up. The Amazon EC2 instances in the VPC are still unable to access the bucket endpoint.

What is the MOST likely cause of this issue?

1. Storage class analytics must be enabled to use private IP addresses.
2. The bucket policy must be configured to all private IP addresses.
3. The EC2 instances need to have an Elastic IP address assigned.
4. The subnet does not have the VPC endpoint as a target in the route table.

QUESTION 54

A company is implementing cross-account access from a production account to a development account. An IAM role must be created and a permissions policy must be attached.

According to the AWS shared responsibility model, who is responsible for creating the IAM role and attaching the policy?

1. A CloudOps Administrator is responsible for creating the role and attaching the policy.
2. A CloudOps Administrator is responsible for creating the role, and AWS is responsible for attaching the policy to the role.

3. AWS is responsible for creating the role and attaching the policy.
4. AWS is responsible for creating the role, and a CloudOps Administrator is responsible for attaching the policy to the role.

QUESTION 55

An Amazon S3 bucket hold sensitive data. A CloudOps Administrator has been tasked with monitoring all object upload and download activity relating to the bucket. Monitoring must include tracking the AWS account of the caller, the IAM user role of the caller, the time of the API call, and the IP address of the API.

What should the CloudOps Administrator do to meet the requirements?

1. Enable data event logging in AWS CloudTrail.
2. Enable management event logging in AWS CloudTrail.
3. Configure Amazon Inspector bucket event logging.
4. Configure Amazon Inspector user event logging.

QUESTION 56

An application running on an Amazon EC2 instance processes data and saves log files to an Amazon S3 bucket. A CloudOps Administrator is tasked with allowing the instance to access the bucket.

How can this be configured for optimum security?

1. Apply an S3 bucket policy to allow access from all EC2 instances.
2. Create an IAM role for Amazon S3 access and attach it to the EC2 instance.
3. Create an IAM user and delegate access to the EC2 instance.
4. Store access keys in an Amazon Machine Image (AMI).

QUESTION 57

A company runs an application on-premises that generates many gigabytes of data files each day. The company requires that the files are stored on the AWS cloud, but the most recent files should be available locally for low latency access.

Which AWS service is most suitable for these requirements?

1. AWS Storage Gateway
2. Amazon EBS
3. Amazon S3
4. Amazon EFS

QUESTION 58

A company runs an Amazon RDS MySQL DB instance in a production account. Each week a backup of the database must be copied to a separate development account for testing.

What is the MOST cost-effective way to meet this requirement?

1. Copy an automated RDS snapshot to the development account using the copy-db-snapshot command with the AWS CLI.
2. Create a multi-AZ standby of the RDS database in the development account and take a manual snapshot using the create-db-snapshot AWS CLI command.
3. Use the Amazon S3 cross-region replication (CRR) to copy the automated backup to the development account.
4. Create a manual RDS snapshot with the create-db-snapshot CLI command and share it with the development account, create a copy in the development account.

QUESTION 59

A company's AWS bill has been increasing and an investigation has shown that many unauthorized services are being used across their AWS accounts.

Which service can the company use to restrict access to AWS services across accounts?

1. AWS Cost Explorer
2. AWS Organizations
3. AWS Config
4. AWS Budgets

QUESTION 60

A company runs a resource-intensive daily reporting job on a production Amazon RDS database. The performance of the database is affected when the reporting job is running, and this has resulted in user complaints.

How can a CloudOps Administrator resolve the performance issues?

1. Create a copy of the database using a snapshot and run the reporting against the copy.
2. Create an Amazon RDS read replica and run the reporting job against the read replica.
3. Enable Multi-AZ mode on Amazon RDS and run the reporting on the standby instance.
4. Enable Auto Scaling for the RDS database and ensure the maximum instances is greater than one.

QUESTION 61

A company runs a critical business application on Amazon EC2 instances in an Auto Scaling group with a database running MySQL on an Amazon EC2 instance. The company wishes to increase the availability and durability of the database layer whilst minimizing application changes.

How can these requirements be met?

1. Configure multi-AZ for the existing database instance to create a standby replica in a separate availability zone.
2. Launch a read replica of the existing database and create an Application Load Balancer (ALB) to evenly distribute connections.
3. Migrate the database to an Amazon RDS Aurora DB instance and create an Aurora Replica in another Availability Zone.
4. Create an Amazon RDS Microsoft SQL DB instance and enable multi-AZ replication. Back up the existing data and import it into the new database.

QUESTION 62

A company has created a static website using an Amazon S3 bucket. The static website configuration was enabled, and content has been uploaded. However, upon testing access to the site the following error message was received:

"HTTP 403 Forbidden"

What needs to be done to resolve the error?

1. Remove the default bucket policy that denies read access to the bucket.
2. Configure cross-region replication (CRR) on the bucket.
3. Add a bucket policy that grants everyone read access to the bucket.
4. Add a bucket policy that grants everyone read access to the bucket objects.

QUESTION 63

A company has deployed a new web application. Following the release, penetration testing revealed a cross-site scripting vulnerability that could expose user data.
Which AWS service will mitigate this issue?

1. AWS WAF
2. AWS Shield Standard

3. AWS KMS
4. Amazon GuardDuty

QUESTION 64

A company has two AWS accounts and has configured a VPC peering connection between them. The VPCs have non-overlapping CIDR blocks. The company requires that instances in the private subnets of each VPC can ping instances in the private subnets of the other VPC.

What action should be taken to meet this requirement?

1. Ensure that both accounts are linked and are part of consolidated billing to create a file sharing network, and then enable VPC peering.
2. Add a route to the VPC route tables of each VPC that points to the IP address range of the other VPC.
3. Modify the CIDR blocks so they are matching to facilitate full connectivity between the two VPCs.
4. Create a virtual private gateway within each VPC and then link the VPGs to enable bi-directional connectivity.

QUESTION 65

A company has configured a backup of their VPC in another Region. Data will be replicated from the primary region to the secondary region. Company policy mandates that all data must be encrypted and must not traverse the public internet.

How should the CloudOps Administrator connect the two VPCs while meeting the compliance requirements?

1. Configure an AWS Managed VPN between each VPC, then configure the route tables.
2. Configure NAT gateways in both VPCs, then configure the route tables.
3. Configure an internet gateway in each VPC and use these as the targets for the VPC route tables.
4. Configure inter-region VPC peering between the two VPCs, then configure route tables.

SET 2: PRACTICE QUESTIONS AND ANSWERS

QUESTION 1

A company is testing a new application which is expected to receive a large amount of traffic. The application runs on Amazon EC2 instances in an Auto Scaling group and uses an Amazon RDS Multi-AZ database. Static content is hosted in an Amazon S3 bucket. During performance testing the application response time increased significantly.

How can a CloudOps Administrator increase the performance and scalability of the application?

1. Serve the static content from the EC2 instances backed by an Amazon EFS filesystem.
2. Move the database from Amazon RDS to Amazon ElastiCache for Memcached.
3. Use Amazon CloudFront to cache the static content.
4. Use Amazon Route 53 with geolocation routing.

Answer: 3

Explanation:

The only answer that will improve performance and scalability is to cache the static content in Amazon CloudFront. This will improve response times for the static content, especially for global users who are farther from the Region where the data is hosted.

CORRECT: "Use Amazon CloudFront to cache the static content" is the correct answer.

INCORRECT: "Serve the static content from the EC2 instances backed by an Amazon EFS filesystem" is incorrect. This does not improve scalability or performance.

INCORRECT: "Move the database from Amazon RDS to Amazon ElastiCache for Memcached" is incorrect. ElastiCache is not a persistent data store so you can't use it to move the data. You could use it in front of the RDS database to improve performance but that is a different answer.

INCORRECT: "Use Amazon Route 53 with geolocation routing" is incorrect. This could be used if you had multiple implementations of the application in different Regions and needed to direct traffic according to the location of the user. That is not the case in this scenario.

References:

https://aws.amazon.com/blogs/networking-and-content-delivery/amazon-s3-amazon-cloudfront-a-match-made-in-the-cloud/

Save time with our exam-specific cheat sheets:

https://digitalcloud.training/certification-training/aws-certified-sysops-administrator-associate/amazon-cloudfront/

QUESTION 2

A CloudOps Administrator created an AWS CloudFormation template and attempted to use it for the first time to create a new stack. The stack creation failed with a status of ROLLBACK_COMPLETE. The issues in the template have been resolved and the administrator wishes to continue with the stack deployment.

How can the administrator continue?

1. Relaunch the template to create a new stack.
2. Run the execute-change-set command.
3. Perform an update-stack action on the failed stack.
4. Run a validate-template command.

Answer: 1

Explanation:

The ROLLBACK_COMPLETE status indicates the successful removal of one or more stacks after a failed stack creation or after an explicitly canceled stack creation. Any resources that were created during the create stack action are deleted.

This status exists only after a failed stack creation. It signifies that all operations from the partially created stack have been appropriately cleaned up. When in this state, only a delete operation can be performed.

CORRECT: "Relaunch the template to create a new stack" is the correct answer.

INCORRECT: "Run the execute-change-set command" is incorrect. You cannot create a change set for a stack in the ROLLBACK_COMPLETE state.

INCORRECT: "Perform an update-stack action on the failed stack" is incorrect. You cannot update a stack in the ROLLBACK_COMPLETE state.

INCORRECT: "Run a validate-template command" is incorrect. This will only validate the JSON or YAML code in the template file is correct.

References:

https://docs.aws.amazon.com/AWSCloudFormation/latest/UserGuide/using-cfn-describing-stacks.html

Save time with our exam-specific cheat sheets:

https://digitalcloud.training/certification-training/aws-certified-sysops-administrator-associate/aws-cloudformation/

QUESTION 3

A CloudOps Administrator has started to use Amazon Inspector to assess Amazon EC2 instances for security and compliance. The Administrator noticed that some security findings are missing for some instances.

Which action should the Administrator take to attempt to resolve this issue?

1. Generate the missing security findings list manually by logging in to the affected EC2 instances and running CLI commands.
2. Verify that the unified agent for Amazon CloudWatch is installed on the instances and collecting the necessary metrics.
3. Move the instances to a public subnet and attach an Elastic IP address to ensure connectivity to the Amazon Inspector service.
4. Verify that the Amazon Inspector agent is installed and running on the affected instances and then restart the agent.

Answer: 4

Explanation:

The Amazon Inspector agent is an entity that collects installed package information and software configuration for an Amazon EC2 instance. Though not required in all cases, you should install the Amazon Inspector agent on each of your target Amazon EC2 instances in order to fully assess their security.

In this case the Administrator should verify that the agent is installed and install it if necessary. If it is already installed then restarting the agent may cause the information to be sent to the telemetry service.

CORRECT: "Verify that the Amazon Inspector agent is installed and running on the affected instances and then restart the agent" is the correct answer.

INCORRECT: "Generate the missing security findings list manually by logging in to the affected EC2 instances and running CLI commands" is incorrect. This is unnecessary, the agent should take care of sending the information to the Inspector service.

INCORRECT: "Verify that the unified agent for Amazon CloudWatch is installed on the instances and collecting the necessary metrics" is incorrect. You do not need the Amazon CloudWatch agent to send data to Amazon Inspector.

INCORRECT: "Move the instances to a public subnet and attach an Elastic IP address to ensure connectivity to the Amazon Inspector service" is incorrect. This is not necessary. Though you do need to be able to connect to the public endpoint for Amazon Inspector, this can be from a private subnet using a NAT Gateway or NAT instance.

References:

https://docs.aws.amazon.com/inspector/latest/userguide/inspector_agents.html

QUESTION 4

A team of Data Analysts launched an Amazon RedShift Spectrum cluster. When the team attempts to use the query editor to query data, they received an "[Amazon](500310) Invalid operation: AwsClientException: Failed connect to datacatalog.us-west-2.amazonaws.com:443" error.

How can this issue be resolved?

1. Enhanced VPC Routing is enabled and must be disabled when using the query editor.
2. There is insufficient capacity in the cluster, use Elastic resize to adjust capacity.
3. The cluster login credentials are incorrect; specify the correct credentials and try again.
4. The cluster nodes are running in multiple Availability Zones, launch nodes in a single AZ only.

Answer: 1

Explanation:

After creating your cluster, you can immediately run queries by using the query editor on the Amazon Redshift console. One of the limitations of the cluster query editor is that you cannot use the query editor with enhanced VPC routing. If enhanced VPC routing is turned on it could result in the error mentioned in the question. The resolution is to disable enhanced VPC routing.

CORRECT: "Enhanced VPC Routing is enabled and must be disabled when using the query editor" is the correct answer.

INCORRECT: "There is insufficient capacity in the cluster, use Elastic resize to adjust capacity" is incorrect. The error generated is unlikely to be due to a cluster capacity issue.

INCORRECT: "The cluster login credentials are incorrect; specify the correct credentials and try again" is incorrect. This error generated does not indicate that the credentials are incorrect, it is more indicative of a connectivity issue.

INCORRECT: "The cluster nodes are running in multiple Availability Zones, launch nodes in a single AZ only" is incorrect. The issue is related to connectivity to the RedShift Spectrum endpoints, it is nothing to do with the cluster nodes running in different AZs.

References:

https://docs.aws.amazon.com/redshift/latest/mgmt/query-editor.html

QUESTION 5

A group of systems administrators use IAM access keys to manage Amazon EC2 instances using the AWS CLI. The company policy mandates that access keys are automatically disabled after 60 days.

Which solution can be used to automate this process?

1. Create an Amazon CloudWatch alarm to trigger an AWS Lambda function that disables keys older than 60 days.
2. Use an AWS Config rule to identify noncompliant keys. Create a custom AWS Systems Manager Automation document for remediation.
3. Configure Amazon Inspector to provide security best practice recommendations and automatically disable the keys.
4. Create a script that checks the key age and disables keys older than 60 days. Use a cron job on an Amazon EC2 instance to execute the script.

Answer: 2

Explanation:

This solution can be implemented by adding an automatic remediation to the AWS Config access-keys-rotated rule. This AWS Config rule checks whether the active access keys are rotated within the number of days specified in maxAccessKeyAge. The rule is NON_COMPLIANT if the access keys have not been rotated for more than maxAccessKeyAge number of days.

The automatic remediation can be configured to execute an AWS Systems Manager automation document that resolves the IAM user name and then disables and creates new access keys using the API.

CORRECT: "Use an AWS Config rule to identify noncompliant keys. Create a custom AWS Systems Manager Automation document for remediation" is the correct answer.

INCORRECT: "Create an Amazon CloudWatch alarm to trigger an AWS Lambda function that disables keys older than 60 days" is incorrect. CloudWatch alarms must be triggered by a metric breach. In this case there is no metric to track.

INCORRECT: "Configure Amazon Inspector to provide security best practice recommendations and automatically disable the keys" is incorrect. Amazon Inspector does not automatically disable access keys.

INCORRECT: "Create a script that checks the key age and disables keys older than 60 days. Use a cron job on an Amazon EC2 instance to execute the script" is incorrect. This is not a cost-effective solution as the EC2 instance is running continuously.

References:

https://aws.amazon.com/blogs/mt/managing-aged-access-keys-through-aws-config-remediations/
https://docs.aws.amazon.com/config/latest/developerguide/access-keys-rotated.html

Save time with our exam-specific cheat sheets:

https://digitalcloud.training/certification-training/aws-certified-sysops-administrator-associate/aws-config/

QUESTION 6

An application is deployed on three separate environments using AWS CloudFormation. The environments, development, test, and production, each require unique credentials to access external services.

Which option provides a secure means for providing the required credentials with a MINIMUM of operational overhead?

1. Use parameters to pass the credentials to the CloudFormation template. Use the user data script to insert the parameterized credentials into the EC2 instances.
2. Use AWS Systems Manager Parameter Store to store the credentials as secure strings. Pass an environment tag as a parameter to the CloudFormation template. Use the user data script to insert the environment tag in the EC2 instances.
3. Use a separate CloudFormation template for each environment. In the Resources section, include a user data script for each EC2 instance. Use the user data script to insert the proper credentials for the environment into the EC2 instances.
4. Use separate Amazon Machine Images (AMIs) for each environment with the required credentials. Pass the environment tag as a parameter to the CloudFormation template and us mappings to map the environment tag to the proper AMI.

Answer: 2

Explanation:

AWS Systems Manager Parameter Store provides secure, hierarchical storage for configuration data management and secrets management. You can store data such as passwords, database strings, Amazon Machine Image (AMI) IDs, and license codes as parameter values. In AWS CloudFormation parameters enable you to input custom values to your template each time you create or update a stack.

For this scenario you can input the environment name as a parameter when launching CloudFormation and have CloudFormation pass this value to the EC2 instances in the user data script at launch. The EC2 instances can use this information to connect to AWS Systems Manager Parameter Store and retrieve the applicable application credentials.

CORRECT: "Use AWS Systems Manager Parameter Store to store the credentials as secure strings. Pass an environment tag as a parameter to the CloudFormation template. Use the user data script to insert the environment tag in the EC2 instances" is the correct answer.

INCORRECT: "Use parameters to pass the credentials to the CloudFormation template. Use the user data script to insert the parameterized credentials into the EC2 instances" is incorrect. This would mean entering the credentials and passing them to EC2 insecurely. It's better to store the credentials in a secure service such as SSM Parameter Store.

INCORRECT: "Use a separate CloudFormation template for each environment. In the Resources section, include a user data script for each EC2 instance. Use the user data script to insert the proper credentials for the environment into the EC2 instances" is incorrect. This would also mean passing the credentials using a user data script which is not encrypted. This is not a secure solution.

INCORRECT: "Use separate Amazon Machine Images (AMIs) for each environment with the required credentials. Pass the environment tag as a parameter to the CloudFormation template and us mappings to map the environment tag to the proper AMI" is incorrect. This requires storing the credentials on the AMI which is not secure.

References:

https://docs.aws.amazon.com/systems-manager/latest/userguide/systems-manager-parameter-store.html

https://docs.aws.amazon.com/AWSCloudFormation/latest/UserGuide/parameters-section-structure.html

Save time with our exam-specific cheat sheets:

https://digitalcloud.training/certification-training/aws-certified-sysops-administrator-associate/aws-systems-manager/

QUESTION 7

A group of Developer have been given access to a separate AWS account to work on a new project. The Developers require full administrative access to create IAM policies and roles in the account, but corporate policies require that they are blocked from using a few specific AWS services.

What is the BEST way to grant the Developers privileges in the new account while still ensuring compliance with corporate policies?

1. Create a service control policy in AWS Organizations and apply it to the new account.
2. Create a customer managed policy in IAM and apply it to all users within the new account.
3. Create a job-specific policy in IAM and apply it to all users within the new account.
4. Create an IAM group for the Developers and apply a policy restricting access to the specific services.

Answer: 1

Explanation:

If the Developers are provided with full administrative access, then the only way to ensure compliance with the corporate policy is to use an AWS Organizations SCP to restrict the API actions relating to use of the specific restricted services.

Service control policies (SCPs) are a type of organization policy that you can use to manage permissions in your organization. SCPs offer central control over the maximum available permissions for all accounts in your organization.

This is the only way you can ensure that the Developers don't modify policies and gain the access to the restricted services.

CORRECT: "Create a service control policy in AWS Organizations and apply it to the new account" is the correct answer.

INCORRECT: "Create a customer managed policy in IAM and apply it to all users within the new account" is incorrect. This will not ensure compliance as the Developers have full administrative control and can change policies.

INCORRECT: "Create a job-specific policy in IAM and apply it to all users within the new account" is incorrect. This will not ensure compliance as the Developers have full administrative control and can change policies.

INCORRECT: "Create an IAM group for the Developers and apply a policy restricting access to the specific services" is incorrect. This will not ensure compliance as the Developers have full administrative control and can change policies.

References:

https://docs.aws.amazon.com/organizations/latest/userguide/orgs_manage_policies_type-auth.html

Save time with our exam-specific cheat sheets:

https://digitalcloud.training/certification-training/aws-certified-sysops-administrator-associate/aws-organizations/

QUESTION 8

The performance of an Amazon RDS MySQL database has been suffering during a recent busy period. A CloudOps Administrator noticed that database queries were running more slowly than is acceptable. Amazon CloudWatch metrics show that the CPU utilization was reaching close to 100%.

Which action should the Administrator take to resolve this issue?

1. Configure Amazon CloudFront to cache database queries and reduce load on RDS.
2. Scale horizontally by adding additional RDS MySQL nodes to offload write requests.
3. Enable the Multi-AZ feature for the RDS instance to enable extra capacity.
4. Modify the RDS MySQL instance so it is a larger instance type.

Answer: 4

Explanation:

There are two ways to scale a database when you need more capacity to serve reads. The first option is to use a Read Replica which can be a target for queries. This scales the database horizontally and is possibly the best solution for this specific scenario. However, it was not provided as an answer.

The other way to scale the database is to modify RDS to use a larger instance type. This will provide more CPU and RAM and enable the database to perform better.

Note that you cannot scale writes horizontally, so for use cases where the writes need to be scaled, you only have the single option of scaling up by changing instance types.

CORRECT: "Modify the RDS MySQL instance so it is a larger instance type" is the correct answer.

INCORRECT: "Configure Amazon CloudFront to cache database queries and reduce load on RDS" is incorrect. You cannot use CloudFront in front of a database to cache queries. CloudFront would be placed in front of your application servers or ELBs to cache certain content such as images and videos.

INCORRECT: "Scale horizontally by adding additional RDS MySQL nodes to offload write requests" is incorrect. You cannot offload writes to additional RDS MySQL nodes. There is only ever a single writable node in RDS even in a multi-AZ deployment.

INCORRECT: "Enable the Multi-AZ feature for the RDS instance to enable extra capacity" is incorrect. This does enable you to use the extra capacity for reading or writing, it is simply a replicated copy of the primary database used for disaster recovery.

References:

https://aws.amazon.com/blogs/database/scaling-your-amazon-rds-instance-vertically-and-horizontally/

Save time with our exam-specific cheat sheets:

https://digitalcloud.training/certification-training/aws-certified-sysops-administrator-associate/amazon-rds/

QUESTION 9

A CloudOps Administrator has an AWS CloudFormation template created from an infrastructure stack deployed in us-east-1. The Administrator attempts to use the template to launch a stack in us-west-1. The stack partially deploys but then errors and rolls back.

What are the most likely reasons for the failure of the stack deployment? (Select TWO.)

1. The template referenced an IAM user that is not available in us-west-1.
2. The template referenced an Amazon Machine Image (AMI) that is not available in us-west-1.
3. The template did not have the proper level of permissions to deploy the resources in us-west-1.
4. The template referenced services that do not exist in us-west-1.
5. CloudFormation templates can be used only to deploy stacks in a single Region.

Answer: 2, 4

Explanation:

The most likely reasons for the stack creation failure are that the AMI that is referenced is not available in the new Region or the template references resources such as VPC IDs that are not relevant in the Region. As the stack has been created from infrastructure in another Region these are both possibilities.

CORRECT: "The template referenced an Amazon Machine Image (AMI) that is not available in us-west-1" is the correct answer.

CORRECT: "The template referenced services that do not exist in us-west-1" is also a correct answer.

INCORRECT: "The template referenced an IAM user that is not available in us-west-1" is incorrect. IAM is a global users and user accounts can be used globally.

INCORRECT: "The template did not have the proper level of permissions to deploy the resources in us-west-1" is incorrect. Permissions are not assigned to templates; they are passed in to CloudFormation when launching the template.

INCORRECT: "CloudFormation templates can be used only to deploy stacks in a single Region" is incorrect. You can use a CloudFormation template to deploy stacks in any region as long as the template is configured correctly.

References:

https://docs.aws.amazon.com/AWSCloudFormation/latest/UserGuide/stacks.html

Save time with our exam-specific cheat sheets:

https://digitalcloud.training/certification-training/aws-certified-sysops-administrator-associate/aws-cloudformation/

QUESTION 10

A CloudOps Administrator is preparing for the release of a new application running on a fleet of Amazon EC2 instances. The Administrator needs to test an Amazon CloudWatch alarm that is configured to send an SNS notification when the CPU hits 70% utilization to ensure the notification is delivered successfully.

How should the Administrator test that the alarm triggers the notification?

1. Use the set-alarm-state command in AWS CloudTrail to invoke the Amazon SNS notification.
2. Send custom metrics reporting that the CPU is running at 80% utilization to AWS CloudTrail.
3. Manually configure the CPU to 80% utilization using the EC2 Management Console.
4. Use the set-alarm-state command in the AWS CLI for CloudWatch.

Answer: 4

Explanation:

You can use the Amazon CloudWatch CLI command set-alarm-state to set the state of an alarm for testing purposes. When the updated state differs from the previous value, the action configured for the appropriate state is invoked. For example, if your alarm is configured to send an Amazon SNS message when an alarm is triggered, temporarily changing the alarm state to ALARM sends an SNS message.

CORRECT: "Use the set-alarm-state command in the AWS CLI for CloudWatch" is the correct answer.

INCORRECT: "Use the set-alarm-state command in AWS CloudTrail to invoke the Amazon SNS notification" is incorrect. This command is an Amazon CloudWatch command, it is not used with AWS CloudTrail.

INCORRECT: "Send custom metrics reporting that the CPU is running at 80% utilization to AWS CloudTrail" is incorrect. You cannot send custom metrics to CloudTrail as this service is used for recording API actions not performance metrics.

INCORRECT: "Manually configure the CPU to 80% utilization using the EC2 Management Console" is incorrect. You cannot manually configure CPU utilization through the EC2 Management Console.

References:

https://docs.aws.amazon.com/cli/latest/reference/cloudwatch/set-alarm-state.html

Save time with our exam-specific cheat sheets:

https://digitalcloud.training/certification-training/aws-certified-sysops-administrator-associate/amazon-cloudwatch/

QUESTION 11

A company is connected to an Amazon VPC from an on-premises data center with a VPN connection. A CloudOps Administrator attempted to ping an Amazon EC2 instance in a private subnet with the IP 172.31.10.10 and did not receive a response. The ping command was issued from a computer in the data center with the IP address 3.104.75.244. VPC Flow Logs were enabled and showed the following entries:

2 123456789010 eni-1234abcd 3.104.75.244 172.31.10.10 0 0 1 4 336 1432917027 1432917142 ACCEPT OK

2 123456789010 eni-1234abcd 172.31.10.10 3.104.75.244 0 0 1 4 336 1432917094 1432917142 REJECT OK

What is the most likely cause of the issue?

1. The EC2 security group rules need to be modified to allow inbound traffic from the on-premises computer.
2. The EC2 security group rules need to be modified to allow outbound traffic to the on-premises computer.
3. The network ACL rules need to be modified to allow inbound traffic from the on-premises computer.
4. The network ACL rules need to be modified to allow outbound traffic to the on-premises computer.

Answer: 4

Explanation:

The VPC Flow Log entries show that the inbound connection is accepted and should therefore reach the destination but the outbound connection from the instance to the on-premises computer (172.31.10.10 -> 3.104.75.244 0) was rejected. Security groups are stateful so would allow any return traffic for connections that were accepted inbound. However, Network ACLs are stateless so there must be an entry to allow inbound traffic and an entry to allow the outbound return traffic. In this case it looks like the Network ACL is not configured with the rule to allow the outbound return traffic.

The following diagram shows the packets for a connection to a web server and the response from the web server with source and destination ports. Note the comments about the difference between stateful and stateless firewalls.

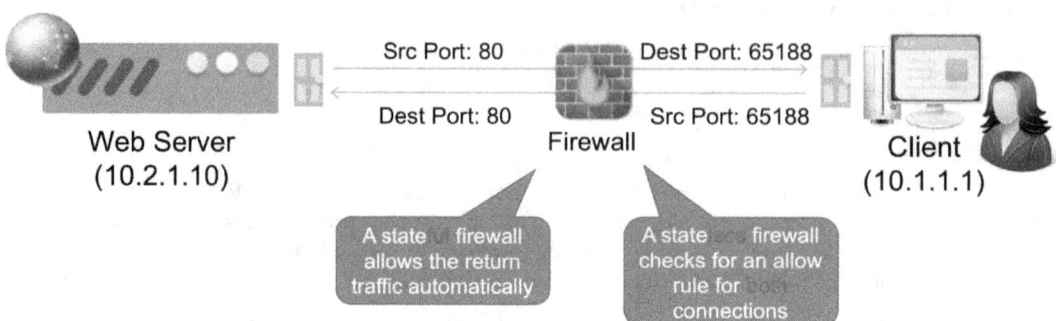

CORRECT: "The network ACL rules need to be modified to allow outbound traffic to the on-premises computer" is the correct answer.

INCORRECT: "The EC2 security group rules need to be modified to allow inbound traffic from the on-premises computer" is incorrect. The inbound connection was accepted so this is unlikely to be the issue.

INCORRECT: "The EC2 security group rules need to be modified to allow outbound traffic to the on-premises computer" is incorrect. Security groups are stateful and will automatically allow the return traffic.

INCORRECT: "The network ACL rules need to be modified to allow inbound traffic from the on-premises computer" is incorrect. The inbound connection was accepted so this is unlikely to be the issue.

References:

https://docs.aws.amazon.com/vpc/latest/userguide/vpc-network-acls.html

Save time with our exam-specific cheat sheets:

https://digitalcloud.training/certification-training/aws-certified-sysops-administrator-associate/amazon-virtual-private-cloud-vpc/

QUESTION 12

A CloudOps Administrator needs to know the number of objects in an Amazon S3 bucket and noticed a discrepancy between an Amazon CloudWatch report and the output of the AWS CLI.

Which S3 feature can the Administrator use to get a definitive answer?

1. Amazon S3 analytics
2. Amazon S3 inventory
3. AWS Management Console
4. Object tags

Answer: 2

Explanation:

Amazon S3 inventory provides comma-separated values (CSV), Apache optimized row columnar (ORC) or Apache Parquet (Parquet) output files that list your objects and their corresponding metadata on a daily or weekly basis for an S3 bucket or a shared prefix. The inventory reports will provide a definitive answer to the Administrator for how many objects there are in the bucket.

CORRECT: "Amazon S3 inventory" is the correct answer.

INCORRECT: "Amazon S3 analytics" is incorrect. This service is used for analyzing access patterns to help you decide which S3 storage class is best for your data.

INCORRECT: "AWS Management Console" is incorrect. You cannot see a count of the number of objects in a bucket using the management console.

INCORRECT: "Object tags" is incorrect. Tags will not assist with counting the number of objects in the bucket.

References:

https://docs.aws.amazon.com/AmazonS3/latest/dev/storage-inventory.html

Save time with our exam-specific cheat sheets:

https://digitalcloud.training/certification-training/aws-certified-sysops-administrator-associate/amazon-s3/

QUESTION 13

A company is preparing for an audit to become accredited. To be compliant, encryption keys must be rotated a minimum of once every 365 days.

Which action should be taken to meet this requirement with the LEAST amount of operational overhead?

1. Import key material into customer master keys (CMKs) in AWS KMS. Create an AWS Lambda function to rotate the keys.
2. Use AWS-managed customer master keys (CMKs) and enable automatic key rotation.
3. Use customer-managed customer master keys (CMKs) in AWS KMS and enable automatic key rotation.
4. Use customer-managed customer master keys (CMKs) in AWS KMS and enforce key rotation with AWS Trusted Advisor.

Answer: 3

Explanation:

In AWS KMS automatic key rotation is disabled by default on customer managed CMKs. When you enable (or re-enable) key rotation, AWS KMS automatically rotates the CMK 365 days after the enable date and every 365 days thereafter.

CORRECT: "Use customer-managed customer master keys (CMKs) in AWS KMS and enable automatic key rotation" is the correct answer.

INCORRECT: "Use AWS-managed customer master keys (CMKs) and enable automatic key rotation" is incorrect. You cannot manage key rotation for AWS managed CMKs. AWS KMS automatically rotates AWS managed CMKs every three years (1095 days).

INCORRECT: "Import key material into customer master keys (CMKs) in AWS KMS. Create an AWS Lambda function to rotate the keys" is incorrect. If you import key material you cannot have AWS automatically rotate the keys, hence the need for AWS Lambda. However, this answer has more operational overhead so is not the best response.

INCORRECT: "Use customer-managed customer master keys (CMKs) in AWS KMS and enforce key rotation with AWS Trusted Advisor" is incorrect. You cannot enforce key rotation using Trusted Advisor.

References:

https://docs.aws.amazon.com/kms/latest/developerguide/rotate-keys.html

Save time with our exam-specific cheat sheets:

https://digitalcloud.training/certification-training/aws-certified-sysops-administrator-associate/aws-kms-and-aws-cloudhsm/

QUESTION 14

A CloudOps Administrator has received a request from the security department to enforce server-side encryption on all new objects uploaded to the digitalcloud-encrypted bucket.

How can the Administrator enforce encryption on all objects uploaded to the bucket?

1. Add the following policy statement to the bucket:
   {

```
"Version": "2012-10-17",
"Id": "PutObjPolicy",
"Statement": [
  {
    "Sid": "DenyUnEncryptedObjectUploads",
    "Effect": "Deny",
    "Principal": "*",
    "Action": "s3:PutObject",
    "Resource": "arn:aws:s3:::digitalcloud-encrypted/*",
    "Condition": {
      "Null": {
        "s3:x-amz-server-side-encryption": "true"
      }
    }
  }
]
}
```

2. Add the following policy statement to the IAM user permissions policy:

```
{
"Version": "2012-10-17",
"Id": "PutObjPolicy",
"Statement": [
  {
    "Sid": "DenyUnEncryptedObjectUploads",
    "Effect": "Deny",
    "Principal": "*",
    "Action": "s3:PutObject",
    "Resource": "arn:aws:s3:::digitalcloud-encrypted/",
    "Condition": {
      "Null": {
        "s3:x-amz-server-side-encryption": "true"
      }
    }
  }
]
}
```

3. Enable Amazon S3 default encryption on the objects.
4. Generate a presigned URL for the Amazon S3 PUT operation with server-side encryption flag set and send the URL to the user.

Answer: 1

Explanation:

The key requirement is to enforce encryption on new objects that are uploaded to the bucket. There is no requirement to encrypt existing objects in the bucket. Therefore, the solution must ensure that you cannot upload unencrypted objects to the bucket.

There are two solutions to this requirement. The first is to enable default encryption on the bucket (not the objects). This will ensure that all newly uploaded objects are encrypted by default.

The other way, which is represented in the correct answer to this question, is to use a bucket policy to enforce encryption by requiring that the server-side-encryption header is set to "true".

CORRECT: "Add the following policy statement to the bucket:..." is the correct answer.

INCORRECT: "Add the following policy statement to the IAM user permissions policy:..." is incorrect. The policy should be added as a bucket policy. The resource must also include /* on the end to be applicable to all objects uploaded.

INCORRECT: "Enable Amazon S3 default encryption on the objects" is incorrect. You cannot enable default encryption on objects, you enable it at the bucket level.

INCORRECT: "Generate a presigned URL for the Amazon S3 PUT operation with server-side encryption flag set and send the URL to the user" is incorrect. The bucket policy is the way to enforce the server-side encryption flag.

References:

https://docs.aws.amazon.com/AmazonS3/latest/user-guide/default-bucket-encryption.html

https://aws.amazon.com/blogs/security/how-to-prevent-uploads-of-unencrypted-objects-to-amazon-s3/

Save time with our exam-specific cheat sheets:

https://digitalcloud.training/certification-training/aws-certified-sysops-administrator-associate/amazon-s3/

QUESTION 15

A company needs a way to share Amazon RDS database snapshots of an encrypted database across different AWS accounts they own. The database must be encrypted at rest in the destination accounts.

How can the Administrator share the snapshots?

1. Take an unencrypted snapshot of the RDS database. Share the snapshot with the AWS accounts and then launch an encrypted database from the snapshot.
2. Update the key policy to grant access to the target accounts. Copy the snapshot using the CMK and then share the snapshot with the target accounts.
3. Take an encrypted snapshot of the RDS database. Share the snapshot with the AWS accounts and then then launch an encrypted database from the snapshot.
4. Create a new unencrypted RDS instance from the encrypted snapshot, copy the database contents to a file and then share the file with the AWS accounts.

Answer: 2

Explanation:

The key policy must be updated to grant access to the target accounts. A (non-default) KMS key must be used to enable this to work. You can then copy the snapshot using the customer managed key, and then share the snapshot with the target accounts.

CORRECT: "Update the key policy to grant access to the target accounts. Copy the snapshot using the CMK and then share the snapshot with the target accounts" is the correct answer.

INCORRECT: "Take an unencrypted snapshot of the RDS database. Share the snapshot with the AWS accounts and then launch an encrypted database from the snapshot" is incorrect. You cannot take an unencrypted snapshot of an encrypted database and you cannot launch an encrypted database from an unencrypted snapshot.

INCORRECT: "Take an encrypted snapshot of the RDS database. Share the snapshot with the AWS accounts and then then launch an encrypted database from the snapshot" is incorrect. You cannot share the snapshot without first updating the KMS key policy to grant permissions to the target accounts and copy the snapshot with the CMK before sharing it.

INCORRECT: "Create a new unencrypted RDS instance from the encrypted snapshot, copy the database contents to a file and then share the file with the AWS accounts" is incorrect. You cannot create an unencrypted database from an encrypted snapshot.

References:

https://aws.amazon.com/premiumsupport/knowledge-center/share-encrypted-rds-snapshot-kms-key/

Save time with our exam-specific cheat sheets:

https://digitalcloud.training/certification-training/aws-certified-sysops-administrator-associate/amazon-rds/

QUESTION 16

Users in a company have reported issues connecting to an application server running on an Amazon EC2 instance using it's DNS hostname and a custom port (8121). The DNS name resolves to a private IP address within the Amazon VPC.

Which log type will confirm whether users are trying to connect to the correct port?

1. AWS CloudTrail logs
2. Elastic Load Balancer access logs
3. Amazon S3 access logs
4. VPC Flow Logs

Answer: 4

Explanation:

VPC Flow Logs is a feature that enables you to capture information about the IP traffic going to and from network interfaces in your VPC. Flow log data can be published to Amazon CloudWatch Logs or Amazon S3. After you've created a flow log, you can retrieve and view its data in the chosen destination.

By default, the log line format for a flow log record is a space-separated string that has the following set of fields in the following order:

<version> <account-id> <interface-id> <srcaddr> <dstaddr> <srcport> <dstport> <protocol> <packets> <bytes> <start> <end> <action> <log-status>

As you can see the flow log records capture the destination address and the destination port so it will be easy to identify if the users are entering the correct port number.

CORRECT: "VPC Flow Logs" is the correct answer.

INCORRECT: "AWS CloudTrail logs" is incorrect. CloudTrail captures API activity not traffic flow data.

INCORRECT: "Elastic Load Balancer access logs" is incorrect. There is no mention of an ELB so the VPC Flow Logs are the best source of data in this scenario.

INCORRECT: "Amazon S3 access logs" is incorrect. S3 access logs are used to record requests to S3, they will not capture traffic going over the network to an EC2 server.

References:

https://docs.aws.amazon.com/vpc/latest/userguide/flow-logs.html

Save time with our exam-specific cheat sheets:

https://digitalcloud.training/certification-training/aws-certified-sysops-administrator-associate/amazon-virtual-private-cloud-vpc/

QUESTION 17

A CloudOps Administrator needs to verify that security best practices are being followed with the AWS account root user.

How can the Administrator check?

1. Change the root user password by using the AWS CLI regularly.
2. Periodically use the AWS CLI to rotate access keys and secret keys for the root user.
3. Use AWS Trusted Advisor security checks to review the configuration of the root user.
4. Periodically run reports using AWS Artifact that verify that security standards are being met.

Answer: 3

Explanation:

AWS Trusted Advisor is an online tool that provides you real time guidance to help you provision your resources following AWS best practices. This service can be used to run various checks that verify compliance for the root account. This can include checking that MFA is being used for example.

CORRECT: "Use AWS Trusted Advisor security checks to review the configuration of the root user" is the correct answer.

INCORRECT: "Change the root user password by using the AWS CLI regularly" is incorrect. Using the AWS CLI to change the root user password is not a security best practice.

INCORRECT: "Periodically use the AWS CLI to rotate access keys and secret keys for the root user" is incorrect. Access keys should be rotated but using the AWS CLI is not the most secure method of implementing this best practice.

INCORRECT: "Periodically run reports using AWS Artifact that verify that security standards are being met" is incorrect. AWS Artifact provides information about compliance of the AWS platform, not the customer accounts.

References:

https://aws.amazon.com/premiumsupport/technology/trusted-advisor/

QUESTION 18

A serverless application uses an AWS Lambda function that is expected to receive a large increase in traffic during a promotional event. A CloudOps Administrator needs to configure the Lambda function to scale and handle the increase in traffic.

How can the Administrator accomplish this?

1. Create additional Lambda functions and configure them as targets for a Network Load Balancer (NLB).
2. Configure AWS Application Auto Scaling to scale concurrent executions.
3. Ensure the concurrency limit for the Lambda function is higher than the expected simultaneous function executions.
4. Increase the amount of memory available to the Lambda function.

Answer: 3

Explanation:

The first time you invoke your function, AWS Lambda creates an instance of the function and runs its handler method to process the event. When the function returns a response, it stays active and waits to process additional events. If you invoke the function again while the first event is being processed, Lambda initializes another instance, and the function processes the two events concurrently. As more events come in, Lambda routes them to available instances and creates new instances as needed. When the number of requests decreases, Lambda stops unused instances to free up scaling capacity for other functions.

Your functions' *concurrency* is the number of instances that serve requests at a given time. For an initial burst of traffic, your functions' cumulative concurrency in a Region can reach an initial level of between 500 and 3000, which varies per Region.

After the initial burst, your functions' concurrency can scale by an additional 500 instances each minute. This continues until there are enough instances to serve all requests, or until a concurrency limit is reached. When requests come in faster than your function can scale, or when your function is at maximum concurrency, additional requests fail with a throttling error (429 status code).

To ensure the Lambda function scales to handle the increased load, the Administrator must ensure that the concurrency limit is higher than the expected traffic.

CORRECT: "Ensure the concurrency limit for the Lambda function is higher than the expected simultaneous function executions" is the correct answer.

INCORRECT: "Create additional Lambda functions and configure them as targets for a Network Load Balancer (NLB)" is incorrect. You cannot configure Lambda functions as targets for NLBs (use ALBs) and you should not scale across different functions. Instead, use Lambda's built-in concurrency scaling features to scale to different instances of the function.

INCORRECT: "Configure AWS Application Auto Scaling to scale concurrent executions" is incorrect. You can use AWS Application Auto Scaling with AWS Lambda to adjusting provisioned concurrency levels according to utilization. This is used to avoid latency when scaling quickly is required. However, latency is not mentioned in this question and provisioned concurrency is also not being used.

INCORRECT: "Increase the amount of memory available to the Lambda function" is incorrect. This increases the amount of memory (and CPU) assigned to each instance of the function. However, you still need to ensure that the concurrency limits are high enough to ensure enough instances of the function are able to execute.

References:

https://docs.aws.amazon.com/lambda/latest/dg/invocation-scaling.html

QUESTION 19

A company runs a critical production application that uses an Amazon RDS MySQL database. The CloudOps Administrator needs to ensure that downtime is kept to a minimum in the event o fa database failure. Any changes that are required must not impact the customer experience during business hours.

Which action will make the database MORE highly available?

1. Modify the instance type to one with redundant Elastic Network Interfaces (ENIs).
2. Create an Amazon RDS DB cluster. Migrate all data to the new cluster.
3. Create a read replica from the existing database outside of business hours.
4. Modify the DB instance outside of business hours to be a Multi-AZ deployment.

Answer: 4

Explanation:

When you provision a Multi-AZ DB Instance, Amazon RDS automatically creates a primary DB Instance and synchronously replicates the data to a standby instance in a different Availability Zone (AZ). When you initially configured Multi-AZ, the replication can cause performance degradation on the master database. Therefore, the changes should be made outside of business hours to reduce the impact of customer experience.

CORRECT: "Modify the DB instance outside of business hours to be a Multi-AZ deployment" is the correct answer.

INCORRECT: "Modify the instance type to one with redundant Elastic Network Interfaces (ENIs)" is incorrect. This will not protect against a broad range of failure scenarios so Multi-AZ would provide a better degree of HA.

INCORRECT: "Create an Amazon RDS DB cluster. Migrate all data to the new cluster" is incorrect. You do not create "clusters" with RDS. You must create Multi-AZ database deployments and this can be enabled for existing RDS databases at any time.

INCORRECT: "Create a read replica from the existing database outside of business hours" is incorrect. Read replicas are primarily used for scaling database queries. Multi-AZ should be used for disaster recovery.

References:

https://aws.amazon.com/rds/features/multi-az/

Save time with our exam-specific cheat sheets:

https://digitalcloud.training/certification-training/aws-certified-sysops-administrator-associate/amazon-rds/

QUESTION 20

An application records highly sensitive customer data to several Amazon S3 buckets. The S3 buckets are secured with bucket policies. There have been reports of attempts at unauthorized access and the security team have requested that information about which buckets are being targeted and by whom is gathered.

Which steps should a CloudOps Administrator gather the requested information? (Select TWO.)

1. Configure Amazon S3 Server Access Logging on all of the affected S3 buckets and store the logs in a separate, dedicated bucket.
2. Configure Amazon S3 Analytics on all of the affected S3 buckets and generate a report showing the unauthorized access attempts.
3. Use Amazon Athena to query the S3 Server Access Logs for HTTP 403 errors, and determine the IAM user or role making the requests.
4. Use Amazon Athena to query the S3 Server Access Logs for HTTP 503 errors and determine the IAM user or role making the requests.
5. Use Amazon Athena to query S3 Analytics reports for HTTP 403 errors and determine the IAM user or role making the requests.

Answer: 1, 3

Explanation:

Server access logging provides detailed records for the requests that are made to a bucket. There access logs should be recorded to a separate, dedicated bucket. Access logs include information such as the requester, the remote IP (IP address of the requester), and the bucket that is being accessed.

Amazon Athena is a serverless query service that makes it easy to analyze large amounts of data stored in Amazon S3 using Standard SQL. This service can be used to run SQL queries looking for the required data in the access logs bucket. The SQL query should look for 403 errors as these relate to unauthorized access.

CORRECT: "Configure Amazon S3 Server Access Logging on all of the affected S3 buckets and store the logs in a separate, dedicated bucket" is the correct answer.

CORRECT: "Use Amazon Athena to query the S3 Server Access Logs for HTTP 403 errors and determine the IAM user or role making the requests" is the correct answer.

INCORRECT: "Configure Amazon S3 Analytics on all of the affected S3 buckets and generate a report showing the unauthorized access attempts" is incorrect. This service analyzes usage patterns to help determine the best storage class to place your data in. It does not record access information.

INCORRECT: "Use Amazon Athena to query the S3 Server Access Logs for HTTP 503 errors and determine the IAM user or role making the requests" is incorrect. 503 errors relate to service unavailable; the Administrator should be looking for 403s (unauthorized access).

INCORRECT: "Use Amazon Athena to query S3 Analytics reports for HTTP 403 errors and determine the IAM user or role making the requests" is incorrect. Athena should be used to look for 403 errors in the server access logging bucket.

References:

https://docs.aws.amazon.com/AmazonS3/latest/dev/LogFormat.html

https://aws.amazon.com/blogs/aws/amazon-athena-interactive-sql-queries-for-data-in-amazon-s3/

Save time with our exam-specific cheat sheets:

https://digitalcloud.training/certification-training/aws-certified-sysops-administrator-associate/amazon-s3/

QUESTION 21

A CloudOps Administrator manages an Auto Scaling group of Amazon EC2 instances in an Amazon VPC. The EC2 instances use a NAT instance to access the internet.

Based on the shared responsibility model, AWS is responsible for managing which element of this deployment?

1. Configuring the route table with the NAT instance ID.
2. Managing scaling policies for the Auto Scaling group.
3. Managing the health of the underlying EC2 hosts.
4. Ensuring high availability of the NAT instance.

Answer: 3

Explanation:

AWS are responsible for security "of" the cloud. This includes managing the health of the underlying EC2 hosts on which your instances are running. AWS are not responsible for the tasks listed in the other answers as these relate to security "in" the cloud and are customer responsibilities.

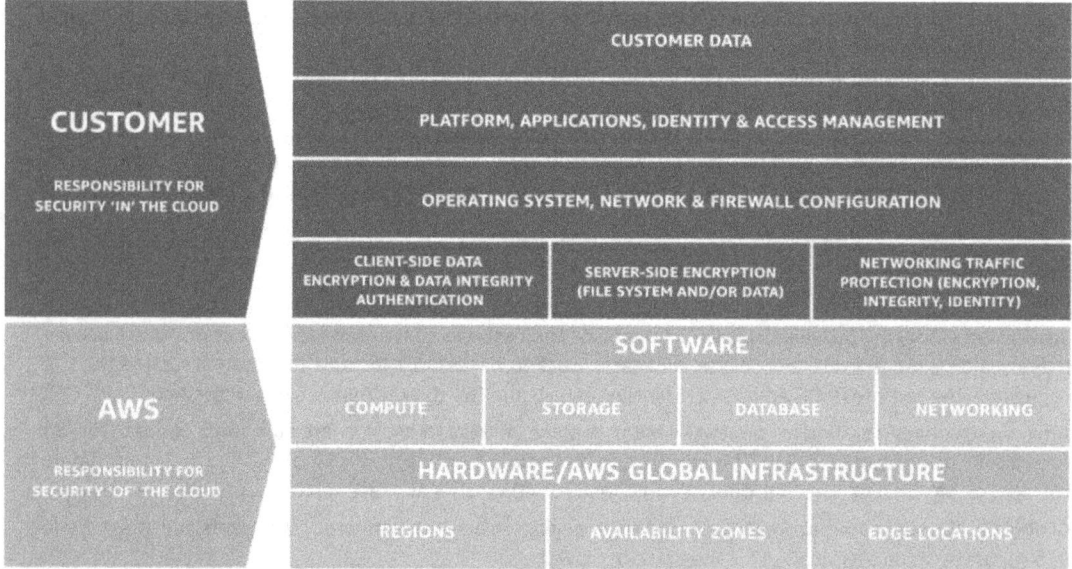

CORRECT: "Managing the health of the underlying EC2 hosts" is the correct answer.

INCORRECT: "Configuring the route table with the NAT instance ID" is incorrect. Customers are responsible for configuring route tables, AWS provides the underlying routing functions.

INCORRECT: "Managing scaling policies for the Auto Scaling group" is incorrect. Customers are responsible for managing the scaling policies with an ASG to ensure the right number of instances to service demand.

INCORRECT: "Ensuring high availability of the NAT instance" is incorrect. NAT instances are customer managed solutions, they are not highly available by default.

References:

https://aws.amazon.com/compliance/shared-responsibility-model/

Save time with our exam-specific cheat sheets:

https://digitalcloud.training/certification-training/aws-certified-sysops-administrator-associate/amazon-ec2/

QUESTION 22

A CloudOps Administrator manages a group of Amazon EC2 Linux instances that use an Amazon RDS database. The EC2 instances use a NAT gateway to access the internet.

Based on the shared responsibility model, AWS is responsible for managing which element of this deployment?

1. Configuring the route table with the NAT gateway ID.
2. Configuring encryption settings for RDS database data.
3. Ensuring high availability of the NAT gateway.
4. Managing the health of the Linux operating systems.

Answer: 3

Explanation:

AWS are responsible for security "of" the cloud. NAT gateways are AWS managed devices which are highly available within an Availability Zone (AZ). Therefore, AWS are responsible for managing the availability of the NAT gateway. AWS are not responsible for the tasks listed in the other answers as these relate to security "in" the cloud and are customer responsibilities.

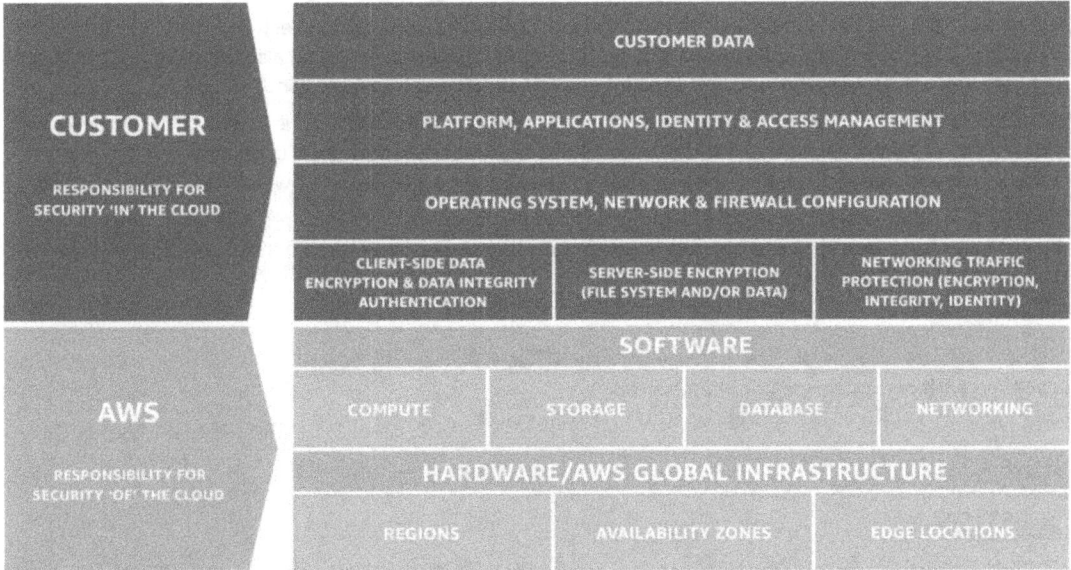

CORRECT: "Ensuring high availability of the NAT gateway" is the correct answer.

INCORRECT: "Configuring the route table with the NAT gateway ID" is incorrect. Though NAT gateway are AWS managed devices, customers are still responsible for provisioning them correctly and configuring route tables.

INCORRECT: "Configuring encryption settings for RDS database data" is incorrect. RDS is a managed service but customers are still responsible for encrypting data.

INCORRECT: "Managing the health of the Linux operating systems" is incorrect. The operating systems of EC2 instances are managed by customers, not AWS.

References:

https://aws.amazon.com/compliance/shared-responsibility-model/

Save time with our exam-specific cheat sheets:

https://digitalcloud.training/certification-training/aws-certified-sysops-administrator-associate/amazon-virtual-private-cloud-vpc/

QUESTION 23

An application is being deployed that hosts highly sensitive data that must not be leaked outside of the company. A security team has asked a CloudOps Administrator to configure the environment to address this concern.

How can the Administrator ensure that the servers in the VPC cannot send traffic to the internet?

1. Ensure that the servers do not have Elastic IP addresses.
2. Create a blackhole NAT gateway that prevents outbound access.
3. Use instance stores to ensure there is no persistent data.
4. Launch the EC2 instances in private subnets.

Answer: 4

Explanation:

The easiest way to solve this issue is to launch the EC2 instances into a private subnet. The subnet should not have a NAT gateway or NAT instance entry in the subnet route table. This ensures that there is no possibility that the instances can connect to the internet and inadvertently leak sensitive data.

CORRECT: "Launch the EC2 instances in private subnets" is the correct answer.

INCORRECT: "Ensure that the servers do not have Elastic IP addresses" is incorrect. An elastic IP is one type of public IP. The instances should not have a public IP or an EIP and they should also not have a route to a NAT gateway or internet gateway. Just ensuring they don't have EIPs alone will not suffice.

INCORRECT: "Create a blackhole NAT gateway that prevents outbound access" is incorrect. The "blackhole" is an artifact of having removed a NAT gateway from a route table. This is not a configuration that you would purposely create to configure routing. Simply not having a NAT gateway will achieve the same goal.

INCORRECT: "Use instance stores to ensure there is no persistent data" is incorrect. This does not prevent the instances from accessing the internet, it just means that data is not stored persistently on the volumes attached to the EC2 instances.

References:

https://docs.aws.amazon.com/vpc/latest/userguide/VPC_Subnets.html

Save time with our exam-specific cheat sheets:

https://digitalcloud.training/certification-training/aws-certified-sysops-administrator-associate/amazon-ec2/

QUESTION 24

A CloudOps Administrator made some changes to a production AWS CloudFormation stack and the update failed and then returned the error UPDATE_ROLLBACK_FAILED. The Administrator needs to return the CloudFormation stack back to its previous working state without the loss of existing resources.

How can this be accomplished?

1. Correct the error that caused the failure, then select the Continue Update Rollback action in the console.
2. Delete the stack, then recreate the stack with the original working template.
3. Select the Update Stack action with a working template in the console.
4. Use the AWS CLI to manually change the stack status to UPDATE_COMPLETE, then continue updating the stack with a working template.

Answer: 1

Explanation:

A stack's state is set to UPDATE_ROLLBACK_FAILED when CloudFormation cannot roll back all changes during an update.

The AWS CloudFormation continue update rollback can then be used. This can be initiated from the AWS CloudFormation console or with the continue-update-rollback command in the AWS Command Line Interface (CLI). This functionality is enabled for all the stacks in the UPDATE_ROLLBACK_FAILED state.

For example, if the stack is in the UPDATE_ROLLBACK_FAILED state due to a service limit violation, you can request a limit increase or delete resources to stay within the limit and then use the continue update rollback functionality to reinitiate the rollback and bring the stack to the UPDATE_ROLLBACK_COMPLETE state.

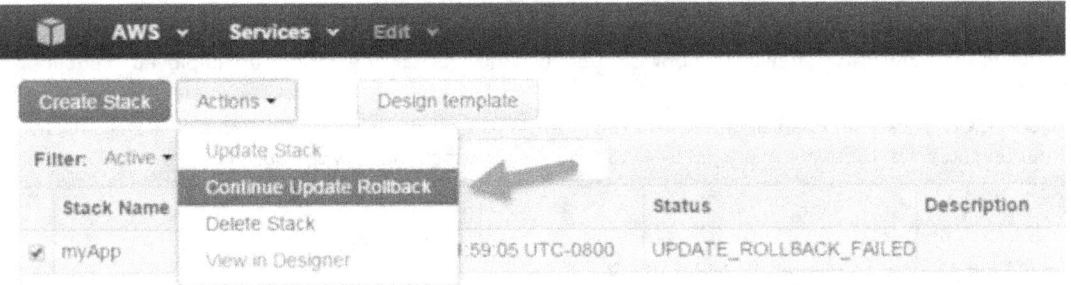

CORRECT: "Correct the error that caused the failure, then select the Continue Update Rollback action in the console" is the correct answer.

INCORRECT: "Delete the stack, then recreate the stack with the original working template" is incorrect. This would destroy the existing resources which should be avoided as this is a production stack

INCORRECT: "Select the Update Stack action with a working template in the console" is incorrect. This is not an option when in the UPDATE_ROLLBACK_FAILED state.

INCORRECT: "Use the AWS CLI to manually change the stack status to UPDATE_COMPLETE, then continue updating the stack with a working template" is incorrect. The status cannot be changed to UPDATE_COMPLETE as the reason for the rollback failure has not yet been addresses.

References:

https://aws.amazon.com/blogs/devops/continue-rolling-back-an-update-for-aws-cloudformation-stacks-in-the-update_rollback_failed-state/

Save time with our exam-specific cheat sheets:

https://digitalcloud.training/certification-training/aws-certified-sysops-administrator-associate/aws-cloudformation/

QUESTION 25

A CloudOps Administrator has created a new Amazon VPC in the us-east-1 Region. A development site will be deployed running on Amazon EC2 instances. The application requires both incoming and outgoing connectivity to the internet.

Which combination of steps are required to provide internet connectivity to the EC2 instances? (Select TWO.)

1. Add a NAT gateway to a public subnet.
2. Add a NAT gateway to a private subnet.
3. Attach an Elastic IP address to the internet gateway.
4. Add an entry to the route table for the subnet that points to the internet gateway.
5. Create an internet gateway and attach it to the VPC.

Answer: 4, 5

Explanation:

The only combination of actions that will result in a working solution with incoming and outgoing internet access of the EC2 instances is to attach an internet gateway and add an entry to the route table that points to it.

This solution indicates that the EC2 instances will be deployed in public subnets with public IP addresses. They will then be able to directly send traffic to the internet gateway to access the internet.

CORRECT: "Add an entry to the route table for the subnet that points to the internet gateway" is the correct answer.

CORRECT: "Create an internet gateway and attach it to the VPC" is also a correct answer.

INCORRECT: "Add a NAT gateway to a public subnet" is incorrect. A NAT gateway provides outbound internet connectivity for instances in public subnets, it does not provide inbound access to instances from the internet.

INCORRECT: "Add a NAT gateway to a private subnet" is incorrect. NAT gateways are deployed in public subnets.

INCORRECT: "Attach an Elastic IP address to the internet gateway" is incorrect. You cannot attach EIPs to internet gateways, these are managed by AWS. You simply attach the IGW to your VPC.

References:

https://docs.aws.amazon.com/vpc/latest/userguide/VPC_Internet_Gateway.html

Save time with our exam-specific cheat sheets:

https://digitalcloud.training/certification-training/aws-certified-sysops-administrator-associate/amazon-virtual-private-cloud-vpc/

QUESTION 26

An application generates data that must be archived for at least 7 years. Amazon Glacier will be used for archiving the data. What configuration option should be used to meet the compliance requirement?

1. A Glacier data retrieval policy.
2. A Glacier vault lock policy.
3. A Glacier vault access policy.
4. A Glacier vault notification.

Answer: 2

Explanation:

S3 Glacier Vault Lock allows you to easily deploy and enforce compliance controls for individual S3 Glacier vaults with a vault lock policy. You can specify controls such as "write once read many" (WORM) in a vault lock policy and lock the policy from future edits. Once locked, the policy can no longer be changed.

S3 Glacier enforces the controls set in the vault lock policy to help achieve your compliance objectives, for example, for data retention. You can deploy a variety of compliance controls in a vault lock policy using the AWS Identity and Access Management (IAM) policy language.

CORRECT: "A Glacier vault lock policy" is the correct answer.

INCORRECT: "A Glacier data retrieval policy" is incorrect. Data retrieval policies allow you to set data retrieval quotas and manage the data retrieval activities across your AWS account in each AWS Region.

INCORRECT: "A Glacier vault access policy" is incorrect. An Amazon S3 Glacier vault access policy is a resource-based policy that you can use to manage permissions to your vault

INCORRECT: "A Glacier vault notification" is incorrect. You can set a notification configuration on a vault so that when a job completes a message is sent to an Amazon Simple Notification Service (Amazon SNS) topic.

References:

https://docs.aws.amazon.com/amazonglacier/latest/dev/vault-lock.html

Save time with our exam-specific cheat sheets:

https://digitalcloud.training/certification-training/aws-certified-sysops-administrator-associate/amazon-s3-glacier/

QUESTION 27

A company has deployed an application on Amazon EC2 instances behind an Application Load Balancer (ALB). There have been reports of errors from users who have attempted to use the application. The CloudOps Administrator noticed an increase in the **HTTPCode_ELB_5XX_Count** Amazon CloudWatch metric for the load balancer.

What is a possible cause for this increase?

1. The ALB is associated with private subnets within the VPC.
2. The service limits for ALBs in the VPC has been exceeded.
3. The ALB security group does not allow inbound traffic from the users.
4. The target group of the ALB does not contain healthy EC2 instances.

Answer: 4

Explanation:

The error "HTTPCode_ELB_5XX_Count" records the number of HTTP 5XX server error codes that originate from the load balancer. This count does not include any response codes generated by the targets. This metric indicates that the instances are not healthy and available to respond to incoming connection requests.

CORRECT: "The target group of the ALB does not contain healthy EC2 instances" is the correct answer.

INCORRECT: "The ALB is associated with private subnets within the VPC" is incorrect. This is not a reason why the targets would not be available. If this is an internal ALB this is a correct configuration.

INCORRECT: "The service limits for ALBs in the VPC has been exceeded" is incorrect. This would mean the ALB could not be created in the first place. The errors indicate the ALB is operational, but the targets are not healthy.

INCORRECT: "The ALB security group does not allow inbound traffic from the users" is incorrect. This would not result in 5XX errors. The clients would simply not be able to connect.

References:

https://docs.aws.amazon.com/elasticloadbalancing/latest/application/load-balancer-cloudwatch-metrics.html

Save time with our exam-specific cheat sheets:

https://digitalcloud.training/certification-training/aws-certified-sysops-administrator-associate/elastic-load-balancing/

QUESTION 28

A company uses AWS Organizations with consolidated billing for several AWS accounts. The CEO is concerned about rising costs and has asked a CloudOps Administrator to determine what is causing the increase.

What is the MOST comprehensive tool that will accomplish this task?

1. AWS Trusted Advisor
2. Cost allocation tags
3. AWS Cost Explorer
4. Resource groups

Answer: 3

Explanation:

Cost Explorer is a tool that enables you to view and analyze your costs and usage. You can explore your usage and costs using the main graph, the Cost Explorer cost and usage reports, or the Cost Explorer RI reports.

You can view data for up to the last 12 months, forecast how much you're likely to spend for the next 12 months, and get recommendations for what Reserved Instances to purchase. You can use Cost Explorer to identify areas that need further inquiry and see trends that you can use to understand your costs.

CORRECT: "AWS Cost Explorer" is the correct answer.

INCORRECT: "AWS Trusted Advisor" is incorrect. This service is used for providing real-time guidance on best practices. This guidance does include cost management, but it does not give the view of individual costs for tracking.

INCORRECT: "Cost allocation tags" is incorrect. Cost allocation tags are useful for tracking the usage and costs associated with individual resources.

INCORRECT: "Resource groups" is incorrect. These can be used to group resources, but do not provide the reporting required.

References:

https://docs.aws.amazon.com/awsaccountbilling/latest/aboutv2/ce-what-is.html

QUESTION 29

A CloudOps Administrator manages a web application that is deployed in an on-premises data center and on Amazon EC2 instances. There have been crashes reported across on-premises servers and EC2 instances and the Administrator suspects a memory leak.

What is the SIMPLEST way to track both the EC2 memory utilization and on-premises server memory utilization over time?

1. Write a script or use a third-party application to report memory utilization for both EC2 instances and on-premises servers.
2. Use the Amazon CloudWatch agent for EC2 instances to report MemoryUtilization metrics to CloudWatch. Use third-party software for the on-premises servers.
3. Create an Auto Scaling group for both on-premises servers and EC2 instances and monitor the memory utilization metrics reported by the ASG.
4. Use the Amazon CloudWatch agent for both EC2 instances and on-premises servers to report MemoryUtilization metrics to CloudWatch.

Answer: 4

Explanation:

The unified CloudWatch agent enables you to collect metrics and logs from Amazon EC2 instances and on-premises servers. The agent enables the collection of more system-level metrics from Amazon EC2 instances across operating systems. The metrics can include in-guest metrics, in addition to the metrics for EC2 instances. System-level metrics are also collected for on-premises servers. The system-level metrics include memory utilization.

CORRECT: "Use the Amazon CloudWatch agent for both EC2 instances and on-premises servers to report MemoryUtilization metrics to CloudWatch" is the correct answer.

INCORRECT: "Write a script or use a third-party application to report memory utilization for both EC2 instances and on-premises servers" is incorrect. This is not necessary as you could use the unified CloudWatch agent which would be a simpler solution.

INCORRECT: "Use the Amazon CloudWatch agent for EC2 instances to report MemoryUtilization metrics to CloudWatch. Use third-party software for the on-premises servers" is incorrect. The simplest solution would be to use the CloudWatch agent for both on-premises servers and EC2 instances.

INCORRECT: "Create an Auto Scaling group for both on-premises servers and EC2 instances and monitor the memory utilization metrics reported by the ASG" is incorrect. Auto Scaling groups cannot be used for on-premises servers and also do not report memory utilization metrics for instances.

References:

https://docs.aws.amazon.com/AmazonCloudWatch/latest/monitoring/Install-CloudWatch-Agent.html

Save time with our exam-specific cheat sheets:

https://digitalcloud.training/certification-training/aws-certified-sysops-administrator-associate/amazon-cloudwatch/

QUESTION 30

A CloudOps Administrator needs to provide internet access for several Amazon EC2 instances in a private subnet. The Administrator has deployed a NAT instance using an amzn-ami-vpc-nat AMI, updated security groups, and configured the appropriate route within the route table. The instances still cannot access the internet.

What should be done to resolve the issue?

1. Configure a VPN and route via the company proxy server.
2. Delete the NAT instance and replace it with an internet gateway.
3. Start/stop the NAT instance so it is launched on a different host.
4. Disable source/destination checks on the NAT instance.

Answer: 4

Explanation:

Each EC2 instance performs source/destination checks by default. This means that the instance must be the source or destination of any traffic it sends or receives. However, a NAT instance must be able to send and receive traffic when the source or destination is not itself. Therefore, you must disable source/destination checks on the NAT instance.

You can disable the SrcDestCheck attribute for a NAT instance that's either running or stopped using the console or the command line. This is the most likely cause of the issues here as all other steps required to launch a NAT instance have been followed.

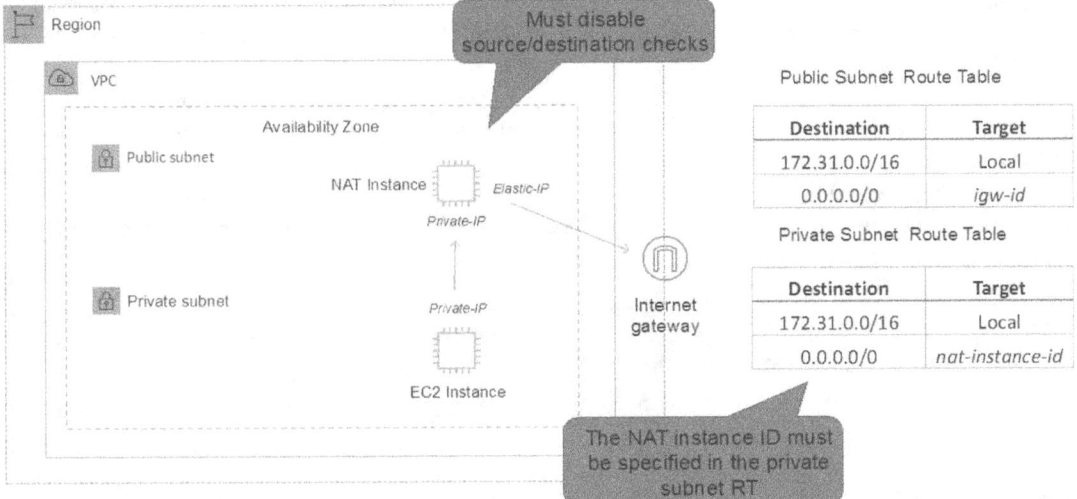

CORRECT: "Disable source/destination checks on the NAT instance" is the correct answer.

INCORRECT: "Configure a VPN and route via the company proxy server" is incorrect. This is not the best solution as you must then forward traffic via a company network. It would be better to use the NAT instance that has been deployed so the internet gateway can be leveraged within AWS.

INCORRECT: "Delete the NAT instance and replace it with an internet gateway" is incorrect. You cannot replace a NAT instance with an internet gateway for instances in a private subnet.

INCORRECT: "Start/stop the NAT instance so it is launched on a different host" is incorrect. The issue is unlikely to be related to the host the instance is running on.

References:

https://docs.aws.amazon.com/vpc/latest/userguide/VPC_NAT_Instance.html

Save time with our exam-specific cheat sheets:

https://digitalcloud.training/certification-training/aws-certified-sysops-administrator-associate/amazon-virtual-private-cloud-vpc/

QUESTION 31

A company run an application on Amazon EC2 instances in an Auto Scaling group. The Auto Scaling group is configured to terminate EC2 instances on scale-in events. A CloudOps Administrator needs to retain the application logs from the instances that have been terminated.

Which action should the Administrator take to achieve this objective?
1. Configure the unified CloudWatch agent to stream the logs to Amazon CloudWatch Logs.
2. Configure a script to capture application logs and run the script once every hour using cron.
3. Configure an Amazon CloudWatch Events rule to transfer the logs to Amazon S3 when the EC2 state changes to terminated.
4. Configure VPC Flow Logs for the subnet hosting the EC2 instance and publish the data to Amazon S3.

Answer: 1

Explanation:

The best solution is to use the unified CloudWatch agent to stream the logs to Amazon CloudWatch Logs. This configuration can be used to capture custom metrics and deliver them to CloudWatch Logs in real-time. When an instance is terminated the log stream should be up to date to the point of termination. The data can then be used for subsequent troubleshooting and analysis.

CORRECT: "Configure the unified CloudWatch agent to stream the logs to Amazon CloudWatch Logs" is the correct answer.

INCORRECT: "Configure a script to capture application logs and run the script once every hour using cron" is incorrect. It is unnecessary to use a script as the unified CloudWatch agent can capture and deliver custom metrics.

INCORRECT: "Configure an Amazon CloudWatch Events rule to transfer the logs to Amazon S3 when the EC2 state changes to terminated" is incorrect. You cannot configure a copy event for log files using CloudWatch Events.

INCORRECT: "Configure VPC Flow Logs for the subnet hosting the EC2 instance and publish the data to Amazon S3" is incorrect. This would not capture the application logs, just network communications on the subnet.

References:

https://docs.aws.amazon.com/AmazonCloudWatch/latest/monitoring/Install-CloudWatch-Agent.html

Save time with our exam-specific cheat sheets:

https://digitalcloud.training/certification-training/aws-certified-sysops-administrator-associate/amazon-cloudwatch/

QUESTION 32

An application uses Amazon EC2 instances to process messages from an Amazon Simple Queue Service (SQS) queue. Amazon EC2 Auto Scaling scales in and out based on CPU utilization. A CloudOps Administrator notices that the number of messages in the SQS queue are increasing significantly.

Which action will remediate the issue?

1. Deploy an Elastic Load Balancer (ELB) to balance the load more evenly across the EC2 instances.
2. Change the scaling policy to scale based upon the number of messages in the Amazon SQS queue.
3. Change the scaling policy to scale based upon the memory utilization of the EC2 instances.
4. Increase the retention period of the Amazon SQS queue so messages are not lost.

Answer: 2

Explanation:

In this scenario the application should scale based on the number of messages in the queue as using CPU utilization is not effective and messages are backing up in the queue and not being processed quickly.

Using the number of messages in the queue as the basis for scaling will more accurately adjust the application according to the actual demand curve. You can configure an EC2 Auto Scaling group to scale using a target tracking policy that is based on a custom metric that tracks the number of messages in the queue.

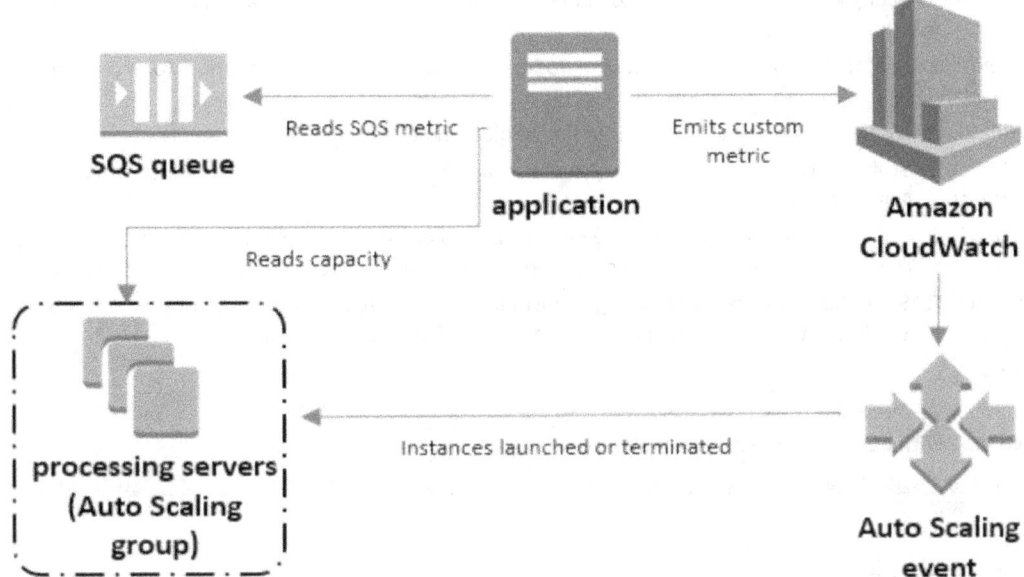

CORRECT: "Change the scaling policy to scale based upon the number of messages in the Amazon SQS queue" is the correct answer.

INCORRECT: "Deploy an Elastic Load Balancer (ELB) to balance the load more evenly across the EC2 instances" is incorrect. You cannot use an ELB to distribute load from an SQS queue. EC2 instances poll the queue to find messages so this does not work.

INCORRECT: "Change the scaling policy to scale based upon the memory utilization of the EC2 instances" is incorrect. You cannot scale based on memory utilization and there's no reason to believe this would be any more accurate than CPU utilization.

INCORRECT: "Increase the retention period of the Amazon SQS queue so messages are not lost" is incorrect. This will ensure messages are not lost but it won't remediate the issue of having messages backing up in the queue and not being processed quickly.

References:

https://docs.aws.amazon.com/autoscaling/ec2/userguide/as-using-sqs-queue.html

Save time with our exam-specific cheat sheets:

https://digitalcloud.training/certification-training/aws-certified-sysops-administrator-associate/amazon-ec2-auto-scaling/

QUESTION 33

A web application for a popular online store is using Amazon ElastiCache with Memcached for frequently used data. Performance has been poor for a couple of weeks and complaints about the user experience have been reported. The metric data for the Amazon EC2 instances and the Amazon RDS instance appear normal, but the eviction count metrics are high.

What can a CloudOps Administrator do to address this issue and resolve the performance issues?

1. Scale the Memcached cluster by adding read replicas.
2. Scale the Memcached cluster by increasing CPU capacity.
3. Scale the RDS instance by changing instance types.
4. Scale the Memcached cluster by adding additional nodes.

Answer: 4

Explanation:

Evictions occur when memory is over filled or greater than the maxmemory setting in the cache, resulting in the engine selecting keys to evict in order to manage its memory. The keys that are chosen are based on the eviction policy that is selected.

Therefore, the best solution is to add additional nodes which will provide more memory for storing the frequently used data and should lower the eviction count metrics.

CORRECT: "Scale the Memcached cluster by adding additional nodes" is the correct answer.

INCORRECT: "Scale the Memcached cluster by adding read replicas" is incorrect. You cannot add read replicas to a Memcached cluster.

INCORRECT: "Scale the Memcached cluster by increasing CPU capacity" is incorrect. This would not increase the memory. The memory must be increased so there's more space to store the frequently used data.

INCORRECT: "Scale the RDS instance by changing instance types" is incorrect. The metrics for RDS are normal. The issue lies in the Memcached layer having insufficient memory available.

References:

https://aws.amazon.com/caching/best-practices/

Save time with our exam-specific cheat sheets:

https://digitalcloud.training/certification-training/aws-certified-sysops-administrator-associate/amazon-elasticache/

QUESTION 34

A CloudOps Administrator creating a system that will run analytics on financial data for several hours a night, 5 days a week. The analysis is expected to run for the same duration and cannot be interrupted once it is started. The system will be required for a minimum of 1 year.

What should the CloudOps Administrator configure to ensure the EC2 instances are available when they are needed?

1. Savings Plans
2. On-Demand Instances
3. Regional Reserved Instances
4. On-Demand Capacity Reservations

Answer: 4

Explanation:

On-Demand Capacity Reservations enable you to reserve compute capacity for your Amazon EC2 instances in a specific Availability Zone for any duration. This gives you the ability to create and manage Capacity Reservations independently from the billing discounts offered by Savings Plans or Regional Reserved Instances.

By creating Capacity Reservations, you ensure that you always have access to EC2 capacity when you need it, for as long as you need it. You can create Capacity Reservations at any time, without entering a one-year or three-year term commitment, and the capacity is available immediately.

The table below shows the difference between capacity reservations and other options:

	Capacity Reservations	Zonal Reserved Instances	Regional Reserved Instances	Savings Plans
Term	No commitment required. Can be created and canceled as needed.	Requires a fixed one-year or three-year commitment		
Capacity benefit	Capacity reserved in a specific Availability Zone.		No capacity reserved.	
Billing discount	No billing discount. †	Provides a billing discount.		
Instance Limits	Your On-Demand Instance limits per Region apply.	Default is 20 per Availability Zone. You can request a limit increase.	Default is 20 per Region. You can request a limit increase.	No limit.

CORRECT: "On-Demand Capacity Reservations" is the correct answer.

INCORRECT: "Regional Reserved Instances" is incorrect. This type of reservation does not reserve capacity.

INCORRECT: "On-Demand Instances" is incorrect. This does not provide any kind of capacity reservation.

INCORRECT: "Savings Plans" is incorrect. This pricing option does not provide a capacity reservation.

References:

https://docs.aws.amazon.com/AWSEC2/latest/UserGuide/ec2-scheduled-instances.html

Save time with our exam-specific cheat sheets:

https://digitalcloud.training/certification-training/aws-solutions-architect-associate/compute/amazon-ec2/

QUESTION 35

An application encrypts data using an AWS KMS customer master key (CMK) with imported key material. The CMK is referenced by an alias in the application code. Company policy mandates that the CMK must be rotated every 6 months

What is the process to rotate the key?

1. Import new key material into a new CMK, update the key alias to point to the new CMK.
2. Enable automatic key rotation for the CMK and specify a period of 6 months.
3. Delete the current key material and import new material into the existing CMK.
4. Use an AWS managed CMK with automatic rotation every 6 months. Update the alias.

Answer: 1

Explanation:

When you import key material into a CMK, the CMK is permanently associated with that key material. You can reimport the same key material, but you cannot import different key material into that CMK. Also, you cannot enable automatic key rotation for a CMK with imported key material. However, you can manually rotate a CMK with imported key material.

Therefore, the best solution is to create a new CMK and import new key material into it. The alias in the application code can then be updated to point to the new CMK.

CORRECT: "Import new key material into a new CMK, update the key alias to point to the new CMK" is the correct answer.

INCORRECT: "Enable automatic key rotation for the CMK and specify a period of 6 months" is incorrect. You cannot enable automatic key rotation for a CMK with imported key material.

INCORRECT: "Delete the current key material and import new material into the existing CMK" is incorrect. You cannot import new key material into a CMK.

INCORRECT: "Use an AWS managed CMK with automatic rotation every 6 months. Update the alias" is incorrect. You cannot manage key rotation for AWS owned CMKs and they are automatically rotated every 365 days.

References:

https://docs.aws.amazon.com/kms/latest/developerguide/importing-keys.html

Save time with our exam-specific cheat sheets:

https://digitalcloud.training/certification-training/aws-certified-sysops-administrator-associate/aws-kms-and-aws-cloudhsm/

QUESTION 36

A university is using a distributed computing application to run complex calculations on a fleet of Amazon EC2 instances. The calculations will be running for at least 1 year. The application uses 2 control nodes and between 8 and 24 worker nodes as required. The control nodes run continuously while the worker nodes run for 8 hours a day and are launched when required.

What is the MOST cost-effective pricing model for the application? (Select TWO.)

1. Use Reserved Instances for the control nodes.
2. Use Dedicated Hosts for the control nodes.
3. Use Reserved Instances for the worker nodes.
4. Use Spot Instances for the worker nodes and On-Demand Instances if there is no Spot availability.
5. Use Spot Instances for the control nodes and On-Demand Instances if there is no Spot availability.

Answer: 1, 4

Explanation:

The worker nodes run continuously and will run for at least 1 year so using reserved instances would be the most cost-effective choice as these instances cannot risk being terminated. For the worker nodes, a mixture of Spot and on-demand would make the most sense. Spot can be used when there is capacity which will provide a significant cost saving. When there is no Spot capacity available on-demand instances can be used.

CORRECT: "Use Reserved Instances for the control nodes" is the correct answer.

CORRECT: "Use Spot Instances for the worker nodes and On-Demand Instances if there is no Spot availability" is also a correct answer.

INCORRECT: "Use Dedicated Hosts for the control nodes" is incorrect. This would not be cost-effective and is not required for this scenario.

INCORRECT: "Use Reserved Instances for the worker nodes" is incorrect. As the worker nodes are variable in number and only run for 8 hours a day, this would not make sense.

INCORRECT: "Use Spot Instances for the control nodes and On-Demand Instances if there is no Spot availability" is incorrect. The control nodes run continuously for the whole year so Spot instances would not be suitable as the instances could be terminated from time to time.

References:

https://aws.amazon.com/ec2/pricing/

Save time with our exam-specific cheat sheets:

https://digitalcloud.training/certification-training/aws-certified-sysops-administrator-associate/amazon-ec2/

QUESTION 37

A company's website has been running slowly during busy periods. The website runs on Amazon EC2 instances and uses and Amazon RDS database. The CloudOps Administrator suspects the issue is related to high CPU usage on a component of this application.

How should the CloudOps Administrator investigate which component is causing the performance bottleneck?

1. Use AWS CloudTrail to review the API usage metrics for each component.
2. Use Amazon Inspector to view the detailed resource usage for each component.
3. Use Amazon CloudWatch Logs and Amazon Athena to search for utilization data.
4. Use Amazon CloudWatch metrics to examine the resource usage of each component.

Answer: 4

Explanation:

Metrics are data about the performance of your systems. By default, several services provide free metrics for resources (such as Amazon EC2 instances, Amazon EBS volumes, and Amazon RDS DB instances). You can also enable detailed monitoring for some resources, such as your Amazon EC2 instances, or publish your own application metrics. Amazon CloudWatch can load all the metrics in your account (both AWS resource metrics and application metrics that you provide) for search, graphing, and alarms.

CORRECT: "Use Amazon CloudWatch metrics to examine the resource usage of each component" is the correct answer.

INCORRECT: "Use AWS CloudTrail to review the API usage metrics for each component" is incorrect. CloudTrail records API actions, not performance metrics.

INCORRECT: "Use Amazon Inspector to view the detailed resource usage for each component" is incorrect. Amazon Inspector is an automated security assessment service that helps improve the security and compliance of applications deployed on AWS.

INCORRECT: "Use Amazon CloudWatch Logs and Amazon Athena to search for utilization data" is incorrect. Utilization data is not recorded in log files in CloudWatch Logs.

References:

https://docs.aws.amazon.com/AmazonCloudWatch/latest/monitoring/working_with_metrics.html

Save time with our exam-specific cheat sheets:

https://digitalcloud.training/certification-training/aws-certified-sysops-administrator-associate/amazon-cloudwatch/

QUESTION 38

A CloudOps Administrator manages a website for an online store that uses an Application Load Balancer (ALB). The Administrator detected many 404 errors occurring from a single source IP address every few seconds and suspects a bot is scraping data from the website.

Which service should the Administrator use to block the suspected malicious activity?

1. AWS CloudTrail
2. AWS WAF
3. Amazon Inspector
4. AWS Shield Standard

Answer: 2

Explanation:

AWS WAF is a web application firewall that lets you monitor the HTTP and HTTPS requests that are forwarded to an Amazon CloudFront distribution, an Amazon API Gateway REST API, or an Application Load Balancer. AWS WAF also lets you control access to your content.

Based on conditions that you specify, such as the IP addresses that requests originate from or the values of query strings, API Gateway, CloudFront or an Application Load Balancer responds to requests either with the requested content or with an HTTP 403 status code (Forbidden).

CORRECT: "AWS WAF" is the correct answer.

INCORRECT: "AWS CloudTrail" is incorrect. CloudTrail is an auditing service that records API activity, it does not function as a web firewall.

INCORRECT: "Amazon Inspector" is incorrect. Inspector is a security assessment service; it will not block malicious traffic.

INCORRECT: "AWS Shield Standard" is incorrect. This service provides distributed denial of service (DDoS) protection. In this case it doesn't look like a DDoS attack, just a competitor scraping data.

References:

https://docs.aws.amazon.com/waf/latest/developerguide/what-is-aws-waf.html

Save time with our exam-specific cheat sheets:

https://digitalcloud.training/certification-training/aws-certified-sysops-administrator-associate/aws-waf-and-shield/

QUESTION 39

A critical Amazon EC2 instance has stopped responding. The CloudOps Administrator checked the EC2 management console and noticed that the system status checks are impaired

What first step should the CloudOps Administrator take to resolve this issue?

1. Reboot the EC2 instance so it can be launched on a new host.
2. Terminate the EC2 instance and launch a replacement in another AZ.
3. Stop and then start the EC2 instance so that it can be launched on a new host.
4. Take a snapshot, create an AMI, and launch a new instance from the AMI.

Answer: 3

Explanation:

System status checks monitor the AWS systems on which your instance runs. These checks detect underlying problems with your instance that require AWS involvement to repair. When a system status check fails, you can choose to wait for AWS to fix the issue, or you can resolve it yourself.

For instances backed by Amazon EBS, you can stop and start the instance yourself, which in most cases results in the instance being migrated to a new host. For instances backed by instance store, you can terminate and replace the instance.

The following are examples of problems that can cause system status checks to fail:

- Loss of network connectivity.
- Loss of system power.
- Software issues on the physical host.
- Hardware issues on the physical host that impact network reachability.

CORRECT: "Stop and then start the EC2 instance so that it can be launched on a new host" is the correct answer.

INCORRECT: "Reboot the EC2 instance so it can be launched on a new host" is incorrect. Rebooting the instance will not cause it to move to a different host server.

INCORRECT: "Terminate the EC2 instance and launch a replacement in another AZ" is incorrect. This is unnecessary. A better solution is to simply stop and start the instance as this will cause it to move to a different host.

INCORRECT: "Take a snapshot, create an AMI, and launch a new instance from the AMI" is incorrect. This is unnecessary. A better solution is to simply stop and start the instance as this will cause it to move to a different host.

References:

https://docs.aws.amazon.com/AWSEC2/latest/UserGuide/monitoring-system-instance-status-check.html

Save time with our exam-specific cheat sheets:

https://digitalcloud.training/certification-training/aws-certified-sysops-administrator-associate/amazon-ec2/

QUESTION 40

A CloudOps Administrator plans to use a single AWS CloudFormation template to create and manage stacks across multiple AWS accounts and regions with a single operation.

What feature of AWS CloudFormation will help the Administrator to accomplish this?

1. StackSets
2. Change sets
3. Nested stacks
4. Stack policies

Answer: 1

Explanation:

A *stack set* lets you create stacks in AWS accounts across regions by using a single AWS CloudFormation template. All the resources included in each stack are defined by the stack set's AWS CloudFormation template. As you create the stack set, you specify the template to use, as well as any parameters and capabilities that template requires.

After you've defined a stack set, you can create, update, or delete stacks in the target accounts and Regions you specify. When you create, update, or delete stacks, you can also specify operation preferences, such as the order of regions in which you want the operation to be performed, the failure tolerance beyond which stack operations stop, and the number of accounts in which operations are performed on stacks concurrently.

CORRECT: "StackSets" is the correct answer.

INCORRECT: "Change sets" is incorrect as changes sets allow you to preview updates to a stack before actually making the changes.

INCORRECT: "Nested stacks" is incorrect as *Nested stacks* are stacks created as part of other stacks.

INCORRECT: "Stack policies" is incorrect. A stack policy is a JSON document that defines the AWS CloudFormation stack update actions that AWS CloudFormation users can perform and the resources that the actions apply to.

References:

https://docs.aws.amazon.com/AWSCloudFormation/latest/UserGuide/stacksets-concepts.html

Save time with our exam-specific cheat sheets:

https://digitalcloud.training/certification-training/aws-certified-sysops-administrator-associate/aws-cloudformation/

QUESTION 41

A consulting company deploy applications for many customers in a single AWS account and AWS Region. The consultants use a base AWS CloudFormation template that configures a new VPC for each application. When a consultant attempted to deploy an application for a new customer, it failed to deploy. A CloudOps Administrator has been asked to determine the cause of the failure.

What is most likely to be the problem?

1. The account has reached the default limit for VPCs allowed.
2. The Amazon Machine Image used is not available in that region.
3. The AWS CloudFormation template needs to be updated to the latest version.
4. Scheduled maintenance is occurring on the region and it is temporarily unavailable.

Answer: 1

Explanation:

By default, you can only have up to five nondefault VPCs per AWS account per AWS Region. It is therefore very likely that this limit has been exceeded. The resolution is to complete a form to request a limit increase.

CORRECT: "The account has reached the default limit for VPCs allowed" is the correct answer.

INCORRECT: "The Amazon Machine Image used is not available in that region" is incorrect. The same template has been used to launch other VPCs in the region without difficulties, so this is unlikely to be the issue.

INCORRECT: "The AWS CloudFormation template needs to be updated to the latest version" is incorrect. The version of the template would not prevent the deployment.

INCORRECT: "Scheduled maintenance is occurring on the region and it is temporarily unavailable" is incorrect. Entire regions are not taken out of service for maintenance.

References:

https://aws.amazon.com/vpc/details/

Save time with our exam-specific cheat sheets:

https://digitalcloud.training/certification-training/aws-certified-sysops-administrator-associate/amazon-virtual-private-cloud-vpc/

QUESTION 42

A CloudOps Administrator created an Amazon Route 53 health check using a String Matching condition. The String Matching condition is searching for /html at the end of the page to ensure it fully loads. After enabling the health check, the administrator received an alert stating that the health check failed. However, the page loads successfully when navigating directly to it.

What is the MOST likely cause of the health check failure?

1. The search string is not in the first 5120 bytes of the response body.
2. The search string is not HTML-encoded.
3. The search string should not include the forward slash (/).
4. The search string must be longer than 4 characters.

Answer: 1

Explanation:

With HTTP_STR_MATCH Amazon Route 53 tries to establish a TCP connection. If successful, Route 53 submits an HTTP request and searches the first 5,120 bytes of the response body for the string that you specify in SearchString.

If the response body contains the value that you specify in Search string, Route 53 considers the endpoint healthy. If not, or if the endpoint doesn't respond, Route 53 considers the endpoint unhealthy. The search string must appear entirely within the first 5,120 bytes of the response body.

CORRECT: "The search string is not in the first 5120 bytes of the response body" is the correct answer.

INCORRECT: "The search string is not HTML-encoded" is incorrect. The search string does not need to be HTML encoded.

INCORRECT: "The search string should not include the forward slash (/)" is incorrect. If you don't include a forward slash, Route 53 will just add it in anyway.

INCORRECT: "The search string must be longer than 4 characters" is incorrect. There is no minimum length for the search string.

References:

https://docs.aws.amazon.com/Route53/latest/APIReference/API_HealthCheckConfig.html

https://docs.aws.amazon.com/Route53/latest/DeveloperGuide/health-checks-creating-values.html

Save time with our exam-specific cheat sheets:

https://digitalcloud.training/certification-training/aws-certified-sysops-administrator-associate/amazon-route-53/

QUESTION 43

The owner of an AWS Service Catalog portfolio shared the portfolio with a second AWS account. The second

AWS account is managed by a different CloudOps Administrator.

Which action will the Administrator of the second account be able to perform?

1. Add a product from the imported portfolio to a local portfolio.
2. Add new products to the imported portfolio.
3. Change the launch role for the products contained in the imported portfolio.
4. Remove products from the imported portfolio.

Answer: 1

Explanation:

A recipient administrator can add imported products to local portfolios. The products will stay in sync with the shared portfolio. However, the recipient administrator cannot upload or add products to the imported portfolio or remove products from the imported portfolio.

CORRECT: "Add a product from the imported portfolio to a local portfolio" is the correct answer.

INCORRECT: "Add new products to the imported portfolio" is incorrect. As explained above, this is not allowed.

INCORRECT: "Change the launch role for the products contained in the imported portfolio" is incorrect. A recipient administrator cannot add launch constraints to or remove launch constraints from the imported portfolio.

INCORRECT: "Remove products from the imported portfolio" is incorrect. As explained above, this is not allowed.

References:

https://docs.aws.amazon.com/servicecatalog/latest/adminguide/catalogs_portfolios_sharing.html

QUESTION 44

A company manages a fleet of Amazon EC2 instances in a VPC and wishes to remove their public IP addresses to protect them from internet-based threats. Some applications still require access to Amazon S3 buckets. A CloudOps Administrator has been tasked with providing continued access to the S3 buckets.

Which solutions can the Administrator recommend? (Select TWO.)

1. Deploy a NAT gateway in a public subnet and configure the route tables in the VPC appropriately.
2. Configure the internet gateway to route connections to S3 using private IP addresses.
3. Add an outbound rule in the security groups of the EC2 instances for Amazon S3 using private IP addresses.
4. Set up AWS Direct Connect and configure a virtual interface between the EC2 instances and the S3 buckets.
5. Create a VPC endpoint in the VPC and configure the route tables appropriately.

Answer: 1, 5

Explanation:

Amazon S3 is a public service and there are two ways you can connect to it from EC2 instances with only private IP addresses. The first option is to deploy a NAT gateway in a public subnet and configure routes to the NAT gateway in the subnets where the instances are running.

The second option is to create a VPC endpoint of the gateway endpoint type. This VPC endpoint requires that you configure the route tables with an entry pointing to the gateway and will enable access to S3 using only private IP addresses.

CORRECT: "Deploy a NAT gateway in a public subnet and configure the route tables in the VPC appropriately" is the correct answer.

CORRECT: "Create a VPC endpoint in the VPC and configure the route tables appropriately" is also a correct answer.

INCORRECT: "Configure the internet gateway to route connections to S3 using private IP addresses" is incorrect. You cannot configure the internet gateway and you cannot route connections to S3 using private IP addresses unless you use a VPC endpoint.

INCORRECT: "Add an outbound rule in the security groups of the EC2 instances for Amazon S3 using private IP addresses" is incorrect. You cannot add rules to security groups to force traffic to use private IP addresses.

INCORRECT: "Set up AWS Direct Connect and configure a virtual interface between the EC2 instances and the S3 buckets" is incorrect. You cannot create VIFs between a VPC and an AWS public service.

References:

https://docs.aws.amazon.com/vpc/latest/userguide/vpc-endpoints-s3.html

Save time with our exam-specific cheat sheets:

https://digitalcloud.training/certification-training/aws-certified-sysops-administrator-associate/amazon-virtual-private-cloud-vpc/

QUESTION 45

A developer is receiving access denied errors when attempting to list the objects in an Amazon S3 bucket. The developer us using the IAM user account "arn:aws:iam::513259117252:user/paul". The following S3 bucket policy has been applied to the bucket:

```
{
  "Id": "Policy1597781793102",
  "Version": "2012-10-17",
  "Statement": [
    {
      "Sid": "Stmt1597781787330",
      "Action": [
        "s3:List*"
      ],
      "Effect": "Allow",
      "Resource": "arn:aws:s3:::dcttestbucket/*",
      "Principal": {
        "AWS": [
          "arn:aws:iam::513259117252:user/paul"
        ]
      }
    }
  ]
}
```

How can a CloudOps Administrator modify the S3 bucket policy to fix the issue?

1. Change the "Resource" from "arn:aws:s3:::dcttestbucket/*" to "arn:aws:s3:::dcttestbucket".
2. Change the "Principal" from "arn:aws:iam::513259117252:user/paul" to "arn:aws:iam::513259117252:role/paul".
3. Change the "Action" from "s3:List*" to "s3:ListBucket".
4. Change the "Effect" from "Allow" to "Deny".

Answer: 1

Explanation:

The bucket policy is not correctly formed. The /* applies the policy only to the objects. However, the s3:ListBucket action must be allowed at the bucket level. Removing the trailing / and the wildcard should fix this issue.

CORRECT: "Change the "Resource" from "arn:aws:s3:::dcttestbucket/*" to "arn:aws:s3:::dcttestbucket"" is the correct answer.

INCORRECT: "Change the "Principal" from "arn:aws:iam::513259117252:user/paul" to "arn:aws:iam::513259117252:role/paul"" is incorrect. The IAM principal being used is a user account so the principal statement is correct in the policy.

INCORRECT: "Change the "Action" from "s3:List*" to "s3:ListBucket"" is incorrect. This would only provide the s3:ListBucket and would therefore remove the s3:ListObject permissions.

INCORRECT: "Change the "Effect" from "Allow" to "Deny"" is incorrect. This would not achieve the desired outcome.

References:

https://aws.amazon.com/premiumsupport/knowledge-center/s3-access-denied-listobjects-sync/

Save time with our exam-specific cheat sheets:

https://digitalcloud.training/certification-training/aws-certified-sysops-administrator-associate/amazon-s3/

QUESTION 46

A manager in a company needs to see a breakdown of costs in an AWS account on a project by project basis. The manager would like to view this information in AWS Cost Explorer.

Which combination of configuration updates should be applied? (Select TWO.)

1. Activate cost allocation tags.
2. Enable server access logging.
3. Activate consolidated billing.
4. Create and apply resource tags.
5. Enable AWS Budgets.

Answer: 1, 4

Explanation:

Cost Allocation Tags appear on the console after you've enabled Cost Explorer, Budgets, AWS Cost and Usage reports, or legacy reports. After you activate the AWS services, they appear on your cost allocation report. You can then use the tags on your cost allocation report to track your AWS costs. Tags are not applied to resources that were created before the tags were created.

In addition to activating cost allocation tags, the actual resource tags must be created and applied to the relevant resources. Tags are key-value pairs that allow you to organize your AWS resources into groups. In this case the resources would be grouped by project.

CORRECT: "Activate cost allocation tags" is the correct answer.

CORRECT: "Create and apply resource tags" is also a correct answer.

INCORRECT: "Enable server access logging" is incorrect. This feature of Amazon S3 logs access requests to S3 buckets and objects.

INCORRECT: "Activate consolidated billing" is incorrect. Consolidated billing is used across multiple accounts to provide a single bill.

INCORRECT: "Enable AWS Budgets" is incorrect as this service is used for setting budgets and receiving notifications when the budgets are likely to be exceeded.

References:

https://docs.aws.amazon.com/awsaccountbilling/latest/aboutv2/custom-tags.html

QUESTION 47

A company's CloudOps Administrator received a notification from AWS that an Amazon EC2 instance is on a degraded host that is scheduled for retirement. The scheduled retirement occurs during business-critical hours.

What can be done to MINIMIZE disruption?

1. Restart the EC2 instance as immediately to ensure the application is not taken offline when the host is retired.
2. Write an AWS Lambda function to migrate the EC2 instance between hosts. Run the function prior to the scheduled retirement and outside of business hours.
3. Restart the instance outside business hours to perform the system maintenance before the scheduled retirement.
4. Stop/start the instance outside business hours to move to a new host before the scheduled retirement.

Answer: 4

Explanation:

When you stop and start an Amazon EC2 instance it is typically moved to a different underlying host. This is the best way to ensure that the instance is moved off of the host that is scheduled for retirement.

CORRECT: "Stop/start the instance outside business hours to move to a new host before the scheduled retirement" is the correct answer.

INCORRECT: "Restart the EC2 instance as immediately to ensure the application is not taken offline when the host is retired" is incorrect. It is not necessary to take immediate action as AWS has notified of an upcoming event. Also, restarting does not solve the issue as the instance would not move to a different host.

INCORRECT: "Write an AWS Lambda function to migrate the EC2 instance between hosts. Run the function prior to the scheduled retirement and outside of business hours" is incorrect. You cannot use a Lambda function to migrate an instance between hosts as there is no API action that controls this.

INCORRECT: "Restart the instance outside business hours to perform the system maintenance before the scheduled retirement" is incorrect. Restarting does not solve the issue as the instance would not move to a different host.

References:

https://docs.aws.amazon.com/AWSEC2/latest/UserGuide/Stop_Start.html

Save time with our exam-specific cheat sheets:

https://digitalcloud.training/certification-training/aws-certified-sysops-administrator-associate/amazon-ec2/

QUESTION 48

An application has been deployed that stores configuration files in an Amazon S3 bucket. A history of revisions of the configuration files must be maintained in case a rollback is required.

How can a CloudOps Administrator configure the S3 bucket to meet these requirements?

1. Enable versioning on the S3 bucket.
2. Enable a lifecycle policy on the S3 bucket.
3. Enable cross-origin resource sharing on the S3 bucket.
4. Enable object tagging on the S3 bucket.

Answer: 1

Explanation:

Versioning is a means of keeping multiple variants of an object in the same bucket. You can use versioning to preserve, retrieve, and restore every version of every object stored in your Amazon S3 bucket.

With versioning, you can easily recover from both unintended user actions and application failures. When you enable versioning for a bucket, if Amazon S3 receives multiple write requests for the same object simultaneously, it stores all of the objects.

CORRECT: "Enable versioning on the S3 bucket" is the correct answer.

INCORRECT: "Enable a lifecycle policy on the S3 bucket" is incorrect. Lifecycle policies are used to move data between different storage classes, they do not retain copies of versions of files.

INCORRECT: "Enable cross-origin resource sharing on the S3 bucket" is incorrect. CORS is not related to retaining copies of versions of an object on S3.

INCORRECT: "Enable object tagging on the S3 bucket" is incorrect. Tagging adds metadata to your objects, it does not assist with retaining versions.

References:

https://docs.aws.amazon.com/AmazonS3/latest/dev/Versioning.html

Save time with our exam-specific cheat sheets:

https://digitalcloud.training/certification-training/aws-certified-sysops-administrator-associate/amazon-s3/

QUESTION 49

Each IT staff member in a company uses a unique IAM user account. Permissions are applied to users using IAM policies and IAM groups. The security team has requested that staff members should log in with their on-premises Active Directory user accounts instead of their IAM user accounts when accessing the AWS Management Console.

Which solution can a CloudOps Administrator implement to the requirements of the security team?

1. Implement a VPN tunnel and configure an Active Directory connector.
2. Use the IAM connector to synchronize the on-premises Active Directory.
3. Enable an Active Directory federation in an Amazon Route 53 private zone.
4. Implement a two-way trust relationship between AWS IAM and Active Directory.

Answer: 1

Explanation:

AD Connector is designed to give you an easy way to establish a trusted relationship between your Active Directory and AWS. When AD Connector is configured, the trust allows you to:

- Sign in to AWS applications such as Amazon WorkSpaces, Amazon WorkDocs, and Amazon WorkMail by using your Active Directory credentials.
- Seamlessly join Windows instances to your Active Directory domain either through the Amazon EC2 launch wizard or programmatically through the EC2 Simple System Manager (SSM) API.
- Provide federated sign-in to the AWS Management Console by mapping Active Directory identities to AWS Identity and Access Management (IAM) roles.

This solution will result in users' using their on-premises Active Directory user accounts to login to AWS IAM. They would then be able to access the AWS Management Console.

CORRECT: "Implement a VPN tunnel and configure an Active Directory connector" is the correct answer.

INCORRECT: "Use the IAM connector to synchronize the on-premises Active Directory" is incorrect. There is no such thing as an IAM connector.

INCORRECT: "Enable an Active Directory federation in an Amazon Route 53 private zone" is incorrect. You cannot federate Active Directory to an Amazon Route 53 hosted zone.

INCORRECT: "Implement a two-way trust relationship between AWS IAM and Active Directory" is incorrect. You cannot implement a two-way trust relationship between IAM and AD.

References:

https://aws.amazon.com/blogs/security/how-to-connect-your-on-premises-active-directory-to-aws-using-ad-connector/

QUESTION 50

A security team has identified some malicious connection requests from an IP address. They have requested that the IP address should be explicitly denied for both ingress and egress requests for all services in an Amazon VPC immediately.

How can this be quickly achieved?

1. Install a host-based firewall on each Amazon EC2 instance and block the IP address.
2. Remove the Internet Gateway from the VPC and use a NAT gateway instead.
3. Add a rule to the Security Groups attached to the instances in the affected subnets.
4. Add a rule to the Network Access Control Lists for all subnets in the VPC.

Answer: 4

Explanation:

A *network access control list (ACL)* is an optional layer of security for your VPC that acts as a firewall for controlling traffic in and out of one or more subnets. You can add both allow and deny rules to Network ACLs and in this case a deny rule can be applied for the IP address identified by the security team. The rule can be created as an inbound and outbound rule to prevent all communications with the IP address.

CORRECT: "Add a rule to the Network Access Control Lists for all subnets in the VPC" is the correct answer.

INCORRECT: "Install a host-based firewall on each Amazon EC2 instance and block the IP address" is incorrect. This is not a quick solution and requires more complexity and effort than blocking the traffic at the subnet level.

INCORRECT: "Remove the Internet Gateway from the VPC and use a NAT gateway instead" is incorrect. This will break all communications with the Internet. You cannot replace an internet gateway with a NAT gateway.

INCORRECT: "Add a rule to the Security Groups attached to the instances in the affected subnets" is incorrect. You cannot add deny rules to security groups.

References:

https://docs.aws.amazon.com/vpc/latest/userguide/vpc-network-acls.html

Save time with our exam-specific cheat sheets:

https://digitalcloud.training/certification-training/aws-certified-sysops-administrator-associate/amazon-virtual-private-cloud-vpc/

QUESTION 51

A CloudOps Administrator created a script that generates custom Amazon CloudWatch metrics. The EC2 instance on which the script was run had a misconfigured clock resulting in timestamps on the logs that were set to 30 minutes in the past.

What will be the result of this situation?

1. Amazon CloudWatch will not capture the data because it is in the past.
2. Amazon CloudWatch will correct the time when recording the timestamp.
3. Amazon CloudWatch will accept the custom metric data and record it.
4. Amazon CloudWatch creates its own timestamps and ignores metric timestamps.

Answer: 3

Explanation:

Each metric data point must be associated with a time stamp. The time stamp can be up to two weeks in the past and up to two hours into the future. If you do not provide a time stamp, CloudWatch creates a time stamp for you based on the time the data point was received.

CORRECT: "Amazon CloudWatch will accept the custom metric data and record it" is the correct answer.

INCORRECT: "Amazon CloudWatch will not capture the data because it is in the past" is incorrect. This is not the behavior of CloudWatch.

INCORRECT: "Amazon CloudWatch will correct the time when recording the timestamp" is incorrect. This is not the behavior of CloudWatch.

INCORRECT: "Amazon CloudWatch creates its own timestamps and ignores metric timestamps" is incorrect. This is not the behavior of CloudWatch.

References:

https://docs.aws.amazon.com/AmazonCloudWatch/latest/monitoring/cloudwatch_concepts.html

Save time with our exam-specific cheat sheets:

https://digitalcloud.training/certification-training/aws-certified-sysops-administrator-associate/amazon-cloudwatch/

QUESTION 52

A company recently performed a security audit of its AWS cloud-based applications. An application that uses an Amazon SQS queue was flagged for review as the IAM policy attached the queue allowed more access than required.

Who is responsible for correcting the issue?

1. AWS Premium Support
2. The Amazon SQS team
3. The AWS IAM team
4. The CloudOps Administrator

Answer: 4

Explanation:

This question is related to the shared responsibility model. It is important to understand that security in the cloud is the responsibility of the customer. In this case it is the customer's responsibility to apply IAM permissions policies to their SQS queue that restricts access appropriately.

CORRECT: "The CloudOps Administrator" is the correct answer.

INCORRECT: "AWS Premium Support" is incorrect. AWS are responsible for security of the cloud platform; they are not responsible for applying policies to resources.

INCORRECT: "The Amazon SQS team" is incorrect. AWS are responsible for security of the cloud platform; they are not responsible for applying policies to resources.

INCORRECT: "The AWS IAM team" is incorrect. AWS are responsible for security of the cloud platform; they are not responsible for applying policies to resources.

References:

https://aws.amazon.com/compliance/shared-responsibility-model/

QUESTION 53

For security reasons the connectivity to an Amazon S3 bucket must remain within the AWS network using private IP addresses. A VPC endpoint has been created and an endpoint policy with the correct permissions has been set up. The Amazon EC2 instances in the VPC are still unable to access the bucket endpoint.

What is the MOST likely cause of this issue?

1. Storage class analytics must be enabled to use private IP addresses.
2. The bucket policy must be configured to all private IP addresses.
3. The EC2 instances need to have an Elastic IP address assigned.
4. The subnet does not have the VPC endpoint as a target in the route table.

Answer: 4

Explanation:

A VPC endpoint enables you to privately connect your VPC to supported AWS services. Instances in your VPC do not require public IP addresses to communicate with resources in the service. Traffic between your

VPC and the other service does not leave the Amazon network.

Amazon S3 uses a gateway endpoint. When configuring the gateway endpoint the following tasks must be performed:

1. Create the endpoint within the VPC
2. Attach an endpoint policy
3. Add a route to the endpoint to the route table

In this case, it is likely that the route table has not been updated so the EC2 instances are not sending requests to the endpoint.

CORRECT: "The subnet does not have the VPC endpoint as a target in the route table" is the correct answer.

INCORRECT: "Storage class analytics must be enabled to use private IP addresses" is incorrect. Analytics has no relevance to connectivity using a gateway endpoint.

INCORRECT: "The bucket policy must be configured to all private IP addresses" is incorrect. This is not the most likely solution it's unlikely that the bucket policy would have previously been configured to restrict private IP addresses.

INCORRECT: "The EC2 instances need to have an Elastic IP address assigned" is incorrect. Elastic IPs are public addresses and this solution is designed to use private addresses.

References:

https://docs.aws.amazon.com/vpc/latest/userguide/vpce-gateway.html

Save time with our exam-specific cheat sheets:

https://digitalcloud.training/certification-training/aws-certified-sysops-administrator-associate/amazon-virtual-private-cloud-vpc/

QUESTION 54

A company is implementing cross-account access from a production account to a development account. An IAM role must be created and a permissions policy must be attached.

According to the AWS shared responsibility model, who is responsible for creating the IAM role and attaching the policy?

1. A CloudOps Administrator is responsible for creating the role and attaching the policy.
2. A CloudOps Administrator is responsible for creating the role, and AWS is responsible for attaching the policy to the role.
3. AWS is responsible for creating the role and attaching the policy.
4. AWS is responsible for creating the role, and a CloudOps Administrator is responsible for attaching the policy to the role.

Answer: 1

Explanation:

This question is related to the shared responsibility model. It is important to understand that security in the cloud is the responsibility of the customer. In this case it is the customer's responsibility to create the IAM role and attach a permissions policy to it.

CORRECT: "A CloudOps Administrator is responsible for creating the role and attaching the policy" is the correct answer.

INCORRECT: "A CloudOps Administrator is responsible for creating the role, and AWS is responsible for attaching the policy to the role" is incorrect. AWS are not responsible for attaching policies to roles.

INCORRECT: "AWS is responsible for creating the role and attaching the policy" is incorrect. AWS is not responsible for creating the role or attaching the policy

INCORRECT: "AWS is responsible for creating the role, and a CloudOps Administrator is responsible for attaching the policy to the role" is incorrect. AWS are not responsible for creating the role.

References:

https://docs.aws.amazon.com/IAM/latest/UserGuide/tutorial_cross-account-with-roles.html https://aws.amazon.com/compliance/shared-responsibility-model/

Save time with our exam-specific cheat sheets:

https://digitalcloud.training/certification-training/aws-certified-sysops-administrator-associate/aws-iam/

QUESTION 55

An Amazon S3 bucket hold sensitive data. A CloudOps Administrator has been tasked with monitoring all object upload and download activity relating to the bucket. Monitoring must include tracking the AWS account of the caller, the IAM user role of the caller, the time of the API call, and the IP address of the API.

What should the CloudOps Administrator do to meet the requirements?

1. Enable data event logging in AWS CloudTrail.
2. Enable management event logging in AWS CloudTrail.
3. Configure Amazon Inspector bucket event logging.
4. Configure Amazon Inspector user event logging.

Answer: 1

Explanation:

Data events provide visibility into the resource operations performed on or within a resource. These are also known as data plane operations. Data events are often high-volume activities.

The following two data types are recorded:

- Amazon S3 object-level API activity (for example, GetObject, DeleteObject, and PutObject API operations).
- AWS Lambda function execution activity (the Invoke API).

Data events are disabled by default when you create a trail. To record CloudTrail data events, you must explicitly add the supported resources or resource types for which you want to collect activity to a trail.

CORRECT: "Enable data event logging in AWS CloudTrail" is the correct answer.

INCORRECT: "Enable management event logging in AWS CloudTrail" is incorrect. Management events provide visibility into management operations that are performed on resources in your AWS account. These are also known as control plane operations and are enabled by default. In this case the Administrator needs to enable data events logging.

INCORRECT: "Configure Amazon Inspector bucket event logging" is incorrect. Inspector does not record API activity, use CloudTrail instead.

INCORRECT: "Configure Amazon Inspector user event logging" is incorrect. Inspector does not record API activity, use CloudTrail instead.

References:

https://docs.aws.amazon.com/awscloudtrail/latest/userguide/logging-data-events-with-cloudtrail.html#logging-data-events

https://docs.aws.amazon.com/awscloudtrail/latest/userguide/logging-management-events-with-cloudtrail.html#logging-management-events

Save time with our exam-specific cheat sheets:

https://digitalcloud.training/certification-training/aws-certified-sysops-administrator-associate/aws-cloudtrail/

QUESTION 56

An application running on an Amazon EC2 instance processes data and saves log files to an Amazon S3 bucket. A CloudOps Administrator is tasked with allowing the instance to access the bucket.

How can this be configured for optimum security?

1. Apply an S3 bucket policy to allow access from all EC2 instances.
2. Create an IAM role for Amazon S3 access and attach it to the EC2 instance.

3. Create an IAM user and delegate access to the EC2 instance.
4. Store access keys in an Amazon Machine Image (AMI).

Answer: 2

Explanation:

Applications that run on an EC2 instance must include AWS credentials in their AWS API requests. You could have your developers store AWS credentials directly within the EC2 instance and allow applications in that instance to use those credentials. But developers would then have to manage the credentials and ensure that they securely pass the credentials to each instance and update each EC2 instance when it's time to rotate the credentials. That's a lot of additional work.

Instead, you can and should use an IAM role to manage *temporary* credentials for applications that run on an EC2 instance. When you use a role, you don't have to distribute long-term credentials (such as a user name and password or access keys) to an EC2 instance. Instead, the role supplies temporary permissions that applications can use when they make calls to other AWS resources. When you launch an EC2 instance, you specify an IAM role to associate with the instance. Applications that run on the instance can then use the role-supplied temporary credentials to sign API requests.

CORRECT: "Create an IAM role for Amazon S3 access and attach it to the EC2 instance" is the correct answer.

INCORRECT: "Apply an S3 bucket policy to allow access from all EC2 instances" is incorrect. This does not represent optimum security as it opens the bucket to many EC2 instances.

INCORRECT: "Create an IAM user and delegate access to the EC2 instance" is incorrect. You cannot delegate using IAM user accounts, you should use an IAM role.

INCORRECT: "Store access keys in an Amazon Machine Image (AMI)" is incorrect. This is not the most secure solution, using roles is a best practice for security.

References:

https://docs.aws.amazon.com/IAM/latest/UserGuide/id_roles_use_switch-role-ec2.html

Save time with our exam-specific cheat sheets:

https://digitalcloud.training/certification-training/aws-certified-sysops-administrator-associate/aws-iam/

QUESTION 57

A company runs an application on-premises that generates many gigabytes of data files each day. The company requires that the files are stored on the AWS cloud, but the most recent files should be available locally for low latency access.

Which AWS service is most suitable for these requirements?

1. AWS Storage Gateway
2. Amazon EBS
3. Amazon S3
4. Amazon EFS

Answer: 1

Explanation:

AWS Storage Gateway Volume Gateways offer two modes: Cached and stored. With cached volumes, the Storage Gateway service stores the full volume in its Amazon S3 service bucket, and a portion of the volume—your recently accessed data—is retained in the gateway's local cache for low-latency access.

This would be suitable for the requirements in this scenario.

CORRECT: "AWS Storage Gateway" is the correct answer.

INCORRECT: "Amazon EBS" is incorrect. Amazon EBS is not accessible from on-premises and offers no local caching feature.

INCORRECT: "Amazon S3" is incorrect. Amazon S3 does not offer a local caching feature.

INCORRECT: "Amazon EFS" is incorrect. Amazon EFS does not offer a local caching feature.

References:

https://aws.amazon.com/storagegateway/volume/

Save time with our exam-specific cheat sheets:

https://digitalcloud.training/certification-training/aws-certified-sysops-administrator-associate/aws-storage-gateway/

QUESTION 58

A company runs an Amazon RDS MySQL DB instance in a production account. Each week a backup of the database must be copied to a separate development account for testing.

What is the MOST cost-effective way to meet this requirement?

1. Copy an automated RDS snapshot to the development account using the copy-db-snapshot command with the AWS CLI.
2. Create a multi-AZ standby of the RDS database in the development account and take a manual snapshot using the create-db-snapshot AWS CLI command.
3. Use the Amazon S3 cross-region replication (CRR) to copy the automated backup to the development account.
4. Create a manual RDS snapshot with the create-db-snapshot CLI command and share it with the development account, create a copy in the development account.

Answer: 4

Explanation:

Using Amazon RDS, you can share a manual DB snapshot in the following ways:

- Sharing a manual DB snapshot, whether encrypted or unencrypted, enables authorized AWS accounts to copy the snapshot.
- Sharing an unencrypted manual DB snapshot enables authorized AWS accounts to directly restore a DB instance from the snapshot instead of taking a copy of it and restoring from that.

You can share a manual snapshot with up to 20 other AWS accounts. You can also share an unencrypted manual snapshot as public, which makes the snapshot available to all AWS accounts.

CORRECT: "Create a manual RDS snapshot with the create-db-snapshot CLI command and share it with the development account, create a copy in the development account" is the correct answer.

INCORRECT: "Copy an automated RDS snapshot to the development account using the copy-db-snapshot command with the AWS CLI" is incorrect. You cannot copy an automated DB snapshot.

INCORRECT: "Create a multi-AZ standby of the RDS database in the development account and take a manual snapshot using the create-db-snapshot AWS CLI command" is incorrect. You cannot create multi-AZ standby instances in another account.

INCORRECT: "Use the Amazon S3 cross-region replication (CRR) to copy the automated backup to the development account" is incorrect. You cannot use CRR to copy any snapshots. Snapshots exist on S3 but you cannot directly work with them.

References:

https://docs.aws.amazon.com/AmazonRDS/latest/UserGuide/USER_ShareSnapshot.html

Save time with our exam-specific cheat sheets:

https://digitalcloud.training/certification-training/aws-certified-sysops-administrator-associate/amazon-rds/

QUESTION 59

A company's AWS bill has been increasing and an investigation has shown that many unauthorized services are being used across their AWS accounts.

Which service can the company use to restrict access to AWS services across accounts?

1. AWS Cost Explorer
2. AWS Organizations
3. AWS Config
4. AWS Budgets

Answer: 2

Explanation:

In AWS Organizations service control policies (SCPs) are a type of organization policy that you can use to manage permissions in your organization. SCPs offer central control over the maximum available permissions for all accounts in your organization.

With SCPs the company can restrict the API actions for the services they need to restrict access to. This will prevent those services from being available for use. The policies can be applied centrally across all accounts in the organization.

CORRECT: "AWS Organizations" is the correct answer.

INCORRECT: "AWS Cost Explorer" is incorrect. Cost explorer is used for visually exploring the costs in AWS accounts. It cannot be used to restrict access to services.

INCORRECT: "AWS Config" is incorrect. This service is used to assess, audit, and evaluate the configurations of AWS resources.

INCORRECT: "AWS Budgets" is incorrect. This service will alert on usage but will not prevent access to services.

References:

https://docs.aws.amazon.com/organizations/latest/userguide/orgs_manage_policies_type-auth.html

Save time with our exam-specific cheat sheets:

https://digitalcloud.training/certification-training/aws-certified-sysops-administrator-associate/aws-organizations/

QUESTION 60

A company runs a resource-intensive daily reporting job on a production Amazon RDS database. The performance of the database is affected when the reporting job is running, and this has resulted in user complaints.

How can a CloudOps Administrator resolve the performance issues?

1. Create a copy of the database using a snapshot and run the reporting against the copy.
2. Create an Amazon RDS read replica and run the reporting job against the read replica.
3. Enable Multi-AZ mode on Amazon RDS and run the reporting on the standby instance.
4. Enable Auto Scaling for the RDS database and ensure the maximum instances is greater than one.

Answer: 2

Explanation:

This is a good use case for an Amazon RDS read replica. When you create a read replica the master database asynchronously replicates to it. The read replica has a separate endpoint that can be used for queries. In this case, the read replica can be used as the target for the reporting job and this will completely offload the pressure of the reporting job from the master database.

CORRECT: "Create an Amazon RDS read replica and run the reporting job against the read replica" is the correct answer.

INCORRECT: "Create a copy of the database using a snapshot and run the reporting against the copy" is incorrect. It is not practical to use this method as the reporting job runs daily so a new copy would need to be instantiated every day.

INCORRECT: "Enable Multi-AZ mode on Amazon RDS and run the reporting on the standby instance" is incorrect. You cannot use a multi-AZ standby for offloading reads from the master DB.

INCORRECT: "Enable Auto Scaling for the RDS database and ensure the maximum instances is greater than one" is incorrect. There is no such thing as Auto Scaling for Amazon RDS instances.

References:

https://aws.amazon.com/rds/features/read-replicas/

Save time with our exam-specific cheat sheets:

https://digitalcloud.training/certification-training/aws-certified-sysops-administrator-associate/amazon-rds/

QUESTION 61

A company runs a critical business application on Amazon EC2 instances in an Auto Scaling group with a database running MySQL on an Amazon EC2 instance. The company wishes to increase the availability and durability of the database layer whilst minimizing application changes.

How can these requirements be met?

1. Configure multi-AZ for the existing database instance to create a standby replica in a separate availability zone.
2. Launch a read replica of the existing database and create an Application Load Balancer (ALB) to evenly distribute connections.
3. Migrate the database to an Amazon RDS Aurora DB instance and create an Aurora Replica in another Availability Zone.
4. Create an Amazon RDS Microsoft SQL DB instance and enable multi-AZ replication. Back up the existing data and import it into the new database.

Answer: 3

Explanation:

Aurora Replicas are independent endpoints in an Aurora DB cluster, best used for scaling read operations and increasing availability. Up to 15 Aurora Replicas can be distributed across the Availability Zones that a DB cluster spans within an AWS Region.

To increase availability, you can use Aurora Replicas as failover targets. That is, if the primary instance fails, an Aurora Replica is promoted to the primary instance.

CORRECT: "Migrate the database to an Amazon RDS Aurora DB instance and create an Aurora Replica in another Availability Zone" is the correct answer.

INCORRECT: "Configure multi-AZ for the existing database instance to create a standby replica in a separate availability zone" is incorrect. You cannot configure multi-AZ for a database running on Amazon EC2.

INCORRECT: "Launch a read replica of the existing database and create an Application Load Balancer (ALB) to evenly distribute connections" is incorrect. You cannot create a read replica of a database running on EC2 and you cannot use ELBs with databases.

INCORRECT: "Create an Amazon RDS Microsoft SQL DB instance and enable multi-AZ replication. Back up the existing data and import it into the new database" is incorrect. This is a change in architecture as the DB is Microsoft SQL rather than MySQL. Therefore, this is not the best answer.

References:

https://docs.aws.amazon.com/AmazonRDS/latest/AuroraUserGuide/Aurora.Replication.html

Save time with our exam-specific cheat sheets:

https://digitalcloud.training/certification-training/aws-certified-sysops-administrator-associate/amazon-rds/

QUESTION 62

A company has created a static website using an Amazon S3 bucket. The static website configuration was enabled, and content has been uploaded. However, upon testing access to the site the following error message was received:

"HTTP 403 Forbidden"

What needs to be done to resolve the error?
1. Remove the default bucket policy that denies read access to the bucket.
2. Configure cross-region replication (CRR) on the bucket.
3. Add a bucket policy that grants everyone read access to the bucket.
4. Add a bucket policy that grants everyone read access to the bucket objects.

Answer: 4

Explanation:

The most likely explanation is that the bucket policy does not grant the s3:GetObject permission. To use GET, you must have READ access to the object. If you grant READ access to the anonymous user, you can return the object without using an authorization header.

In this case, the bucket policy may not be configured to provide anonymous users with read access to the objects in the bucket.

CORRECT: "Add a bucket policy that grants everyone read access to the bucket objects" is the correct answer.

INCORRECT: "Remove the default bucket policy that denies read access to the bucket" is incorrect. There is not default policy that denies read access.

INCORRECT: "Configure cross-region replication (CRR) on the bucket" is incorrect. This will not assist with resolving access denied error messages, it just copies the objects to a bucket in another region.

INCORRECT: "Add a bucket policy that grants everyone read access to the bucket" is incorrect. In this case the object-level permissions are more relevant as the website users must able to perform the s3:GetObject API action to retrieve the objects.

References:

https://aws.amazon.com/premiumsupport/knowledge-center/s3-troubleshoot-403/

https://docs.aws.amazon.com/AmazonS3/latest/API/API_GetObject.html

Save time with our exam-specific cheat sheets:

https://digitalcloud.training/certification-training/aws-certified-sysops-administrator-associate/amazon-s3/

QUESTION 63

A company has deployed a new web application. Following the release, penetration testing revealed a cross-site scripting vulnerability that could expose user data.
Which AWS service will mitigate this issue?
1. AWS WAF
2. AWS Shield Standard
3. AWS KMS
4. Amazon GuardDuty

Answer: 1

Explanation:

AWS WAF is a web application firewall that helps protect your web applications or APIs against common web exploits that may affect availability, compromise security, or consume excessive resources.

AWS WAF gives you control over how traffic reaches your applications by enabling you to create security rules that block common attack patterns, such as SQL injection or cross-site scripting, and rules that filter out specific traffic patterns you define.

This is the most appropriate service to use for mitigating web attacks using cross-site scripting techniques.

CORRECT: "AWS WAF" is the correct answer.

INCORRECT: "AWS Shield Standard" is incorrect. This service is used for preventing Distributed Denial of Service (DDoS) attacks, not cross-site scripting attacks.

INCORRECT: "AWS KMS" is incorrect. This service is used for creating and managing encryption keys.

INCORRECT: "Amazon GuardDuty" is incorrect. This service analyzes and processes VPC Flow Logs, AWS

CloudTrail management event logs, Cloudtrail S3 data event logs, and DNS logs. It will not mitigate a cross-site scripting attack.

References:

https://aws.amazon.com/waf/

Save time with our exam-specific cheat sheets:

https://digitalcloud.training/certification-training/aws-certified-sysops-administrator-associate/aws-waf-and-shield/

QUESTION 64

A company has two AWS accounts and has configured a VPC peering connection between them. The VPCs have non-overlapping CIDR blocks. The company requires that instances in the private subnets of each VPC can ping instances in the private subnets of the other VPC.

What action should be taken to meet this requirement?

1. Ensure that both accounts are linked and are part of consolidated billing to create a file sharing network, and then enable VPC peering.
2. Add a route to the VPC route tables of each VPC that points to the IP address range of the other VPC.
3. Modify the CIDR blocks so they are matching to facilitate full connectivity between the two VPCs.
4. Create a virtual private gateway within each VPC and then link the VPGs to enable bi-directional connectivity.

Answer: 2

Explanation:

A VPC peering connection is a networking connection between two VPCs that enables you to route traffic between them using private IPv4 addresses or IPv6 addresses. Instances in either VPC can communicate with each other as if they are within the same network.

You can create a VPC peering connection between your own VPCs, or with a VPC in another AWS account. The VPCs can be in different regions (also known as an inter-region VPC peering connection).

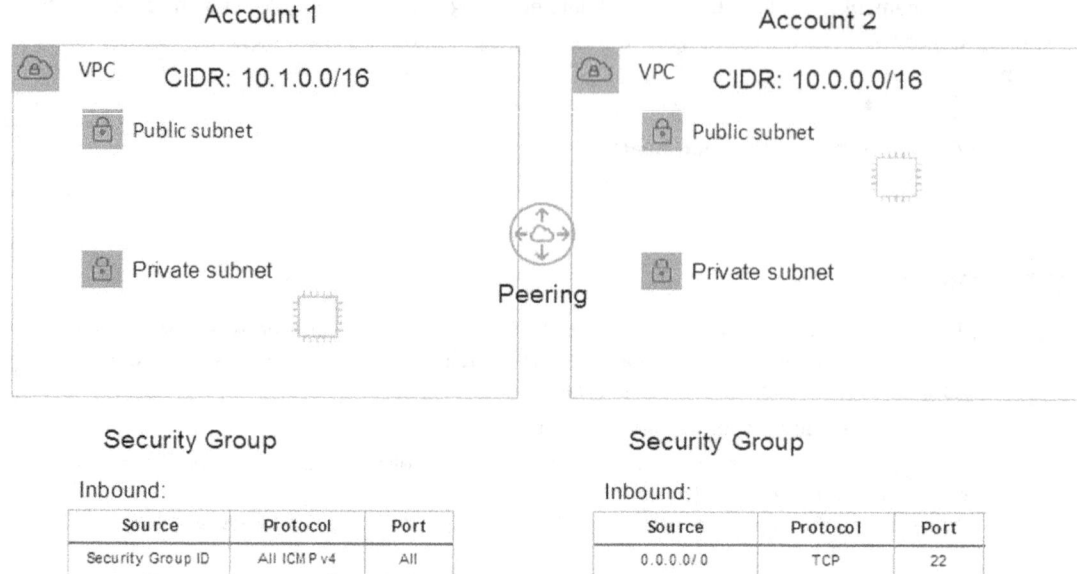

To enable the flow of traffic between the VPCs using private IP addresses, the owner of each VPC in the VPC peering connection must manually add a route to one or more of their VPC route tables that points to the IP address range of the other VPC (the peer VPC).

CORRECT: "Add a route to the VPC route tables of each VPC that points to the IP address range of the other VPC" is the correct answer.

INCORRECT: "Ensure that both accounts are linked and are part of consolidated billing to create a file sharing network, and then enable VPC peering" is incorrect. Consolidated billing has nothing to do with network connectivity.

INCORRECT: "Modify the CIDR blocks so they are matching to facilitate full connectivity between the two VPCs" is incorrect. You cannot use VPC peering with VPCs that have overlapping CIDR blocks, the ranges must be non-overlapping.

INCORRECT: "Create a virtual private gateway within each VPC and then link the VPGs to enable bi-directional connectivity" is incorrect. VPGs are used with VPN connections to on-premises data centers. They are not used between VPCs and are not related to VPC peering.

References:

https://docs.aws.amazon.com/vpc/latest/peering/what-is-vpc-peering.html

Save time with our exam-specific cheat sheets:

https://digitalcloud.training/certification-training/aws-certified-sysops-administrator-associate/amazon-virtual-private-cloud-vpc/

QUESTION 65

A company has configured a backup of their VPC in another Region. Data will be replicated from the primary region to the secondary region. Company policy mandates that all data must be encrypted and must not traverse the public internet.

How should the CloudOps Administrator connect the two VPCs while meeting the compliance requirements?

1. Configure an AWS Managed VPN between each VPC, then configure the route tables.
2. Configure NAT gateways in both VPCs, then configure the route tables.
3. Configure an internet gateway in each VPC and use these as the targets for the VPC route tables.
4. Configure inter-region VPC peering between the two VPCs, then configure route tables.

Answer: 4

Explanation:

Inter-Region VPC Peering provides a simple and cost-effective way to share resources between regions or replicate data for geographic redundancy. Inter-Region VPC Peering encrypts inter-region traffic with no single point of failure or bandwidth bottleneck.

Traffic using Inter-Region VPC Peering always stays on the global AWS backbone and never traverses the public internet, thereby reducing threat vectors, such as common exploits and DDoS attacks.

CORRECT: "Configure inter-region VPC peering between the two VPCs, then configure route tables" is the correct answer.

INCORRECT: "Configure an AWS Managed VPN between each VPC, then configure the route tables" is incorrect. Using AWS Managed VPN connections between two VPCs is not a best practice solution.

INCORRECT: "Configure NAT gateways in both VPCs, then configure the route tables" is incorrect. You cannot use NAT gateways for creating a private, encrypted connection between two VPCs.

INCORRECT: "Configure an internet gateway in each VPC and use these as the targets for the VPC route tables" is incorrect. You cannot create a private, encrypted connection between two VPCs using internet gateways.

References:

https://docs.aws.amazon.com/vpc/latest/peering/what-is-vpc-peering.html

Save time with our exam-specific cheat sheets:

https://digitalcloud.training/certification-training/aws-certified-sysops-administrator-associate/amazon-virtual-private-cloud-vpc/

SET 3: PRACTICE QUESTIONS ONLY

For training purposes, go directly to Set 3: Practice Questions, Answers & Explanations

QUESTION 1

A CloudOps Administrator has configured an Amazon EC2 instance in a public subnet for remote access over SSH. The Administrator is able to establish an SSH connection from an on-premises network via the internet but is unable to ping the instance.

What is the most likely reason for this?

1. The instance does not have an Elastic IP address.
2. The instance is in a VPC that does not have an internet gateway.
3. The instance's security group does not allow ICMP traffic.
4. The instance is behind a NAT gateway.

QUESTION 2

A company needs to improve the security of passwords by forcing all IAM users to rotate their passwords on a regular basis.

Which action should be taken take to implement this?

1. Configure multi-factor authentication for all IAM users.
2. Set up a password policy to enable password expiration for IAM users.
3. Use Amazon SNS to send regular notifications that passwords must be changed.
4. Set up an access key policy to enable expiration for access keys.

QUESTION 3

A company is deploying AWS Single Sign-On (SSO). A CloudOps Administrator has created an AWS SSO directory in an AWS Organizations master account and enabled full access. What is the next step to configure the single sign-on functionality?

1. Create IAM roles in each account to be used by AWS SSO and associate users with these roles using AWS SSO.
2. Create permission sets in AWS SSO and associate the permission sets with Directory Service users or groups.
3. Create IAM users in the master account and use AWS SSO to associate the users with the accounts they will access.
4. Create service control policies (SCPs) in Organizations and associate the SCPs with Directory Service users or groups.

QUESTION 4

The security team has notified a CloudOps Administrator that there may be a vulnerable version of software installed on some Amazon EC2 instances. How can the Administrator verify if the vulnerable software is installed on the EC2 instances with the LEAST operational overhead?

1. Create and run an Amazon Inspector assessment template.
2. Connect to each instance using SSH and check the software version.
3. Use AWS CloudTrail to verify Amazon EC2 API activity in the account.
4. Write some custom code that uses AWS Lambda to check the instances.

QUESTION 5

A company is developing some new applications in a development account. The costs associated with the account have been rising management acre concerned. A CloudOps Administrator has been tasked with configuring alerts that will notify management when the accounts' costs or usage are forecasted to exceed a specified spending amount.

Which AWS service should the Administrator use?

1. AWS Cost Explorer
2. AWS Trusted Advisor
3. AWS Budgets
4. AWS Cost and Usage report

QUESTION 6

A CloudOps Administrator has been tasked with setting up a record set in Amazon Route 53 to point to an Application Load Balancer (ALB). The hosted zone and the ALB are in different accounts.

What is the MOST cost-effective and efficient solution to this requirement?

1. Create an Application Load Balancer in the same account as the hosted zone and forward connections cross-account to the other ALB.
2. Create an alias record in the hosted zone pointing to the Application Load Balancer.
3. Create an asynchronous replica of the hosted zone in the account with the Application Load Balancer.
4. Create a CNAME record in the hosted zone pointing to an alias record to the Application Load Balancer.

QUESTION 7

A Company has identified that a security vulnerability affects a version of MariaDB that is being used with an Amazon RDS database instance.

Who is responsible for ensuring that the patch is applied to the database?

1. Amazon Web Services (AWS).
2. The database vendor.
3. The security department the company.
4. The company's CloudOps Administrator.

QUESTION 8

A Company stores a large volume of non-critical log files in an Amazon S3 bucket. An Amazon EC2 instance processes files from the bucket on a daily basis. Which storage option will be the MOST cost-effective for this scenario?

1. Amazon Glacier.
2. Amazon S3 Standard-Infrequent Access.
3. Amazon Instance Store.
4. Amazon S3 Standard.

QUESTION 9

A security vulnerability has been discovered that impacts a version of Linux that is running on some Amazon EC2 instances in a VPC. How can a CloudOps Administrator mitigate the exposure with the LEAST disruption?

1. Shut down and then restart the instances so they change underlying hosts.
2. Use Amazon Inspector to produce a report with best practice recommendations.
3. Redeploy the EC2 instances using an updated AMI through AWS CloudFormation.
4. Use AWS Systems Manager to patch the Linux operating systems.

QUESTION 10

A CloudOps team in a company would like to make AWS maintenance events that may affect their resources visible in their existing operations dashboard. What should a CloudOps Administrator do to include this data?

1. Use an AWS Lambda function that queries Amazon CloudWatch Events for state changes in AWS infrastructure.
2. Integrate the AWS Service Health Dashboard's RSS feed into the company's existing operations dashboard.
3. Use Amazon Inspector to send notifications of upcoming maintenance events to the Operations team distribution list.
4. Use the AWS Health API to query for upcoming maintenance events and include this data in the operations dashboard.

QUESTION 11

A company runs an application that uses Amazon EC2 instances behind an Application Load Balancer (ALB). Customers access the application using a custom DNS domain name. Reports have been received about errors when connecting to the application using the DNS name.

The administrator has confirmed:

- The security groups and network ACLs are correctly configured.
- An Amazon Route 53 Alias record is setup correctly pointing the custom DNS name to the ALB.
- The load balancer target group shows no healthy instances.

What first step should the CloudOps Administrator take to troubleshoot this issue?

1. Review the VPC Flow Logs, looking for any API errors.
2. Review the load balancer target group health check configuration.
3. Review the load balancer access logs, looking for any issues or errors.
4. Review the load balancer listener configuration.

QUESTION 12

A company's security team requested that all Amazon EBS volumes should be encrypted with a specific AWS KMS customer master key (CMK). A CloudOps Administrator is tasked with verifying that the security team's request has been implemented.

What is the MOST efficient way for the Administrator to verify the correct encryption key is being used?

1. Use AWS Config to configure the encrypted-volumes managed rule and specify the key ID of the CMK.
2. Create an AWS Lambda function to run on a daily schedule, and have the function run the aws ec2 describe-volumes --filters encrypted command.
3. Log in to the AWS Management Console on a daily schedule, then filter the list of volumes by encryption status, then export this list.
4. Create an AWS Organizations SCP that only allows encrypt API actions that use the specific KMS CMK.

QUESTION 13

The security team in a company is concerned about the security of AWS CloudTrail logs. The key requirements are to keep a record of any deletions or modifications to the log files.

Which steps should a CloudOps Administrator take to meet these requirements? (Select TWO.)

1. Enable the CloudTrail log file integrity check in AWS Config Rules.
2. Add an SNS notification to CloudWatch Logs for any delete actions.
3. Enable Amazon S3 MFA Delete for the CloudTrail S3 bucket.
4. Enable CloudTrail log file integrity validation.

5. Restrict all access to the CloudTrail S3 bucket.

QUESTION 14

A company is deploying a new website that hosts dynamic content. Due to licensing restrictions the content must not be accessible by users in specific countries or regions. How can a CloudOps Administrator enforce the content restrictions? (Choose TWO.)

1. Security group restriction
2. Amazon CloudFront geo-restriction
3. AWS Shield geo-restriction
4. Amazon Route 53 geolocation routing
5. Network ACL restriction

QUESTION 15

A CloudOps Administrator typically manages an Amazon EC2 instance using SSH from the corporate network. The Administrator is working from home and attempting to connect to the EC2 instance but is receiving a connection timeout error.

What is the most likely cause of the connection timeout?

1. The key pair the Administrator is using does not allow connections from the home network.
2. The Administrators' home network does not have a route to the internet gateway in its route table.
3. The IAM role associated with the EC2 instance does not allow SSH connections from the home network.
4. The security group is not allowing inbound traffic from the home network on the SSH port.

QUESTION 16

A legacy application is deployed on an Amazon EC2 m1.large instance and the CPU utilization is over 90% resulting in high latency. The application can only be scaled vertically. How can a CloudOps Administrator resolve the performance issues?

1. Change the Amazon EBS volume to Provisioned IOPS.
2. Add additional m1.large instances to the application.
3. Add a read replica to offload queries from the instance.
4. Upgrade to a compute-optimized instance.

QUESTION 17

A corporate application is used by remote workers and is hosted on Amazon EC2 instances behind an Application Load Balancer (ALB). User authentication is handled at the individual EC2 instance level. Once a user is authenticated; all requests from that user must go to the same EC2 instance.

Which feature of the Elastic Load Balancer must a CloudOps Administrator use to control the behavior?

1. TCP listeners
2. Sticky sessions
3. Deregistration delay
4. Cross-zone load balancing

QUESTION 18

A company needs to track the allocation of Reserved instance discounts in the company's consolidated bill.

Which AWS tool can be used to find this information?

1. AWS Budgets
2. Amazon Inspector

3. AWS Organizations
4. AWS Cost and Usage report

QUESTION 19

A manager has requested a report that provides a detailed history of all API activity for a specific user over the last several months of employment. AWS CloudTrail is enabled in the account.

What is the MOST efficient method for a CloudOps Administrator to generate the required report?

1. Using the AWS management Console, search for the user name in the CloudTrail history. Then filter by API and download the report in CSV format.
2. Locate the CloudTrail logs in the appropriate Amazon S3 bucket. Use Amazon Athena to extract the information needed to generate the report.
3. Use the CloudTrail digest files stored in the company's Amazon S3 bucket. then send the logs to Amazon QuickSight to create the report.
4. Using the AWS management Console, search for the API activity in the CloudTrail history. Then filter by user name and download the report in CSV format.

QUESTION 20

A CloudOps Administrator noticed a large increase in the number of requests against an Amazon SQS queue. The administrator is concerned about rising costs associated with the queue and needs to identify the source of the calls.

What should the CloudOps Administrator use to validate the calls made to SQS?

1. Amazon CloudWatch
2. AWS Cost Explorer
3. AWS CloudTrail
4. Amazon SQS Access Logs

QUESTION 21

A CloudOps Administrator needs to restrict access to a bucket that is currently accessed by users in other AWS accounts. The Administrator requires that the bucket is only accessible to users in the same account.

How can this be achieved?

1. Move the S3 bucket to the S3 One Zone-IA storage class and disable versioning.
2. Create Amazon S3 presigned URLs for accessing objects in the bucket.
3. Create an object policy that restricts access to only users in the same account.
4. Change the bucket access control list (ACL) to restrict access to the bucket owner.

QUESTION 22

A Company is planning to deploy a workload that requires Payment Card Industry (PCI) compliance. The security team has requested information on the PCI compliance status of the AWS infrastructure.

Which AWS tool will provide the necessary information?

1. Amazon CloudWatch
2. AWS OpsWorks
3. AWS Artifact
4. AWS GuardDuty

QUESTION 23

The manager of a CloudOps team needs to ensure Administrators do not accidentally terminate several critical Amazon EC2 instances.

How can this be accomplished?

1. Use AWS Systems Manager to restrict EC2 termination.
2. Enable termination protection on the EC2 instances.
3. Use AWS Config to restrict EC2 termination.
4. Use CloudTrail to restrict the terminate-instances API call.

QUESTION 24

A CloudOps Administrator attempted to launch an Amazon EC2 instance and received the following error:

"InstanceLimitExceeded "Your quota allows for 0 more running instance(s).""

What action should the Administrator take to resolve this issue and launch the EC2 instances?

1. Open a case with AWS Support requesting an increase of the EC2 instance limit.
2. Try to launch the EC2 instances into another availability zone.
3. Launch the EC2 instances by using the run-instances CLI command.
4. Use the AWS management console to increase the limits for the region.

QUESTION 25

A CloudOps Administrator manages some critical applications that run on several Amazon EC2 instances. The Administrator needs to ensure that the EC2 instances are automatically recovered if they become impaired due to an underlying hardware failure.

Which service can the Administrator use to monitor and recover the EC2 instances?

1. Amazon EC2 Systems Manager
2. AWS OpsWorks
3. Amazon CloudWatch
4. AWS CloudFormation

QUESTION 26

A CloudOps Administrator has deployed a fleet of Amazon EC2 instances using an EC2 Auto Scaling group. The instances must be configured to send local logs to Amazon CloudWatch and the solution must minimize operational overhead.

Which action should the Administrator take to meet this requirement?

1. Configure AWS Config to forward events to CloudWatch.
2. Install and configure the unified CloudWatch agent.
3. Create a script that forwards events to CloudWatch.
4. Install and configure the Amazon Inspector agent.

QUESTION 27

According to the shared responsibility model, for which of the following Amazon EC2 activities is AWS responsible? (Select TWO.)

1. Patching the guest operating system.
2. Patching the hypervisor.
3. Monitoring EBS volume utilization.
4. Configuring security groups.
5. Maintaining network infrastructure.

QUESTION 28

An Amazon EC2 instance was launched from a Microsoft Windows 2012 AMI and is inaccessible using Remote Desktop Protocol (RDP), or over the network. Another instance was deployed using a different AMI but the same configuration options and is functioning normally.

Which next step should a CloudOps Administrator take to troubleshoot the problem?

1. Use Amazon CloudWatch Events to gather operating system log files for analysis.
2. Use VPC Flow Logs to gather operating system log files for analysis.
3. Use AWS CloudTrail to gather operating system log files for analysis.
4. Use EC2Rescue to gather operating system log files for analysis.

QUESTION 29

A bespoke application must be installed on a fleet of Amazon EC2 instances. The application is updated frequently and can be installed automatically. How can the application be deployed on new EC2 instances?

1. Use AWS Config to detect application updates and trigger an update process.
2. Create a script that downloads and installs the application using EC2 user data.
3. Use AWS Systems Manager to inject the application into an AMI.
4. Create an AWS CloudFormation stack and use a change set to deploy to EC2.

QUESTION 30

An application that uses an Amazon ElastiCache Memcached cluster is receiving a larger increase in traffic. A CloudOps Administrator needs to use a larger instance type with more memory. What does the Administrator need to do to implement this change?

1. Modify the existing cache cluster using the ModifyCacheCluster API.
2. Specify a new CacheNodeType with the ModifyCacheParameterGroup API.
3. Create a new cache cluster with a new node type using the CreateCacheCluster API.
4. Use the CreateReplicationGroup API and specify a new CacheNodeType.

QUESTION 31

An application running on Amazon EC2 was moved from a public subnet to a private subnet to increase security. Since the move the instance has been unable to automatically update. What needs to be done to allow the automatic updates to complete successfully?

1. Modify the instance security group to allow traffic from the internet into the private subnet.
2. Set up a NAT gateway in a public subnet and add a route to the private subnet route table.
3. Add a Network Load Balancer to a public subnet and configure the EC2 instance as a target.
4. Set up a NAT gateway in a private subnet and add a route to the public subnet route table.

QUESTION 32

A company is deploying an application on Amazon EC2 instances in multiple Availability Zones. The instances will access and share data using file system interfaces. The volume of data is small but expected to increase significantly over time.

What is the MOST scalable storage solution for these requirements?

1. Create an Amazon S3 bucket and a VPC endpoint, mount the bucket to the instances.
2. Create an Amazon EFS filesystem and create mount targets in multiple subnets.
3. Use Amazon EBS multi-attach to connect the EC2 instances to a single volume.
4. Deploy an AWS Storage Gateway cached volume on Amazon EC2.

QUESTION 33

A company uses an AWS Storage Gateway volume gateway. The virtual machine running the storage gateway must be rebooted. What is the correct process for rebooting the VM?

1. Reboot the gateway, then reboot the virtual machine.
2. Stop the virtual machine, restart the gateway, then turn on the virtual machine.
3. Synchronize the gateway, then reboot the virtual machine.
4. Stop the gateway, reboot the virtual machine, then restart the gateway.

QUESTION 34

A company is planning to migrate over 80 TB of data to Amazon S3. The company has a 50-Mbps internet connection that is heavily utilized. What is the MOST efficient method of transferring this data to Amazon S3?

1. Amazon S3 Transfer Acceleration
2. AWS Direct Connect
3. AWS Managed VPN
4. AWS Snowball

QUESTION 35

A CloudOps Administrator needs to receive an email whenever critical, production Amazon EC2 instances reach 80% CPU utilization. How can this be achieved?

1. Create an Amazon CloudWatch alarm and configure an Amazon SNS notification.
2. Create an Amazon CloudWatch alarm and configure an Amazon SES notification.
3. Create an Amazon CloudWatch Events rule that triggers an Amazon SNS notification.
4. Create an Amazon CloudWatch Events rule that triggers an Amazon SES notification.

QUESTION 36

A CloudOps Administrator launched an Amazon EC2 instance and noticed it went from the pending state to the terminated state immediately after starting it. What is a possible cause of this issue?

1. The limit on the number of instances that can be launched in the Region has been exceeded.
2. AWS does not currently have enough available On-Demand capacity to service the request.
3. The root EBS volume is encrypted and the Administrator does not have permissions to access the KMS key for decryption.
4. The API action for launching the specific instance type has been restricted in the AWS account.

QUESTION 37

An EBS-backed Amazon EC2 instance has a data volume with a status of *impaired*. I/O has also been disabled due to data consistency issues. Which first step should a CloudOps Administrator take to recover the volume?

1. Perform a consistency check on the volume attached to the instance.
2. Recreate the volume by restoring an Amazon EBS snapshot.
3. Change the volume to a general purpose SSD volume type.
4. Attach an Elastic Fabric Adapter (EFA) to the instance and restart I/O.

QUESTION 38

An Amazon EBS volume has a status of error. What can a CloudOps Administrator do to bring the volume back online?

1. Enable I/O using the enable-volume-io API.
2. Perform a consistency check using the fsck command.
3. Create a new volume from a recent snapshot.
4. Take a snapshot and then create a new volume from the snapshot.

QUESTION 39

An Amazon EC2 Auto Scaling group failed to launch an EC2 instance with the error message "The AMI ID ami-0c23bcf3g31a58706 does not exist". What action should be taken to resolve the issue and enable the ASG to launch new instances?

1. Add an alias for the AMI ID pointing to a valid AMI.

2. Create a new AMI with the same AMI ID.
3. Update the launch configuration with a valid AMI ID.
4. Create a new launch configuration using a valid AMI.

QUESTION 40

An Amazon EC2 Auto Scaling group is set to scale-out when CPU utilization reaches 80%. The CPU utilization has reached 90% and the following error message was received "8 instance(s) are already running. Launching EC2 instance failed".

What action should be taken to allow the Auto Scaling group to launch additional instances?

1. Increase the account limits for EBS General Purpose (SSD) storage.
2. Request an EC2 service quota increase for the Region.
3. Configure a scheduled scaling policy with the current date and time.
4. Disable the scaling policies and manually launch EC2 instances.

QUESTION 41

An Amazon EFS file system is used by several Amazon EC2 instances. The data stored on the file system is sensitive and a manager has asked for the data to be encrypted at rest. How can a CloudOps Administrator enable encryption for the EFS file system?

1. Enable encryption on the existing EFS volume using the AWS tools for Windows PowerShell.
2. Create a new EFS volume with encryption enabled and copy the data from the original volume.
3. Enable encryption on the existing EFS volume by using the AWS Command Line interface.
4. Create an SSL/TLS certificate using Amazon Certificate Manager (ACM) and attach it to the EFS volume.

QUESTION 42

An Amazon EBS gp2 volume is running low on space. How can this be resolved with MINIMAL effort?

1. Change to an io1 volume type and then modify the volume size.
2. Create a new, larger volume, and migrate the data.
3. Create a snapshot and restore it to a larger gp2 volume.
4. Use the Elastic Volumes feature to modify the volume size.

QUESTION 43

Users of a web application that is served using Amazon CloudFront have complained about receiving 4XX and 5XX errors. A CloudOps Administrator wants to monitor for elevated error rates in Amazon CloudFront. Which metric should be monitored?

1. CacheHitRate
2. OriginLatency
3. Requests
4. TotalErrorRate

QUESTION 44

An application running on Amazon EC2 instances needs to store log files in an Amazon S3 bucket. What is the MOST secure method of granting access to the bucket?

1. Create an IAM role with the required privileges and associate it with the EC2 instance.
2. Create an IAM user with the required privileges, generate an access key and embed the key in the application code.
3. Create an IAM role with the required privileges and embed the role credentials in the application code.

4. Create an IAM user with the required privileges, generate a key pair and embed the key pair in the application code.

QUESTION 45

A CloudOps Administrator has created an Amazon S3 bucket for storing files associated with current troubleshooting and analysis. To ensure the bucket doesn't get too large the administrator wants to automatically delete files older than 6 months. How can this be achieved?

1. Use Amazon CloudWatch Events to delete objects older than 6 months.
2. Run a script on an Amazon EC2 instance that identifies and deletes old files.
3. Implement lifecycle policies to expire objects older than 6 months.
4. Create and object versioning rule that expires objects older than 6 months.

QUESTION 46

An application uploads periodic logs to an Amazon S3 bucket. The logs must be immediately available but are not frequently accessed. Which lifecycle rule should be created for cost-efficiency?

1. Transition the objects to S3 Standard-IA after 30 days.
2. Transition the objects to S3 Glacier after immediately.
3. Transition the objects to S3 Intelligent-Tiering after 30 days.
4. Transition the objects to S3 Standard-IA immediately.

QUESTION 47

A company runs a static website on Amazon S3. A CloudOps Administrator noticed that the S3 bucket is receiving a very high rate of read operations. What can the Administrator do to minimize latency and reduce the load on the S3 bucket?

1. Use cross-region replication (CRR) to replicate the data to another region.
2. Create an Amazon CloudFront distribution with the S3 bucket as the origin.
3. Migrate to a bucket in an AWS Region that is closer to the end users.
4. Use Amazon ElastiCache Redis to cache the static data from the S3 bucket.

QUESTION 48

A web application running on HTTP has been launched in an Amazon VPC. The application runs on Amazon EC2 instances across multiple Availability Zones behind an Application Load Balancer. A security group and network ACL has been created for the load balancer allowing inbound traffic on port 80. During testing the web application is found to be inaccessible from the internet.

What additional action must be taken to make the web application accessible form the internet?

1. Add a rule to the security group allowing outbound traffic on ports 1024 through 65535.
2. Add a rule to the security group allowing all outbound traffic to 0.0.0.0/0.
3. Add a rule to the network ACL allowing outbound traffic on ports 1024 through 65535.
4. Add a rule to the network ACL allowing outbound traffic on port 80 to any destination.

QUESTION 49

A security team has identified an attack on web applications running on Amazon EC2. The attack uses malformed HTTP headers. Which AWS service or feature can be used to prevent this type of attack from reaching the EC2 instances?

1. Amazon Security Group rules
2. Application Load Balancer (ALB)
3. Network Access Control List (NACL)
4. AWS Web Application Firewall (WAF)

QUESTION 50

An application has been deployed on Amazon EC2 instances behind an Application Load Balancer (ALB). Users have complained that they must log in several times each hour. What can be done to reduce the number of times users must log in to the application?

1. Add targets in multiple Availability Zones.
2. Enable HTTP/2 on the Application Load Balancer.
3. Enable sticky sessions on the Target Group.
4. Configure health checks on the Application Load Balancer.

QUESTION 51

A CloudOps Administrator has created an Amazon VPC with an IPv6 CIDR block. Amazon EC2 instances in the VPC should be able to connect to IPv6 domains on the internet but connectivity from the internet should be restricted.

What must be configured to enable the required connectivity?

1. Create an egress-only internet gateway and add a route to the route table pointing to the gateway for the target ::/0
2. Create an egress-only internet gateway and add a route to the route table pointing to the gateway for the target 0.0.0.0/0
3. Create an internet gateway and add a route to the route table pointing to the gateway for the target ::/0
4. Create a NAT gateway and add a route to the route table pointing to the gateway for the target 0.0.0.0/0

QUESTION 52

A manager has asked a CloudOps Administrator to add high availability to an existing Amazon RDS instance. How can this requirement be achieved?

1. Use the ModifyDBInstance API action with the ReplicaMode value.
2. Create a new DB instance with multi-AZ enabled and migrate data.
3. Create a Read Replica and use DNS failover for high availability.
4. Modify the RDS instance using the console and enabled multi-AZ.

QUESTION 53

A security consultant has identified unnecessary security group and network ACL rules that pose a security risk. What steps should a CloudOps Administrator take to resolve the security vulnerabilities?

1. Contact AWS Support and notify them of the vulnerabilities.
2. Create an AWS WAF web ACL that protects resources from web attacks.
3. Remove the unnecessary security group rules and network ACL rules.
4. Use Amazon Inspector to identify security best practices and rectify issues.

QUESTION 54

A CloudOps Administrator has been tasked with configuring protection for an Amazon RDS database. The solution must be cost-effective, protect against table corruption, and retain backups for 30 days. How can these requirements be achieved?

1. Use the Database Migration Service to synchronize data with another RDS instance.
2. Create a read replica of the RDS instance in another Availability Zone.
3. Take daily snapshots of the RDS database and store them on Amazon S3.
4. Enabled automated backups and configure a 30-day backup retention period.

QUESTION 55

A company runs and Amazon Aurora database instance. According to the AWS Shared Responsibility Model, which of the following actions are the responsibility of the customer?

1. Scheduling maintenance, patches, and other updates.
2. Provisioning the underlying server hardware.
3. Managing network infrastructure for the database.
4. Executing maintenance, patches, and other updates.

QUESTION 56

A CloudOps Administrator is monitoring an Amazon Aurora database and received a "inaccessible-encryption-credentials" DB instance status message and has become inaccessible. What is the explanation for this error?

1. The AWS KMS key used to encrypt or decrypt the DB instance can't be accessed.
2. The DB instance has reached its storage capacity allocation.
3. AWS IAM database authentication is being enabled or disabled for this DB instance.
4. Enhanced Monitoring is being enabled or disabled for this DB instance.

QUESTION 57

A database runs on Amazon Aurora and is experiencing some performance issues. A CloudOps Administrator needs to monitor memory utilization and OS level metrics. How can the Administrator access these metrics?

1. Use Amazon CloudWatch to view the standard metrics for RDS.
2. Enable enhanced monitoring and view the metrics in the RDS console.
3. Install the unified CloudWatch agent on the RDS instance to generate the metrics.
4. Enable detailed monitoring for the RDS instance to increase metric frequency.

QUESTION 58

A CloudOps Administrator attempted to deploy an AWS CloudFormation StackSet across multiple AWS accounts. The stack operation failed, and the stack instance status is OUTDATED. What could be a possible cause of this error?

1. The deployment was run without specifying a CloudFormation template.
2. The deployment was run with insufficient permissions in the target account.
3. The deployment is trying to create resources in other accounts in a different region.
4. The deployment requires multi-factor authentication and a token was not provided.

QUESTION 59

An Amazon Elastic Beanstalk environment was deployed with a configuration file that runs a series of commands. The environment creation completed with the message *"Create environment operation is complete, but with command timeouts"*. How can this issue be resolve so future deployments avoid this issue?

1. Use a larger instance type with more CPU.
2. Increase the command timeout period.
3. Configure a worker environment.
4. Use the high availability preset.

QUESTION 60

A user is attempting to connect to an Amazon Linux instance using SSH and is experiencing errors. A CloudOps Administrator has checked the configuration including key pairs, security groups, and network

ACLs and confirmed that the user can connect to other instances in the same subnet. What can the Administrator do to further troubleshoot the issue?

1. Check that there is an internet gateway attached to the VPC.
2. Use Trusted Advisor to check the SSH configuration.
3. Run the AWSSupport-TroubleshootSSH automation.
4. Attach an Elastic IP address to the instance.

QUESTION 61

An AWS Lambda function has been connected to an Amazon VPC and is no longer able to connect to an external service on the internet. How can this issue be resolved?

1. Update the function code to avoid the VPC and connect directly.
2. Add an entry to the subnet route table pointing to a NAT gateway.
3. Enable enhanced VPC routing for the AWS Lambda function.
4. Create a virtual private gateway (VGW) to the subnet.

QUESTION 62

A manager has requested that Developers using a dedicated testing account should only be able to use the t2.micro instance type. A CloudOps Administrator has created an AWS Organizations SCP and applied it to the correct OU. However, Developers are still able to launch other instance types. What needs to be corrected in the SCP policy statement?

```
{
  "Version": "2012-10-17",
  "Statement": [
    {
      "Sid": "RequireMicroInstanceType",
      "Effect": "Deny",
      "Action": "ec2:RunInstances",
      "Resource": "arn:aws:ec2:*:*:instance/*",
      "Condition": {
        "StringEquals":{
          "ec2:InstanceType":"t2.micro"
        }
      }
    }
  ]
}
```

1. Change the Resource statement to "arn:aws:ec2:*:*:t2.micro/*"
2. Change the Effect statement from Deny to Allow
3. Change the Condition statement to StringNotEquals
4. Change the date in the version statement to the current date

QUESTION 63

An Amazon S3 bucket has been created for storing sensitive company data. The following bucket policy has been applied:

```
{
    "Version": "2012-10-17",
    "Id": "Policy12345663434343",
    "Statement": [
      {
        "Sid": "New policy",
        "Principal": "*",
        "Action": "s3:*",
        "Effect": "Deny",
        "Resource": ["arn:aws:s3:::examplebucket1",
                     "arn:aws:s3:::examplebucket1/*"],
        "Condition": {
          "StringNotEquals": {
            "aws:SourceVpce": "vpce-2bd1s1209"
          }
        }
      }
    ]
}
```

What will be the effect of this bucket policy?
1. Access is restricted to connections coming from a specific VPC endpoint.
2. Access is restricted to Amazon EC2 instances in a specific VPC.
3. Access is restricted to connections coming from a VPC in a different account.
4. Access is restricted to servers connecting over an AWS Direct Connect connection.

QUESTION 64

The following Service Control Policy (SCP) has been applied to an Organizational Unit (OU) containing an AWS Organizations member account. What will be the effect of this policy?

```json
{
    "Version": "2012-10-17",
    "Statement": [
      {
        "Sid": "RestrictEC2ForRoot",
        "Effect": "Deny",
        "Action": [
          "ec2:*"
        ],
        "Resource": [
          "*"
        ],
        "Condition": {
          "StringLike": {
            "aws:PrincipalArn": [
              "arn:aws:iam::*:root"
            ]
          }
        }
      }
    ]
}
```

1. Nothing, it is not possible to restrict root user actions.
2. The root user will not be able to perform any ec2 actions.
3. All users will be restricted from performing any ec2 actions.
4. The root user will not be able to login to EC2 instances.

QUESTION 65

A VPC peering connection has been established between two VPCs in different AWS Regions in the same account. A CloudOps Administrator is attempting to update the security group configuration to allow inbound connections over HTTP from a security group in the second Region and is unable to complete the configuration. What could be the cause of the issue?

1. The Administrator must manually copy the security group ID and paste it in.
2. The Administrator has not yet configured the route tables appropriately.
3. The VPC peering connection is not in an active state.
4. You cannot enter the security group ID of a security group from another Region.

SET 3: PRACTICE QUESTIONS AND ANSWERS

QUESTION 1

A CloudOps Administrator has configured an Amazon EC2 instance in a public subnet for remote access over SSH. The Administrator is able to establish an SSH connection from an on-premises network via the internet but is unable to ping the instance.

What is the most likely reason for this?

1. The instance does not have an Elastic IP address.
2. The instance is in a VPC that does not have an internet gateway.
3. The instance's security group does not allow ICMP traffic.
4. The instance is behind a NAT gateway.

Answer: 3

Explanation:

The most likely explanation is that the instance's security group does not have a rule allowing the Internet Control Message Protocol (ICMP). This protocol must be allowed for ICMP ping requests to be successful.

CORRECT: "The instance's security group does not allow ICMP traffic" is the correct answer.

INCORRECT: "The instance does not have an Elastic IP address" is incorrect. This does not matter; the instance must have a public IP address as an SSH connection has been established.

INCORRECT: "The instance is in a VPC that does not have an internet gateway" is incorrect. If this is the case, no connections would be possible.

INCORRECT: "The instance is behind a NAT gateway" is incorrect. If this is the case, no connections would be possible.

References:

https://docs.aws.amazon.com/vpc/latest/userguide/VPC_SecurityGroups.html

Save time with our exam-specific cheat sheets:

https://digitalcloud.training/certification-training/aws-certified-sysops-administrator-associate/amazon-virtual-private-cloud-vpc/

QUESTION 2

A company needs to improve the security of passwords by forcing all IAM users to rotate their passwords on a regular basis.

Which action should be taken take to implement this?

1. Configure multi-factor authentication for all IAM users.
2. Set up a password policy to enable password expiration for IAM users.
3. Use Amazon SNS to send regular notifications that passwords must be changed.
4. Set up an access key policy to enable expiration for access keys.

Answer: 2

Explanation:

You can grant IAM users the permission to change their own passwords for signing in to the AWS Management Console. You can do this in one of two ways:

- Allow all IAM users in the account to change their own passwords.
- Allow only selected IAM users to change their own passwords. In this scenario, you disable the option for all users to change their own passwords and you use an IAM policy to grant permissions

to only some users to change their own passwords and optionally other credentials like their own access keys.

CORRECT: "Set up a password policy to enable password expiration for IAM users" is the correct answer.

INCORRECT: "Set up an access key policy to enable expiration for access keys" is incorrect. There is no policy that can be configured to expire access keys and the questions asks to force password rotation.

INCORRECT: "Configure multi-factor authentication for all IAM users" is incorrect. MFA does not ensure that passwords are rotated.

INCORRECT: "Use Amazon SNS to send regular notifications that passwords must be changed" is incorrect. This would not force password rotation; it would simply advise users to do it.

References:

https://docs.aws.amazon.com/IAM/latest/UserGuide/id_credentials_passwords_enable-user-change.html

Save time with our exam-specific cheat sheets:

https://digitalcloud.training/certification-training/aws-certified-sysops-administrator-associate/aws-iam/

QUESTION 3

A company is deploying AWS Single Sign-On (SSO). A CloudOps Administrator has created an AWS SSO directory in an AWS Organizations master account and enabled full access. What is the next step to configure the single sign-on functionality?

1. Create IAM roles in each account to be used by AWS SSO and associate users with these roles using AWS SSO.
2. Create permission sets in AWS SSO and associate the permission sets with Directory Service users or groups.
3. Create IAM users in the master account and use AWS SSO to associate the users with the accounts they will access.
4. Create service control policies (SCPs) in Organizations and associate the SCPs with Directory Service users or groups.

Answer: 2

Explanation:

Permission sets define the level of access that users and groups have to an AWS account. Permission sets are stored in AWS SSO and provisioned to the AWS account as IAM roles.

You can assign more than one permission set to a user. Users who have multiple permission sets must choose one when they sign into the user portal. (Users will see these as IAM roles). For this scenario, the Administrator must next create the permissions sets and then associate the permission set with the user accounts or groups.

CORRECT: "Create permission sets in AWS SSO and associate the permission sets with Directory Service users or groups" is the correct answer.

INCORRECT: "Create IAM roles in each account to be used by AWS SSO and associate users with these roles using AWS SSO" is incorrect. Rather than directly creating roles the Administrator must create permission sets which act like roles.

INCORRECT: "Create IAM users in the master account and use AWS SSO to associate the users with the accounts they will access" is incorrect. Users do not need to be created in the master account. The user in the source account will assume a role via a permission sets which will then provide the permissions granted in the attached policy.

INCORRECT: "Create service control policies (SCPs) in Organizations and associate the SCPs with Directory Service users or groups" is incorrect. SCPs are used for controlling the available API actions in an account, they are not used for SSO.

References:

https://docs.aws.amazon.com/singlesignon/latest/userguide/permissionsets.html

QUESTION 4

The security team has notified a CloudOps Administrator that there may be a vulnerable version of software installed on some Amazon EC2 instances. How can the Administrator verify if the vulnerable software is installed on the EC2 instances with the LEAST operational overhead?

1. Create and run an Amazon Inspector assessment template.
2. Connect to each instance using SSH and check the software version.
3. Use AWS CloudTrail to verify Amazon EC2 API activity in the account.
4. Write some custom code that uses AWS Lambda to check the instances.

Answer: 1

Explanation:

Amazon Inspector helps you discover potential security issues by using security rules to analyze your AWS resources. Amazon Inspector monitors and collects behavioral data (telemetry) about your resources.

To get started, you create an *assessment target* (a collection of the AWS resources that you want Amazon Inspector to analyze). Next, you create an *assessment template* (a blueprint that you use to configure your assessment). You use the template to start an *assessment run*, which is the monitoring and analysis process that results in a set of findings.

CORRECT: "Create and run an Amazon Inspector assessment template" is the correct answer.

INCORRECT: "Connect to each instance using SSH and check the software version" is incorrect. This is very manual and not the most effective method.

INCORRECT: "Use AWS CloudTrail to verify Amazon EC2 API activity in the account" is incorrect. API activity will not identify software installed on an EC2 instance.

INCORRECT: "Write some custom code that uses AWS Lambda to check the instances" is incorrect. This is possible but more time consuming than just using the Inspector template.

References:

https://docs.aws.amazon.com/inspector/latest/userguide/inspector_assessments.html

QUESTION 5

A company is developing some new applications in a development account. The costs associated with the account have been rising management acre concerned. A CloudOps Administrator has been tasked with configuring alerts that will notify management when the accounts' costs or usage are forecasted to exceed a specified spending amount.

Which AWS service should the Administrator use?

1. AWS Cost Explorer
2. AWS Trusted Advisor
3. AWS Budgets
4. AWS Cost and Usage report

Answer: 3

Explanation:

AWS Budgets gives you the ability to set custom budgets that alert you when your costs or usage exceed (or are forecasted to exceed) your budgeted amount.

With AWS Budgets you can set custom cost and usage budgets to more easily manage your AWS spend. You can monitor your budget status from the AWS Budgets dashboard or AWS Budgets reports.

CORRECT: "AWS Budgets" is the correct answer.

INCORRECT: "AWS Cost Explorer" is incorrect. AWS Cost Explorer does provide forecasting, but AWS Budgets should be used for alerting for specific spending budgets.

INCORRECT: "AWS Cost and Usage report" is incorrect. This report provides detailed data about AWS billing delivered to an S3 bucket. It does not provide budgets and alerting.

INCORRECT: "AWS Trusted Advisor" is incorrect. This service provides recommendations for several areas including cost. It is not used for alerting based on spending budgets.

References:

https://aws.amazon.com/aws-cost-management/aws-budgets

QUESTION 6

A CloudOps Administrator has been tasked with setting up a record set in Amazon Route 53 to point to an Application Load Balancer (ALB). The hosted zone and the ALB are in different accounts.

What is the MOST cost-effective and efficient solution to this requirement?

1. Create an Application Load Balancer in the same account as the hosted zone and forward connections cross-account to the other ALB.
2. Create an alias record in the hosted zone pointing to the Application Load Balancer.
3. Create an asynchronous replica of the hosted zone in the account with the Application Load Balancer.
4. Create a CNAME record in the hosted zone pointing to an alias record to the Application Load Balancer.

Answer: 2

Explanation:

It is possible to create an Alias record that points to a resource in another account. In this case the fully qualified domain name of the ALB must be obtained and then entered when creating the record set. This is the most cost-effective option as you do not pay for Alias records and there is minimal configuration required.

CORRECT: "Create an alias record in the hosted zone pointing to the Application Load Balancer" is the correct answer.

INCORRECT: "Create an Application Load Balancer in the same account as the hosted zone and forward connections cross-account to the other ALB" is incorrect. This would not be cost-effective or efficient.

INCORRECT: "Create an asynchronous replica of the hosted zone in the account with the Application Load Balancer" is incorrect. This is not something that is possible with Route 53.

INCORRECT: "Create a CNAME record in the hosted zone pointing to an alias record to the Application Load Balancer" is incorrect. CNAMEs records do incur costs and this is a less efficient solution as there is more complexity.

References:

https://docs.aws.amazon.com/Route53/latest/DeveloperGuide/resource-record-sets-values-alias.html#rrsets-values-alias-alias-target

Save time with our exam-specific cheat sheets:

https://digitalcloud.training/certification-training/aws-certified-sysops-administrator-associate/amazon-route-53/

QUESTION 7

A Company has identified that a security vulnerability affects a version of MariaDB that is being used with an Amazon RDS database instance.

Who is responsible for ensuring that the patch is applied to the database?

1. Amazon Web Services (AWS).
2. The database vendor.
3. The security department the company.
4. The company's CloudOps Administrator.

Answer: 1

Explanation:

Amazon RDS is a managed database service and AWS are responsible for patching the DB instance's underlying hardware, underlying operating system (OS), and database engine version.

Required patching is automatically scheduled only for patches that are related to security and instance reliability. Such patching occurs infrequently (typically once every few months) and seldom requires more than a fraction of your maintenance window.

CORRECT: "Amazon Web Services (AWS)" is the correct answer.

INCORRECT: "The database vendor" is incorrect. The database vendor may release patches, but they are not responsible for applying them.

INCORRECT: "The security department the company" is incorrect. Amazon RDS is a managed database and AWS will patch the underlying DB software.

INCORRECT: "The company's CloudOps Administrator " is incorrect. Amazon RDS is a managed database and AWS will patch the underlying DB software.

References:

https://docs.aws.amazon.com/AmazonRDS/latest/UserGuide/USER_UpgradeDBInstance.Maintenance.html

QUESTION 8

A Company stores a large volume of non-critical log files in an Amazon S3 bucket. An Amazon EC2 instance processes files from the bucket on a daily basis. Which storage option will be the MOST cost-effective for this scenario?

1. Amazon Glacier.
2. Amazon S3 Standard-Infrequent Access.
3. Amazon Instance Store.
4. Amazon S3 Standard.

Answer: 4

Explanation:

As the data is being frequently accessed the Amazon S3 Standard storage class is the best choice for this particular use case.

	S3 Standard	S3 Intelligent-Tiering*	S3 Standard-IA	S3 One Zone-IA†	S3 Glacier	S3 Glacier Deep Archive
Designed for durability	99.999999999% (11 9's)	99.999999999% (11 9's)	99.999999999% (11 9's)	99.999999999% (11 9's)	99.999999999% (11 9's)	99.999999999% (11 9's)
Designed for availability	99.99%	99.9%	99.9%	99.5%	99.99%	99.99%
Availability SLA	99.9%	99%	99%	99%	99.9%	99.9%
Availability Zones	≥3	≥3	≥3	1	≥3	≥3
Minimum capacity charge per object	N/A	N/A	128KB	128KB	40KB	40KB
Minimum storage duration charge	N/A	30 days	30 days	30 days	90 days	180 days
Retrieval fee	N/A	N/A	per GB retrieved	per GB retrieved	per GB retrieved	per GB retrieved
First byte latency	milliseconds	milliseconds	milliseconds	milliseconds	select minutes or hours	select hours
Storage type	Object	Object	Object	Object	Object	Object
Lifecycle transitions	Yes	Yes	Yes	Yes	Yes	Yes

CORRECT: "Amazon S3 Standard" is the correct answer.

INCORRECT: "Amazon S3 Standard-Infrequent Access" is incorrect as the data is being frequently accessed and there would be additional retrieval costs.

INCORRECT: "Amazon Glacier" is incorrect as the data is being frequently accessed so it cannot be archived.

INCORRECT: "Amazon Instance Store" is incorrect as this is an ephemeral block storage volume associated with EC2 instances. It is not suitable for this use case.

References:

https://aws.amazon.com/s3/storage-classes/

Save time with our exam-specific cheat sheets:

https://digitalcloud.training/certification-training/aws-certified-sysops-administrator-associate/amazon-s3/

QUESTION 9

A security vulnerability has been discovered that impacts a version of Linux that is running on some Amazon EC2 instances in a VPC. How can a CloudOps Administrator mitigate the exposure with the LEAST disruption?

1. Shut down and then restart the instances so they change underlying hosts.
2. Use Amazon Inspector to produce a report with best practice recommendations.
3. Redeploy the EC2 instances using an updated AMI through AWS CloudFormation.
4. Use AWS Systems Manager to patch the Linux operating systems.

Answer: 4

Explanation:

AWS Systems Manager Patch Manager automates the process of patching managed instances with both security related and other types of updates. You can use Patch Manager to apply patches for both operating systems and applications.

CORRECT: "Use AWS Systems Manager to patch the Linux operating systems" is the correct answer.

INCORRECT: "Shut down and then restart the instances so they change underlying hosts" is incorrect. The vulnerability is with the EC2 instance OS so moving hosts will not change anything.

INCORRECT: "Use Amazon Inspector to produce a report with best practice recommendations" is incorrect. This will not mitigate the exposure.

INCORRECT: "Redeploy the EC2 instances using an updated AMI through AWS CloudFormation" is incorrect. This would cause more disruption than patching the existing EC2 instances.

References:

https://docs.aws.amazon.com/systems-manager/latest/userguide/systems-manager-patch.html

Save time with our exam-specific cheat sheets:

https://digitalcloud.training/certification-training/aws-certified-sysops-administrator-associate/aws-systems-manager/

QUESTION 10

A CloudOps team in a company would like to make AWS maintenance events that may affect their resources visible in their existing operations dashboard. What should a CloudOps Administrator do to include this data?

1. Use an AWS Lambda function that queries Amazon CloudWatch Events for state changes in AWS infrastructure.
2. Integrate the AWS Service Health Dashboard's RSS feed into the company's existing operations dashboard.
3. Use Amazon Inspector to send notifications of upcoming maintenance events to the Operations team distribution list.

4. Use the AWS Health API to query for upcoming maintenance events and include this data in the operations dashboard.

Answer: 4

Explanation:

The AWS Health API provides programmatic access to the AWS Health information that is presented in the Personal Health Dashboard. You can use these API operations to get information about events that affect your AWS resources:

- DescribeEvents: Summary information about events.
- DescribeEventDetails: Detailed information about one or more events.
- DescribeAffectedEntities: Information about AWS resources that are affected by one or more events.

CORRECT: "Use the AWS Health API to query for upcoming maintenance events and include this data in the operations dashboard" is the correct answer.

INCORRECT: "Use an AWS Lambda function that queries Amazon CloudWatch Events for state changes in AWS infrastructure" is incorrect. You cannot query CloudWatch Events, it triggers Lambda and not the other way around. Also, it cannot report on AWS infrastructure changes, only state changes in a customer's AWS resources.

INCORRECT: "Integrate the AWS Service Health Dashboard's RSS feed into the company's existing operations dashboard" is incorrect. The service health dashboard does not show upcoming events that may affect your resources, only a general view of current status.

INCORRECT: "Use Amazon Inspector to send notifications of upcoming maintenance events to the Operations team distribution list" is incorrect. Inspector does not notify on maintenance events.

References:

https://docs.aws.amazon.com/health/latest/ug/getting-started-api.html

QUESTION 11

A company runs an application that uses Amazon EC2 instances behind an Application Load Balancer (ALB). Customers access the application using a custom DNS domain name. Reports have been received about errors when connecting to the application using the DNS name.

The administrator has confirmed:

- The security groups and network ACLs are correctly configured.
- An Amazon Route 53 Alias record is setup correctly pointing the custom DNS name to the ALB.
- The load balancer target group shows no healthy instances.

What first step should the CloudOps Administrator take to troubleshoot this issue?

1. Review the VPC Flow Logs, looking for any API errors.
2. Review the load balancer target group health check configuration.
3. Review the load balancer access logs, looking for any issues or errors.
4. Review the load balancer listener configuration.

Answer: 2

Explanation:

The best first step is to check the load balancer target group health check configuration to understand why there are no healthy instances. The application will not work until the instances are healthy and accessible via the load balancer.

CORRECT: "Review the load balancer target group health check configuration" is the correct answer.

INCORRECT: "Review the VPC Flow Logs, looking for any API errors" is incorrect. API errors are not logged in VPC Flow Logs, they are logged in CloudTrail.

INCORRECT: "Review the load balancer access logs, looking for any issues or errors" is incorrect. The application is not accessible because there are no healthy issues. The first thing to check is why the instances are unhealthy. There is unlikely to be evidence for this in the load balancer access logs.

INCORRECT: "Review the load balancer listener configuration" is incorrect. There's no reason to believe the listener is at fault. The instances are not healthy so that issue must be addressed first.

References:

https://docs.aws.amazon.com/elasticloadbalancing/latest/application/target-group-health-checks.html

Save time with our exam-specific cheat sheets:

https://digitalcloud.training/certification-training/aws-certified-sysops-administrator-associate/elastic-load-balancing/

QUESTION 12

A company's security team requested that all Amazon EBS volumes should be encrypted with a specific AWS KMS customer master key (CMK). A CloudOps Administrator is tasked with verifying that the security team's request has been implemented.

What is the MOST efficient way for the Administrator to verify the correct encryption key is being used?

1. Use AWS Config to configure the encrypted-volumes managed rule and specify the key ID of the CMK.
2. Create an AWS Lambda function to run on a daily schedule, and have the function run the aws ec2 describe-volumes --filters encrypted command.
3. Log in to the AWS Management Console on a daily schedule, then filter the list of volumes by encryption status, then export this list.
4. Create an AWS Organizations SCP that only allows encrypt API actions that use the specific KMS CMK.

Answer: 1

Explanation:

The AWS Config encrypted-volumes rule Checks whether the EBS volumes that are in an attached state are encrypted. If you specify the ID of a KMS key for encryption using the kmsId parameter, the rule checks if the EBS volumes in an attached state are encrypted with that KMS key.

CORRECT: "Use AWS Config to configure the encrypted-volumes managed rule and specify the key ID of the CMK" is the correct answer.

INCORRECT: "Create an AWS Lambda function to run on a daily schedule, and have the function run the aws ec2 describe-volumes --filters encrypted command" is incorrect. This is not an efficient solution.

INCORRECT: "Log in to the AWS Management Console on a daily schedule, then filter the list of volumes by encryption status, then export this list" is incorrect. This is not an efficient solution.

INCORRECT: "Create an AWS Organizations SCP that only allows encrypt API actions that use the specific KMS CMK" is incorrect. This is not possible. You cannot restrict API actions by KMS key.

References:

https://docs.aws.amazon.com/config/latest/developerguide/encrypted-volumes.html

Save time with our exam-specific cheat sheets:

https://digitalcloud.training/certification-training/aws-certified-sysops-administrator-associate/aws-config/

QUESTION 13

The security team in a company is concerned about the security of AWS CloudTrail logs. The key requirements are to keep a record of any deletions or modifications to the log files.

Which steps should a CloudOps Administrator take to meet these requirements? (Select TWO.)

1. Enable the CloudTrail log file integrity check in AWS Config Rules.
2. Add an SNS notification to CloudWatch Logs for any delete actions.
3. Enable Amazon S3 MFA Delete for the CloudTrail S3 bucket.
4. Enable CloudTrail log file integrity validation.

5. Restrict all access to the CloudTrail S3 bucket.

Answer: 3,4

Explanation:

To determine whether a log file was modified, deleted, or unchanged after CloudTrail delivered it, you can use CloudTrail log file integrity validation. This feature is built using industry standard algorithms: SHA-256 for hashing and SHA-256 with RSA for digital signing.

This makes it computationally infeasible to modify, delete or forge CloudTrail log files without detection. You can use the AWS CLI to validate the files in the location where CloudTrail delivered them.

Configuring multi-factor authentication (MFA) ensures that any attempt to change the versioning state of your bucket or permanently delete an object version requires additional authentication. This helps prevent any operation that could compromise the integrity of your log files, even if a user acquires the password of an IAM user that has permissions to permanently delete Amazon S3 objects.

CORRECT: "Enable CloudTrail log file integrity validation" is the correct answer.

CORRECT: "Enable Amazon S3 MFA Delete for the CloudTrail S3 bucket" is the correct answer.

INCORRECT: "Add an SNS notification to CloudWatch Logs for any delete actions" is incorrect. CloudWatch Logs is a different service to CloudTrail and the question is asking to secure the logs generated by CloudTrail logs.

INCORRECT: "Enable the CloudTrail log file integrity check in AWS Config Rules" is incorrect. This setting is enabled in CloudTrail not in AWS Config.

INCORRECT: "Restrict all access to the CloudTrail S3 bucket" is incorrect. This is unnecessary and may restrict legitimate access requests.

References:

https://docs.aws.amazon.com/awscloudtrail/latest/userguide/cloudtrail-log-file-validation-intro.html

Save time with our exam-specific cheat sheets:

https://digitalcloud.training/certification-training/aws-certified-sysops-administrator-associate/amazon-s3/

QUESTION 14

A company is deploying a new website that hosts dynamic content. Due to licensing restrictions the content must not be accessible by users in specific countries or regions. How can a CloudOps Administrator enforce the content restrictions? (Choose TWO.)

1. Security group restriction
2. Amazon CloudFront geo-restriction
3. AWS Shield geo-restriction
4. Amazon Route 53 geolocation routing
5. Network ACL restriction

Answer: 2,4

Explanation:

With Amazon CloudFront you can use *geo restriction*, also known as *geo blocking*, to prevent users in specific geographic locations from accessing content that you're distributing through a CloudFront web distribution.

Amazon Route 53 geolocation routing lets you choose the resources that serve your traffic based on the geographic location of your users, meaning the location that DNS queries originate from. For example, you might want all queries from Europe to be routed to an ELB load balancer in the Frankfurt region.

CORRECT: "Amazon CloudFront geo-restriction" is the correct answer.

CORRECT: "Amazon Route 53 geolocation routing" is also a correct answer.

INCORRECT: "Security group restriction" is incorrect. You cannot block traffic with security groups so the only way this would work is to allow only the IP ranges of all allowed countries which would be an administrative challenge.

INCORRECT: "AWS Shield geo-restriction" is incorrect. AWS Shield is used for mitigating DDoS attacks, it does not do geo-restriction.

INCORRECT: "Network ACL restriction" is incorrect. You would need to add every restricted IP range which would be administratively difficult.

References:

https://docs.aws.amazon.com/AmazonCloudFront/latest/DeveloperGuide/georestrictions.html

https://docs.aws.amazon.com/Route53/latest/DeveloperGuide/routing-policy.html#routing-policy-geo

Save time with our exam-specific cheat sheets:

https://digitalcloud.training/certification-training/aws-certified-sysops-administrator-associate/amazon-cloudfront/

https://digitalcloud.training/certification-training/aws-certified-sysops-administrator-associate/amazon-route-53/

QUESTION 15

A CloudOps Administrator typically manages an Amazon EC2 instance using SSH from the corporate network. The Administrator is working from home and attempting to connect to the EC2 instance but is receiving a connection timeout error.

What is the most likely cause of the connection timeout?

1. The key pair the Administrator is using does not allow connections from the home network.
2. The Administrators' home network does not have a route to the internet gateway in its route table.
3. The IAM role associated with the EC2 instance does not allow SSH connections from the home network.
4. The security group is not allowing inbound traffic from the home network on the SSH port.

Answer: 4

Explanation:

The most likely explanation is that the security group attached to the EC2 instance allows SSH from the corporate network, but it does not allow the protocol from the IP range of the home network. In this case the Administrator simply needs to modify the security group to allow the IP range of the home network.

CORRECT: "The security group is not allowing inbound traffic from the home network on the SSH port" is the correct answer.

INCORRECT: "The key pair the Administrator is using does not allow connections from the home network" is incorrect. Key pairs do not restrict network connections based on location; they are public/private key files used to authenticate.

INCORRECT: "The Administrators' home network does not have a route to the internet gateway in its route table" is incorrect. The home network just needs an internet connection as the Amazon EC2 instance has a public IP to connect to. A route to an internet gateway is not required.

INCORRECT: "The IAM role associated with the EC2 instance does not allow SSH connections from the home network" is incorrect. IAM roles can be configured with conditions such as source IP address for resources that support resource-based policies, but this is not the case with Amazon EC2.

References:

https://docs.aws.amazon.com/vpc/latest/userguide/VPC_SecurityGroups.html

Save time with our exam-specific cheat sheets:

https://digitalcloud.training/certification-training/aws-certified-sysops-administrator-associate/amazon-virtual-private-cloud-vpc/

QUESTION 16

A legacy application is deployed on an Amazon EC2 m1.large instance and the CPU utilization is over 90%

resulting in high latency. The application can only be scaled vertically. How can a CloudOps Administrator resolve the performance issues?

1. Change the Amazon EBS volume to Provisioned IOPS.
2. Add additional m1.large instances to the application.
3. Add a read replica to offload queries from the instance.
4. Upgrade to a compute-optimized instance.

Answer: 4

Explanation:

The instance type being used is a memory optimized instance and the CPU is a bottleneck for the performance of the application. As the application can only scale vertically the best resolution is to change to a compute optimized instance which will have more CPUs to run the application.

CORRECT: "Upgrade to a compute-optimized instance" is the correct answer.

INCORRECT: "Change the Amazon EBS volume to Provisioned IOPS" is incorrect. The CPU is constrained, not the storage, so this will not be effective.

INCORRECT: "Add additional m1.large instances to the application" is incorrect. The application can only scale vertically and adding additional instances would be scaling horizontally.

INCORRECT: "Add a read replica to offload queries from the instance" is incorrect. This is not an RDS database, so you cannot add a read replica.

References:

https://aws.amazon.com/ec2/instance-types/

Save time with our exam-specific cheat sheets:

https://digitalcloud.training/certification-training/aws-certified-sysops-administrator-associate/amazon-ec2/

QUESTION 17

A corporate application is used by remote workers and is hosted on Amazon EC2 instances behind an Application Load Balancer (ALB). User authentication is handled at the individual EC2 instance level. Once a user is authenticated; all requests from that user must go to the same EC2 instance.

Which feature of the Elastic Load Balancer must a CloudOps Administrator use to control the behavior?

1. TCP listeners
2. Sticky sessions
3. Deregistration delay
4. Cross-zone load balancing

Answer: 2

Explanation:

Sticky sessions are a mechanism to route requests to the same target in a target group. This is useful for servers that maintain state information in order to provide a continuous experience to clients. To use sticky sessions, the clients must support cookies.

You enable sticky sessions at the target group level. You can also set the duration for the stickiness of the load balancer-generated cookie, in seconds. The duration is set with each request. Therefore, if the client sends a request before each duration period expires, the sticky session continues.

CORRECT: "Sticky sessions" is the correct answer.

INCORRECT: "TCP listeners" is incorrect. A TCP listener is used with a Network Load Balancer (NLB) to listen for incoming connection requests.

INCORRECT: "Deregistration delay" is incorrect. This is the time period in which the load balancer stops sending requests to targets that are deregistering.

INCORRECT: "Cross-zone load balancing" is incorrect. This is used to enable even distribution across targets in multiple AZs. It does not bind a user to an instance.

References:

https://docs.aws.amazon.com/elasticloadbalancing/latest/application/load-balancer-target-groups.html

Save time with our exam-specific cheat sheets:

https://digitalcloud.training/certification-training/aws-certified-sysops-administrator-associate/elastic-load-balancing/

QUESTION 18

A company needs to track the allocation of Reserved instance discounts in the company's consolidated bill.

Which AWS tool can be used to find this information?

1. AWS Budgets
2. Amazon Inspector
3. AWS Organizations
4. AWS Cost and Usage report

Answer: 4

Explanation:

The AWS Cost and Usage Report contains the most comprehensive set of data about your AWS costs and usage, including additional information regarding AWS services, pricing, and reservations. By using the AWS Cost and Usage report, you can gain a wealth of reservation-related insights about the Amazon Resource Name (ARN) for a reservation, the number of reservations, the number of units per reservation, and more. It can help you do the following:

- **Calculate savings** – Each hourly line item of usage contains the discounted rate that was charged, as well as the public On-Demand rate for that usage type at that time. You can quantify your savings by calculating the difference between the public On-Demand rates and the rates you were charged.
- **Track the allocation of Reserved Instance discounts** – Each line item of usage that receives a discount contains information about where the discount came from. This makes it easier to trace which instances are benefitting from specific reservations.

CORRECT: "AWS Cost and Usage report" is the correct answer.

INCORRECT: "AWS Organizations" is incorrect. Even though Organizations is used to get a consolidated bill, the AWS Cost and Usage report tool is still required to analyze this information.

INCORRECT: "AWS Budgets" is incorrect. This tool is used for alerting on spending limits, it does not provide this level of reporting.

INCORRECT: "Amazon Inspector" is incorrect. This tool provides best practice recommendations, it does not provide this level of reporting.

References:

https://docs.aws.amazon.com/whitepapers/latest/cost-optimization-reservation-models/aws-cost-and-usage-report.html

QUESTION 19

A manager has requested a report that provides a detailed history of all API activity for a specific user over the last several months of employment. AWS CloudTrail is enabled in the account.

What is the MOST efficient method for a CloudOps Administrator to generate the required report?

1. Using the AWS management Console, search for the user name in the CloudTrail history. Then filter by API and download the report in CSV format.
2. Locate the CloudTrail logs in the appropriate Amazon S3 bucket. Use Amazon Athena to extract the information needed to generate the report.
3. Use the CloudTrail digest files stored in the company's Amazon S3 bucket. then send the logs to Amazon QuickSight to create the report.

4. Using the AWS management Console, search for the API activity in the CloudTrail history. Then filter by user name and download the report in CSV format.

Answer: 2

Explanation:

Using Athena with CloudTrail logs is a powerful way to enhance your analysis of AWS service activity. For example, you can use queries to identify trends and further isolate activity by attributes, such as source IP address or user.

For example the following query will look at the top events initiated by root from the beginning of the year. It will show whether these were direct root activities or whether they were invoked by an AWS service (and, if so, which one) to perform an activity.

```
select count (*) as TotalEvents, eventname, useridentity.invokedby
from cloudtrail_logs
where eventtime >= '2017-01-01T00:00:00Z'
and useridentity.type = 'Root'
group by useridentity.username, eventname, useridentity.invokedby
order by TotalEvents desc;
```

For this specific scenario the root user can be replaced by the user name of the specific user the manager needs to audit.

CORRECT: "Locate the CloudTrail logs in the appropriate Amazon S3 bucket. Use Amazon Athena to extract the information needed to generate the report" is the correct answer.

INCORRECT: "Using the AWS management Console, search for the user name in the CloudTrail history. Then filter by API and download the report in CSV format" is incorrect. This is not the most efficient method of reporting.

INCORRECT: "Use the CloudTrail digest files stored in the company's Amazon S3 bucket. then send the logs to Amazon QuickSight to create the report" is incorrect. Digest files are used to verify the integrity of CloudTrail logs that are delivered to an S3 bucket. They cannot be used for auditing a users' API activity.

INCORRECT: "Using the AWS management Console, search for the API activity in the CloudTrail history. Then filter by user name and download the report in CSV format" is incorrect. This is not the most efficient method of reporting.

References:

https://docs.aws.amazon.com/athena/latest/ug/cloudtrail-logs.html

Save time with our exam-specific cheat sheets:

https://digitalcloud.training/certification-training/aws-certified-sysops-administrator-associate/aws-cloudtrail/

QUESTION 20

A CloudOps Administrator noticed a large increase in the number of requests against an Amazon SQS queue. The administrator is concerned about rising costs associated with the queue and needs to identify the source of the calls.

What should the CloudOps Administrator use to validate the calls made to SQS?

1. Amazon CloudWatch
2. AWS Cost Explorer
3. AWS CloudTrail
4. Amazon SQS Access Logs

Answer: 3

Explanation:

The administrator needs to identify the source of API calls made to an Amazon SQS queue. Therefore, the correct service to use is AWS CloudTrail as it is an auditing service that keeps a record of API calls made. This includes the source of the API call.

CORRECT: "AWS CloudTrail" is the correct answer.

INCORRECT: "Amazon CloudWatch" is incorrect. This service is used for performance monitoring not auditing API activity.

INCORRECT: "AWS Cost Explorer" is incorrect. Cost explorer will not identify the source of the API calls, so it is the wrong tool to use.

INCORRECT: "Amazon SQS Access Logs" is incorrect. There is no such thing as access logs for SQS, logging for SQS uses CloudTrail.

References:

https://docs.aws.amazon.com/AWSSimpleQueueService/latest/SQSDeveloperGuide/sqs-logging-using-cloudtrail.html

Save time with our exam-specific cheat sheets:

https://digitalcloud.training/certification-training/aws-certified-sysops-administrator-associate/aws-cloudtrail/

QUESTION 21

A CloudOps Administrator needs to restrict access to a bucket that is currently accessed by users in other AWS accounts. The Administrator requires that the bucket is only accessible to users in the same account.

How can this be achieved?

1. Move the S3 bucket to the S3 One Zone-IA storage class and disable versioning.
2. Create Amazon S3 presigned URLs for accessing objects in the bucket.
3. Create an object policy that restricts access to only users in the same account.
4. Change the bucket access control list (ACL) to restrict access to the bucket owner.

Answer: 4

Explanation:

The bucket ACL can be used to provide cross-account access to an Amazon S3 bucket. To restrict cross-account access that has been granted in this way, simply remove the entry for the other account from the ACL.

The image below shows a bucket ACL with only a single account (the bucket owner) specified:

CORRECT: "Change the bucket access control list (ACL) to restrict access to the bucket owner" is the correct answer.

INCORRECT: "Move the S3 bucket to the S3 One Zone-IA storage class and disable versioning" is incorrect. Changing storage classes will not restrict access to the bucket.

INCORRECT: "Create Amazon S3 presigned URLs for accessing objects in the bucket" is incorrect. Presigned URLs can be used for temporary access to the bucket, this is not the best method of restricting access as you would need to distribute the URLs.

INCORRECT: "Create an object policy that restricts access to only users in the same account" is incorrect. You cannot create object policies, only bucket policies and IAM policies.

References:

https://docs.aws.amazon.com/AmazonS3/latest/user-guide/set-bucket-permissions.html

Save time with our exam-specific cheat sheets:

https://digitalcloud.training/certification-training/aws-certified-sysops-administrator-associate/amazon-s3/

QUESTION 22

A Company is planning to deploy a workload that requires Payment Card Industry (PCI) compliance. The security team has requested information on the PCI compliance status of the AWS infrastructure.

Which AWS tool will provide the necessary information?

1. Amazon CloudWatch
2. AWS OpsWorks
3. AWS Artifact
4. AWS GuardDuty

Answer: 3

Explanation:

AWS Artifact is your go-to, central resource for compliance-related information that matters to you. It provides on-demand access to AWS' security and compliance reports and select online agreements.

Reports available in AWS Artifact include our Service Organization Control (SOC) reports, Payment Card Industry (PCI) reports, and certifications from accreditation bodies across geographies and compliance verticals that validate the implementation and operating effectiveness of AWS security controls.

CORRECT: "AWS Artifact" is the correct answer.

INCORRECT: "Amazon CloudWatch" is incorrect. This service is used for performance monitoring.

INCORRECT: "AWS OpsWorks" is incorrect. This service provides managed implementations of Chef and Puppet.

INCORRECT: "AWS GuardDuty" is incorrect. This service provides monitoring of workloads on AWS.

References:

https://aws.amazon.com/artifact/

QUESTION 23

The manager of a CloudOps team needs to ensure Administrators do not accidentally terminate several critical Amazon EC2 instances.

How can this be accomplished?

1. Use AWS Systems Manager to restrict EC2 termination.
2. Enable termination protection on the EC2 instances.
3. Use AWS Config to restrict EC2 termination.
4. Use CloudTrail to restrict the terminate-instances API call.

Answer: 2

Explanation:

To prevent your instance from being accidentally terminated using Amazon EC2, you can enable *termination protection* for the instance.

The DisableApiTermination attribute controls whether the instance can be terminated using the console, CLI, or API. By default, termination protection is disabled for your instance.

You can set the value of this attribute when you launch the instance, while the instance is running, or while the instance is stopped (for Amazon EBS-backed instances).

CORRECT: "Enable termination protection on the EC2 instances" is the correct answer.

INCORRECT: "Use AWS Systems Manager to restrict EC2 termination" is incorrect. Termination protection should be configured in EC2.

INCORRECT: "Use AWS Config to restrict EC2 termination" is incorrect. Config cannot be used to enable termination protection, but it could be used to check if it's enabled.

INCORRECT: "Use CloudTrail to restrict the terminate-instances API call" is incorrect. You cannot use CloudTrail to limit API calls, it just audits API activity.

References:

https://docs.aws.amazon.com/AWSEC2/latest/UserGuide/terminating-instances.html#Using_ChangingDisableAPITermination

Save time with our exam-specific cheat sheets:

https://digitalcloud.training/certification-training/aws-certified-sysops-administrator-associate/amazon-ec2/

QUESTION 24

A CloudOps Administrator attempted to launch an Amazon EC2 instance and received the following error:

"InstanceLimitExceeded "Your quota allows for 0 more running instance(s).""

What action should the Administrator take to resolve this issue and launch the EC2 instances?

1. Open a case with AWS Support requesting an increase of the EC2 instance limit.
2. Try to launch the EC2 instances into another availability zone.
3. Launch the EC2 instances by using the run-instances CLI command.
4. Use the AWS management console to increase the limits for the region.

Answer: 1

Explanation:

The InstanceLimitExceeded error indicates that you reached the limit on the number of running On-Demand instances that you can launch in a Region. You can request an instance limit increase on a per-Region basis.

CORRECT: "Open a case with AWS Support requesting an increase of the EC2 instance limit" is the correct answer.

INCORRECT: "Try to launch the EC2 instances into another availability zone" is incorrect. The instance limits are applied at the region level so changing AZs will not resolve this issue.

INCORRECT: "Launch the EC2 instances by using the run-instances CLI command" is incorrect. It doesn't matter how you launch the instances, if the limit is exceeded the request will fail.

INCORRECT: "Use the AWS management console to increase the limits for the region" is incorrect. You cannot manually adjust the limits yourself; you must contact AWS support to request an increase.

References:

https://aws.amazon.com/premiumsupport/knowledge-center/ec2-InstanceLimitExceeded-error/

Save time with our exam-specific cheat sheets:

https://digitalcloud.training/certification-training/aws-certified-sysops-administrator-associate/amazon-ec2/

QUESTION 25

A CloudOps Administrator manages some critical applications that run on several Amazon EC2 instances. The Administrator needs to ensure that the EC2 instances are automatically recovered if they become impaired due to an underlying hardware failure.

Which service can the Administrator use to monitor and recover the EC2 instances?

1. Amazon EC2 Systems Manager
2. AWS OpsWorks
3. Amazon CloudWatch
4. AWS CloudFormation

Answer: 3

Explanation:

Using Amazon CloudWatch alarm actions, you can create alarms that automatically stop, terminate, reboot, or recover your EC2 instances.

You can use the stop or terminate actions to help you save money when you no longer need an instance to be running.

You can use the reboot and recover actions to automatically reboot those instances or recover them onto new hardware if a system impairment occurs.

CORRECT: "Amazon CloudWatch" is the correct answer.

INCORRECT: "Amazon EC2 Systems Manager" is incorrect. Systems Manager does not monitor the underlying hardware. EC2 status checks monitor the underlying hardware and CloudWatch can respond to status check alarms and restart instances.

INCORRECT: "AWS OpsWorks" is incorrect. This service is used for configuration management using Chef or Puppet.

INCORRECT: "AWS CloudFormation" is incorrect. This service does not respond to EC2 status checks.

References:

https://docs.aws.amazon.com/AmazonCloudWatch/latest/monitoring/UsingAlarmActions.html

Save time with our exam-specific cheat sheets:

https://digitalcloud.training/certification-training/aws-certified-sysops-administrator-associate/amazon-cloudwatch/

QUESTION 26

A CloudOps Administrator has deployed a fleet of Amazon EC2 instances using an EC2 Auto Scaling group. The instances must be configured to send local logs to Amazon CloudWatch and the solution must minimize operational overhead.

Which action should the Administrator take to meet this requirement?

1. Configure AWS Config to forward events to CloudWatch.
2. Install and configure the unified CloudWatch agent.
3. Create a script that forwards events to CloudWatch.
4. Install and configure the Amazon Inspector agent.

Answer: 2

Explanation:

The unified CloudWatch agent enables you to do the following:

- Collect more system-level metrics from Amazon EC2 instances across operating systems. The metrics can include in-guest metrics, in addition to the metrics for EC2 instances.
- Collect system-level metrics from on-premises servers. These can include servers in a hybrid environment as well as servers not managed by AWS.
- Retrieve custom metrics from your applications or services using the StatsD and collectd protocols.
- Collect logs from Amazon EC2 instances and on-premises servers, running either Linux or Windows Server.

CORRECT: "Install and configure the unified CloudWatch agent" is the correct answer.

INCORRECT: "Configure AWS Config to forward events to CloudWatch" is incorrect. AWS Config is not involved with collecting log files.

INCORRECT: "Create a script that forwards events to CloudWatch" is incorrect. This solution does not minimize operational overhead as the script must be created and managed on each EC2 instance. Using an agent is a better solution.

INCORRECT: "Install and configure the Amazon Inspector agent" is incorrect. Amazon Inspector reports on best practice compliance of AWS resources, it does not collect logs.

References:

https://docs.aws.amazon.com/AmazonCloudWatch/latest/monitoring/Install-CloudWatch-Agent.html

Save time with our exam-specific cheat sheets:

https://digitalcloud.training/certification-training/aws-certified-sysops-administrator-associate/amazon-cloudwatch/

QUESTION 27

According to the shared responsibility model, for which of the following Amazon EC2 activities is AWS responsible? (Select TWO.)

1. Patching the guest operating system.
2. Patching the hypervisor.
3. Monitoring EBS volume utilization.
4. Configuring security groups.
5. Maintaining network infrastructure.

Answer: 2,5

Explanation:

AWS is responsible for "Security of the Cloud". This includes protecting the infrastructure that runs all of the services offered in the AWS Cloud. This infrastructure is composed of the hardware, software, networking, and facilities that run AWS Cloud services.

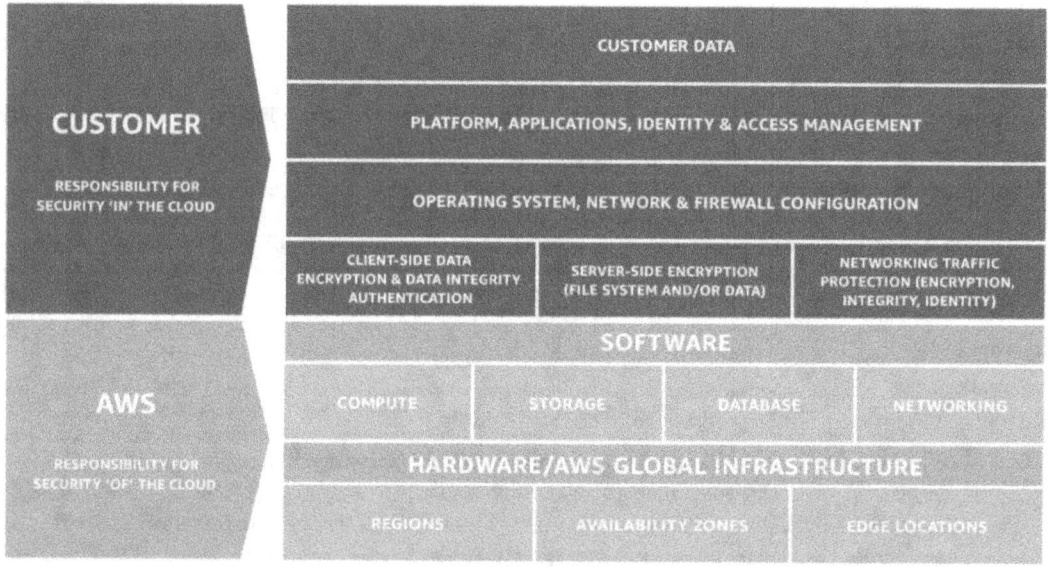

CORRECT: "Patching the hypervisor" is the correct answer.

CORRECT: "Maintaining network infrastructure" is also a correct answer.

INCORRECT: "Patching the guest operating system" is incorrect. AWS are not responsible for patching guest OSs with Amazon EC2.

INCORRECT: "Monitoring EBS volume utilization" is incorrect. It is up to the customer to monitor the EBS volume utilization.

INCORRECT: "Configuring security groups" is incorrect. This is a customer responsibility.

References:

https://aws.amazon.com/compliance/shared-responsibility-model/

QUESTION 28

An Amazon EC2 instance was launched from a Microsoft Windows 2012 AMI and is inaccessible using Remote Desktop Protocol (RDP), or over the network. Another instance was deployed using a different AMI but the same configuration options and is functioning normally.

Which next step should a CloudOps Administrator take to troubleshoot the problem?

1. Use Amazon CloudWatch Events to gather operating system log files for analysis.
2. Use VPC Flow Logs to gather operating system log files for analysis.
3. Use AWS CloudTrail to gather operating system log files for analysis.
4. Use EC2Rescue to gather operating system log files for analysis.

Answer: 4

Explanation:

EC2Rescue for EC2 Windows is a convenient, straightforward, GUI-based troubleshooting tool that can be run on your Amazon EC2 Windows Server instances to troubleshoot operating system-level issues and collect advanced logs and configuration files for further analysis. EC2Rescue simplifies and expedites the troubleshooting of EC2 Windows instances.

CORRECT: "Use EC2Rescue to gather operating system log files for analysis" is the correct answer.

INCORRECT: "Use Amazon CloudWatch Events to gather operating system log files for analysis" is incorrect. You cannot collect operating system log files using CloudWatch Events as this service tracks resource state changes.

INCORRECT: "Use VPC Flow Logs to gather operating system log files for analysis" is incorrect. VPC Flow Logs can be used to collect network traffic data but they cannot be used to collect operating system log files.

INCORRECT: "Use AWS CloudTrail to gather operating system log files for analysis" is incorrect. CloudTrail records API activity, it cannot be used to collect operating system log files.

References:

https://aws.amazon.com/premiumsupport/knowledge-center/ec2rescue-windows-troubleshoot/

Save time with our exam-specific cheat sheets:

https://digitalcloud.training/certification-training/aws-certified-sysops-administrator-associate/aws-systems-manager/

QUESTION 29

A bespoke application must be installed on a fleet of Amazon EC2 instances. The application is updated frequently and can be installed automatically. How can the application be deployed on new EC2 instances?

1. Use AWS Config to detect application updates and trigger an update process.
2. Create a script that downloads and installs the application using EC2 user data.
3. Use AWS Systems Manager to inject the application into an AMI.
4. Create an AWS CloudFormation stack and use a change set to deploy to EC2.

Answer: 2

Explanation:

An up to date version of the application must be installed on new EC2 instances. A simple solution for this is to run a script that downloads the latest binaries for the application and installs it through EC2 user data. This will ensure that all new instances have the latest software installed.

CORRECT: "Create a script that downloads and installs the application using EC2 user data" is the correct answer.

INCORRECT: "Use AWS Config to detect application updates and trigger an update process" is incorrect. AWS Config can be used to detect configuration of AWS resources. However, it would be better to just install the application at system startup rather than detect it's missing.

INCORRECT: "Use AWS Systems Manager to inject the application into an AMI" is incorrect. You can patch

AMIs using Systems Manager but adding an application is not possible.

INCORRECT: "Create an AWS CloudFormation stack and use a change set to deploy to EC2" is incorrect. You cannot use change sets to deploy applications to newly created instances.

References:

https://docs.aws.amazon.com/AWSEC2/latest/UserGuide/user-data.html

Save time with our exam-specific cheat sheets:

https://digitalcloud.training/certification-training/aws-certified-sysops-administrator-associate/amazon-ec2/

QUESTION 30

An application that uses an Amazon ElastiCache Memcached cluster is receiving a larger increase in traffic. A CloudOps Administrator needs to use a larger instance type with more memory. What does the Administrator need to do to implement this change?

1. Modify the existing cache cluster using the ModifyCacheCluster API.
2. Specify a new CacheNodeType with the ModifyCacheParameterGroup API.
3. Create a new cache cluster with a new node type using the CreateCacheCluster API.
4. Use the CreateReplicationGroup API and specify a new CacheNodeType.

Answer: 3

Explanation:

With Amazon ElastiCache Memcached engine you cannot modify the node type. The way to scale up is to create a new cluster and specify the new node type. You can then update the endpoint configuration in your application to point to the new endpoints and then delete the old cache cluster.

CORRECT: "Create a new cache cluster with a new node type using the CreateCacheCluster API " is the correct answer.

INCORRECT: "Modify the existing cache cluster using the ModifyCacheCluster API" is incorrect. This is possible for Redis but not for Memcached.

INCORRECT: "Specify a new CacheNodeType with the ModifyCacheParameterGroup API" is incorrect. You cannot specify node types with this API operation.

INCORRECT: "Use the CreateReplicationGroup API and specify a new CacheNodeType" is incorrect. You cannot specify node types with this API operation.

References:

https://docs.aws.amazon.com/AmazonElastiCache/latest/mem-ug/Scaling.html#Scaling.Memcached.Vertically.API

https://docs.aws.amazon.com/AmazonElastiCache/latest/mem-ug/Clusters.Create.API.html#Clusters.Create.API.Memcached

Save time with our exam-specific cheat sheets:

https://digitalcloud.training/certification-training/aws-certified-sysops-administrator-associate/amazon-elasticache/

QUESTION 31

An application running on Amazon EC2 was moved from a public subnet to a private subnet to increase security. Since the move the instance has been unable to automatically update. What needs to be done to allow the automatic updates to complete successfully?

1. Modify the instance security group to allow traffic from the internet into the private subnet.
2. Set up a NAT gateway in a public subnet and add a route to the private subnet route table.
3. Add a Network Load Balancer to a public subnet and configure the EC2 instance as a target.
4. Set up a NAT gateway in a private subnet and add a route to the public subnet route table.

Answer: 2

Explanation:

The instance is unable to automatically update as it cannot access the internet from the private subnet. To resolve this situation simply create a NAT gateway in a public subnet and then add a route to the private subnet route table that points to the NAT gateway for all internet traffic. This allow outbound communications only so does not expose the instance to any incoming traffic from the internet.

CORRECT: "Set up a NAT gateway in a public subnet and add a route to the private subnet route table" is the correct answer.

INCORRECT: "Set up a NAT gateway in a private subnet and add a route to the public subnet route table" is incorrect. The NAT gateway must be created in a public subnet.

INCORRECT: "Modify the instance security group to allow traffic from the internet into the private subnet" is incorrect. Security groups do not control traffic at the subnet level (Network ACLs do).

INCORRECT: "Add a Network Load Balancer to a public subnet and configure the EC2 instance as a target" is incorrect. An NLB distributes incoming connections. In this case the instance needs outbound connectivity to the internet.

References:

https://docs.aws.amazon.com/vpc/latest/userguide/vpc-nat-gateway.html

Save time with our exam-specific cheat sheets:

https://digitalcloud.training/certification-training/aws-certified-sysops-administrator-associate/amazon-virtual-private-cloud-vpc/

QUESTION 32

A company is deploying an application on Amazon EC2 instances in multiple Availability Zones. The instances will access and share data using file system interfaces. The volume of data is small but expected to increase significantly over time.

What is the MOST scalable storage solution for these requirements?

1. Create an Amazon S3 bucket and a VPC endpoint, mount the bucket to the instances.
2. Create an Amazon EFS filesystem and create mount targets in multiple subnets.
3. Use Amazon EBS multi-attach to connect the EC2 instances to a single volume.
4. Deploy an AWS Storage Gateway cached volume on Amazon EC2.

Answer: 2

Explanation:

The Amazon Elastic File System (EFS) provides filesystem interfaces to connect multiple instances from multiple availability zones to a single filesystem using the NFS protocol. It is highly scalable and is the most suitable service for these requirements.

CORRECT: "Create an Amazon EFS filesystem and create mount targets in multiple subnets" is the correct answer.

INCORRECT: "Create an Amazon S3 bucket and a VPC endpoint, mount the bucket to the instances" is incorrect. You cannot mount an S3 bucket to EC2 instances using file system interfaces as it is an object-based storage system that you access using a REST API.

INCORRECT: "Use Amazon EBS multi-attach to connect the EC2 instances to a single volume" is incorrect. You cannot use EBS multi-attach across availability zones.

INCORRECT: "Deploy an AWS Storage Gateway cached volume on Amazon EC2" is incorrect. Storage gateways are used by on-premises servers and cached volumes use iSCSI (block-based), not file system interfaces such as SMB/CIFS or NFS.

References:

https://docs.aws.amazon.com/efs/latest/ug/performance.html

Save time with our exam-specific cheat sheets:

https://digitalcloud.training/certification-training/aws-certified-sysops-administrator-associate/amazon-efs/

QUESTION 33

A company uses an AWS Storage Gateway volume gateway. The virtual machine running the storage gateway must be rebooted. What is the correct process for rebooting the VM?

1. Reboot the gateway, then reboot the virtual machine.
2. Stop the virtual machine, restart the gateway, then turn on the virtual machine.
3. Synchronize the gateway, then reboot the virtual machine.
4. Stop the gateway, reboot the virtual machine, then restart the gateway.

Answer: 4

Explanation:

You might need to shutdown or reboot your VM for maintenance, such as when applying a patch to your hypervisor. Before you shutdown the VM, you must first stop the gateway.

- For file gateway, you just shutdown your VM.
- For volume and tape gateways, stop the gateway, reboot the VM, then start the gateway.

CORRECT: "Stop the gateway, reboot the virtual machine, then restart the gateway" is the correct answer.

INCORRECT: "Reboot the gateway, then reboot the virtual machine" is incorrect. This is not the correct process.

INCORRECT: "Stop the virtual machine, restart the gateway, then turn on the virtual machine" is incorrect. This is not the correct process.

INCORRECT: "Synchronize the gateway, then reboot the virtual machine" is incorrect. This is not the correct process.

References:

https://docs.aws.amazon.com/storagegateway/latest/userguide/MaintenanceShutDown-common.html

Save time with our exam-specific cheat sheets:

https://digitalcloud.training/certification-training/aws-certified-sysops-administrator-associate/aws-storage-gateway/

QUESTION 34

A company is planning to migrate over 80 TB of data to Amazon S3. The company has a 50-Mbps internet connection that is heavily utilized. What is the MOST efficient method of transferring this data to Amazon S3?

1. Amazon S3 Transfer Acceleration
2. AWS Direct Connect
3. AWS Managed VPN
4. AWS Snowball

Answer: 4

Explanation:

In this scenario there is a large quantity of data and a limited amount of bandwidth available. Therefore, it is best to avoid using the internet link. AWS Snowball is a physical device onto which you can load your data, and have it securely transferred to AWS. This will be the most efficient method of transferring the data.

CORRECT: "AWS Snowball" is the correct answer.

INCORRECT: "Amazon S3 Transfer Acceleration" is incorrect. This service is used for accelerating uploads. It costs more to use this service and you still need a decent amount of internet bandwidth, so it is not the most efficient method for this scenario.

INCORRECT: "AWS Direct Connect" is incorrect. This takes weeks to setup and should be used if you have ongoing requirements for consistent bandwidth and latency to AWS. It is not the best choice for an individual requirement.

INCORRECT: "AWS Managed VPN" is incorrect. This relies on the internet links to create an encrypted tunnel to a VPC. It is not useful in this scenario.

References:

https://aws.amazon.com/snowball/

QUESTION 35

A CloudOps Administrator needs to receive an email whenever critical, production Amazon EC2 instances reach 80% CPU utilization. How can this be achieved?

1. Create an Amazon CloudWatch alarm and configure an Amazon SNS notification.
2. Create an Amazon CloudWatch alarm and configure an Amazon SES notification.
3. Create an Amazon CloudWatch Events rule that triggers an Amazon SNS notification.
4. Create an Amazon CloudWatch Events rule that triggers an Amazon SES notification.

Answer: 1

Explanation:

The way to achieve this requirement is to create an Amazon CloudWatch alarm and associate an Amazon SNS topic. The SNS topic can send an email to the CloudOps Administrator.

CORRECT: "Create an Amazon CloudWatch alarm and configure an Amazon SNS notification" is the correct answer.

INCORRECT: "Create an Amazon CloudWatch alarm and configure an Amazon SES notification" is incorrect. The Administrator should use SNS not SE.

INCORRECT: "Create an Amazon CloudWatch Events rule that triggers an Amazon SNS notification" is incorrect. CloudWatch alarms should be used as CloudWatch Events is used for state changes not metric breaches.

INCORRECT: "Create an Amazon CloudWatch Events rule that triggers an Amazon SES notification" is incorrect. CloudWatch alarms should be used as CloudWatch Events is used for state changes not metric breaches.

References:

https://docs.aws.amazon.com/AmazonCloudWatch/latest/monitoring/US_SetupSNS.html

Save time with our exam-specific cheat sheets:

https://digitalcloud.training/certification-training/aws-certified-sysops-administrator-associate/amazon-cloudwatch/

QUESTION 36

A CloudOps Administrator launched an Amazon EC2 instance and noticed it went from the pending state to the terminated state immediately after starting it. What is a possible cause of this issue?

1. The limit on the number of instances that can be launched in the Region has been exceeded.
2. AWS does not currently have enough available On-Demand capacity to service the request.
3. The root EBS volume is encrypted and the Administrator does not have permissions to access the KMS key for decryption.
4. The API action for launching the specific instance type has been restricted in the AWS account.

Answer: 3

Explanation:

The following are a few reasons why an instance might immediately terminate:

- You've reached your EBS volume limit.
- An EBS snapshot is corrupt.

- The root EBS volume is encrypted and you do not have permissions to access the KMS key for decryption.
- The instance store-backed AMI that you used to launch the instance is missing a required part (an image.part.*xx* file).

CORRECT: "The root EBS volume is encrypted and the Administrator does not have permissions to access the KMS key for decryption" is the correct answer.

INCORRECT: "The limit on the number of instances that can be launched in the Region has been exceeded" is incorrect. This would result in an InstanceLimitExceeded error.

INCORRECT: "AWS does not currently have enough available On-Demand capacity to service the request" is incorrect. This would result in an InsufficientInstanceCapacity error.

INCORRECT: "The API action for launching the specific instance type has been restricted in the AWS account" is incorrect. This would result an access denied error.

References:

https://docs.aws.amazon.com/AWSEC2/latest/UserGuide/troubleshooting-launch.html#troubleshooting-launch-internal

Save time with our exam-specific cheat sheets:

https://digitalcloud.training/certification-training/aws-certified-sysops-administrator-associate/amazon-ebs/

QUESTION 37

An EBS-backed Amazon EC2 instance has a data volume with a status of *impaired*. I/O has also been disabled due to data consistency issues. Which first step should a CloudOps Administrator take to recover the volume?

1. Perform a consistency check on the volume attached to the instance.
2. Recreate the volume by restoring an Amazon EBS snapshot.
3. Change the volume to a general purpose SSD volume type.
4. Attach an Elastic Fabric Adapter (EFA) to the instance and restart I/O.

Answer: 1

Explanation:

The simplest option is to enable I/O and then perform a data consistency check on the volume while the volume is still attached to its Amazon EC2 instance. The steps are:

1. Stop any applications from using the volume.
2. Enable I/O on the volume.
3. Check the data on the volume.

CORRECT: "Perform a consistency check on the volume attached to the instance" is the correct answer.

INCORRECT: "Recreate the volume by restoring an Amazon EBS snapshot" is incorrect. This is not the first step as the snapshot my not be fully up to date so recovering the existing volume should be attempted first.

INCORRECT: "Change the volume to a general purpose SSD volume type" is incorrect. There is no reason to change volume types when data consistency is the issue.

INCORRECT: "Attach an Elastic Fabric Adapter (EFA) to the instance and restart I/O" is incorrect. Attaching an EFA is not a useful step for this scenario.

References:

https://docs.aws.amazon.com/AWSEC2/latest/UserGuide/monitoring-volume-status.html

Save time with our exam-specific cheat sheets:

https://digitalcloud.training/certification-training/aws-certified-sysops-administrator-associate/amazon-ebs/

QUESTION 38

An Amazon EBS volume has a status of error. What can a CloudOps Administrator do to bring the volume back online?

1. Enable I/O using the enable-volume-io API.
2. Perform a consistency check using the fsck command.
3. Create a new volume from a recent snapshot.
4. Take a snapshot and then create a new volume from the snapshot.

Answer: 3

Explanation:

The error status indicates that the underlying hardware related to your EBS volume has failed, and the data associated with the volume is unrecoverable. If you have an EBS snapshot of the volume, you can restore that volume from your snapshot.

CORRECT: "Create a new volume from a recent snapshot" is the correct answer.

INCORRECT: "Enable I/O using the enable-volume-io API" is incorrect. You cannot enable I/O for a volume in this state.

INCORRECT: "Perform a consistency check using the fsck command" is incorrect. You cannot bring the volume online so you cannot run a consistency check on it.

INCORRECT: "Take a snapshot and then create a new volume from the snapshot" is incorrect. The data is not accessible so it is no longer possible to create an EBS snapshot.

References:

https://aws.amazon.com/premiumsupport/knowledge-center/ebs-error-status/

Save time with our exam-specific cheat sheets:

https://digitalcloud.training/certification-training/aws-certified-sysops-administrator-associate/amazon-ebs/

QUESTION 39

An Amazon EC2 Auto Scaling group failed to launch an EC2 instance with the error message "The AMI ID ami-0c23bcf3g31a58706 does not exist". What action should be taken to resolve the issue and enable the ASG to launch new instances?

1. Add an alias for the AMI ID pointing to a valid AMI.
2. Create a new AMI with the same AMI ID.
3. Update the launch configuration with a valid AMI ID.
4. Create a new launch configuration using a valid AMI.

Answer: 4

Explanation:

This error message indicates that the AMI might have been deleted after creating the launch configuration. As it is not possible to update launch configurations a new launch configuration must be created that has a valid AMI ID.

CORRECT: "Create a new launch configuration using a valid AMI" is the correct answer.

INCORRECT: "Add an alias for the AMI ID pointing to a valid AMI" is incorrect. You cannot add aliases to AMIs.

INCORRECT: "Create a new AMI with the same AMI ID" is incorrect. You cannot choose the AMI ID you use when creating an AMI.

INCORRECT: "Update the launch configuration with a valid AMI ID" is incorrect. You cannot update launch configurations.

References:

https://docs.aws.amazon.com/autoscaling/ec2/userguide/ts-as-ami.html

Save time with our exam-specific cheat sheets:

https://digitalcloud.training/certification-training/aws-certified-sysops-administrator-associate/amazon-ec2-auto-scaling/

QUESTION 40

An Amazon EC2 Auto Scaling group is set to scale-out when CPU utilization reaches 80%. The CPU utilization has reached 90% and the following error message was received "8 instance(s) are already running. Launching EC2 instance failed".

What action should be taken to allow the Auto Scaling group to launch additional instances?

1. Increase the account limits for EBS General Purpose (SSD) storage.
2. Request an EC2 service quota increase for the Region.
3. Configure a scheduled scaling policy with the current date and time.
4. Disable the scaling policies and manually launch EC2 instances.

Answer: 2

Explanation:

This error message indicates that you have reached the limit on the number of instances that you can launch in a Region. When you create your AWS account, we set default limits on the number of instances you can run on a per-Region basis. You can request a quota increase on a per-Region basis.

CORRECT: "Request an EC2 service quota increase for the Region." is the correct answer.

INCORRECT: "Increase the account limits for EBS General Purpose (SSD) storage" is incorrect. This error message is not due to an EBS limit being reached.

INCORRECT: "Configure a scheduled scaling policy with the current date and time" is incorrect. This will not help and the EC2 quota limit has been reached anyway.

INCORRECT: "Disable the scaling policies and manually launch EC2 instances" is incorrect. This will not help as the EC2 quota limit has been reached.

References:

https://docs.aws.amazon.com/autoscaling/ec2/userguide/ts-as-instancelaunchfailure.html#ts-as-capacity-3

Save time with our exam-specific cheat sheets:

https://digitalcloud.training/certification-training/aws-certified-sysops-administrator-associate/amazon-ec2-auto-scaling/

QUESTION 41

An Amazon EFS file system is used by several Amazon EC2 instances. The data stored on the file system is sensitive and a manager has asked for the data to be encrypted at rest. How can a CloudOps Administrator enable encryption for the EFS file system?

1. Enable encryption on the existing EFS volume using the AWS tools for Windows PowerShell.
2. Create a new EFS volume with encryption enabled and copy the data from the original volume.
3. Enable encryption on the existing EFS volume by using the AWS Command Line interface.
4. Create an SSL/TLS certificate using Amazon Certificate Manager (ACM) and attach it to the EFS volume.

Answer: 2

Explanation:

Amazon EFS supports two forms of encryption for file systems, encryption of data in transit and encryption at rest. You can enable encryption of data at rest when creating an Amazon EFS file system. You can enable encryption of data in transit when you mount the file system. You cannot enable encryption for a volume after it has been created.

CORRECT: "Create a new EFS volume with encryption enabled and copy the data from the original volume" is the correct answer.

INCORRECT: "Enable encryption on the existing EFS volume using the AWS tools for Windows PowerShell" is incorrect. You cannot enable encryption for a volume after it has been created.

INCORRECT: "Enable encryption on the existing EFS volume by using the AWS Command Line interface" is incorrect. You cannot enable encryption for a volume after it has been created.

INCORRECT: "Create an SSL/TLS certificate using Amazon Certificate Manager (ACM) and attach it to the EFS volume" is incorrect. You cannot associate SSL/TLS certificates with EFS volumes, and they are used for encryption in transit not encryption at rest.

References:

https://docs.aws.amazon.com/efs/latest/ug/encryption.html

Save time with our exam-specific cheat sheets:

https://digitalcloud.training/certification-training/aws-certified-sysops-administrator-associate/amazon-efs/

QUESTION 42

An Amazon EBS gp2 volume is running low on space. How can this be resolved with MINIMAL effort?

1. Change to an io1 volume type and then modify the volume size.
2. Create a new, larger volume, and migrate the data.
3. Create a snapshot and restore it to a larger gp2 volume.
4. Use the Elastic Volumes feature to modify the volume size.

Answer: 4

Explanation:

With Elastic Volumes, you can dynamically modify the size, performance, and volume type of your Amazon EBS volumes without detaching them.

Use the following process when modifying a volume:

1. (Optional) Before modifying a volume that contains valuable data, it is a best practice to create a snapshot of the volume in case you need to roll back your changes.
2. Request the volume modification.
3. Monitor the progress of the volume modification.
4. If the size of the volume was modified, extend the volume's file system to take advantage of the increased storage capacity.

CORRECT: "Use the Elastic Volumes feature to modify the volume size" is the correct answer.

INCORRECT: "Change to an io1 volume type and then modify the volume size" is incorrect. It is not necessary to change volume types as all volume types support size modifications.

INCORRECT: "Create a new, larger volume, and migrate the data" is incorrect. This is not the simplest way to resolve the issue as it involves data migration.

INCORRECT: "Create a snapshot and restore it to a larger gp2 volume" is incorrect. There is no need to create a new volume, just modify the existing volume.

References:

https://docs.aws.amazon.com/AWSEC2/latest/UserGuide/requesting-ebs-volume-modifications.html

Save time with our exam-specific cheat sheets:

https://digitalcloud.training/certification-training/aws-certified-sysops-administrator-associate/amazon-ebs/

QUESTION 43

Users of a web application that is served using Amazon CloudFront have complained about receiving 4XX and 5XX errors. A CloudOps Administrator wants to monitor for elevated error rates in Amazon CloudFront. Which metric should be monitored?

1. CacheHitRate
2. OriginLatency
3. Requests
4. TotalErrorRate

Answer: 4

Explanation:

The TotalErrorRate metric shows the percentage of all viewer requests for which the response's HTTP status code is 4xx or 5xx. This can be used to determine if there is indeed an elevation in the rate of errors that are being generated.

CORRECT: "TotalErrorRate" is the correct answer.

INCORRECT: "CacheHitRate" is incorrect. This measures the percentage of all cacheable requests for which CloudFront served the content from its cache.

INCORRECT: "OriginLatency" is incorrect. This measures the total time spent, in milliseconds, from when CloudFront receives a request to when it starts providing a response to the network (not the viewer), for requests that are served from the origin, not the CloudFront cache.

INCORRECT: "Requests" is incorrect. This measures the total number of viewer requests received by CloudFront, for all HTTP methods and for both HTTP and HTTPS requests.

References:

https://docs.aws.amazon.com/AmazonCloudFront/latest/DeveloperGuide/programming-cloudwatch-metrics.html

Save time with our exam-specific cheat sheets:

https://digitalcloud.training/certification-training/aws-certified-sysops-administrator-associate/amazon-cloudfront/

QUESTION 44

An application running on Amazon EC2 instances needs to store log files in an Amazon S3 bucket. What is the MOST secure method of granting access to the bucket?

1. Create an IAM role with the required privileges and associate it with the EC2 instance.
2. Create an IAM user with the required privileges, generate an access key and embed the key in the application code.
3. Create an IAM role with the required privileges and embed the role credentials in the application code.
4. Create an IAM user with the required privileges, generate a key pair and embed the key pair in the application code.

Answer: 1

Explanation:

The most secure method of granting this access is to use an IAM role that is associated with an instance profile attached to the EC2 instance. This method ensures there are no credentials stored in the application code.

CORRECT: "Create an IAM role with the required privileges and associate it with the EC2 instance" is the correct answer.

INCORRECT: "Create an IAM user with the required privileges, generate an access key and embed the key in the application code" is incorrect. This is not secure as an access key is embedded in the application code

INCORRECT: "Create an IAM role with the required privileges and embed the role credentials in the application code" is incorrect. There are no credentials associated with a role that you can embed in the code.

INCORRECT: "Create an IAM user with the required privileges, generate a key pair and embed the key pair in the application code" is incorrect. You cannot use a key pair to authenticate to an Amazon S3 bucket.

References:

https://docs.aws.amazon.com/AWSEC2/latest/UserGuide/iam-roles-for-amazon-ec2.html

Save time with our exam-specific cheat sheets:

https://digitalcloud.training/certification-training/aws-certified-sysops-administrator-associate/aws-iam/

QUESTION 45

A CloudOps Administrator has created an Amazon S3 bucket for storing files associated with current troubleshooting and analysis. To ensure the bucket doesn't get too large the administrator wants to automatically delete files older than 6 months. How can this be achieved?

1. Use Amazon CloudWatch Events to delete objects older than 6 months.
2. Run a script on an Amazon EC2 instance that identifies and deletes old files.
3. Implement lifecycle policies to expire objects older than 6 months.
4. Create and object versioning rule that expires objects older than 6 months.

Answer: 3

Explanation:

You can add rules in an S3 Lifecycle configuration to tell Amazon S3 to transition objects to another Amazon S3 storage class or to expire the objects. In this case the Administrator should create a lifecycle policy that expires the objects that are older than 6 months.

CORRECT: "Implement lifecycle policies to expire objects older than 6 months" is the correct answer.

INCORRECT: "Use Amazon CloudWatch Events to delete objects older than 6 months" is incorrect. You cannot use CloudWatch Events to expire objects based on age.

INCORRECT: "Run a script on an Amazon EC2 instance that identifies and deletes old files." is incorrect. This is not the best solution when you could just a lifecycle policy instead,

INCORRECT: "Create and object versioning rule that expires objects older than 6 months" is incorrect. You cannot use versioning to expire objects based on age.

References:

https://docs.aws.amazon.com/AmazonS3/latest/dev/lifecycle-transition-general-considerations.html

Save time with our exam-specific cheat sheets:

https://digitalcloud.training/certification-training/aws-certified-sysops-administrator-associate/amazon-s3/

QUESTION 46

An application uploads periodic logs to an Amazon S3 bucket. The logs must be immediately available but are not frequently accessed. Which lifecycle rule should be created for cost-efficiency?

1. Transition the objects to S3 Standard-IA after 30 days.
2. Transition the objects to S3 Glacier after immediately.
3. Transition the objects to S3 Intelligent-Tiering after 30 days.
4. Transition the objects to S3 Standard-IA immediately.

Answer: 1

Explanation:

The log files must be immediately available so Glacier cannot be used. However, cost savings are required so moving the files to S3 Standard-IA is the best answer. Before you transition objects from the S3 Standard or S3 Standard-IA storages classes to S3 Standard-IA or S3 One Zone-IA, you must store them at least 30 days in the S3 Standard storage class.

CORRECT: "Transition the objects to S3 Standard-IA after 30 days" is the correct answer.

INCORRECT: "Transition the objects to S3 Glacier after immediately" is incorrect. Glacier does not provide immediate access.

INCORRECT: "Transition the objects to S3 Intelligent-Tiering after 30 days" is incorrect. As the usage pattern is known to be infrequent this is not the best choice.

INCORRECT: "Transition the objects to S3 Standard-IA immediately" is incorrect. You cannot transition the objects immediately after they are stored in S3 Standard, you must wait 30 days.

References:

https://docs.aws.amazon.com/AmazonS3/latest/dev/lifecycle-transition-general-considerations.html

Save time with our exam-specific cheat sheets:

https://digitalcloud.training/certification-training/aws-certified-sysops-administrator-associate/amazon-s3/

QUESTION 47

A company runs a static website on Amazon S3. A CloudOps Administrator noticed that the S3 bucket is receiving a very high rate of read operations. What can the Administrator do to minimize latency and reduce the load on the S3 bucket?

1. Use cross-region replication (CRR) to replicate the data to another region.
2. Create an Amazon CloudFront distribution with the S3 bucket as the origin.
3. Migrate to a bucket in an AWS Region that is closer to the end users.
4. Use Amazon ElastiCache Redis to cache the static data from the S3 bucket.

Answer: 2

Explanation:

Amazon CloudFront can be used to cache the static content in Edge Locations around the world. This reduces the load on the S3 bucket as well as reducing latency for users by moving the data closer to them.

CORRECT: "Create an Amazon CloudFront distribution with the S3 bucket as the origin" is the correct answer.

INCORRECT: "Use cross-region replication (CRR) to replicate the data to another region" is incorrect. This could be used to get a copy of the data closer to users in another region. However, the Administrator would then need a method of directing users to the copy of the data and that is not mentioned in the answer.

INCORRECT: "Migrate to a bucket in an AWS Region that is closer to the end users" is incorrect. The question does not state that the users are in one location so they could be globally distributed.

INCORRECT: "Use Amazon ElastiCache Redis to cache the static data from the S3 bucket" is incorrect. ElastiCache cannot be used to cache data from S3 bucket.

References:

https://aws.amazon.com/premiumsupport/knowledge-center/cloudfront-serve-static-website/

Save time with our exam-specific cheat sheets:

https://digitalcloud.training/certification-training/aws-certified-sysops-administrator-associate/amazon-s3/

https://digitalcloud.training/certification-training/aws-certified-sysops-administrator-associate/amazon-cloudfront/

QUESTION 48

A web application running on HTTP has been launched in an Amazon VPC. The application runs on Amazon EC2 instances across multiple Availability Zones behind an Application Load Balancer. A security group and network ACL has been created for the load balancer allowing inbound traffic on port 80. During testing the web application is found to be inaccessible from the internet.

What additional action must be taken to make the web application accessible form the internet?

1. Add a rule to the security group allowing outbound traffic on ports 1024 through 65535.
2. Add a rule to the security group allowing all outbound traffic to 0.0.0.0/0.
3. Add a rule to the network ACL allowing outbound traffic on ports 1024 through 65535.
4. Add a rule to the network ACL allowing outbound traffic on port 80 to any destination.

Answer: 3

Explanation:

Network ACLs are stateless firewalls which means you need a rule for each connection – inbound and outbound. When inbound connections are made the source port is dynamically set to a port in the 1024-65535 range. Therefore, the resolution is to create a rule that allows outbound connections to that port range to any destination.

CORRECT: "Add a rule to the network ACL allowing outbound traffic on ports 1024 through 65535" is the correct answer.

INCORRECT: "Add a rule to the security group allowing outbound traffic on ports 1024 through 65535" is incorrect. Security groups are stateful, so an outbound rule is unnecessary.

INCORRECT: "Add a rule to the security group allowing all outbound traffic to 0.0.0.0/0" is incorrect. Security groups are stateful, so an outbound rule is unnecessary.

INCORRECT: "Add a rule to the network ACL allowing outbound traffic on port 80 to any destination" is incorrect. The return traffic will go back to the high numbered port dynamically assigned by the client; it does not go back to port 80.

References:

https://docs.aws.amazon.com/vpc/latest/userguide/vpc-network-acls.html

Save time with our exam-specific cheat sheets:

https://digitalcloud.training/certification-training/aws-certified-sysops-administrator-associate/amazon-virtual-private-cloud-vpc/

QUESTION 49

A security team has identified an attack on web applications running on Amazon EC2. The attack uses malformed HTTP headers. Which AWS service or feature can be used to prevent this type of attack from reaching the EC2 instances?

1. Amazon Security Group rules
2. Application Load Balancer (ALB)
3. Network Access Control List (NACL)
4. AWS Web Application Firewall (WAF)

Answer: 2

Explanation:

An application load balancer will block malformed requests that do not meet the HTTP specification with a HTTP 400: Bad request error. An ALB can be placed in front of the EC2 web applications and this will prevent the attack from reaching the instances.

The ALB attribute "Drop Invalid Header Fields" setting can be used to control if invalid header fields are removed by the load balancer.

Edit load balancer attributes

Delete Protection	☐ Enable
Idle timeout	60 seconds
HTTP/2	☑ Enable
Drop Invalid Header Fields	☑ Enable
Desync mitigation mode	⦿ Defensive ○ Strictest ○ Monitor
Access logs	☐ Enable

See the documentation for more information.

CORRECT: "Application Load Balancer (ALB)" is the correct answer.

INCORRECT: "AWS Web Application Firewall (WAF)" is incorrect. AWS WAF cannot be used to protect EC2 instances directly. It can be used in front of CloudFront distributions, ALBs and API Gateways.

INCORRECT: "Amazon Security Group rules" is incorrect. You cannot stop malformed HTTP requests from reaching and instance using security group rules without blocking all traffic.

INCORRECT: "Network Access Control List (NACL)" is incorrect. You cannot stop malformed HTTP requests from reaching and instance using Network ACLs without blocking all traffic.

References:

https://docs.aws.amazon.com/elasticloadbalancing/latest/application/load-balancer-troubleshooting.html#http-400-issues

Save time with our exam-specific cheat sheets:

https://digitalcloud.training/certification-training/aws-certified-sysops-administrator-associate/elastic-load-balancing/

QUESTION 50

An application has been deployed on Amazon EC2 instances behind an Application Load Balancer (ALB). Users have complained that they must log in several times each hour. What can be done to reduce the number of times users must log in to the application?

1. Add targets in multiple Availability Zones.
2. Enable HTTP/2 on the Application Load Balancer.
3. Enable sticky sessions on the Target Group.
4. Configure health checks on the Application Load Balancer.

Answer: 3

Explanation:

Sticky sessions are a mechanism to route requests to the same target in a target group. This is useful for servers that maintain state information in order to provide a continuous experience to clients. To use sticky sessions, the clients must support cookies.

When sticky sessions in enabled connections from an individual client are routed to the same back-end EC2 instance for the duration of the session. This will reduce the need to authenticate multiple times in an hour.

CORRECT: "Enable sticky sessions on the Target Group." is the correct answer.

INCORRECT: "Configure health checks on the Application Load Balancer." is incorrect. Health checks are not the issue here and they are configured on the target group.

INCORRECT: "Add targets in multiple Availability Zones." is incorrect. The issue is unlikely to be due to an Availability Zone being unavailable and more likely due to connections being routed to multiple instances.

INCORRECT: "Enable HTTP/2 on the Application Load Balancer." is incorrect. This will not solve the authentication issue.

References:

https://docs.aws.amazon.com/elasticloadbalancing/latest/application/load-balancer-target-groups.html#sticky-sessions

Save time with our exam-specific cheat sheets:

https://digitalcloud.training/certification-training/aws-certified-sysops-administrator-associate/elastic-load-balancing/

QUESTION 51

A CloudOps Administrator has created an Amazon VPC with an IPv6 CIDR block. Amazon EC2 instances in the VPC should be able to connect to IPv6 domains on the internet but connectivity from the internet should be restricted.

What must be configured to enable the required connectivity?

1. Create an egress-only internet gateway and add a route to the route table pointing to the gateway for the target ::/0
2. Create an egress-only internet gateway and add a route to the route table pointing to the gateway for the target 0.0.0.0/0
3. Create an internet gateway and add a route to the route table pointing to the gateway for the target ::/0
4. Create a NAT gateway and add a route to the route table pointing to the gateway for the target 0.0.0.0/0

Answer: 1

Explanation:

An egress-only internet gateway is a horizontally scaled, redundant, and highly available VPC component that allows outbound communication over IPv6 from instances in your VPC to the internet and prevents the internet from initiating an IPv6 connection with your instances.

A route must be added to the route table pointing to the gateway. For IPv6 the target should be configured as ::/0 which is the equivalent of the 0.0.0.0/0 (IPv4) address.

CORRECT: "Create an egress-only internet gateway and add a route to the route table pointing to the gateway for the target ::/0" is the correct answer.

INCORRECT: "Create an egress-only internet gateway and add a route to the route table pointing to the gateway for the target 0.0.0.0/0" is incorrect. This ::/0 address should be used for IPv6 instead of 0.0.0.0/0.

INCORRECT: "Create an internet gateway and add a route to the route table pointing to the gateway for the target ::/0" is incorrect. An internet gateway is used for IPv4, an egress-only gateway must be used for IPv6.

INCORRECT: "Create a NAT gateway and add a route to the route table pointing to the gateway for the target 0.0.0.0/0" is incorrect. A NAT gateway is used for IPv4 connectivity from private subnets to the internet.

References:

https://docs.aws.amazon.com/vpc/latest/userguide/egress-only-internet-gateway.html#egress-only-internet-gateway-working-with

Save time with our exam-specific cheat sheets:

https://digitalcloud.training/certification-training/aws-certified-sysops-administrator-associate/amazon-virtual-private-cloud-vpc/

QUESTION 52

A manager has asked a CloudOps Administrator to add high availability to an existing Amazon RDS instance. How can this requirement be achieved?

1. Use the ModifyDBInstance API action with the ReplicaMode value.
2. Create a new DB instance with multi-AZ enabled and migrate data.
3. Create a Read Replica and use DNS failover for high availability.
4. Modify the RDS instance using the console and enabled multi-AZ.

Answer: 4

Explanation:

Amazon RDS provides high availability and failover support for DB instances using Multi-AZ deployments. Amazon RDS uses several different technologies to provide failover support.

Multi-AZ deployments for MariaDB, MySQL, Oracle, and PostgreSQL DB instances use Amazon's failover technology. SQL Server DB instances use SQL Server Database Mirroring (DBM) or Always On Availability Groups (AGs).

CORRECT: "Modify the RDS instance using the console and enabled multi-AZ" is the correct answer.

INCORRECT: "Use the ModifyDBInstance API action with the ReplicaMode value." is incorrect. This is only relevant to Oracle Enterprise Edition and is used to mount replicas for cross-Region disaster recovery.

INCORRECT: "Create a new DB instance with multi-AZ enabled and migrate data." is incorrect. It is not necessary to create a new DB instance as you can enabled Multi-AZ at any time.

INCORRECT: "Create a Read Replica and use DNS failover for high availability." is incorrect. Read Replicas are only used for queries not writing data so you cannot use them in this manner for HA.

References:

https://docs.aws.amazon.com/AmazonRDS/latest/UserGuide/Concepts.MultiAZ.html

Save time with our exam-specific cheat sheets:

https://digitalcloud.training/certification-training/aws-certified-sysops-administrator-associate/amazon-rds/

QUESTION 53

A security consultant has identified unnecessary security group and network ACL rules that pose a security risk. What steps should a CloudOps Administrator take to resolve the security vulnerabilities?

1. Contact AWS Support and notify them of the vulnerabilities.
2. Create an AWS WAF web ACL that protects resources from web attacks.
3. Remove the unnecessary security group rules and network ACL rules.
4. Use Amazon Inspector to identify security best practices and rectify issues.

Answer: 3

Explanation:

This question is partly technical and partly about the shared responsibility model. The unnecessary rules are part of the security in the cloud which is a customer responsibility so there's no need to contact AWS support. The easiest way to resolve the vulnerability issues is for the CloudOps Administrator to remove the rules.

CORRECT: "Remove the unnecessary security group rules and network ACL rules" is the correct answer.

INCORRECT: "Contact AWS Support and notify them of the vulnerabilities" is incorrect. This is not a responsibility of AWS Support as it constitutes security in the cloud.

INCORRECT: "Create an AWS WAF web ACL that protects resources from web attacks" is incorrect. AWS WAF can assist with protecting certain resources such as CloudFront distributions, ALBs and API Gateways. However, it cannot resolve issues with security group and network ACL rules.

INCORRECT: "Use Amazon Inspector to identify security best practices and rectify issues" is incorrect. Inspector offers best practice guidance, but it will not rectify unnecessary rules.

References:

https://aws.amazon.com/compliance/shared-responsibility-model

Save time with our exam-specific cheat sheets:

https://digitalcloud.training/certification-training/aws-certified-sysops-administrator-associate/amazon-virtual-private-cloud-vpc/

QUESTION 54

A CloudOps Administrator has been tasked with configuring protection for an Amazon RDS database. The solution must be cost-effective, protect against table corruption, and retain backups for 30 days. How can these requirements be achieved?

1. Use the Database Migration Service to synchronize data with another RDS instance.
2. Create a read replica of the RDS instance in another Availability Zone.
3. Take daily snapshots of the RDS database and store them on Amazon S3.
4. Enabled automated backups and configure a 30-day backup retention period.

Answer: 4

Explanation:

Amazon RDS creates and saves automated backups of your DB instance during the backup window of your DB instance. RDS creates a storage volume snapshot of your DB instance, backing up the entire DB instance and not just individual databases.

RDS saves the automated backups of your DB instance according to the backup retention period that you specify which can be up to 35 days.

CORRECT: "Enabled automated backups and configure a 30-day backup retention period" is the correct answer.

INCORRECT: "Use the Database Migration Service to synchronize data with another RDS instance" is incorrect. This is not cost-effective as another database instance is running. It also does not protect against database corruption.

INCORRECT: "Create a read replica of the RDS instance in another Availability Zone" is incorrect. As the data is replicated from the master asynchronously this does not protect against database corruption.

INCORRECT: "Take daily snapshots of the RDS database and store them on Amazon S3" is incorrect. This will cost more as automated backups up to the size of the allocated storage are included in the cost of the instance whereas manual snapshots are not.

References:

https://docs.aws.amazon.com/AmazonRDS/latest/UserGuide/USER_WorkingWithAutomatedBackups.html

Save time with our exam-specific cheat sheets:

https://digitalcloud.training/certification-training/aws-certified-sysops-administrator-associate/amazon-rds/

QUESTION 55

A company runs and Amazon Aurora database instance. According to the AWS Shared Responsibility Model, which of the following actions are the responsibility of the customer?

1. Scheduling maintenance, patches, and other updates.
2. Provisioning the underlying server hardware.
3. Managing network infrastructure for the database.
4. Executing maintenance, patches, and other updates.

Answer: 1

Explanation:

Amazon Aurora is a managed service and AWS will take care of executing maintenance, patches and other updates. However, customers are responsible for configuring the maintenance window in which these updates will take place.

CORRECT: "Scheduling maintenance, patches, and other updates." is the correct answer.

INCORRECT: "Executing maintenance, patches, and other updates" is incorrect. AWS are responsible for executing these activities.

INCORRECT: "Provisioning the underlying server hardware" is incorrect. AWS are responsible for the server hardware.

INCORRECT: "Managing network infrastructure for the database" is incorrect. AWS are responsible for the networking infrastructure that makes the database available.

References:

https://docs.aws.amazon.com/AmazonRDS/latest/AuroraUserGuide/USER_UpgradeDBInstance.Maintenance.html

QUESTION 56

A CloudOps Administrator is monitoring an Amazon Aurora database and received a "inaccessible-encryption-credentials" DB instance status message and has become inaccessible. What is the explanation for this error?

1. The AWS KMS key used to encrypt or decrypt the DB instance can't be accessed.
2. The DB instance has reached its storage capacity allocation.
3. AWS IAM database authentication is being enabled or disabled for this DB instance.
4. Enhanced Monitoring is being enabled or disabled for this DB instance.

Answer: 1

Explanation:

This can occur if the KMS key is unavailable and the underlying EC2 host changes for any reason, RDS attempts to save logs to support a future point-in-time-restore, or if automated backups are enabled.

To recover from an inaccessible-encryption-credentials state, the RDS instance must be restored from backup or point-in-time. However, the original KMS key must be available for the restore to complete successfully.

CORRECT: "The AWS KMS key used to encrypt or decrypt the DB instance can't be accessed" is the correct answer.

INCORRECT: "The DB instance has reached its storage capacity allocation" is incorrect. This would cause a "storage-full" status.

INCORRECT: "AWS IAM database authentication is being enabled or disabled for this DB instance" is incorrect. This would cause a "configuring-iam-database-auth" status.

INCORRECT: "Enhanced Monitoring is being enabled or disabled for this DB instance" is incorrect. This would cause a "configuring-enhanced-monitoring" status.

References:

https://aws.amazon.com/blogs/database/securing-data-in-amazon-rds-using-aws-kms-encryption/

https://docs.aws.amazon.com/AmazonRDS/latest/AuroraUserGuide/Overview.DBInstance.Status.html

Save time with our exam-specific cheat sheets:

https://digitalcloud.training/certification-training/aws-certified-sysops-administrator-associate/aws-kms-and-aws-cloudhsm/

QUESTION 57

A database runs on Amazon Aurora and is experiencing some performance issues. A CloudOps Administrator needs to monitor memory utilization and OS level metrics. How can the Administrator access these metrics?

1. Use Amazon CloudWatch to view the standard metrics for RDS.
2. Enable enhanced monitoring and view the metrics in the RDS console.
3. Install the unified CloudWatch agent on the RDS instance to generate the metrics.
4. Enable detailed monitoring for the RDS instance to increase metric frequency.

Answer: 2

Explanation:

Amazon RDS provides metrics in real time for the operating system (OS) that your DB instance runs on. You can view the metrics for your DB instance using the console. Also, you can consume the Enhanced Monitoring JSON output from Amazon CloudWatch Logs in a monitoring system of your choice. You can enable and disable Enhanced Monitoring using the AWS Management Console, AWS CLI, or RDS API.

CORRECT: "Enable enhanced monitoring and view the metrics in the RDS console." is the correct answer.

INCORRECT: "Use Amazon CloudWatch to view the standard metrics for RDS" is incorrect. OS level and memory utilization metrics are not standard RDS metrics.

INCORRECT: "Install the unified CloudWatch agent on the RDS instance to generate the metrics" is incorrect. You cannot install this agent on RDS as you do not have access to the underlying operating system. When you enable enhanced monitoring, AWS install an agent on the OS.

INCORRECT: "Enable detailed monitoring for the RDS instance to increase metric frequency" is incorrect. This will not generate the required metrics as they are not standard metrics. This setting also applies to EC2, not RDS.

References:

https://docs.aws.amazon.com/AmazonRDS/latest/AuroraUserGuide/USER_Monitoring.OS.html

Save time with our exam-specific cheat sheets:

https://digitalcloud.training/certification-training/aws-certified-sysops-administrator-associate/amazon-rds/

QUESTION 58

A CloudOps Administrator attempted to deploy an AWS CloudFormation StackSet across multiple AWS accounts. The stack operation failed, and the stack instance status is OUTDATED. What could be a possible cause of this error?

1. The deployment was run without specifying a CloudFormation template.
2. The deployment was run with insufficient permissions in the target account.
3. The deployment is trying to create resources in other accounts in a different region.
4. The deployment requires multi-factor authentication and a token was not provided.

Answer: 2

Explanation:

There can be several common causes for stack operation failure.

- Insufficient permissions in a target account for creating resources that are specified in your template.
- The AWS CloudFormation template might have errors. Validate the template in AWS CloudFormation and fix errors before trying to create your stack set.
- The template could be trying to create global resources that must be unique but aren't, such as S3 buckets.
- A specified target account number doesn't exist. Check the target account numbers that you specified on the **Set deployment options** page of the wizard.
- The administrator account does not have a trust relationship with the target account.
- The maximum number of a resource that is specified in your template already exists in your target account. For example, you might have reached the limit of allowed IAM roles in a target account, but the template creates more IAM roles.
- You have reached the maximum number of stacks that are allowed in a stack set.

CORRECT: "The deployment was run with insufficient permissions in the target account." is the correct answer.

INCORRECT: "The deployment was run without specifying a CloudFormation template" is incorrect. You cannot start a deployment without a template.

INCORRECT: "The deployment is trying to create resources in other accounts in a different region" is incorrect. StackSets can be run across accounts and regions.

INCORRECT: "The deployment requires multi-factor authentication and a token was not provided" is incorrect. This is not the case as StackSets do not use MFA.

References:

https://docs.aws.amazon.com/AWSCloudFormation/latest/UserGuide/stacksets-troubleshooting.html

Save time with our exam-specific cheat sheets:

https://digitalcloud.training/certification-training/aws-certified-sysops-administrator-associate/aws-cloudformation/

QUESTION 59

An Amazon Elastic Beanstalk environment was deployed with a configuration file that runs a series of commands. The environment creation completed with the message "*Create environment operation is* complete, but with command timeouts". How can this issue be resolve so future deployments avoid this issue?

1. Use a larger instance type with more CPU.
2. Increase the command timeout period.
3. Configure a worker environment.
4. Use the high availability preset.

Answer: 2

Explanation:

An application may take a long time to deploy if you use configuration files that run commands on the instance, download large files, or install packages. Increase the command timeout to give the application more time to start running during deployments.

CORRECT: "Increase the command timeout period." is the correct answer.

INCORRECT: "Use a larger instance type with more CPU" is incorrect. The issue is how long the instance took to run the commands. Using more CPU power is unlikely to resolve this issue as it could be delays in downloading files or calling external services that is causing the delay.

INCORRECT: "Configure a worker environment" is incorrect. Worker environments are a different type of deployment and you wouldn't choose this to resolve an issue in deployment.

INCORRECT: "Use the high availability preset" is incorrect. This would create a HA deployment but would not resolve the issue.

References:

https://docs.aws.amazon.com/elasticbeanstalk/latest/dg/troubleshooting-envcreate.html

Save time with our exam-specific cheat sheets:

https://digitalcloud.training/certification-training/aws-certified-sysops-administrator-associate/aws-elastic-beanstalk/

QUESTION 60

A user is attempting to connect to an Amazon Linux instance using SSH and is experiencing errors. A CloudOps Administrator has checked the configuration including key pairs, security groups, and network ACLs and confirmed that the user can connect to other instances in the same subnet. What can the Administrator do to further troubleshoot the issue?

1. Check that there is an internet gateway attached to the VPC.
2. Use Trusted Advisor to check the SSH configuration.
3. Run the AWSSupport-TroubleshootSSH automation.
4. Attach an Elastic IP address to the instance.

Answer: 3

Explanation:

AWSSupport-TroubleshootSSH installs the Amazon EC2Rescue tool and then checks for and corrects some issues that cause remote connection errors when connecting to a Linux machine through SSH. Run the AWSSupport-TroubleshootSSH automation to automatically repair issues by subnet, S3 buckets, or IAM role.

CORRECT: "Run the AWSSupport-TroubleshootSSH automation" is the correct answer.

INCORRECT: "Check that there is an internet gateway attached to the VPC" is incorrect. The user would be unable to connect to other instances in the same subnet if an internet gateway was not attached.

INCORRECT: "Use Trusted Advisor to check the SSH configuration" is incorrect. Trusted Advisor will not advise on SSH configuration issues.

INCORRECT: "Attach an Elastic IP address to the instance" is incorrect. The instance does not necessarily need an Elastic IP address. A public IP address will do, and other instances are contactable so the subnet must be configured to automatically assign public IP addresses.

References:

https://aws.amazon.com/premiumsupport/knowledge-center/ec2-ssh-errors-automation-workflow/

Save time with our exam-specific cheat sheets:

https://digitalcloud.training/certification-training/aws-certified-sysops-administrator-associate/aws-systems-manager/

QUESTION 61

An AWS Lambda function has been connected to an Amazon VPC and is no longer able to connect to an external service on the internet. How can this issue be resolved?

1. Update the function code to avoid the VPC and connect directly.
2. Add an entry to the subnet route table pointing to a NAT gateway.
3. Enable enhanced VPC routing for the AWS Lambda function.
4. Create a virtual private gateway (VGW) to the subnet.

Answer: 2

Explanation:

When you connect a function to a VPC, all outbound requests go through your VPC. To connect to the internet, configure your VPC to send outbound traffic from the function's subnet to a NAT gateway in a public subnet.

CORRECT: "Add an entry to the subnet route table pointing to a NAT gateway" is the correct answer.

INCORRECT: "Update the function code to avoid the VPC and connect directly" is incorrect. This is not possible. Once the function is connected to a VPC all traffic goes via the VPC.

INCORRECT: "Enable enhanced VPC routing for the AWS Lambda function" is incorrect. There is no such thing in relation to Lambda (it exists for Amazon RedShift).

INCORRECT: "Create a virtual private gateway (VGW) to the subnet" is incorrect. A VGW is used for connecting to an on-premises network using an AWS Managed VPN.

References:

https://docs.aws.amazon.com/lambda/latest/dg/troubleshooting-networking.html

Save time with our exam-specific cheat sheets:

https://digitalcloud.training/certification-training/aws-certified-sysops-administrator-associate/amazon-virtual-private-cloud-vpc/

QUESTION 62

A manager has requested that Developers using a dedicated testing account should only be able to use the t2.micro instance type. A CloudOps Administrator has created an AWS Organizations SCP and applied it to the correct OU. However, Developers are still able to launch other instance types. What needs to be corrected in the SCP policy statement?

```
{
  "Version": "2012-10-17",
  "Statement": [
    {
      "Sid": "RequireMicroInstanceType",
      "Effect": "Deny",
      "Action": "ec2:RunInstances",
      "Resource": "arn:aws:ec2:*:*:instance/*",
      "Condition": {
        "StringEquals":{
          "ec2:InstanceType":"t2.micro"
        }
      }
    }
  ]
}
```

1. Change the Resource statement to "arn:aws:ec2:*:*:t2.micro/*"
2. Change the Effect statement from Deny to Allow
3. Change the Condition statement to StringNotEquals
4. Change the date in the version statement to the current date

Answer: 3

Explanation:

The Condition statement should use the StringNotEquals as this is policy uses a deny effect. This change will result in denying any ec2:RunInstances requests where the ec2:InstanceType is not t2.micro.

CORRECT: "Change the Condition statement to StringNotEquals" is the correct answer.

INCORRECT: "Change the Resource statement to "arn:aws:ec2:*:*:t2.micro/*"" is incorrect. This is not the correct syntax.

INCORRECT: "Change the Effect statement from Deny to Allow" is incorrect. This would not deny the ability to launch other instance types.

INCORRECT: "Change the date in the version statement to the current date" is incorrect. This is not necessary and will not resolve the issue.

References:

https://docs.aws.amazon.com/organizations/latest/userguide/orgs_manage_policies_scps_examples.html#examples_config

Save time with our exam-specific cheat sheets:

https://digitalcloud.training/certification-training/aws-certified-sysops-administrator-associate/aws-organizations/

QUESTION 63

An Amazon S3 bucket has been created for storing sensitive company data. The following bucket policy has been applied:

```
{
    "Version": "2012-10-17",
    "Id": "Policy12345663434343",
    "Statement": [
      {
        "Sid": "New policy",
        "Principal": "*",
        "Action": "s3:*",
        "Effect": "Deny",
        "Resource": ["arn:aws:s3:::examplebucket1",
                     "arn:aws:s3:::examplebucket1/*"],
        "Condition": {
          "StringNotEquals": {
            "aws:SourceVpce": "vpce-2bd1s1209"
          }
        }
      }
    ]
}
```

What will be the effect of this bucket policy?

1. Access is restricted to connections coming from a specific VPC endpoint.
2. Access is restricted to Amazon EC2 instances in a specific VPC.
3. Access is restricted to connections coming from a VPC in a different account.
4. Access is restricted to servers connecting over an AWS Direct Connect connection.

Answer: 1

Explanation:

The bucket policy restricts access to a specific bucket, examplebucket1, only from the VPC endpoint with the ID vpce-2bd1s1209. The policy denies all access to the bucket if the specified endpoint is not being used. The aws:SourceVpce condition is used to specify the endpoint. The aws:SourceVpce condition does not require an Amazon Resource Name (ARN) for the VPC endpoint resource, only the VPC endpoint ID.

CORRECT: "Access is restricted to connections coming from a specific VPC endpoint" is the correct answer.

INCORRECT: "Access is restricted to Amazon EC2 instances in a specific VPC" is incorrect. The ID relates to a VPC endpoint not a VPC.

INCORRECT: "Access is restricted to connections coming from a VPC in a different account" is incorrect. The ID relates to a VPC endpoint not a VPC.

INCORRECT: "Access is restricted to servers connecting over an AWS Direct Connect connection" is incorrect. The ID relates to a VPC endpoint not an AWS Direct Connect connection.

References:

https://docs.aws.amazon.com/AmazonS3/latest/dev/example-bucket-policies-vpc-endpoint.html

Save time with our exam-specific cheat sheets:

https://digitalcloud.training/certification-training/aws-certified-sysops-administrator-associate/amazon-virtual-private-cloud-vpc/

QUESTION 64

The following Service Control Policy (SCP) has been applied to an Organizational Unit (OU) containing an AWS Organizations member account. What will be the effect of this policy?

```json
{
    "Version": "2012-10-17",
    "Statement": [
      {
        "Sid": "RestrictEC2ForRoot",
        "Effect": "Deny",
        "Action": [
          "ec2:*"
        ],
        "Resource": [
          "*"
        ],
        "Condition": {
          "StringLike": {
            "aws:PrincipalArn": [
              "arn:aws:iam::*:root"
            ]
          }
        }
      }
    ]
}
```

1. Nothing, it is not possible to restrict root user actions.
2. The root user will not be able to perform any ec2 actions.
3. All users will be restricted from performing any ec2 actions.
4. The root user will not be able to login to EC2 instances.

Answer: 2

Explanation:

The policy restricts all access to the specified actions for the root user in the account. The actions that are restricted are included in the "Action": [" ec2:*"] statement which will restrict all EC2 actions.

CORRECT: "The root user will not be able to perform any ec2 actions." is the correct answer.

INCORRECT: "Nothing, it is not possible to restrict root user actions" is incorrect. This is incorrect, SCPs can be used to restrict root user actions in member accounts (but not in the master account).

INCORRECT: "All users will be restricted from performing any ec2 actions" is incorrect. Only the root user will be restricted based on the aws:PrincipalArn statement.

INCORRECT: "The root user will not be able to login to EC2 instances" is incorrect. This policy does not affect logging in to EC2 instances as that does not involve an API action.

References:

https://docs.aws.amazon.com/organizations/latest/userguide/orgs_manage_policies_scps_examples.html

Save time with our exam-specific cheat sheets:

https://digitalcloud.training/certification-training/aws-certified-sysops-administrator-associate/aws-organizations/

QUESTION 65

A VPC peering connection has been established between two VPCs in different AWS Regions in the same account. A CloudOps Administrator is attempting to update the security group configuration to allow inbound connections over HTTP from a security group in the second Region and is unable to complete the configuration. What could be the cause of the issue?

1. The Administrator must manually copy the security group ID and paste it in.
2. The Administrator has not yet configured the route tables appropriately.
3. The VPC peering connection is not in an active state.
4. You cannot enter the security group ID of a security group from another Region.

Answer: 4

Explanation:

It is not possible to enter the security group ID of a security group in a different Region. Therefore, the security group should be configured using network address ranges instead.

Requirements for configuring security groups:

- The peer VPC can be a VPC in your account, or a VPC in another AWS account. To reference a security group in another AWS account, include the account number in **Source** or **Destination** field; for example, 123456789012/sg-1a2b3c4d.
- You cannot reference the security group of a peer VPC that's in a different region. Instead, use the CIDR block of the peer VPC.
- To reference a security group in a peer VPC, the VPC peering connection must be in the active state.

CORRECT: "You cannot enter the security group ID of a security group from another Region" is the correct answer.

INCORRECT: "The Administrator must manually copy the security group ID and paste it in" is incorrect. This is not correct as you cannot enter security groups from a different Region.

INCORRECT: "The Administrator has not yet configured the route tables appropriately" is incorrect. The configuration of security groups is not reliant on setting up the route tables.

INCORRECT: "The VPC peering connection is not in an active state" is incorrect. Even if the VPC peering connection is active this configuration is not possible.

References:

https://docs.aws.amazon.com/vpc/latest/peering/vpc-peering-security-groups.html

Save time with our exam-specific cheat sheets:

https://digitalcloud.training/certification-training/aws-certified-sysops-administrator-associate/amazon-virtual-private-cloud-vpc/

SET 4: PRACTICE QUESTIONS ONLY

For training purposes, go directly to Set 4: Practice Questions, Answers & Explanations

QUESTION 1

A popular web application uses an Amazon DynamoDB table for storing customer transaction data. A CloudOps Administrator needs to add disaster recovery protection for the DynamoDB table. The table should be replicated to another AWS Region.

What should the CloudOps Administrator do to meet this requirement?

1. Enable a scheduled on-demand backup.
2. Enable DynamoDB Streams and add a global secondary index (GSI).
3. Enable point-in-time recovery to a second AWS Region.
4. Enable DynamoDB Streams and add a Global Table Region.

QUESTION 2

A company manager is concerned about an increase in monthly costs associated with a developer AWS account. A large team of over 60 developers use the account and the manager needs to determine the costs incurred per developer.

What should a CloudOps Administrator do to collect this information? (Select TWO.)

1. Activate the createdBy tag in the account.
2. Analyze the usage with AWS Cost Explorer.
3. Analyze the API usage with AWS CloudTrail.
4. Configure AWS Config to track resource usage.
5. Create a billing alarm in AWS Budgets.

QUESTION 3

A company stores sensitive data in a private Amazon S3 bucket. The data must be accessible to Amazon EC2 instances in an Amazon VPC, and all traffic must traverse the AWS private network.

What actions should a CloudOps Administrator take to meet these requirements and ensure the traffic does not traverse the internet?

1. Create a gateway VPC endpoint and create an IAM policy with a conditional statement limiting access to the VPC endpoint ID.
2. Create a gateway VPC endpoint and attach an S3 bucket policy with a conditional statement limiting access to the VPC endpoint ID.
3. Create an interface VPC endpoint service and associate a network load balancer. Attach an S3 bucket policy with a conditional statement limiting access to the VPC endpoint ID.
4. Create a NAT gateway in the VPC and update the VPC route table to send all Amazon S3 traffic through the NAT gateway.

QUESTION 4

A custom application is running in a single AWS region in the United States. The application runs on a fleet of Amazon EC2 instances behind a Network Load Balancer. The application provides an SFTP endpoint to users.

Recently, the application has been launched for users in Europe and the European users have reported high latency and connection instability. A CloudOps Administrator must improve performance and stability for the application.

What should the CloudOps Administrator do to meet these requirements?

1. Create an Auto Scaling group in an AWS Region in Europe.
2. Create a new Network Load Balancer in an AWS Region in Europe.
3. Create an accelerator in AWS Global Accelerator and update the DNS record.
4. Create an Amazon CloudFront distribution and update the DNS record.

QUESTION 5

A stateless web application runs on a fleet of Amazon EC2 instances. Amazon Route 53 is used to direct incoming traffic using a multivalue answer routing policy. A CloudOps Administrator attempted to add more instances ahead of an expected increase in demand and experienced an InstanceLimitExceeded error.

What should the CloudOps Administrator do to resolve this error?

1. Add new EC2 instances in a placement group.
2. Use Service Quotas to request an EC2 quota increase.
3. Launch the EC2 instances in a different Availability Zone.
4. Launch new EC2 instances in another VPC.

QUESTION 6

A web application runs on Amazon EC2 instances in an Auto Scaling group behind an Application Load Balancer (ALB). A CloudOps Administrator wants to set an alarm that triggers when all instances in the associated target group are unhealthy.

Which condition should be used with the alarm?

1. AWS/EC2 StatusCheckFailed_Instance <= 0
2. AWS/EC2 StatusCheckFailed_System >= 1
3. AWS/ApplicationELB HealthyHostCount <= 0
4. AWS/ApplicationELB UnhealthyHostCount >= 1

QUESTION 7

A company has multiple accounts that are managed using AWS Organizations. A CloudOps Administrator must setup a shared S3 bucket in a central account and grant read-only access for all users in any account within the AWS Organization. There should be no public access to the S3 bucket data.

Which parameters should the Administrator use to MOST efficiently accomplish this goal?

1. Specify all account numbers within an array as the principal.
2. Specify '*' as the principal and aws:PrincipalOrgId as a condition.
3. Specify the organization's master account as the principal.
4. Specify aws:PrincipalOrgId as the principal with the organization ID value.

QUESTION 8

A web application will be deployed that uses separate microservices running on different Amazon EC2 instances. A CloudOps Administrator has been tasked with configuring the infrastructure to route connection requests to the appropriate EC2 endpoints.

How can this be accomplished with the LEAST administrative effort?

1. Use Amazon CloudFront and forward the host header to the origin.
2. Use AWS Global Accelerator with a weighted routing policy.
3. Use a Network Load Balancer (NLB) and do path-based routing.
4. Use an Application Load Balancer (ALB) and do path-based routing.

QUESTION 9

A security team requires that AWS CloudTrail is always enabled in an AWS account. The security team has enabled CloudTrail in the account and have asked a CloudOps Administrator to ensure that if it is disabled, it is immediately and automatically re-enabled.

How can the CloudOps Administrator accomplish this requirement without writing any custom code?

1. Configure Amazon Inspector to analyze the account configuration and initiate an AWS Lambda function that re-enables CloudTrail if it is disabled.
2. Create an AWS Config rule that is invoked when the CloudTrail configuration changes. Configure the rule to invoke an AWS Lambda function to re-enable CloudTrail.
3. Create an Amazon EventBridge (Amazon CloudWatch Events) hourly rule with a schedule pattern to run an AWS Systems Manager Automation document to enable CloudTrail.
4. Create an AWS Config rule that is invoked when the CloudTrail configuration changes. Apply the AWS-ConfigureCloudTrailLogging automatic remediation action.

QUESTION 10

A CloudOps Administrator noticed an unusual number of requests to an application that runs behind an Application Load Balancer (ALB). The administrator would like to identify the IP addresses of the clients that accessed the ALB.

Which logs should the administrator use to find this information?

1. EC2 Auto Scaling logs
2. Elastic Load Balancer access logs
3. AWS CloudTrail logs
4. Amazon CloudWatch Logs

QUESTION 11

A company has several production accounts that are managed using AWS Organizations. The company policy mandates that Amazon S3 buckets should never be deleted.

What is the SIMPLEST approach a CloudOps Administrator can take to enforce this policy?

1. Set up MFA Delete on all the S3 buckets to prevent the buckets from being deleted.
2. Create an IAM group that has an IAM policy to deny the s3:DeleteBucket action on all buckets in all accounts.
3. Use service control policies to deny the s3:DeleteBucket action on all buckets in all accounts.
4. Use an Access Control List to deny the s3:DeleteBucket action at the organization level to apply the policy to all accounts.

QUESTION 12

A company runs a web application that runs from Amazon EC2 instances in a VPC. The application is fronted by an Application Load Balancer (ALB) and an Amazon CloudFront distribution. The backend uses an Amazon DynamoDB table. A CloudOps Administrator needs to investigate HTTP Layer 7 status codes from the web application.

Which log sources contain the status codes? (Select TWO.)

1. VPC Flow Logs
2. Amazon CloudTrail logs
3. ALB access logs
4. CloudFront access logs
5. Amazon DynamoDB logs

QUESTION 13

A company is running a production application across subnets in different AWS accounts within the same Region. To ensure high availability of the application, the CloudOps Administrator needs to be able to map Availability Zones across accounts.

Which actions will obtain this information? (Select TWO.)

1. Call the DescribeAvailabilityZones API operation and match the response of zoneId between the two AWS accounts.
2. Call the Describe AvailabilityZones API operation and match the response of zoneName between the two AWS accounts.
3. Call the Describe Subnets API operation and match the response of availabilityZoneName between the two AWS accounts.
4. Call the Describe Subnets API operation and match the response of availabilityZoneId between the two AWS accounts.
5. Call the Describe Subnets API operation and match the response of defaultForAz between the two AWS accounts.

QUESTION 14

A company runs a web application on several Amazon EC2 instances in an Auto Scaling group. The EC2 instances share a file system that is delivered using Amazon EFS. Though the volume of data does not change much, during periods of heavy utilization users have reported that file retrieval latency increases.

Which action should a CloudOps Administrator take to improve the performance of the file system?

1. Enable encryption in transit on the file system.
2. Configure the file system for Provisioned Throughput.
3. Remove any unused files from the file system.
4. Configure the file system for Bursting Throughput.

QUESTION 15

A CloudOps Administrator manages an Amazon Elasticsearch Service (Amazon ES) domain that is configured with a public endpoint. Users connect to the Amazon ES domain over AWS Site-to-Site VPN connections from multiple branch offices. The Administrator needs to ensure that Amazon ES can be accessed only from the branch offices while preserving existing data.

Which solution will meet these requirements?

1. Configure an identity-based access policy on Amazon ES. Add an allow statement to the policy that includes the Amazon Resource Name (ARN) for each branch office VPN connection.
2. Reconfigure the Amazon ES domain in private subnets in a VPC. Configure an IP-based domain access policy on Amazon ES and allow the private IP CIDR blocks from each branch office network.
3. Configure an IP-based domain access policy on Amazon ES. Add an allow statement to the policy that includes the private IP CIDR blocks from each branch office network.
4. Reconfigure the Amazon ES domain in private subnets in a VPC. Create a security group that allows inbound traffic from the branch office CIDR blocks.

QUESTION 16

The security policy of a company requires that all objects that are uploaded to Amazon S3 buckets must be encrypted.

Which of the following actions can be taken to meet the security policy requirements? (Select TWO.)

1. Implement an AWS Config rule that defines an S3 bucket access control list (ACL) that enforces default encryption.

2. Implement Object access control list (ACL) to deny unencrypted objects from being uploaded to the S3 bucket.
3. Implement S3 server access logs and configure an event notification. Trigger an AWS Lambda function that checks the logs for object creation events and deletes any unencrypted objects.
4. Implement Amazon S3 default encryption to make sure that any object being uploaded is encrypted before it is stored.
5. Implement S3 bucket policies to deny unencrypted objects from being uploaded to the buckets.

QUESTION 17

A company is planning to deploy an Amazon Elasticsearch Service (Amazon ES) cluster that will analyze data produced by a fleet of Amazon EC2 instances. A CloudOps Administrator must deploy an Amazon ES cluster in a highly available production-grade deployment.

Which Amazon ES configuration should the CloudOps Administrator use to meet this requirement?

1. Use a cluster of four data nodes across two AWS Regions. Deploy four dedicated master nodes in each Region.
2. Use a cluster of six data nodes across three Availability Zones. Use six dedicated master nodes.
3. Use a cluster of six data nodes across three Availability Zones. Use three dedicated master nodes.
4. Use a cluster of eight data nodes across two Availability Zones. Deploy four master nodes in a failover AWS Region.

QUESTION 18

A fleet of Amazon EC2 instances read and write data to a shared Amazon EFS file system. The security team have raised concerns that the file system is not encrypted.

How can a CloudOps Administrator resolve the issue?

1. Create a new EFS file system with encryption enabled and copy all data from the original file system.
2. Enable encryption of data in transit when mounting the file system to each EC2 instance.
3. Enable encryption on the existing EFS file system by using the AWS Command Line Interface (AWS CLI).
4. Modify the existing EFS file system through the AWS Management Console and enable AES-256 encryption.

QUESTION 19

A company needs to find a way to securely share an object from an Amazon S3 bucket that does not have public access enabled. The users who will be accessing the object do not have an AWS account.

What is the MOST operationally efficient solution that will meet this requirement?

1. Attach an S3 bucket policy that only allows object downloads from the users' IP addresses.
2. Create an IAM role that has access to the object. Instruct the users to assume the role.
3. Create an application that distributes signed cookies to the users and control access through the cookies.
4. Generate a presigned URL for the object. Share the URL with the users.

QUESTION 20

A CloudOps Administrator is deploying a new website that will run on Amazon EC2 instances in an Auto Scaling group behind an Application Load Balancer (ALB). The website's apex domain name is example.com and this name must resolve to the ALB.

What type of record set should the Administrator create in Amazon Route 53?

1. CNAME

2. ALIAS
3. SOA
4. TXT

QUESTION 21

An Amazon EC2 instance that processes large data files has an attached 1 TB General Purpose SSD (gp2) Amazon EBS volume. Amazon CloudWatch metrics on the instance show a consistent 3,000 VolumeReadOps. A CloudOps Administrator must improve the I/O performance while ensuring data integrity.

Which action will meet these requirements?

1. Increase the EBS volume to a 2 TB General Purpose SSD (gp2) volume.
2. Change the instance type to a bare metal instance.
3. Change the instance type to a Burstable Performance instance.
4. Move the data that resides on the EBS volume to the instance store.

QUESTION 22

An application runs on four Amazon EC2 instances. The application requires that a minimum of four instances must be always running to support application demand. A CloudOps Administrator must design a highly available, fault-tolerant architecture that continues to meet these requirements even if one Availability Zone becomes unavailable.

Which configuration meets these requirements?

1. Deploy two Auto Scaling groups in two Availability Zones with a minimum capacity of two instances in each group.
2. Deploy an Auto Scaling group across two Availability Zones with a minimum capacity of four instances.
3. Deploy an Auto Scaling group across three Availability Zones with a minimum capacity of six instances.
4. Deploy an Auto Scaling group across three Availability Zones with a minimum capacity of four instances.

QUESTION 23

A website is used by users in several countries. The company has implemented the website on Amazon EC2 instances in different Regions and countries. Each Regional website contains content that is specific to the country in which it is located.

A CloudOps Administrator must implement a solution that will automatically send users to the appropriate Regional website, depending on each user's location, from a single URL.

Which solution meets these requirements?

5. AWS Global Accelerator with a network load balancer.
6. Application Load Balancer with cross-zone load balancing.
7. Amazon CloudFront with cross-origin resource sharing (CORS).
8. Amazon Route 53 with a geolocation routing policy.

QUESTION 24

A CloudOps Administrator is deploying a website that must be directly accessible from the internet. The Amazon EC2 instance is running in a subnet that is configured to auto assign public IP addresses. The subnet route table has the following configuration:

Destination   **Target**

10.0.0.0/16	Local
172.31.0.0/16	pcx-123456123456

Which entry must the Administrator add to the route table to meet the requirement?

1. A route for 0.0.0.0/0 that points to an internet gateway.
2. A route for 0.0.0.0/0 that points to a NAT gateway.
3. A route for 0.0.0.0/0 that points to an egress-only internet gateway.
4. A route for 0.0.0.0/0 that points to an elastic network interface.

QUESTION 25

A critical application running on Amazon EC2 instances occasionally suffers from increased read and write latency to attached Amazon EBS volumes. A CloudOps Administrator is attempting to configure Amazon CloudWatch alarms for the DiskReadBytes metric and the DiskWriteBytes metrics. However, during busy periods when users have experienced performance degradation, the alarms have not changed to the ALARM state.

Which action will ensure that the CloudWatch alarms function correctly?

1. Install and configure the CloudWatch agent on the EC2 instance to capture the desired metrics.
2. Reconfigure the CloudWatch alarms to use the VolumeReadBytes metric and the VolumeWriteBytes metric for the EBS volumes.
3. Install and configure AWS Systems Manager Agent on the EC2 instance to capture the desired metrics.
4. Reconfigure the CloudWatch alarms to use the VolumeReadBytes metric and the VolumeWriteBytes metric for the EC2 instances.

QUESTION 26

An application uses several AWS Lambda functions that each generate a large volume of log data each day in its own Amazon CloudWatch Logs log group. A CloudOps Administrator is troubleshooting application issues and needs to generate a count of application errors, grouped by type, across all the log groups.

What should the administrator do to meet this requirement?

1. Perform an Amazon Athena query that uses the SELECT and GROUP BY keywords.
2. Perform a CloudWatch Logs Insights query that uses the stats command and count function.
3. Perform a CloudWatch Logs search that uses the groupby keyword and count function.
4. Perform an Amazon RDS query that uses the SELECT and GROUP BY keywords.

QUESTION 27

A CloudOps Administrator is deploying a new website running on Amazon EC2 instances. The application requires both incoming and outgoing connectivity to the internet.

Which combination of steps are required to provision the required connectivity? (Select TWO.)

1. Add a NAT gateway to a public subnet and update the route table.
2. Attach a private address to the elastic network interface on the EC2 instance.
3. Attach an Elastic IP address to the internet gateway.
4. Add an entry to the route table for the subnet that points to an internet gateway.
5. Create an internet gateway and attach it to a VPC.

QUESTION 28

A CloudOps Administrator is checking some performance data for an Amazon EC2 instance in Amazon CloudWatch. The administrator reviews the DiskReadBytes metric and notices that the metric shows that 0 bytes have been read during the day.

What is the most likely explanation for the metric value showing 0 bytes?

1. An Amazon EBS volume is not attached to the EC2 instance.
2. Detailed monitoring is not enabled on the EC2 instance.
3. The CloudWatch agent is not installed on the EC2 instance.
4. An instance store volume is not attached to the EC2 instance.

QUESTION 29

A CloudOps Administrator has launched an Amazon EC2 Linux instance in a public subnet. The instance obtained a public IP address, and the administrator needs to connect using an SSH client. When attempting the SSH connection, the connection attempt fails repeatedly with a timeout error.

Which action will allow the CloudOps Administrator to remotely connect to the instance?

1. Update the subnet route table with an entry for the CloudOps Administrator's IP address.
2. Update the instance security group with a rule allowing SSH inbound from the CloudOps Administrator's IP address.
3. Update the network ACL for the subnet to allow port 22 outbound to the CloudOps Administrator's IP address.
4. Update the instance security group with a rule allowing SSH outbound to the CloudOps Administrator's IP address.

QUESTION 30

A CloudOps Administrator has been asked to review an IAM policy that has been created to allow a new hire to access specific AWS services. The following policy is presented:

```
{
    "Version": "2012-10-17",
    "Statement": [
        {
            "Action": [
                "rds:CreateDBInstance",
                "elasticloadbalancing:*",
                "lambda:*",
                "sns:ListTopics*"
            ],
            "Effect": "Allow",
            "Resource": "*"
        }
    ]
}
```

Which actions does this policy allow? (Select TWO.)

1. Delete an Amazon RDS database.
2. Create an IAM role for an AWS Lambda function.
3. Delete an Amazon SNS topic.
4. Describe AWS load balancers.
5. Invoke an AWS Lambda function.

QUESTION 31

A custom application that runs on an Amazon EC2 instance has performance issues due to an application process that erroneously consumes all available CPU resources. The development team are working on a resolution and have asked a CloudOps Administrator to restart the instance when the problem occurs.

How can the administrator automate rebooting the instance if the issue is experienced for more than 2 minutes?

1. Create an Amazon CloudWatch alarm with an action to reboot the instance. Use basic monitoring.
2. Create an Amazon CloudWatch alarm with an action to reboot the instance. Use detailed monitoring.
3. Create an Amazon EventBridge rule that runs an AWS Lambda function on a schedule and reboots the instance.
4. Create an AWS CloudTrail API action that reboots the instance when resources are fully utilized.

QUESTION 32

A company is using AWS CloudTrail and needs to ensure that the log files stored in S3 are not tampered with. The company must be able to determine if log files are modified, deleted, or unchanged.

How can a CloudOps Administrator meet this requirement MOST efficiently?

1. Update the trail and enable log file validation.
2. Update the S3 bucket and enable log file validation.
3. Create an AWS Lambda function that computes an MD5 hash of the log files.
4. Enable default encryption on the S3 bucket.

QUESTION 33

An application uses an Amazon RDS database in a single AWS Region. The company wants to add disaster recovery (DR) capability to the database across geographic locations. A CloudOps Administrator must add DR for the database.

Which solutions offers the lowest recovery time objective (RTO) and recovery point objective (RPO)?

1. Run an AWS Lambda function on a schedule to create and copy snapshots across Regions.
2. Take automated snapshots and replicate them across Regions.
3. Create a Multi-AZ read replica for the database.
4. Create a cross-Region read replica for the database.

QUESTION 34

An eCommerce company run a website that is hosted on burstable performance Amazon EC2 instances in an Auto Scaling group. The website occasionally experiences sustained spikes in sales for a few hours when email promotions are sent out. Users have reported poor performance a couple of hours into these events. A CloudOps Administrator noticed that the CPU utilization is <30% across the fleet and the ASG did not scale as it is configured to scale when CPU utilization is >60%.

How can the CloudOps Administrator resolve the performance issues?

1. Add an Elastic Load Balancer and enable ELB health checks.
2. Create an Amazon CloudFront distribution for the Auto Scaling group.
3. Configure unlimited mode for the EC2 instances.
4. Modify the Auto Scaling group to use EBS-optimized EC2 instances.

QUESTION 35

An application allows users to upload PDF files directly to an Amazon S3 bucket in the us-east-1 Region. Users are located globally, and many remote users have reported slow upload times. A CloudOps Administrator needs to improve the upload speed for the PDF files.

How can this be achieved?
1. Enable S3 Transfer Acceleration for the S3 bucket.
2. Create S3 access points in Regions closer to the users.
3. Enable cross-Region replication for the S3 bucket.
4. Create an accelerator in AWS Global Accelerator.

QUESTION 36

A company runs a highly elastic application across hundreds of Amazon EC2 instances in private subnets. The application uses EC2 Auto Scaling which launches and terminates instances across three Availability Zones (AZs). The application connects to a third-party API over the public internet and the CloudOps Administrator must provide a list of static IP addresses for the third party to whitelist in their firewalls.

Which solution will meet these requirements?

1. Configure a NAT gateway in the public subnet of each AZ. Add a route to the NAT gateway to the route table of each private subnet.
2. Attach an Elastic IP address to each AZ. Associate the Elastic IP with the EC2 instances within each AZ.
3. Attach an Elastic IP address to the internet gateway in the public subnet. Add a route to the internet gateway to the route table of each private subnet.
4. Attach an Elastic IP address to each EC2 instance. Configure a VPC endpoint for outbound traffic.

QUESTION 37

A CloudOps Administrator has launched a new web application and Amazon RDS database instance in private subnets within a VPC. The administrator updated the application with the connection information for the DB. After ensuring the application and DB are fully deployed, the administrator checked the web server logs and noticed that the connection to the database is repeatedly failing.

Which of the following may be causes of the connectivity problems? (Select TWO.)

1. The source used to connect is not authorized in the database security group egress rules.
2. The database instance does not have an Elastic IP address attached.
3. The source used to connect is not authorized in the database security group ingress rules.
4. The wrong DNS name or database endpoint was used to connect.
5. The database is still being created and is not available for connectivity.

QUESTION 38

A popular application uses an Amazon Aurora DB cluster for storing data. The application's usage is highly variable with unpredictable spikes in traffic. Much of the load is database queries and the same query is rarely performed multiple times. The application logs show that performance issues have occurred during peak usage periods when many searches were submitted.

A CloudOps Administrator must improve the performance of the application. Which solution will meet these requirements?

1. Create an Amazon ElastiCache cluster to cache database queries and update the application to check the cache.
2. Implement Aurora Auto Scaling to scale the number of replicas and update the application to use the Aurora reader endpoint.
3. Implement Aurora Auto Scaling to scale the database instance size based on the number of queries submitted.
4. Create RAID 0 arrays for the Aurora database cluster instances to improve I/O performance.

QUESTION 39

A CloudOps Administrator attempts to deploy many EC2 instances to support a large distributed application workload. The instances are being deployed in several batches and on the most recent deployment the administrator received the InstanceLimitExceeded error.

What should the CloudOps Administrator do to resolve this error?

1. Use Service Quotas to request an EC2 quota increase.
2. Use the Amazon EC2 console to request an EBS quota increase.
3. Launch the EC2 instances in a different Availability Zone.
4. Launch new EC2 instances in another VPC within the Region.

QUESTION 40

A company uses several AWS accounts by different business units for development purposes. An additional account is used by security admins purposes. The security admins have requested that they be granted access to review the configuration of Amazon EC2 resources in the development accounts to ensure security best practices are being followed.

Which solution will meet these requirements in the MOST secure manner?

1. Create an IAM policy in each development account that has read-only access to Amazon EC2 resources. Assign the policy to an IAM user. Share the user credentials with the security administrators.
2. Create an IAM policy in each development account that has administrator access to all Amazon EC2 actions. Assign the policy to an IAM user. Share the user credentials with the security administrators.
3. Create an IAM policy in each development account that has read-only access to Amazon EC2 resources. Assign the policy to a cross-account IAM role. Ask the security administrators to assume the role from their account.
4. Create an IAM policy in each development account that has administrator access to Amazon EC2 resources. Assign the policy to a cross-account IAM role. Ask the security administrators to assume the role from their account.

QUESTION 41

A company's management team need to view and track and the cost of separate projects within an AWS account. A CloudOps Administrator must setup the account so that this information can be viewed for each project in AWS Cost Explorer.

What must the administrator do to set this up?

1. Activate cost allocation tags. Tag resources based on the project they are associated with.
2. Use AWS Organizations and enable consolidated billing. Create AWS Cost and Usage Reports.
3. Create billing alerts in AWS Budgets that track the resources associated with each project.
4. Use cost categories to define custom groups that are based on AWS cost and usage dimensions.

QUESTION 42

A company is deploying an internet-facing application in the AWS Cloud that will run behind an Application Load Balancer (ALB). The ALB will be configured with a secure listener. The CloudOps Administrator must ensure that the SSL/TLS certificate used by the listener automatically renews.

Which solution MOST efficiently meets these requirements?

1. Request a public certificate by using AWS Certificate Manager (ACM) and use Email validation. ACM will automatically renew the certificate.
2. Request a public certificate by using AWS Certificate Manager (ACM). Write an AWS Lambda function that automates the renewal of the certificate.
3. Request a public certificate by using AWS Certificate Manager (ACM) and use DNS validation. ACM will automatically renew the certificate.
4. Request a private certificate by using AWS Certificate Manager (ACM) and use DNS validation. ACM will automatically renew the certificate.

QUESTION 43

A company's security team updated their security policy and require that multi-factor authentication (MFA) is implemented for all IAM users. A CloudOps Administrator has created a policy that denies API calls that are not authenticated with MFA.

How can users authenticate with MFA when issuing API calls using the AWS CLI?

1. Add the users who require CLI access to an IAM user group. Use a policy condition to exclude the MFA requirement for the user group.
2. Instruct users to run the *sts get-session-token* AWS CLI command use the returned temporary security credentials to sign API calls.
3. Instruct the users to log into the AWS Management Console with MFA before issuing API calls using the CLI.
4. Users will not be able to use the AWS CLI due to the policy restriction and must use the AWS Management Console.

QUESTION 44

A company is using AWS Organizations and wants to implement tag policies to standardize tags across resources in the organization's accounts. A CloudOps Administrator signs in to the organization's management account with the required permissions but cannot activate tag policies.

Which of the following may resolve this issue?

1. Enable all features for the organization.
2. Enable consolidated billing for the organization.
3. Sign in to each member account and enable tag policies.
4. Enable service control policies (SCPs) first.

QUESTION 45

An application runs in on Amazon EC2 instances in a private subnet and processes images stored in an Amazon S3 bucket. The EC2 instances have an attached IAM role that provides the required permissions to access the bucket. However, the application is unable to initiate connections to the S3 bucket.

Which action will solve this problem MOST securely?

1. Create an S3 gateway endpoint. Configure the route table for the private subnet.
2. Add a bucket policy to the S3 bucket permitting access from the IAM role.
3. Update the route table of the private subnet with a route to the internet gateway.
4. Create a NAT gateway in the private subnet and update the private subnet route table.

QUESTION 46

An AWS Lambda function is used to process data received by a web application and store the processed data in an Amazon RDS database. The credentials for accessing the RDS database are stored in the Lambda function code.

A CloudOps Administrator needs to update the configuration so the database credentials are not stored in plaintext and the password is rotated every 30 days.

Which solution will meet these requirements in the MOST operationally efficient manner?

1. Use AWS Certificate Manager to create a public certificate that automatically rotates every 30 days. Update the RDS database to use certificate-based authentication and configure the Lambda function with the private key.
2. Use AWS Secrets Manager to store credentials for the database. Create a secret in Secrets Manager, select the RDS database, and configure and automatic rotation schedule. Update the Lambda function to use the credentials stored from Secrets Manager.

3. Use AWS Key Management Service (KMS) to create a key that can encrypt the database password. Create a custom Lambda function that rotates the password and uses the KMS key to encrypt it. Store the encrypted password in environment variables.
4. Use AWS Systems Manager Parameter Store to create a secure string to store credentials for the database. Create a custom Lambda function that rotates the password. Use Amazon EventBridge to schedule the custom function to run every 30 days. Update the Lambda function to use the credentials from Parameter Store.

QUESTION 47

A Development account is being used to test a CPU-heavy application. To save costs, a CloudOps Administrator needs a solution to stop Amazon EC2 instances that are not in use in the account

Which solution will meet this requirement?

1. Use Amazon Athena to search AWS CloudTrail logs. Invoke a Lambda function to stop the EC2 instances when there is no API activity.
2. Create an Amazon CloudWatch metric to stop the EC2 instances when the VolumeIdleTime metric is >1800 seconds.
3. Use AWS Config to identify resource state changes and invoke an AWS Lambda function that stops the EC2 instances.
4. Create an Amazon CloudWatch alarm that monitors the CPUUtilization metric and stops the EC2 instances if the utilization is <5% for a 30-minute period.

QUESTION 48

An Amazon RDS database is encrypted using a customer managed AWS KMS key. Snapshots of the database need to be shared with another AWS account owned by the same company. The database must always remain encrypted.

How can a CloudOps Administrator share the encrypted database snapshots?

1. Extract the data from the database snapshot using an AWS Lambda function and write it to an encrypted Amazon S3 bucket. Use a second AWS Lambda function in the target account that retrieves the data from bucket and creates an encrypted snapshot.
2. Add the second AWS account as a key user in the key policy of the customer managed KMS key that is used to encrypt the database. Copy and share the database snapshot with the target account using the KMS key.
3. Create an unencrypted copy of the database snapshot. Share the database snapshot with the target account and use a customer managed KMS key to encrypt the snapshot.
4. Create a copy of the database snapshot and encrypt it with the default AWS KMS encryption key. Add the second AWS account as a key user in the key policy of the KMS key. Copy and share the database snapshot with the target account.

QUESTION 49

A company uses Amazon S3 to store media content that is served through an Amazon CloudFront distribution. The media is consumed by global users but due to agreements in place in certain countries the content should not be viewable there.

What is the MOST cost effective solution to block access in specific countries?

1. Enable the geo restriction feature in the CloudFront distribution and create a blacklist of banned countries.
2. Update a Network ACL with a deny rule based on the IP addresses of the banned countries.
3. Create a secondary origin access identity (OAI). Configure the S3 bucket policy to prevent access from unauthorized countries.
4. Use Amazon Route 53 geolocation routing and route traffic from banned countries to an Amazon EC2 website that returns a 403 Forbidden HTTP response.

QUESTION 50

A CloudOps Administrator us unable to connect to an Amazon EC2 instance which keeps returning a "request timed out" error message. The administrator is connecting from the public IP address of 200.10.11.12 and the instance's private IP address is 172.31.16.25. A VPC flow log has captured the following information:

2 0123456789992 eni-12345c7b2012345678 200.10.11.12 172.31.16.25 0 0 1 4 232 1357101112 1357101182 ACCEPT OK

2 0123456789992 eni-12345c7b2012345678 172.31.16.25 200.10.11.12 0 0 1 4 232 1357101112 1357101182 REJECT OK

What could be the cause of the problem?

1. Security group inbound deny rules.
2. Security group outbound deny rules.
3. Network ACL inbound rules.
4. Network ACL outbound rules.

QUESTION 51

A stateful web applications runs on a fleet of Amazon EC2 instances behind an Application Load Balancer (ALB). The ALB is configured as the origin in an Amazon CloudFront distribution. Users who have recently signed in to the application have reported that they are sometimes asked to re-authenticate.

Which combination of actions should a CloudOps Administrator take to resolve this problem? (Select TWO.)

1. Configure the cache behavior to forward cookies.
2. Enable the slow start duration on the ALB target group.
3. Configure the cache behavior to forward headers.
4. Enable group-level stickiness on the ALB listener rule.
5. Enable sticky sessions on the ALB target group.

QUESTION 52

An application vendor has reported that the latest version of their application is vulnerable to a cross-site scripting (XSS) attack. The CloudOps team has recently updated to the latest version, and it would be difficult to roll back.

Which AWS service can the CloudOps team use to mitigate this issue?

1. AWS Shield Standard
2. AWS Secrets Manager
3. AWS KMS
4. AWS WAF

QUESTION 53

A company uses Amazon ElastiCache Redis as the database for a web application. The database uses a single shard running on a large node which has 20% freeable memory. A CloudOps Administrator has been asked to resize the cluster and add high availability for the database.

Which actions should the administrator perform? (Select TWO.)

1. Add a read replica in a different Availability Zone.
2. Resize the cluster nodes to use extra-large nodes.
3. Add a shard in a different Availability Zone.
4. Enable multithreading and update the application.
5. Enable cluster mode and configure high availability.

QUESTION 54

A company requires a solution for caching content globally and delivering it only to authorized users.

Which solution will meet these requirements?

1. Store the content in an Amazon S3 bucket with public access disabled. Create an Amazon CloudFront distribution that uses an origin access identity (OAI) to access the S3 bucket. Use CloudFront signed URLs to restrict access to the authorized users.
2. Store the content in an Amazon S3 bucket with public access disabled. Create an Amazon CloudFront distribution that uses an origin access identity (OAI) to access the S3 bucket. Use S3 presigned URLs to restrict access to the authorized users.
3. Store the content in an Amazon S3 bucket with public access disabled. Create an IAM role with permissions to the S3 bucket. Create an Amazon CloudFront distribution and assign the IAM role. Use CloudFront signed URLs to restrict access to the authorized users.
4. Store the content in an Amazon S3 bucket with public access enabled. Create an Amazon CloudFront distribution and enable field-level encryption. Use S3 presigned URLs to restrict access to the authorized users.

QUESTION 55

A company manages several applications running across multiple AWS Regions. The applications use Amazon EC2 On-Demand instances and AWS Lambda functions. The CloudOps team must optimize the cost of running the workloads. The overall consumption of compute resources is stable.

Which approach should the CloudOps team use to optimize costs?

1. Purchase Compute Savings Plans based recommendations in Cost Explorer.
2. Purchase Convertible Reserved Instances based on CloudWatch metrics.
3. Purchase EC2 Instance Savings Plans based recommendations in Cost Explorer.
4. Purchase Standard Reserved Instances based on CloudWatch metrics.

QUESTION 56

An application deployed on several Amazon EC2 instances in a VPC requires very low latency between nodes. A CloudOps Administrator has noticed unacceptable latency for inter-node communications and must find a solution to reduce latency.

Which approach should the administrator take?

1. Redeploy the application in a dedicated subnet.
2. Redeploy the application in a single Availability Zone.
3. Redeploy the application in a placement group.
4. Redeploy the application in an Auto Scaling group.

QUESTION 57

A company manages Amazon EC2 instances across several AWS Regions. A CloudOps Administrator has been tasked with ensuring that all instances are appropriately tagged.

What is the MOST operationally efficient way to identify tagged and untagged EC2 instances?

1. Create a tag-based resource group in AWS Resource Groups and choose a resource type of AWS::EC2::Instance.
2. Generate a cost and usage report in AWS Cost Explorer, choose a service type of EC2-Instances and filter by tag.
3. Use Cost Explorer. Choose a service type of EC2-Instances, and group by Resource.
4. Use Tag Editor in AWS Resource Groups. Select all Regions and choose a resource type of AWS::EC2::Instance.
5. Enable AWS Organizations and create a tag policy. Use Tag Policies in AWS Resource Groups to generate a compliance report.

QUESTION 58

A company is using AWS Organizations with multiple AWS accounts. The company has purchases Reserved Instances (RIs) and wants to ensure that each member account only receives discounts associated with RIs they own and not for RIs owned by other accounts.

Which solution will meet these requirements?

1. Purchase RIs in individual member accounts. Disable RI discount sharing in the management account.
2. Purchase RIs in individual member accounts. Disable RI discount sharing in the member accounts.
3. Purchase RIs in the management account. Disable RI discount sharing in the management account.
4. Purchase RIs in the management account. Disable RI discount sharing in the member accounts.

QUESTION 59

A company has an application deployed behind an internet-facing Application Load Balancer (ALB). A CloudOps Administrator is concerned about DDoS attacks and wants to use AWS WAF to implement rate limiting for the ALB.

Which solution will meet these requirements?

1. Create a web ACL with a block default action. Create a rate-based rule to allow the matching traffic. Associate the web ACL with the ALB.
2. Create a web ACL with an allow default action. Create a rate-based rule to block the matching traffic. Associate the web ACL with the ALB.
3. Create a web ACL with a block default action. Create a regular rule to allow the matching traffic with an IP match condition. Associate the web ACL with the ALB.
4. Create a web ACL with an allow default action. Create a regular rule to block the matching traffic with an IP match condition. Associate the web ACL with the ALB.

QUESTION 60

A CloudOps Administrator reviewed the performance of an Amazon CloudFront distribution and noticed the cache hit ratio was less than 20% causing excessive origin requests. The administrator needs to implement configuration changes to increase the cache hit ratio.

Which combination of changes should the administrator implement? (Select TWO.)

1. Modify the cache behavior settings to ensure only required cookies, query strings, and headers are forwarded.
2. Decrease the origin response timeout to cause more objects to be returned from the cache.
3. Change the viewer protocol policy to redirect HTTP to HTTPS to increase security.
4. Restrict allowed HTTP methods to GET and HEAD to limit the methods forwarded to the origin.
5. Use the Cache-Control max-age directive to increase the time objects remain in the cache.

QUESTION 61

A company uses third-party software to collect a large volume of application log files and store them in an Amazon S3 bucket. The company needs a fully managed service to search and analyze the log files and visualize the data using Kibana.

Which solution should the company use?

1. Create an Amazon Kinesis Data Firehose delivery stream to ingest data from the S3 bucket and stream it to the Elasticsearch domain.
2. Create an Amazon Elasticsearch cluster and use AWS Lambda to process the data from the S3 bucket and stream it to the Elasticsearch domain.
3. Create an Amazon DynamoDB table. Use an AWS Lambda function to load data from the S3 bucket to the table.

4. Create Elasticsearch cluster on Amazon EC2 instances and use AWS Lambda to process the data from the S3 bucket and stream it to the Elasticsearch domain.

QUESTION 62

A CloudOps Administrator has deployed an application using an AWS CloudFormation stack set across multiple AWS accounts and Regions. The administrator plans to deploy and updated template and wants to test the update in subset of the accounts and Regions before rolling it out to the entire stack set.

How can the administrator implement the test update?

1. Create a nested stack to deploy the update.
2. Use a change set for the stack set to test the update.
3. Update the stack set and select a single account and Region.
4. Create a separate stack set to test the update.

QUESTION 63

A CloudOps Administrator has created an Amazon CloudFront distribution that uses an Amazon S3 bucket as the origin. The S3 static website endpoint is used as the origin domain name.

When testing access the administrator receives a 403 Access Denied message.

Which action should resolve this issue?

1. Remove the default bucket policy that denies read access to the bucket.
2. Ensure default encryption using the Amazon S3-managed keys.
3. Create a bucket policy that allows public read access for all objects in the bucket.
4. Create a bucket policy that allows public read access to the bucket.

QUESTION 64

A company uses AWS Organizations with consolidated billing. A CloudOps Administrator would like to be alerted if the total billing for all accounts within the organization exceeds a specific threshold.

How can the administrator set this up?

1. Enable the Receive Billing Alerts preference in the payer account and setup a billing alarm in Amazon CloudWatch. Use SNS to send a notification based on the alarm.
2. Enable the Receive Billing Alerts preference in each member account and setup a billing alarm in Amazon CloudWatch in the payer account. Use SNS to send a notification based on the alarm.
3. Enable the Receive Billing Alerts preference in the payer account and setup a billing alarm in AWS Config. Use SNS to send a notification based on the alarm.
4. Enable the Receive Billing Alerts preference in each member account and setup a billing alarm in AWS Config in the payer account. Use SNS to send a notification based on the alarm.

QUESTION 65

A company wants to use an AWS IAM role with a SAML 2.0-compliant identity provider (IdP) and AWS to permit federated users to access the AWS Management Console. The workflow should open the AWS Management Console on behalf of the user.

Which of the following workflow steps should be included?

1. Configure the client to directly call the AssumeRoleWithSAML API.
2. Configure the client to post a SAML assertion and use an AWS SSO endpoint.
3. Configure the client to directly call the AssumeRoleWithWebIdentity API.
4. Configure the client to post a SAML assertion and use an Amazon Cognito endpoint.

SET 4: PRACTICE QUESTIONS AND ANSWERS

QUESTION 1

A popular web application uses an Amazon DynamoDB table for storing customer transaction data. A CloudOps Administrator needs to add disaster recovery protection for the DynamoDB table. The table should be replicated to another AWS Region.

What should the CloudOps Administrator do to meet this requirement?

1. Enable a scheduled on-demand backup.
2. Enable DynamoDB Streams and add a global secondary index (GSI).
3. Enable point-in-time recovery to a second AWS Region.
4. Enable DynamoDB Streams and add a Global Table Region.

Answer: 4

Explanation:

Global tables build on the global Amazon DynamoDB footprint to provide you with a fully managed, multi-region, and multi-active database that delivers fast, local, read and write performance for massively scaled, global applications. Global tables replicate your DynamoDB tables automatically across your choice of AWS Regions.

Global tables use DynamoDB Streams to propagate changes between replicas. A DynamoDB stream is an ordered flow of information about changes to items in a DynamoDB table. Whenever an application creates, updates, or deletes items in the table, streams writes a stream record with the primary key attributes of the items that were modified.

To create a Global table, you must enable DynamoDB Streams and then add an AWS Region to which the table should be replicated.

CORRECT: "Enable DynamoDB Streams and add a Global Table Region" is the correct answer.

INCORRECT: "Enable a scheduled on-demand backup" is incorrect. This will not provide disaster recovery as the data is stored in the same Region. Though you can restore across Regions if there is a Region outage this will not be possible so you would not be protected.

INCORRECT: "Enable DynamoDB Streams and add a global secondary index (GSI)" is incorrect. A GSI is not used to enable disaster recovery.

INCORRECT: "Enable point-in-time recovery to a second AWS Region" is incorrect. You cannot enable PITR to a second AWS Region. Instead, you would need to restore across Regions.

References:

https://aws.amazon.com/blogs/database/how-to-use-amazon-dynamodb-global-tables-to-power-multiregion-architectures/

QUESTION 2

A company manager is concerned about an increase in monthly costs associated with a developer AWS account. A large team of over 60 developers use the account and the manager needs to determine the costs incurred per developer.

What should a CloudOps Administrator do to collect this information? (Select TWO.)

1. Activate the createdBy tag in the account.
2. Analyze the usage with AWS Cost Explorer.
3. Analyze the API usage with AWS CloudTrail.
4. Configure AWS Config to track resource usage.

5. Create a billing alarm in AWS Budgets.

Answer: 1,2

Explanation:

The AWS generated tags createdBy is a tag that AWS defines and applies to supported AWS resources for cost allocation purposes. To use the AWS generated tags, a management account owner must activate it in the Billing and Cost Management console.

The createdBy tag can be used to track the resources created by each individual developer. The manager can then use AWS Cost Explorer to report on the total costs incurred per developer.

CORRECT: "Activate the createdBy tag in the account" is a correct answer.

CORRECT: "Analyze the usage with AWS Cost Explorer" is also a correct answer.

INCORRECT: "Analyze the API usage with AWS CloudTrail" is incorrect. API usage data cannot be used to report on the costs incurred per developer.

INCORRECT: "Configure AWS Config to track resource usage" is incorrect. AWS Config is used for configuration compliance, not cost management.

INCORRECT: "Create a billing alarm in AWS Budgets" is incorrect. You cannot create a billing alarm in AWS Budgets that is triggered on costs incurred per developer.

References:

https://docs.aws.amazon.com/awsaccountbilling/latest/aboutv2/aws-tags.html

QUESTION 3

A company stores sensitive data in a private Amazon S3 bucket. The data must be accessible to Amazon EC2 instances in an Amazon VPC, and all traffic must traverse the AWS private network.

What actions should a CloudOps Administrator take to meet these requirements and ensure the traffic does not traverse the internet?

1. Create a gateway VPC endpoint and create an IAM policy with a conditional statement limiting access to the VPC endpoint ID.
2. Create a gateway VPC endpoint and attach an S3 bucket policy with a conditional statement limiting access to the VPC endpoint ID.
3. Create an interface VPC endpoint service and associate a network load balancer. Attach an S3 bucket policy with a conditional statement limiting access to the VPC endpoint ID.
4. Create a NAT gateway in the VPC and update the VPC route table to send all Amazon S3 traffic through the NAT gateway.

Answer: 2

Explanation:

You can use Amazon S3 bucket policies to control access to buckets from specific virtual private cloud (VPC) endpoints, or specific VPCs. Using a VPC endpoint will ensure that all traffic goes via the AWS private network and does not traverse the internet.

VPC endpoints for Amazon S3 provide two ways to control access to your Amazon S3 data:

- You can control the requests, users, or groups that are allowed through a specific VPC endpoint using an endpoint policy.
- You can control which VPCs or VPC endpoints have access to your buckets by using Amazon S3 bucket policies.

In this case the administrator can configure a gateway endpoint and attach an S3 bucket that only allows access from the VPC endpoint ID. This will ensure that only the EC2 instances using the gateway endpoint will be able to perform actions on the S3 bucket.

CORRECT: "Create a gateway VPC endpoint and attach an S3 bucket policy with a conditional statement limiting access to the VPC endpoint ID" is the correct answer.

INCORRECT: "Create a gateway VPC endpoint and create an IAM policy with a conditional statement limiting access to the VPC endpoint ID" is incorrect. A bucket policy should be used as bucket policies are attached to resources such as S3 buckets.

INCORRECT: "Create an interface VPC endpoint service and associate a network load balancer. Attach an S3 bucket policy with a conditional statement limiting access to the VPC endpoint ID" is incorrect. You cannot use an interface endpoint with an S3 bucket.

INCORRECT: "Create a NAT gateway in the VPC and update the VPC route table to send all Amazon S3 traffic through the NAT gateway" is incorrect. You cannot secure traffic to an S3 bucket by using a NAT gateway.

References:

https://docs.aws.amazon.com/AmazonS3/latest/userguide/example-bucket-policies-vpc-endpoint.html

Save time with our exam-specific cheat sheets:

https://digitalcloud.training/certification-training/aws-certified-sysops-administrator-associate/amazon-virtual-private-cloud-vpc/

QUESTION 4

A custom application is running in a single AWS region in the United States. The application runs on a fleet of Amazon EC2 instances behind a Network Load Balancer. The application provides an SFTP endpoint to users.

Recently, the application has been launched for users in Europe and the European users have reported high latency and connection instability. A CloudOps Administrator must improve performance and stability for the application.

What should the CloudOps Administrator do to meet these requirements?

1. Create an Auto Scaling group in an AWS Region in Europe.
2. Create a new Network Load Balancer in an AWS Region in Europe.
3. Create an accelerator in AWS Global Accelerator and update the DNS record.
4. Create an Amazon CloudFront distribution and update the DNS record.

Answer: 3

Explanation:

AWS Global Accelerator is a networking service that helps you improve the availability and performance of the applications that you offer to your global users. It provides static IP addresses that provide a fixed entry point to your applications and eliminate the complexity of managing specific IP addresses for different AWS Regions and Availability Zones.

AWS Global Accelerator always routes user traffic to the optimal endpoint based on performance, reacting instantly to changes in application health, your user's location, and policies that you configure.

The administrator can create an accelerator that directs traffic to application endpoints in USA and Europe. This will ensure that European users are directed to an endpoint for the application that is geographically closer. Amazon Route 53 must be updated to direct traffic to the accelerator rather than the NLB.

CORRECT: "Create an accelerator in AWS Global Accelerator and update the DNS record" is the correct answer.

INCORRECT: "Create an Auto Scaling group in an AWS Region in Europe" is incorrect. This alone will not help. The ASG should have an NLB in front and a mechanism for directing traffic locally must be used. This could be implemented using Route 53 routing policies or AWS Global Accelerator. AWS GA will assist more with stability as it directs traffic via CloudFront edge locations.

INCORRECT: "Create a new Network Load Balancer in an AWS Region in Europe" is incorrect. As above, there must be a way to dynamically route traffic to the Region and reduce latency and instability.

INCORRECT: "Create an Amazon CloudFront distribution and update the DNS record" is incorrect. CloudFront cannot be used for the SFTP protocol.

References:

https://aws.amazon.com/global-accelerator/faqs/

QUESTION 5

A stateless web application runs on a fleet of Amazon EC2 instances. Amazon Route 53 is used to direct incoming traffic using a multivalue answer routing policy. A CloudOps Administrator attempted to add more instances ahead of an expected increase in demand and experienced an InstanceLimitExceeded error.

What should the CloudOps Administrator do to resolve this error?

1. Add new EC2 instances in a placement group.
2. Use Service Quotas to request an EC2 quota increase.
3. Launch the EC2 instances in a different Availability Zone.
4. Launch new EC2 instances in another VPC.

Answer: 2

Explanation:

The InstanceLimitExceeded error indicates that you reached the limit on the number of running On-Demand instances that you can launch in a Region. You can request an instance limit increase on a per-Region basis.

You can use the **Limits** page in the Amazon EC2 console to request an increase in your Amazon EC2 or Amazon VPC resources, on a per-Region basis. Alternatively, you can request an increase using Service Quotas.

CORRECT: "Use Service Quotas to request an EC2 quota increase" is the correct answer.

INCORRECT: "Add new EC2 instances in a placement group" is incorrect. This will not offer any advantages.

INCORRECT: "Launch the EC2 instances in a different Availability Zone" is incorrect. The limits are per Region so this will not help.

INCORRECT: "Launch new EC2 instances in another VPC" is incorrect. The limits are per Region so this will not help.

References:

https://aws.amazon.com/premiumsupport/knowledge-center/ec2-InstanceLimitExceeded-error/

https://docs.aws.amazon.com/AWSEC2/latest/UserGuide/ec2-resource-limits.html

Save time with our exam-specific cheat sheets:

https://digitalcloud.training/certification-training/aws-certified-sysops-administrator-associate/amazon-ec2/

QUESTION 6

A web application runs on Amazon EC2 instances in an Auto Scaling group behind an Application Load Balancer (ALB). A CloudOps Administrator wants to set an alarm that triggers when all instances in the associated target group are unhealthy.

Which condition should be used with the alarm?

1. AWS/EC2 StatusCheckFailed_Instance <= 0
2. AWS/EC2 StatusCheckFailed_System >= 1
3. AWS/ApplicationELB HealthyHostCount <= 0
4. AWS/ApplicationELB UnhealthyHostCount >= 1

Answer: 3

Explanation:

The alarm condition should be configured to monitor the metrics associated with the health status of the EC2 instances in the ALBs associated target group. The namespace should be AWS/ApplicationELB and the metric should be configured as HealthyHostCount.

This metric monitors the number of targets that are considered healthy (in the TargetGroup dimension). The threshold of <= 0 means that if there are no healthy instances, the alarm will be triggered. If any instances are healthy, the alarm will not be triggered.

CORRECT: "AWS/ApplicationELB HealthyHostCount <= 0" is the correct answer.

INCORRECT: "AWS/ApplicationELB UnhealthyHostCount >= 1" is incorrect. This alarm would trigger when there are 1 or more unhealthy instances, rather than when all instances are unhealthy.

INCORRECT: "AWS/EC2 StatusCheckFailed_Instance <= 0" is incorrect. This metric is associated with the EC2 namespace and reports whether the instance has passed the instance status check in the last minute. Status checks and health checks are separate.

INCORRECT: "AWS/EC2 StatusCheckFailed_System >= 1" is incorrect. This metric is also associated with the EC2 namespace and reports whether the instance has passed the system status check in the last minute.

References:

https://docs.aws.amazon.com/elasticloadbalancing/latest/application/load-balancer-cloudwatch-metrics.html

Save time with our exam-specific cheat sheets:

https://digitalcloud.training/certification-training/aws-certified-sysops-administrator-associate/amazon-cloudwatch/

QUESTION 7

A company has multiple accounts that are managed using AWS Organizations. A CloudOps Administrator must setup a shared S3 bucket in a central account and grant read-only access for all users in any account within the AWS Organization. There should be no public access to the S3 bucket data.

Which parameters should the Administrator use to MOST efficiently accomplish this goal?

1. Specify all account numbers within an array as the principal.
2. Specify '*' as the principal and aws:PrincipalOrgId as a condition.
3. Specify the organization's master account as the principal.
4. Specify aws:PrincipalOrgId as the principal with the organization ID value.

Answer: 2

Explanation:

You can use a condition key, aws:PrincipalOrgID, in policies to require all principals accessing the resource to be from an account (including the master account) in the organization. To set this up for this scenario you must specify '*' as the principal, to allow any user access, and then restrict only to users within the AWS Organization using the condition key. The aws:PrincipalOrgId condition key should be used with the organization ID value specified

CORRECT: "Specify '*' as the principal and aws:PrincipalOrgId as a condition" is the correct answer.

INCORRECT: "Specify aws:PrincipalOrgId as the principal with the organization ID value" is incorrect. The value mentioned is used in a condition, not in the principal.

INCORRECT: "Specify all account numbers within an array as the principal" is incorrect. This is less efficient as you must specify all account numbers and you must come back and add account numbers if new accounts are added to the organization.

INCORRECT: "Specify the organization's master account as the principal" is incorrect. This is the not the correct method and will not grant access for users from other accounts within the organization.

References:

https://aws.amazon.com/blogs/security/control-access-to-aws-resources-by-using-the-aws-organization-of-iam-principals/

Save time with our exam-specific cheat sheets:

https://digitalcloud.training/certification-training/aws-certified-sysops-administrator-associate/aws-organizations/

QUESTION 8

A web application will be deployed that uses separate microservices running on different Amazon EC2 instances. A CloudOps Administrator has been tasked with configuring the infrastructure to route connection requests to the appropriate EC2 endpoints.

How can this be accomplished with the LEAST administrative effort?

1. Use Amazon CloudFront and forward the host header to the origin.
2. Use AWS Global Accelerator with a weighted routing policy.
3. Use a Network Load Balancer (NLB) and do path-based routing.
4. Use an Application Load Balancer (ALB) and do path-based routing.

Answer: 4

Explanation:

You can configure rules for your ALB listener that forward requests based on the URL in the request. This enables you to structure your application as smaller services, and route requests to the correct service based on the content of the URL.

CORRECT: "Use an Application Load Balancer (ALB) and do path-based routing" is the correct answer.

INCORRECT: "Use a Network Load Balancer (NLB) and do path-based routing" is incorrect. You cannot do path-based routing with an NLB.

INCORRECT: "Use Amazon CloudFront and forward the host header to the origin" is incorrect. This does not achieve the statement requirements as it will not direct traffic to the correct endpoint, it simply forwards headers for processing.

INCORRECT: "Use AWS Global Accelerator with a weighted routing policy" is incorrect. This would involve using AWS Route 53 for the routing policy. However, weighted routing will only direct based on configured weights rather than based on which components the traffic should be forwarded to.

References:

https://docs.aws.amazon.com/elasticloadbalancing/latest/application/introduction.html

Save time with our exam-specific cheat sheets:

https://digitalcloud.training/certification-training/aws-certified-sysops-administrator-associate/elastic-load-balancing/

QUESTION 9

A security team requires that AWS CloudTrail is always enabled in an AWS account. The security team has enabled CloudTrail in the account and have asked a CloudOps Administrator to ensure that if it is disabled, it is immediately and automatically re-enabled.

How can the CloudOps Administrator accomplish this requirement without writing any custom code?

1. Configure Amazon Inspector to analyze the account configuration and initiate an AWS Lambda function that re-enables CloudTrail if it is disabled.
2. Create an AWS Config rule that is invoked when the CloudTrail configuration changes. Configure the rule to invoke an AWS Lambda function to re-enable CloudTrail.
3. Create an Amazon EventBridge (Amazon CloudWatch Events) hourly rule with a schedule pattern to run an AWS Systems Manager Automation document to enable CloudTrail.
4. Create an AWS Config rule that is invoked when the CloudTrail configuration changes. Apply the AWS-ConfigureCloudTrailLogging automatic remediation action.

Answer: 4

Explanation:

To ensure that CloudTrail remains enabled in your account, AWS Config provides the cloudtrail-enabled managed rule. If CloudTrail is turned off, the cloudtrail-enabled rule automatically re-enables it by using automatic remediation. AWS Config leverages AWS Systems Manager automation documents to perform the automatic remediation. The AWS-ConfigureCloudTrailLogging document can be used for this purpose.

CORRECT: "Create an AWS Config rule that is invoked when the CloudTrail configuration changes. Apply the AWS-ConfigureCloudTrailLogging automatic remediation action" is the correct answer.

INCORRECT: "Configure Amazon Inspector to analyze the account configuration and initiate an AWS Lambda function that re-enables CloudTrail if it is disabled" is incorrect. Inspector is used to analyze EC2 instances for deviations from best practices.

INCORRECT: "Create an AWS Config rule that is invoked when the CloudTrail configuration changes. Configure the rule to invoke an AWS Lambda function to re-enable CloudTrail" is incorrect. There is no need to use Lambda, and this would require writing custom code.

INCORRECT: "Create an Amazon EventBridge (Amazon CloudWatch Events) hourly rule with a schedule pattern to run an AWS Systems Manager Automation document to enable CloudTrail" is incorrect. AWS Config should be used to identify the configuration changes and then automatically remediate the issue with SSM.

References:

https://docs.aws.amazon.com/prescriptive-guidance/latest/patterns/automatically-re-enable-aws-cloudtrail-by-using-a-custom-remediation-rule-in-aws-config.html

Save time with our exam-specific cheat sheets:

https://digitalcloud.training/certification-training/aws-certified-sysops-administrator-associate/aws-config/

QUESTION 10

A CloudOps Administrator noticed an unusual number of requests to an application that runs behind an Application Load Balancer (ALB). The administrator would like to identify the IP addresses of the clients that accessed the ALB.

Which logs should the administrator use to find this information?

1. EC2 Auto Scaling logs
2. Elastic Load Balancer access logs
3. AWS CloudTrail logs
4. Amazon CloudWatch Logs

Answer: 2

Explanation:

Elastic Load Balancing provides access logs that capture detailed information about requests sent to your load balancer. Each log contains information such as the time the request was received, the client's IP address, latencies, request paths, and server responses. You can use these access logs to analyze traffic patterns and troubleshoot issues.

CORRECT: "Elastic Load Balancer access logs" is the correct answer.

INCORRECT: "EC2 Auto Scaling logs" is incorrect. Auto Scaling uses CloudWatch Logs for logging and the client IP addresses will not be recorded.

INCORRECT: "AWS CloudTrail logs" is incorrect. CloudTrail logs API activity and will not log the client IP addresses.

INCORRECT: "Amazon CloudWatch Logs" is incorrect. CloudWatch Logs will not capture the client IP addresses as with an ALB this information must be captured at the ALB level before the traffic is forwarded to the EC2 instances.

References:

https://docs.aws.amazon.com/elasticloadbalancing/latest/application/load-balancer-access-logs.html

Save time with our exam-specific cheat sheets:

https://digitalcloud.training/certification-training/aws-certified-sysops-administrator-associate/elastic-load-balancing/

QUESTION 11

A company has several production accounts that are managed using AWS Organizations. The company policy mandates that Amazon S3 buckets should never be deleted.

What is the SIMPLEST approach a CloudOps Administrator can take to enforce this policy?
1. Set up MFA Delete on all the S3 buckets to prevent the buckets from being deleted.
2. Create an IAM group that has an IAM policy to deny the s3:DeleteBucket action on all buckets in all accounts.
3. Use service control policies to deny the s3:DeleteBucket action on all buckets in all accounts.
4. Use an Access Control List to deny the s3:DeleteBucket action at the organization level to apply the policy to all accounts.

Answer: 3

Explanation:

Service control policies (SCPs) are a type of organization policy that you can use to manage permissions in your organization. SCPs offer central control over the maximum available permissions for all accounts in your organization. SCPs help you to ensure your accounts stay within your organization's access control guidelines.

In this case the Administrator should apply an SCP that denies the s3:DeleteBucket action on all buckets in all accounts. This will ensure that users are not able to delete buckets in any account within the organization.

CORRECT: "Use service control policies to deny the s3:DeleteBucket action on all buckets in all accounts" is the correct answer.

INCORRECT: "Create an IAM group that has an IAM policy to deny the s3:DeleteBucket action on all buckets in all accounts" is incorrect. Groups are used to apply policies to users, but you cannot have a group that applies to multiple accounts.

INCORRECT: "Set up MFA Delete on all the S3 buckets to prevent the buckets from being deleted" is incorrect. MFA delete will simply require a second factor of authentication; buckets can still be deleted. This is also administratively very complex.

INCORRECT: "Use an Access Control List to deny the s3:DeleteBucket action at the organization level to apply the policy to all accounts" is incorrect. ACLs are applied to subnets and cannot be used to control privileges for Amazon S3.

References:

https://docs.aws.amazon.com/organizations/latest/userguide/orgs_manage_policies_scps.html

Save time with our exam-specific cheat sheets:

https://digitalcloud.training/certification-training/aws-certified-sysops-administrator-associate/aws-organizations/

QUESTION 12

A company runs a web application that runs from Amazon EC2 instances in a VPC. The application is fronted by an Application Load Balancer (ALB) and an Amazon CloudFront distribution. The backend uses an Amazon DynamoDB table. A CloudOps Administrator needs to investigate HTTP Layer 7 status codes from the web application.

Which log sources contain the status codes? (Select TWO.)

1. VPC Flow Logs
2. Amazon CloudTrail logs
3. ALB access logs
4. CloudFront access logs
5. Amazon DynamoDB logs

Answer: 3, 4

Explanation:

The key here is to understand that the administrator must capture status codes at layer 7 of the OSI model. The only logs listed that will contain this information are the ALB access logs and the CloudFront access logs.

More info from AWS below:

ALB access logs: Elastic Load Balancing provides access logs that capture detailed information about requests sent to your load balancer. Each log contains information such as the time the request was received, the client's IP address, latencies, request paths, and server responses. You can use these access logs to analyze traffic patterns and troubleshoot issues.

CloudFront access logs: You can configure CloudFront to create log files that contain detailed information about every user request that CloudFront receives. These are called *standard logs*, also known as *access logs*. If you enable standard logs, you can also specify the Amazon S3 bucket that you want CloudFront to save files in.

CORRECT: "ALB access logs" is a correct answer.

CORRECT: "CloudFront access logs" is also a correct answer.

INCORRECT: "VPC Flow Logs" is incorrect. These logs capture data at layer 4, not layer 7

INCORRECT: "Amazon CloudTrail logs" is incorrect. This service captures API activity data, not layer 7 application data.

INCORRECT: "Amazon DynamoDB logs" is incorrect. DynamoDB can use CloudTrail for logging API activity but does not capture any logs for application layer information.

References:

https://docs.aws.amazon.com/elasticloadbalancing/latest/application/load-balancer-access-logs.html

https://docs.aws.amazon.com/AmazonCloudFront/latest/DeveloperGuide/AccessLogs.html

Save time with our exam-specific cheat sheets:

https://digitalcloud.training/certification-training/aws-certified-sysops-administrator-associate/elastic-load-balancing/

https://digitalcloud.training/certification-training/aws-certified-sysops-administrator-associate/amazon-cloudfront/

QUESTION 13

A company is running a production application across subnets in different AWS accounts within the same Region. To ensure high availability of the application, the CloudOps Administrator needs to be able to map Availability Zones across accounts.

Which actions will obtain this information? (Select TWO.)

1. Call the DescribeAvailabilityZones API operation and match the response of zoneId between the two AWS accounts.
2. Call the Describe AvailabilityZones API operation and match the response of zoneName between the two AWS accounts.
3. Call the Describe Subnets API operation and match the response of availabilityZoneName between the two AWS accounts.
4. Call the Describe Subnets API operation and match the response of availabilityZoneId between the two AWS accounts.
5. Call the Describe Subnets API operation and match the response of defaultForAz between the two AWS accounts.

Answer: 1, 4

Explanation:

When using multiple accounts within a Region it is important to understand that the name of the Availability Zone in each account may map to a different underlying AZ. For instance, us-east-1a may map to a different AZ in one account vs another.

To identify the location of your resources relative to your accounts, you must use the *AZ ID*, which is a unique and consistent identifier for an Availability Zone. For example, use1-az1 is an AZ ID for the us-east-1 Region and it is the same location in every AWS account.

This information can be obtained a few different ways including running the DescribeAvailabilityZones API operation or calling the Describe Subnets API operation.

CORRECT: "Call the DescribeAvailabilityZones API operation and match the response of zoneId between the two AWS accounts" is a correct answer.

CORRECT: "Call the Describe Subnets API operation and match the response of availabilityZoneId between the two AWS accounts" is also a correct answer.

INCORRECT: "Call the Describe AvailabilityZones API operation and match the response of zoneName between the two AWS accounts" is incorrect. Zone ID should be used, not zone name.

INCORRECT: "Call the Describe Subnets API operation and match the response of availabilityZoneName between the two AWS accounts" is incorrect. Zone ID should be used, not zone name.

INCORRECT: "Call the Describe Subnets API operation and match the response of defaultForAz between the two AWS accounts" is incorrect. This property checks whether the subnet is default for the availability zone.

References:

https://docs.aws.amazon.com/ram/latest/userguide/working-with-az-ids.html

Save time with our exam-specific cheat sheets:

https://digitalcloud.training/certification-training/aws-certified-sysops-administrator-associate/amazon-virtual-private-cloud-vpc/

QUESTION 14

A company runs a web application on several Amazon EC2 instances in an Auto Scaling group. The EC2 instances share a file system that is delivered using Amazon EFS. Though the volume of data does not change much, during periods of heavy utilization users have reported that file retrieval latency increases.

Which action should a CloudOps Administrator take to improve the performance of the file system?

1. Enable encryption in transit on the file system.
2. Configure the file system for Provisioned Throughput.
3. Remove any unused files from the file system.
4. Configure the file system for Bursting Throughput.

Answer: 2

Explanation:

There are two throughput modes to choose from for your file system, Bursting Throughput and Provisioned Throughput:

- With *Bursting Throughput* mode, throughput on Amazon EFS scales as the size of your file system in the EFS Standard or One Zone storage class grows.
- With *Provisioned Throughput* mode, you can instantly provision the throughput of your file system (in MiB/s) independent of the amount of data stored.

In this case the file system does not grow much in volume so bursting throughput mode may not result in reducing the latency. Provisioned throughput mode would be the better option as it will ensure that even without any growth in the volume of data, enough throughput is provisioned to reduce the latency.

CORRECT: "Configure the file system for Provisioned Throughput" is the correct answer.

INCORRECT: "Configure the file system for Bursting Throughput" is incorrect as described above.

INCORRECT: "Enable encryption in transit on the file system" is incorrect. Encryption will not reduce latency.

INCORRECT: "Remove any unused files from the file system" is incorrect. This will not assist in reducing latency. In bursting mode this would reduce the performance, in provisioned throughput mode this would make no difference at all.

References:

https://docs.aws.amazon.com/efs/latest/ug/performance.html

Save time with our exam-specific cheat sheets:

https://digitalcloud.training/certification-training/aws-certified-sysops-administrator-associate/amazon-efs/

QUESTION 15

A CloudOps Administrator manages an Amazon Elasticsearch Service (Amazon ES) domain that is configured with a public endpoint. Users connect to the Amazon ES domain over AWS Site-to-Site VPN connections from multiple branch offices. The Administrator needs to ensure that Amazon ES can be accessed only from the branch offices while preserving existing data.

Which solution will meet these requirements?

1. Configure an identity-based access policy on Amazon ES. Add an allow statement to the policy that includes the Amazon Resource Name (ARN) for each branch office VPN connection.
2. Reconfigure the Amazon ES domain in private subnets in a VPC. Configure an IP-based domain access policy on Amazon ES and allow the private IP CIDR blocks from each branch office network.
3. Configure an IP-based domain access policy on Amazon ES. Add an allow statement to the policy that includes the private IP CIDR blocks from each branch office network.
4. Reconfigure the Amazon ES domain in private subnets in a VPC. Create a security group that allows inbound traffic from the branch office CIDR blocks.

Answer: 3

Explanation:

When you create a domain, you specify whether it should have a public endpoint or reside within a VPC. Once created, you cannot switch from one to the other. Instead, you must create a new domain and either manually reindex or migrate your data.

In this case the domain is already created with a public endpoint, and we must preserve the data whilst restricting access to the clients connecting over the VPN connections. IP-based policies restrict access to a domain to one or more IP addresses or CIDR blocks.

Therefore, we can restrict based on the CIDR blocks of the VPN connections and this will have the desired effect.

CORRECT: "Configure an IP-based domain access policy on Amazon ES. Add an allow statement to the policy that includes the private IP CIDR blocks from each branch office network" is the correct answer.

INCORRECT: "Reconfigure the Amazon ES domain in private subnets in a VPC. Configure an IP-based domain access policy on Amazon ES and allow the private IP CIDR blocks from each branch office network" is incorrect. This would not preserve the data and so the data would need to be migrated using a snapshot of other mechanism.

INCORRECT: "Configure an identity-based access policy on Amazon ES. Add an allow statement to the policy that includes the Amazon Resource Name (ARN) for each branch office VPN connection" is incorrect. Identity-based policies are attached to users or roles so cannot be used in this manner.

INCORRECT: "Reconfigure the Amazon ES domain in private subnets in a VPC. Create a security group that allows inbound traffic from the branch office CIDR blocks" is incorrect. This would require migration of the data.

References:

https://docs.aws.amazon.com/elasticsearch-service/latest/developerguide/es-ac.html#es-ac-types-ip

QUESTION 16

The security policy of a company requires that all objects that are uploaded to Amazon S3 buckets must be encrypted.

Which of the following actions can be taken to meet the security policy requirements? (Select TWO.)

1. Implement an AWS Config rule that defines an S3 bucket access control list (ACL) that enforces default encryption.
2. Implement Object access control list (ACL) to deny unencrypted objects from being uploaded to the S3 bucket.
3. Implement S3 server access logs and configure an event notification. Trigger an AWS Lambda function that checks the logs for object creation events and deletes any unencrypted objects.
4. Implement Amazon S3 default encryption to make sure that any object being uploaded is encrypted before it is stored.
5. Implement S3 bucket policies to deny unencrypted objects from being uploaded to the buckets.

Answer: 4, 5

Explanation:

There are several ways to enforce encryption for objects uploaded to an Amazon S3 bucket. Firstly, you can implement default encryption so that all new objects are encrypted when they are stored in the bucket.

However, it is still possible to upload unencrypted objects if the PUT operation contains specific parameters. To enforce encryption of all objects you can use a bucket policy that denies any S3 Put request that does not include the *x-amz-server-side-encryption* header.

There are two possible values for the *x-amz-server-side-encryption* header: AES256, which tells S3 to use S3-managed keys, and aws:kms, which tells S3 to use AWS KMS–managed keys.

CORRECT: "Implement Amazon S3 default encryption to make sure that any object being uploaded is encrypted before it is stored" is a correct answer.

CORRECT: "Implement S3 bucket policies to deny unencrypted objects from being uploaded to the buckets" is also a correct answer.

INCORRECT: "Implement an AWS Config rule that defines an S3 bucket access control list (ACL) that enforces default encryption" is incorrect. Config checks for compliance but does not define ACLs. It is also not possible to enforce default encryption with a bucket ACL.

INCORRECT: "Implement Object access control list (ACL) to deny unencrypted objects from being uploaded to the S3 bucket" is incorrect. This is not possible using an ACL.

INCORRECT: "Implement S3 server access logs and configure an event notification. Trigger an AWS Lambda function that checks the logs for object creation events and deletes any unencrypted objects" is incorrect. The data recorded in these log files does not include the encryption used.

References:

https://aws.amazon.com/blogs/security/how-to-prevent-uploads-of-unencrypted-objects-to-amazon-s3/

Save time with our exam-specific cheat sheets:

https://digitalcloud.training/certification-training/aws-certified-sysops-administrator-associate/amazon-s3/

QUESTION 17

A company is planning to deploy an Amazon Elasticsearch Service (Amazon ES) cluster that will analyze data produced by a fleet of Amazon EC2 instances. A CloudOps Administrator must deploy an Amazon ES cluster in a highly available production-grade deployment.

Which Amazon ES configuration should the CloudOps Administrator use to meet this requirement?

1. Use a cluster of four data nodes across two AWS Regions. Deploy four dedicated master nodes in each Region.
2. Use a cluster of six data nodes across three Availability Zones. Use six dedicated master nodes.
3. Use a cluster of six data nodes across three Availability Zones. Use three dedicated master nodes.
4. Use a cluster of eight data nodes across two Availability Zones. Deploy four master nodes in a failover AWS Region.

Answer: 3

Explanation:

The best practices for the number of dedicated master nodes are the key here. AWS recommend that you have three dedicated master nodes as this provides two backup nodes in the event of a master node failure and the necessary quorum (2) to elect a new master.

AWS recommend that you never choose an even number of dedicated master nodes. Consider the following when choosing the number of dedicated master nodes and they state that four dedicated master nodes are no better than three and can cause issues if you use multiple Availability Zones.

CORRECT: "Use a cluster of six data nodes across three Availability Zones. Use three dedicated master nodes" is the correct answer.

INCORRECT: "Use a cluster of four data nodes across two AWS Regions. Deploy four dedicated master nodes in each Region" is incorrect. As described above AWS do not recommend 4 dedicated master nodes.

INCORRECT: "Use a cluster of six data nodes across three Availability Zones. Use six dedicated master nodes" is incorrect. As described above AWS recommend you do not have an even number of dedicated master nodes.

INCORRECT: "Use a cluster of eight data nodes across two Availability Zones. Deploy four master nodes in a failover AWS Region" is incorrect. Dedicated master nodes should be used in the same Region.

References:

https://docs.aws.amazon.com/elasticsearch-service/latest/developerguide/es-managedomains-dedicatedmasternodes.html

https://docs.aws.amazon.com/elasticsearch-service/latest/developerguide/aes-bp.html

QUESTION 18

A fleet of Amazon EC2 instances read and write data to a shared Amazon EFS file system. The security team have raised concerns that the file system is not encrypted.

How can a CloudOps Administrator resolve the issue?

1. Create a new EFS file system with encryption enabled and copy all data from the original file system.
2. Enable encryption of data in transit when mounting the file system to each EC2 instance.
3. Enable encryption on the existing EFS file system by using the AWS Command Line Interface (AWS CLI).
4. Modify the existing EFS file system through the AWS Management Console and enable AES-256 encryption.

Answer: 1

Explanation:

Amazon EFS supports two forms of encryption for file systems, encryption of data in transit and encryption at rest. You can enable encryption of data at rest when creating an Amazon EFS file system. You can enable encryption of data in transit when you mount the file system.

In this case the file system already exists and is not encrypted so a new file system must be created with encryption enabled. Data must then be copied across and the EC2 instances will need to mount the new file system.

CORRECT: "Create a new EFS file system with encryption enabled and copy all data from the original file system" is the correct answer.

INCORRECT: "Enable encryption of data in transit when mounting the file system to each EC2 instance" is incorrect. File system encryption is encryption of the data at rest. In transit encryption is not file system encryption, it is data connection encryption.

INCORRECT: "Enable encryption on the existing EFS file system by using the AWS Command Line Interface (AWS CLI)" is incorrect. You cannot enable encryption on an existing EFS file system through the CLI of the console.

INCORRECT: "Modify the existing EFS file system through the AWS Management Console and enable AES-256 encryption" is incorrect. You cannot enable encryption on an existing EFS file system through the CLI of the console.

References:

https://docs.aws.amazon.com/efs/latest/ug/encryption.html

Save time with our exam-specific cheat sheets:

https://digitalcloud.training/certification-training/aws-certified-sysops-administrator-associate/amazon-efs/

QUESTION 19

A company needs to find a way to securely share an object from an Amazon S3 bucket that does not have public access enabled. The users who will be accessing the object do not have an AWS account.

What is the MOST operationally efficient solution that will meet this requirement?

1. Attach an S3 bucket policy that only allows object downloads from the users' IP addresses.
2. Create an IAM role that has access to the object. Instruct the users to assume the role.
3. Create an application that distributes signed cookies to the users and control access through the cookies.
4. Generate a presigned URL for the object. Share the URL with the users.

Answer: 4

Explanation:

All objects by default are private. Only the object owner has permission to access these objects. However, the object owner can optionally share objects with others by creating a presigned URL, using their own security credentials, to grant time-limited permission to download the objects.

When you create a presigned URL for your object, you must provide your security credentials, specify a bucket name, an object key, specify the HTTP method (GET to download the object) and expiration date and time. The presigned URLs are valid only for the specified duration.

Anyone who receives the presigned URL can then access the object. For example, if you have a video in your bucket and both the bucket and the object are private, you can share the video with others by generating a presigned URL.

CORRECT: "Generate a presigned URL for the object. Share the URL with the users" is the correct answer.

INCORRECT: "Attach an S3 bucket policy that only allows object downloads from the users' IP addresses" is incorrect. This is not operationally efficient as the users' IP addresses may change and need to be updated.

INCORRECT: " Create an IAM role that has access to the object. Instruct the users to assume the rol " is incorrect. This adds complexity and the users need to be able to assume the IAM role.

INCORRECT: "Create an application that distributes signed cookies to the users and control access through the cookies" is incorrect. Signed cookies are used with CloudFront but not directly with Amazon S3.

References:

https://docs.aws.amazon.com/AmazonS3/latest/userguide/ShareObjectPreSignedURL.html

Save time with our exam-specific cheat sheets:

https://digitalcloud.training/certification-training/aws-certified-sysops-administrator-associate/amazon-s3/

QUESTION 20

A CloudOps Administrator is deploying a new website that will run on Amazon EC2 instances in an Auto Scaling group behind an Application Load Balancer (ALB). The website's apex domain name is example.com and this name must resolve to the ALB.

What type of record set should the Administrator create in Amazon Route 53?

1. CNAME
2. ALIAS
3. SOA

4. TXT

Answer: 2

Explanation:

Amazon Route 53 offers a special type of record called an 'Alias' record that lets you map your zone apex (example.com) DNS name to the DNS name for your ELB load balancer (such as my-loadbalancer-1234567890.us-west-2.elb.amazonaws.com).

IP addresses associated with load balancers can change at any time due to scaling up, scaling down, or software updates. Route 53 responds to each request for an Alias record with one or more IP addresses for the load balancer.

Route 53 supports alias records for three types of load balancers: Application Load Balancers, Network Load Balancers, and Classic Load Balancers.

CORRECT: "ALIAS" is the correct answer.

INCORRECT: "CNAME" is incorrect. You cannot use a zone apex domain name with a CNAME record, you must use a subdomain (e.g., www.example.com).

INCORRECT: "SOA" is incorrect. This is a start of authority record and is not the correct record type to use.

INCORRECT: "TXT" is incorrect. This is a text record and is not the correct record type to use.

References:

https://aws.amazon.com/route53/faqs/

Save time with our exam-specific cheat sheets:

https://digitalcloud.training/certification-training/aws-certified-sysops-administrator-associate/amazon-route-53/

QUESTION 21

An Amazon EC2 instance that processes large data files has an attached 1 TB General Purpose SSD (gp2) Amazon EBS volume. Amazon CloudWatch metrics on the instance show a consistent 3,000 VolumeReadOps. A CloudOps Administrator must improve the I/O performance while ensuring data integrity.

Which action will meet these requirements?

1. Increase the EBS volume to a 2 TB General Purpose SSD (gp2) volume.
2. Change the instance type to a bare metal instance.
3. Change the instance type to a Burstable Performance instance.
4. Move the data that resides on the EBS volume to the instance store.

Answer: 1

Explanation:

General Purpose SSD (gp2) volumes offer cost-effective storage that is ideal for a broad range of workloads. These volumes deliver single-digit millisecond latencies and the ability to burst to 3,000 IOPS for extended periods of time. Between a minimum of 100 IOPS (at 33.33 GiB and below) and a maximum of 16,000 IOPS (at 5,334 GiB and above), baseline performance scales linearly at 3 IOPS per GiB of volume size.

EBS volumes use a credit system in which volumes earn I/O credits at the baseline performance rate of 3 IOPS per GiB of volume size. For example, a 100 GiB gp2 volume has a baseline performance of 300 IOPS. To increase the number of credits earned and the amount of IOPS achievable, increase the size of the volume.

CORRECT: "Increase the EBS volume to a 2 TB General Purpose SSD (gp2) volume" is the correct answer.

INCORRECT: "Change the instance type to a bare metal instance" is incorrect. This will not improve storage performance.

INCORRECT: "Change the instance type to a Burstable Performance instance" is incorrect. This enables bursting of CPU not of storage performance.

INCORRECT: "Move the data that resides on the EBS volume to the instance store" is incorrect. This will leave the data vulnerable to loss as these volumes are non-persistent.

References:

https://docs.aws.amazon.com/AWSEC2/latest/UserGuide/ebs-volume-types.html

Save time with our exam-specific cheat sheets:

https://digitalcloud.training/certification-training/aws-certified-sysops-administrator-associate/amazon-ebs/

QUESTION 22

An application runs on four Amazon EC2 instances. The application requires that a minimum of four instances must be always running to support application demand. A CloudOps Administrator must design a highly available, fault-tolerant architecture that continues to meet these requirements even if one Availability Zone becomes unavailable.

Which configuration meets these requirements?

1. Deploy two Auto Scaling groups in two Availability Zones with a minimum capacity of two instances in each group.
2. Deploy an Auto Scaling group across two Availability Zones with a minimum capacity of four instances.
3. Deploy an Auto Scaling group across three Availability Zones with a minimum capacity of six instances.
4. Deploy an Auto Scaling group across three Availability Zones with a minimum capacity of four instances.

Answer: 3

Explanation:

This is simply a case of ensuring that if an AZ fails the application will still have at least four EC2 instances still running. Therefore, a single Auto Scaling group with a minimum configuration of six instances across three AZs is the most efficient solution. If a single AZ fails, there will still be four instances available to service the application demand.

CORRECT: "Deploy an Auto Scaling group across three Availability Zones with a minimum capacity of six instances" is the correct answer.

INCORRECT: "Deploy two Auto Scaling groups in two Availability Zones with a minimum capacity of two instances in each group" is incorrect. There is no need for multiple ASGs. This will also result in reducing the capacity beneath four instances if a single AZ fails (only two would remain).

INCORRECT: "Deploy an Auto Scaling group across two Availability Zones with a minimum capacity of four instances" is incorrect. If a single AZ fails, there will only be two instances remaining operational.

INCORRECT: "Deploy an Auto Scaling group across three Availability Zones with a minimum capacity of four instances" is incorrect. Assuming the ASG spreads the instances across three AZs this will result in a loss of an instance in the event of an AZ failure and will therefore decrease the number of running instances below four.

References:

https://docs.aws.amazon.com/autoscaling/ec2/userguide/as-add-availability-zone.html

Save time with our exam-specific cheat sheets:

https://digitalcloud.training/certification-training/aws-certified-sysops-administrator-associate/amazon-ec2-auto-scaling/

QUESTION 23

A website is used by users in several countries. The company has implemented the website on Amazon EC2 instances in different Regions and countries. Each Regional website contains content that is specific to the country in which it is located.

A CloudOps Administrator must implement a solution that will automatically send users to the appropriate Regional website, depending on each user's location, from a single URL.

Which solution meets these requirements?

1. AWS Global Accelerator with a network load balancer.
2. Application Load Balancer with cross-zone load balancing.
3. Amazon CloudFront with cross-origin resource sharing (CORS).
4. Amazon Route 53 with a geolocation routing policy.

Answer: 4

Explanation:

Geolocation routing lets you choose the resources that serve your traffic based on the geographic location of your users, meaning the location that DNS queries originate from. For example, you might want all queries from Europe to be routed to an ELB load balancer in the Frankfurt region.

When you use geolocation routing, you can localize your content and present some or all of your website in the language of your users. You can also use geolocation routing to restrict distribution of content to only the locations in which you have distribution rights.

CORRECT: "Amazon Route 53 with a geolocation routing policy" is the correct answer.

INCORRECT: "AWS Global Accelerator with a network load balancer" is incorrect. There is no mechanism here for ensuring that the users are directed to the website in the correct geographic location that contains the localized content.

INCORRECT: "Application Load Balancer with cross-zone load balancing" is incorrect. Cross-zone load balancing works across Availability Zones not Regions.

INCORRECT: "Amazon CloudFront with cross-origin resource sharing (CORS)" is incorrect. This enables websites to connect to content on other websites and is not applicable here.

References:

https://docs.aws.amazon.com/Route53/latest/DeveloperGuide/routing-policy.html

Save time with our exam-specific cheat sheets:

https://digitalcloud.training/certification-training/aws-certified-sysops-administrator-associate/amazon-route-53/

QUESTION 24

A CloudOps Administrator is deploying a website that must be directly accessible from the internet. The Amazon EC2 instance is running in a subnet that is configured to auto assign public IP addresses. The subnet route table has the following configuration:

Destination	Target
10.0.0.0/16	Local
172.31.0.0/16	pcx-123456123456

Which entry must the Administrator add to the route table to meet the requirement?

1. A route for 0.0.0.0/0 that points to an internet gateway.
2. A route for 0.0.0.0/0 that points to a NAT gateway.
3. A route for 0.0.0.0/0 that points to an egress-only internet gateway.
4. A route for 0.0.0.0/0 that points to an elastic network interface.

Answer: 1

Explanation:

If a subnet is associated with a route table that has a route to an internet gateway, it's known as a *public subnet*. If a subnet is associated with a route table that does not have a route to an internet gateway, it's known as a *private subnet*.

In your public subnet's route table, you can specify a route for the internet gateway to all destinations not explicitly known to the route table (0.0.0.0/0 for IPv4 or ::/0 for IPv6).

Alternatively, you can scope the route to a narrower range of IP addresses; for example, the public IPv4 addresses of your company's public endpoints outside of AWS, or the Elastic IP addresses of other Amazon EC2 instances outside your VPC.

In this case the route for 0.0.0.0/0 that points to the internet gateway will ensure the instance is accessible from the internet.

CORRECT: "A route for 0.0.0.0/0 that points to an internet gateway" is the correct answer.

INCORRECT: "A route for 0.0.0.0/0 that points to a NAT gateway" is incorrect. A NAT gateway is used by instances in public subnets for outbound connectivity to the internet.

INCORRECT: "A route for 0.0.0.0/0 that points to an egress-only internet gateway" is incorrect. This type of internet gateway is used for IPv6, not IPv4.

INCORRECT: "A route for 0.0.0.0/0 that points to an elastic network interface" is incorrect. This is not how you enable internet connectivity for a public subnet.

References:

https://docs.aws.amazon.com/vpc/latest/userguide/VPC_Internet_Gateway.html

Save time with our exam-specific cheat sheets:

https://digitalcloud.training/certification-training/aws-certified-sysops-administrator-associate/amazon-virtual-private-cloud-vpc/

QUESTION 25

A critical application running on Amazon EC2 instances occasionally suffers from increased read and write latency to attached Amazon EBS volumes. A CloudOps Administrator is attempting to configure Amazon CloudWatch alarms for the DiskReadBytes metric and the DiskWriteBytes metrics. However, during busy periods when users have experienced performance degradation, the alarms have not changed to the ALARM state.

Which action will ensure that the CloudWatch alarms function correctly?

1. Install and configure the CloudWatch agent on the EC2 instance to capture the desired metrics.
2. Reconfigure the CloudWatch alarms to use the VolumeReadBytes metric and the VolumeWriteBytes metric for the EBS volumes.
3. Install and configure AWS Systems Manager Agent on the EC2 instance to capture the desired metrics.
4. Reconfigure the CloudWatch alarms to use the VolumeReadBytes metric and the VolumeWriteBytes metric for the EC2 instances.

Answer: 2

Explanation:

The DiskReadBytes metric and the DiskWriteBytes metrics are associated with the AWS/EC2 namespace and report on the read and write performance of attached instance store volumes, not EBS volumes.

The correct metrics to use come from the AWS/EBS namespace and are the VolumeReadBytes metric and the VolumeWriteBytes metric. Changing the alarm configuration to use these metrics should result in the correct reporting and will trigger the alarm.

CORRECT: "Reconfigure the CloudWatch alarms to use the VolumeReadBytes metric and the VolumeWriteBytes metric for the EBS volumes" is the correct answer.

INCORRECT: "Reconfigure the CloudWatch alarms to use the VolumeReadBytes metric and the VolumeWriteBytes metric for the EC2 instances" is incorrect. These metrics are associated with the AWS/EBS namespace not the AWS/EC2 namespace.

INCORRECT: "Install and configure AWS Systems Manager Agent on the EC2 instance to capture the desired metrics" is incorrect. This agent does not collect this information and the required information is already being reported through CloudWatch metrics.

INCORRECT: "Install and configure the CloudWatch agent on the EC2 instance to capture the desired metrics" is incorrect. It is not necessary to install the CloudWatch agent as the required information is already being reported through CloudWatch metrics.

References:

https://docs.aws.amazon.com/AWSEC2/latest/UserGuide/using_cloudwatch_ebs.html

Save time with our exam-specific cheat sheets:

https://digitalcloud.training/certification-training/aws-certified-sysops-administrator-associate/amazon-cloudwatch/

QUESTION 26

An application uses several AWS Lambda functions that each generate a large volume of log data each day in its own Amazon CloudWatch Logs log group. A CloudOps Administrator is troubleshooting application issues and needs to generate a count of application errors, grouped by type, across all the log groups.

What should the administrator do to meet this requirement?

1. Perform an Amazon Athena query that uses the SELECT and GROUP BY keywords.
2. Perform a CloudWatch Logs Insights query that uses the stats command and count function.
3. Perform a CloudWatch Logs search that uses the groupby keyword and count function.
4. Perform an Amazon RDS query that uses the SELECT and GROUP BY keywords.

Answer: 2

Explanation:

CloudWatch Logs Insights enables you to interactively search and analyze your log data in Amazon CloudWatch Logs. You can perform queries to help you more efficiently and effectively respond to operational issues. If an issue occurs, you can use CloudWatch Logs Insights to identify potential causes and validate deployed fixes.

A single request can query up to 20 log groups. Queries time out after 15 minutes, if they have not completed. Query results are available for 7 days. For this scenario, the administrator can query multiple log groups at once, and use the stats command count function to calculate aggregate statistics.

CORRECT: "Perform a CloudWatch Logs Insights query that uses the stats command and count function" is the correct answer.

INCORRECT: "Perform an Amazon Athena query that uses the SELECT and GROUP BY keywords" is incorrect. You can connect Athena to CW Logs; however, each log group will be a schema and each log stream a separate table. This would make it difficult to calculate aggregate statistics across log groups.

INCORRECT: "Perform a CloudWatch Logs search that uses the groupby keyword and count function" is incorrect. This would search an individual log group not across log groups.

INCORRECT: "Perform an Amazon RDS query that uses the SELECT and GROUP BY keywords" is incorrect. Amazon RDS is not relevant here as it cannot be used to search CW Logs.

References:

https://docs.aws.amazon.com/AmazonCloudWatch/latest/logs/CWL_QuerySyntax.html

Save time with our exam-specific cheat sheets:

https://digitalcloud.training/certification-training/aws-certified-sysops-administrator-associate/amazon-cloudwatch/

QUESTION 27

A CloudOps Administrator is deploying a new website running on Amazon EC2 instances. The application requires both incoming and outgoing connectivity to the internet.

Which combination of steps are required to provision the required connectivity? (Select TWO.)

1. Add a NAT gateway to a public subnet and update the route table.

2. Attach a private address to the elastic network interface on the EC2 instance.
3. Attach an Elastic IP address to the internet gateway.
4. Add an entry to the route table for the subnet that points to an internet gateway.
5. Create an internet gateway and attach it to a VPC.

Answer: 4, 5

Explanation:

Public subnets allow communication to and from the internet. There are several configuration settings that you must define to enable bi-directional internet connectivity. First, you must create an internet gateway and attach it to the VPC. Then, you must update the route table of the subnet to point to the internet gateway.

Finally, you will need to ensure your instances get public IP addresses and this can be automated by setting the "auto-assign public IP4 addresses" configuration option for the subnet.

CORRECT: "Add an entry to the route table for the subnet that points to an internet gateway" is a correct answer.

CORRECT: "Create an internet gateway and attach it to a VPC" is also a correct answer.

INCORRECT: "Add a NAT gateway to a public subnet and update the route table" is incorrect. NAT gateways are used for outbound connectivity only from private subnets.

INCORRECT: "Attach a private address to the elastic network interface on the EC2 instance" is incorrect. A private IP is automatically assigned to all EC2 instances; a public IP is needed for bi-directional internet connectivity.

INCORRECT: "Attach an Elastic IP address to the internet gateway" is incorrect. Internet gateways are automatically provisioned with connectivity, you do not need to manually assign an EIP.

References:

https://docs.aws.amazon.com/vpc/latest/userguide/VPC_Subnets.html

Save time with our exam-specific cheat sheets:

https://digitalcloud.training/certification-training/aws-certified-sysops-administrator-associate/amazon-virtual-private-cloud-vpc/

QUESTION 28

A CloudOps Administrator is checking some performance data for an Amazon EC2 instance in Amazon CloudWatch. The administrator reviews the DiskReadBytes metric and notices that the metric shows that 0 bytes have been read during the day.

What is the most likely explanation for the metric value showing 0 bytes?

1. An Amazon EBS volume is not attached to the EC2 instance.
2. Detailed monitoring is not enabled on the EC2 instance.
3. The CloudWatch agent is not installed on the EC2 instance.
4. An instance store volume is not attached to the EC2 instance.

Answer: 4

Explanation:

The DiskReadBytes metric shows all bytes read from all instance store volumes available to the instance. It does not show data for Amazon EBS volumes. Therefore, the most likely explanation for the metric value showing 0 bytes is that the EC2 instance is using EBS volumes and does not have any attached instance store volumes.

CORRECT: "An instance store volume is not attached to the EC2 instance" is the correct answer.

INCORRECT: "An Amazon EBS volume is not attached to the EC2 instance" is incorrect. The DiskReadBytes metric shows statistics for instance store volumes, not EBS volumes.

INCORRECT: "Detailed monitoring is not enabled on the EC2 instance" is incorrect. Detailed monitoring will provide more regular reporting of data but does not explain why the values are 0 for an entire day.

INCORRECT: "The CloudWatch agent is not installed on the EC2 instance" is incorrect. You do not need the CloudWatch agent for the DiskReadBytes metric, this is a standard metric that reports statistics for instance store volumes.

References:

https://docs.aws.amazon.com/AWSEC2/latest/UserGuide/viewing_metrics_with_cloudwatch.html

Save time with our exam-specific cheat sheets:

https://digitalcloud.training/certification-training/aws-certified-sysops-administrator-associate/amazon-cloudwatch/

QUESTION 29

A CloudOps Administrator has launched an Amazon EC2 Linux instance in a public subnet. The instance obtained a public IP address, and the administrator needs to connect using an SSH client. When attempting the SSH connection, the connection attempt fails repeatedly with a timeout error.

Which action will allow the CloudOps Administrator to remotely connect to the instance?

1. Update the subnet route table with an entry for the CloudOps Administrator's IP address.
2. Update the instance security group with a rule allowing SSH inbound from the CloudOps Administrator's IP address.
3. Update the network ACL for the subnet to allow port 22 outbound to the CloudOps Administrator's IP address.
4. Update the instance security group with a rule allowing SSH outbound to the CloudOps Administrator's IP address.

Answer: 2

Explanation:

When a timeout error is experienced, this is a good indication that the connectivity issue relates to security group configuration.

To allow the required connectivity the instance's security group will need to be configured with a rule that allows the SSH protocol inbound from the IP address of the CloudOps Administrator. This would be the most secure configuration as it would only allow that single IP address to connect over SSH.

CORRECT: "Update the instance security group with a rule allowing SSH inbound from the CloudOps Administrator's IP address" is the correct answer.

INCORRECT: "Update the subnet route table with an entry for the CloudOps Administrator's IP address" is incorrect. You would not configure the individual IP of the administrator in a route table. If route table configuration was an issue the connection attempt would typically fail quickly rather than timing out.

INCORRECT: "Update the network ACL for the subnet to allow port 22 outbound to the CloudOps Administrator's IP address" is incorrect. This would not assist in allowing inbound connectivity over the SSH port (port 22).

INCORRECT: "Update the instance security group with a rule allowing SSH outbound to the CloudOps Administrator's IP address" is incorrect. Inbound connectivity is required so the rule should be an inbound rule.

References:

https://docs.aws.amazon.com/vpc/latest/userguide/VPC_SecurityGroups.html

Save time with our exam-specific cheat sheets:

https://digitalcloud.training/certification-training/aws-certified-sysops-administrator-associate/amazon-virtual-private-cloud-vpc/

QUESTION 30

A CloudOps Administrator has been asked to review an IAM policy that has been created to allow a new hire to access specific AWS services. The following policy is presented:

```json
{
    "Version": "2012-10-17",
    "Statement": [
        {
            "Action": [
                "rds:CreateDBInstance",
                "elasticloadbalancing:*",
                "lambda:*",
                "sns:ListTopics*"
            ],
            "Effect": "Allow",
            "Resource": "*"
        }
    ]
}
```

Which actions does this policy allow? (Select TWO.)

1. Delete an Amazon RDS database.
2. Create an IAM role for an AWS Lambda function.
3. Delete an Amazon SNS topic.
4. Describe AWS load balancers.
5. Invoke an AWS Lambda function.

Answer: 4, 5

Explanation:

It is important to have a basic understanding of IAM policies for the CloudOps Administrator exam. In this case we simply need to determine actions will be allowed based on the presented policy example. The effect of the policy is "Allow". Let's go through each action statement:

rds:CreateDBInstance – This will allow a user to create an RDS database but not to delete an RDS database.

Elasticloadbalancing:* – This will allow all actions for AWS load balancers.

lambda:* – This will allow all actions for AWS Lambda functions but note that it does not allow the creation of a role for an AWS Lambda function as that would require the iam:CreateRole permission.

sns:ListTopics* – This would allow listing SNS topics but not deletion of an SNS topic.

CORRECT: "Describe AWS load balancers" is a correct answer.

CORRECT: "Invoke an AWS Lambda function" is also a correct answer.

INCORRECT: "Delete an Amazon RDS database" is incorrect as described above.

INCORRECT: "Create an IAM role for an AWS Lambda function" is incorrect as described above.

INCORRECT: "Delete an Amazon SNS topic" is incorrect as described above.

References:

https://docs.aws.amazon.com/IAM/latest/UserGuide/access_policies.html

Save time with our exam-specific cheat sheets:

https://digitalcloud.training/certification-training/aws-certified-sysops-administrator-associate/aws-iam/

QUESTION 31

A custom application that runs on an Amazon EC2 instance has performance issues due to an application process that erroneously consumes all available CPU resources. The development team are working on a resolution and have asked a CloudOps Administrator to restart the instance when the problem occurs.

How can the administrator automate rebooting the instance if the issue is experienced for more than 2 minutes?

1. Create an Amazon CloudWatch alarm with an action to reboot the instance. Use basic monitoring.
2. Create an Amazon CloudWatch alarm with an action to reboot the instance. Use detailed monitoring.
3. Create an Amazon EventBridge rule that runs an AWS Lambda function on a schedule and reboots the instance.
4. Create an AWS CloudTrail API action that reboots the instance when resources are fully utilized.

Answer: 2

Explanation:

Using Amazon CloudWatch alarm actions, you can create alarms that automatically stop, terminate, reboot, or recover your EC2 instances.

You can use the stop or terminate actions to help you save money when you no longer need an instance to be running.

You can use the reboot and recover actions to automatically reboot those instances or recover them onto new hardware if a system impairment occurs.

In this case the instance should be rebooted if the event occurs for more than 2 minutes. Therefore, we must use detailed monitoring which has a frequency of 1 minute as basic monitoring has a frequency of 5 minutes.

CORRECT: "Create an Amazon CloudWatch alarm with an action to reboot the instance. Use detailed monitoring" is the correct answer.

INCORRECT: "Create an Amazon CloudWatch alarm with an action to reboot the instance. Use basic monitoring" is incorrect. Detailed monitoring must be used, or the alarm will not occur for at least 5 minutes.

INCORRECT: "Create an Amazon EventBridge rule that runs an AWS Lambda function on a schedule and reboots the instance" is incorrect. This can be done but this will always reboot the instance based on the schedule rather than reacting to the resource usage.

INCORRECT: "Create an AWS CloudTrail API action that reboots the instance when resources are fully utilized" is incorrect. CloudTrail records API actions rather than initiating them.

References:

https://docs.aws.amazon.com/AmazonCloudWatch/latest/monitoring/UsingAlarmActions.html

Save time with our exam-specific cheat sheets:

https://digitalcloud.training/certification-training/aws-certified-sysops-administrator-associate/amazon-cloudwatch/

QUESTION 32

A company is using AWS CloudTrail and needs to ensure that the log files stored in S3 are not tampered with. The company must be able to determine if log files are modified, deleted, or unchanged.

How can a CloudOps Administrator meet this requirement MOST efficiently?

1. Update the trail and enable log file validation.
2. Update the S3 bucket and enable log file validation.
3. Create an AWS Lambda function that computes an MD5 hash of the log files.
4. Enable default encryption on the S3 bucket.

Answer: 1

Explanation:

To determine whether a log file was modified, deleted, or unchanged after CloudTrail delivered it, you can use CloudTrail log file integrity validation.

This feature is built using industry standard algorithms: SHA-256 for hashing and SHA-256 with RSA for digital signing. This makes it computationally infeasible to modify, delete or forge CloudTrail log files without detection.

To enable log file integrity validation with the CloudTrail console, choose **Yes** for the **Enable log file validation** option when you create or update a trail. By default, this feature is enabled for new trails.

CORRECT: "Update the trail and enable log file validation" is the correct answer.

INCORRECT: "Update the S3 bucket and enable log file validation" is incorrect. Log file validation for CloudTrail log files is enabled by updating the trail.

INCORRECT: "Create an AWS Lambda function that computes an MD5 hash of the log files" is incorrect. You could use event notifications along with Lambda, but it would operationally more complex (less efficient).

INCORRECT: "Enable default encryption on the S3 bucket" is incorrect. Encryption will not ensure log file integrity.

References:

https://docs.aws.amazon.com/awscloudtrail/latest/userguide/cloudtrail-log-file-validation-intro.html

Save time with our exam-specific cheat sheets:

https://digitalcloud.training/certification-training/aws-certified-sysops-administrator-associate/aws-cloudtrail/

QUESTION 33

An application uses an Amazon RDS database in a single AWS Region. The company wants to add disaster recovery (DR) capability to the database across geographic locations. A CloudOps Administrator must add DR for the database.

Which solutions offers the lowest recovery time objective (RTO) and recovery point objective (RPO)?

1. Run an AWS Lambda function on a schedule to create and copy snapshots across Regions.
2. Take automated snapshots and replicate them across Regions.
3. Create a Multi-AZ read replica for the database.
4. Create a cross-Region read replica for the database.

Answer: 4

Explanation:

The RTO relates to how long it takes to restore the DB and the RPO relates to the amount of data loss. A low RTO means a quick recovery and a low RPO means less data loss.

In this case the best solution is to use a cross-Region read replica. The master DB synchronizes changes to the replica using asynchronous replication.

The lag time for replication will be greater than it is for read replicas that are in the same Region as the master. However, it will still mean a lower RPO than the other (valid) methods.

The replica can be promoted to being a standalone database and this will take around 15 minutes. The other (valid) solutions all require creating a new database from a snapshot which will also take time to provision but will result in greater data loss.

CORRECT: "Create a cross-Region read replica for the database" is the correct answer.

INCORRECT: "Run an AWS Lambda function on a schedule to create and copy snapshots across Regions" is incorrect. This will likely result in a higher RTO and RPO.

INCORRECT: "Take automated snapshots and replicate them across Regions" is incorrect. This will likely result in a higher RTO and RPO.

INCORRECT: "Create a Multi-AZ read replica for the database" is incorrect. This is not valid as an option as it is within a single Region and does not provide geographic DR.

References:

https://docs.aws.amazon.com/AmazonRDS/latest/UserGuide/USER_ReadRepl.XRgn.html

Save time with our exam-specific cheat sheets:

https://digitalcloud.training/certification-training/aws-certified-sysops-administrator-associate/amazon-rds/

QUESTION 34

An eCommerce company run a website that is hosted on burstable performance Amazon EC2 instances in an Auto Scaling group. The website occasionally experiences sustained spikes in sales for a few hours when email promotions are sent out. Users have reported poor performance a couple of hours into these events. A CloudOps Administrator noticed that the CPU utilization is <30% across the fleet and the ASG did not scale as it is configured to scale when CPU utilization is >60%.

How can the CloudOps Administrator resolve the performance issues?

1. Add an Elastic Load Balancer and enable ELB health checks.
2. Create an Amazon CloudFront distribution for the Auto Scaling group.
3. Configure unlimited mode for the EC2 instances.
4. Modify the Auto Scaling group to use EBS-optimized EC2 instances.

Answer: 3

Explanation:

The T instance family of burstable instances provides a baseline CPU performance with the ability to burst above the baseline at any time for as long as required. However, burstable instances have a CPU credit balance. Unlimited mode is a credit configuration mode, which allows an instance to burst above the baseline by sustaining high CPU utilization for any period of time whenever required.

It is likely that the CPU credits have been used up by sustained bursting above the baseline for the instances. Enabling unlimited mode will allow the instances to sustain higher CPU utilization through the sales events.

CORRECT: "Configure unlimited mode for the EC2 instances" is the correct answer.

INCORRECT: "Add an Elastic Load Balancer and enable ELB health checks" is incorrect. This would only assist with replacement of EC2 instances that the ELB reports as unhealthy.

INCORRECT: "Create an Amazon CloudFront distribution for the Auto Scaling group" is incorrect. You cannot create a CloudFront distribution for an Auto Scaling group as it is not a supported origin (an ELB would be required).

INCORRECT: "Modify the Auto Scaling group to use EBS-optimized EC2 instances" is incorrect. This would not assist as it is likely that the issue relates to CPU credits being used up causing CPU constraints.

References:

https://docs.aws.amazon.com/AWSEC2/latest/UserGuide/burstable-performance-instances-unlimited-mode.html

Save time with our exam-specific cheat sheets:

https://digitalcloud.training/certification-training/aws-certified-sysops-administrator-associate/amazon-ec2/

QUESTION 35

An application allows users to upload PDF files directly to an Amazon S3 bucket in the us-east-1 Region. Users are located globally, and many remote users have reported slow upload times. A CloudOps Administrator needs to improve the upload speed for the PDF files.

How can this be achieved?

1. Enable S3 Transfer Acceleration for the S3 bucket.
2. Create S3 access points in Regions closer to the users.
3. Enable cross-Region replication for the S3 bucket.
4. Create an accelerator in AWS Global Accelerator.

Answer: 1

Explanation:

Amazon S3 Transfer Acceleration is a bucket-level feature that enables fast, easy, and secure transfers of files over long distances between your client and an S3 bucket. Transfer Acceleration takes advantage of the globally distributed edge locations in Amazon CloudFront. As the data arrives at an edge location, the data is routed to Amazon S3 over an optimized network path.

This solution ensures that remote users of the application will be directed to a local edge location for better performance when uploading the PDF files.

CORRECT: "Enable S3 Transfer Acceleration for the S3 bucket" is the correct answer.

INCORRECT: "Create S3 access points in Regions closer to the users" is incorrect. S3 access points are not used for improving upload speeds.

INCORRECT: " Enable cross-Region replication for the S3 bucket " is incorrect. This would get data already in S3 replicated to Regions closer to the users. It does not help with uploading data.

INCORRECT: "Create an accelerator in AWS Global Accelerator" is incorrect. Global Accelerator works with applications running on EC2 and ELB rather than S3.

References:

https://docs.aws.amazon.com/AmazonS3/latest/userguide/transfer-acceleration.html

Save time with our exam-specific cheat sheets:

https://digitalcloud.training/certification-training/aws-certified-sysops-administrator-associate/amazon-s3/

QUESTION 36

A company runs a highly elastic application across hundreds of Amazon EC2 instances in private subnets. The application uses EC2 Auto Scaling which launches and terminates instances across three Availability Zones (AZs). The application connects to a third-party API over the public internet and the CloudOps Administrator must provide a list of static IP addresses for the third party to whitelist in their firewalls.

Which solution will meet these requirements?

1. Configure a NAT gateway in the public subnet of each AZ. Add a route to the NAT gateway to the route table of each private subnet.
2. Attach an Elastic IP address to each AZ. Associate the Elastic IP with the EC2 instances within each AZ.
3. Attach an Elastic IP address to the internet gateway in the public subnet. Add a route to the internet gateway to the route table of each private subnet.
4. Attach an Elastic IP address to each EC2 instance. Configure a VPC endpoint for outbound traffic.

Answer: 1

Explanation:

When you configure a NAT gateway in a public subnet you must attach an Elastic IP address. All outbound traffic will be subject to network address translation which will change the source IPv4 address to connections to the third-party API to the EIP public IP address.

The EIP address of the NAT gateway can be provided to the third-party company to whitelist in their firewalls.

This solution is very efficient and means there is no requirement to make any ongoing changes as EC2 instances are launched and terminated as they will always use the NAT gateway for internet-bound connections.

CORRECT: "Configure a NAT gateway in the public subnet of each AZ. Add a route to the NAT gateway to the route table of each private subnet" is the correct answer.

INCORRECT: "Attach an Elastic IP address to each AZ. Associate the Elastic IP with the EC2 instances within each AZ" is incorrect. You cannot attach EIPs to an AZ. They can be attached to EC2 instances, NAT gateways, and other network services.

INCORRECT: "Attach an Elastic IP address to the internet gateway in the public subnet. Add a route to the internet gateway to the route table of each private subnet" is incorrect. You cannot attach an EIP to an internet gateway and there is no point adding a route to an internet gateway to a private subnet as instances there will not have public IP addresses.

INCORRECT: "Attach an Elastic IP address to each EC2 instance. Configure a VPC endpoint for outbound traffic" is incorrect. EIPs should not be assigned to instances in private subnets and a VPC endpoint is not used for internet traffic.

References:

https://docs.aws.amazon.com/vpc/latest/userguide/vpc-nat-gateway.html

Save time with our exam-specific cheat sheets:

https://digitalcloud.training/certification-training/aws-certified-sysops-administrator-associate/amazon-virtual-private-cloud-vpc/

QUESTION 37

A CloudOps Administrator has launched a new web application and Amazon RDS database instance in private subnets within a VPC. The administrator updated the application with the connection information for the DB. After ensuring the application and DB are fully deployed, the administrator checked the web server logs and noticed that the connection to the database is repeatedly failing.

Which of the following may be causes of the connectivity problems? (Select TWO.)

1. The source used to connect is not authorized in the database security group egress rules.
2. The database instance does not have an Elastic IP address attached.
3. The source used to connect is not authorized in the database security group ingress rules.
4. The wrong DNS name or database endpoint was used to connect.
5. The database is still being created and is not available for connectivity.

Answer: 3,4

Explanation:

The inability to connect to an Amazon RDS DB instance can have several root causes. Here are a few of the most common reasons:

- The RDS DB instance is in a state other than available, so it can't accept connections.
- The source you use to connect to the DB instance is missing from the sources authorized to access the DB instance in your security group, network access control lists (ACLs), or local firewalls.
- The wrong DNS name or endpoint was used to connect to the DB instance.
- The Multi-AZ DB instance failed over, and the secondary DB instance uses a subnet or route table that doesn't allow inbound connections.
- The user authentication is incorrect.

In this case we know the database instance is fully deployed so the most likely issues are that the security group for the database instance does not have an inbound rule allowing the web server security group on the correct port, or the connection information is incorrect.

CORRECT: "The source used to connect is not authorized in the database security group ingress rules" is a correct answer.

CORRECT: "The wrong DNS name or database endpoint was used to connect" is also a correct answer.

INCORRECT: "The source used to connect is not authorized in the database security group egress rules" is incorrect. Security groups are stateful, so response traffic does not require a rule.

INCORRECT: "The database instance does not have an Elastic IP address attached" is incorrect. The DB instance was launched in a private subnet so does not have any kind of public IP address.

INCORRECT: "The database is still being created and is not available for connectivity" is incorrect. The question states that the application and database are fully deployed.

References:

https://aws.amazon.com/premiumsupport/knowledge-center/rds-cannot-connect/

Save time with our exam-specific cheat sheets:

https://digitalcloud.training/certification-training/aws-certified-sysops-administrator-associate/amazon-rds/

QUESTION 38

A popular application uses an Amazon Aurora DB cluster for storing data. The application's usage is highly variable with unpredictable spikes in traffic. Much of the load is database queries and the same query is rarely performed multiple times. The application logs show that performance issues have occurred during peak usage periods when many searches were submitted.

A CloudOps Administrator must improve the performance of the application. Which solution will meet these requirements?

1. Create an Amazon ElastiCache cluster to cache database queries and update the application to check the cache.
2. Implement Aurora Auto Scaling to scale the number of replicas and update the application to use the Aurora reader endpoint.
3. Implement Aurora Auto Scaling to scale the database instance size based on the number of queries submitted.
4. Create RAID 0 arrays for the Aurora database cluster instances to improve I/O performance.

Answer: 2

Explanation:

Aurora Auto Scaling dynamically adjusts the number of Aurora Replicas provisioned for an Aurora DB cluster using single-master replication. Aurora Auto Scaling is available for both Aurora MySQL and Aurora PostgreSQL.

Aurora Auto Scaling enables your Aurora DB cluster to handle sudden increases in connectivity or workload. When the connectivity or workload decreases, Aurora Auto Scaling removes unnecessary Aurora Replicas so that you don't pay for unused provisioned DB instances.

Applications must be updated to use the reader endpoint so they can take advantage of Aurora Auto Scaling.

CORRECT: "Implement Aurora Auto Scaling to scale the number of replicas and update the application to use the Aurora reader endpoint" is the correct answer.

INCORRECT: "Create an Amazon ElastiCache cluster to cache database queries and update the application to check the cache" is incorrect. In this case the queries are rarely repeated so caching would be ineffective.

INCORRECT: "Implement Aurora Auto Scaling to scale the database instance size based on the number of queries submitted" is incorrect. You cannot scale the instance size using Aurora Auto Scaling, only the number of replicas.

INCORRECT: "Create RAID 0 arrays for the Aurora database cluster instances to improve I/O performance" is incorrect. You cannot use RAID arrays with Aurora DBs as it is a managed service.

References:

https://docs.aws.amazon.com/AmazonRDS/latest/AuroraUserGuide/Aurora.Integrating.AutoScaling.html

Save time with our exam-specific cheat sheets:

https://digitalcloud.training/certification-training/aws-certified-sysops-administrator-associate/amazon-aurora/

QUESTION 39

A CloudOps Administrator attempts to deploy many EC2 instances to support a large distributed application workload. The instances are being deployed in several batches and on the most recent deployment the administrator received the InstanceLimitExceeded error.

What should the CloudOps Administrator do to resolve this error?

1. Use Service Quotas to request an EC2 quota increase.

2. Use the Amazon EC2 console to request an EBS quota increase.
3. Launch the EC2 instances in a different Availability Zone.
4. Launch new EC2 instances in another VPC within the Region.

Answer: 1

Explanation:

The InstanceLimitExceeded error indicates that you reached the limit on the number of running On-Demand instances that you can launch in a Region. You can request an instance limit increase on a per-Region basis.

You can request a quota increase through the Amazon EC2 console and by using Service Quotas.

CORRECT: "Use Service Quotas to request an EC2 quota increase" is the correct answer.

INCORRECT: "Use the Amazon EC2 console to request an EBS quota increase" is incorrect. The administrator must increase the EC2 quota, not the EBS quota.

INCORRECT: "Launch the EC2 instances in a different Availability Zone" is incorrect. The limit applies within the Region so this will not help.

INCORRECT: "Launch new EC2 instances in another VPC within the Region" is incorrect. The limit applies within the Region so this will not help.

References:

https://aws.amazon.com/premiumsupport/knowledge-center/ec2-InstanceLimitExceeded-error/

Save time with our exam-specific cheat sheets:

https://digitalcloud.training/certification-training/aws-certified-sysops-administrator-associate/amazon-ec2/

QUESTION 40

A company uses several AWS accounts by different business units for development purposes. An additional account is used by security admins purposes. The security admins have requested that they be granted access to review the configuration of Amazon EC2 resources in the development accounts to ensure security best practices are being followed.

Which solution will meet these requirements in the MOST secure manner?

1. Create an IAM policy in each development account that has read-only access to Amazon EC2 resources. Assign the policy to an IAM user. Share the user credentials with the security administrators.
2. Create an IAM policy in each development account that has administrator access to all Amazon EC2 actions. Assign the policy to an IAM user. Share the user credentials with the security administrators.
3. Create an IAM policy in each development account that has read-only access to Amazon EC2 resources. Assign the policy to a cross-account IAM role. Ask the security administrators to assume the role from their account.
4. Create an IAM policy in each development account that has administrator access to Amazon EC2 resources. Assign the policy to a cross-account IAM role. Ask the security administrators to assume the role from their account.

Answer: 3

Explanation:

This question is checking that you know how to configure cross-account access and how to do so securely using the principle of least privilege. This can be achieved through the creation of a policy providing permissions to the resources in each development account, associating the policies to roles, and then assuming those roles from the security admins account.

To ensure this solution is secure, read-only permissions should be assigned to the permissions policy as per the requirements of the security team.

CORRECT: "Create an IAM policy in each development account that has read-only access to Amazon EC2 resources. Assign the policy to a cross-account IAM role. Ask the security administrators to assume the role from their account" is the correct answer.

INCORRECT: "Create an IAM policy in each development account that has administrator access to Amazon EC2 resources. Assign the policy to a cross-account IAM role. Ask the security administrators to assume the role from their account" is incorrect. Administrator access provides more permissions than are required by the security team.

INCORRECT: "Create an IAM policy in each development account that has read-only access to Amazon EC2 resources. Assign the policy to an IAM user. Share the user credentials with the security administrators" is incorrect. Sharing credentials is much less secure than using roles.

INCORRECT: "Create an IAM policy in each development account that has administrator access to all Amazon EC2 actions. Assign the policy to an IAM user. Share the user credentials with the security administrators" is incorrect. This answer provides too many permissions and an insecure method of authentication.

References:

https://docs.aws.amazon.com/IAM/latest/UserGuide/tutorial_cross-account-with-roles.html

Save time with our exam-specific cheat sheets:

https://digitalcloud.training/certification-training/aws-certified-sysops-administrator-associate/aws-iam/

QUESTION 41

A company's management team need to view and track and the cost of separate projects within an AWS account. A CloudOps Administrator must setup the account so that this information can be viewed for each project in AWS Cost Explorer.

What must the administrator do to set this up?

1. Activate cost allocation tags. Tag resources based on the project they are associated with.
2. Use AWS Organizations and enable consolidated billing. Create AWS Cost and Usage Reports.
3. Create billing alerts in AWS Budgets that track the resources associated with each project.
4. Use cost categories to define custom groups that are based on AWS cost and usage dimensions.

Answer: 1

Explanation:

A tag is a label that you or AWS assigns to an AWS resource. Each tag consists of a *key* and a *value*. For each resource, each tag key must be unique, and each tag key can have only one value. You can use tags to organize your resources, and cost allocation tags to track your AWS costs on a detailed level.

After you activate cost allocation tags, AWS uses the cost allocation tags to organize your resource costs on your cost allocation report, to make it easier for you to categorize and track your AWS costs.

CORRECT: "Activate cost allocation tags. Tag resources based on the project they are associated with" is the correct answer.

INCORRECT: "Use AWS Organizations and enable consolidated billing. Create AWS Cost and Usage Reports" is incorrect. Cost allocation tags should be used to track costs per project.

INCORRECT: "Create billing alerts in AWS Budgets that track the resources associated with each project" is incorrect. You cannot track resources for each project without first enabling cost allocation tags and tagging the resources.

INCORRECT: "Use cost categories to define custom groups that are based on AWS cost and usage dimensions" is incorrect. You must first activate cost allocation tags to track the project resources before you can use them as dimensions in cost categories rules.

References:

https://docs.aws.amazon.com/awsaccountbilling/latest/aboutv2/cost-alloc-tags.html

QUESTION 42

A company is deploying an internet-facing application in the AWS Cloud that will run behind an Application

Load Balancer (ALB). The ALB will be configured with a secure listener. The CloudOps Administrator must ensure that the SSL/TLS certificate used by the listener automatically renews.

Which solution MOST efficiently meets these requirements?

1. Request a public certificate by using AWS Certificate Manager (ACM) and use Email validation. ACM will automatically renew the certificate.
2. Request a public certificate by using AWS Certificate Manager (ACM). Write an AWS Lambda function that automates the renewal of the certificate.
3. Request a public certificate by using AWS Certificate Manager (ACM) and use DNS validation. ACM will automatically renew the certificate.
4. Request a private certificate by using AWS Certificate Manager (ACM) and use DNS validation. ACM will automatically renew the certificate.

Answer: 3

Explanation:

ACM provides managed renewal for your Amazon-issued SSL/TLS certificates. This means that ACM will either renew your certificates automatically (if you are using DNS validation), or it will send you email notices when expiration is approaching. These services are provided for both public and private ACM certificates.

CORRECT: "Request a public certificate by using AWS Certificate Manager (ACM) and use DNS validation. ACM will automatically renew the certificate" is the correct answer.

INCORRECT: "Request a private certificate by using AWS Certificate Manager (ACM) and use DNS validation. ACM will automatically renew the certificate" is incorrect. A public certificate should be used as this is an internet-facing application.

INCORRECT: "Request a public certificate by using AWS Certificate Manager (ACM) and use Email validation. ACM will automatically renew the certificate" is incorrect. DNS validation should be used when automatic renewal is required.

INCORRECT: "Request a public certificate by using AWS Certificate Manager (ACM). Write an AWS Lambda function that automates the renewal of the certificate" is incorrect. There is no need to use a Lambda function when automatic renewal can be achieved.

References:

https://docs.aws.amazon.com/acm/latest/userguide/managed-renewal.html

QUESTION 43

A company's security team updated their security policy and require that multi-factor authentication (MFA) is implemented for all IAM users. A CloudOps Administrator has created a policy that denies API calls that are not authenticated with MFA.

How can users authenticate with MFA when issuing API calls using the AWS CLI?

1. Add the users who require CLI access to an IAM user group. Use a policy condition to exclude the MFA requirement for the user group.
2. Instruct users to run the *sts get-session-token* AWS CLI command use the returned temporary security credentials to sign API calls.
3. Instruct the users to log into the AWS Management Console with MFA before issuing API calls using the CLI.
4. Users will not be able to use the AWS CLI due to the policy restriction and must use the AWS Management Console.

Answer: 2

Explanation:

If you plan to interact with your resources using the AWS CLI when using an MFA device, then you must create a temporary session. Users will need to run the sts get-session-token AWS CLI command, replacing the variables with information from your account, resources, and MFA device.

The users will then receive an output with temporary credentials and an expiration time (by default, 12 hours). These temporary credentials can then be used to sign API calls using the AWS CLI.

CORRECT: "Instruct users to run the *sts get-session-token* AWS CLI command use the returned temporary security credentials to sign API calls" is the correct answer.

INCORRECT: "Add the users who require CLI access to an IAM user group. Use a policy condition to exclude the MFA requirement for the user group" is incorrect. This does not meet the requirement to authenticate using MFA when using the CLI. You also cannot use an IAM user group in a policy.

INCORRECT: "Instruct the users to log into the AWS Management Console with MFA before issuing API calls using the CLI" is incorrect. It is not necessary to use the console first and this does not negate the need to get session tokens with an MFA device.

INCORRECT: "Users will not be able to use the AWS CLI due to the policy restriction and must use the AWS Management Console" is incorrect. This is not true; you can use MFA with the AWS CLI as described in the explanation above.

References:

https://aws.amazon.com/premiumsupport/knowledge-center/authenticate-mfa-cli/

Save time with our exam-specific cheat sheets:

https://digitalcloud.training/certification-training/aws-certified-sysops-administrator-associate/aws-iam/

QUESTION 44

A company is using AWS Organizations and wants to implement tag policies to standardize tags across resources in the organization's accounts. A CloudOps Administrator signs in to the organization's management account with the required permissions but cannot activate tag policies.

Which of the following may resolve this issue?

1. Enable all features for the organization.
2. Enable consolidated billing for the organization.
3. Sign in to each member account and enable tag policies.
4. Enable service control policies (SCPs) first.

Answer: 1

Explanation:

Tag policies are a type of policy that can help you standardize tags across resources in your organization's accounts. In a tag policy, you specify tagging rules applicable to resources when they are tagged.

Using tag policies requires the following:

- Your organization must have all features enabled.
- You must be signed in to your organization's management account.
- You need the correct IAM permissions for AWS Organizations.

In this case the question states that the administrator has permissions and is signed in to the management account. Therefore, the most likely issue is that all features are not enabled for the organization.

CORRECT: "Enable all features for the organization" is the correct answer.

INCORRECT: "Enable consolidated billing for the organization" is incorrect. All features must be enabled; consolidated billing is not enough.

INCORRECT: "Sign in to each member account and enable tag policies" is incorrect. The administrator is correctly signed in to the management account and does not need to enable tag policies in the member accounts.

INCORRECT: "Enable service control policies (SCPs) first" is incorrect. SCPs do not need to be enabled to use tag policies.

References:

https://docs.aws.amazon.com/organizations/latest/userguide/orgs_manage_policies_tag-policies-preregs.html

Save time with our exam-specific cheat sheets:

https://digitalcloud.training/certification-training/aws-certified-sysops-administrator-associate/aws-organizations/

QUESTION 45

An application runs in on Amazon EC2 instances in a private subnet and processes images stored in an Amazon S3 bucket. The EC2 instances have an attached IAM role that provides the required permissions to access the bucket. However, the application is unable to initiate connections to the S3 bucket.

Which action will solve this problem MOST securely?

1. Create an S3 gateway endpoint. Configure the route table for the private subnet.
2. Add a bucket policy to the S3 bucket permitting access from the IAM role.
3. Update the route table of the private subnet with a route to the internet gateway.
4. Create a NAT gateway in the private subnet and update the private subnet route table.

Answer: 1

Explanation:

In this case there it is likely that the private subnet does not have a NAT gateway configured so it cannot communicate with the public S3 endpoints. The S3 gateway endpoint will enable private connectivity to S3.

With gateway endpoints you must update the route table with a route to the service as it uses addresses that are outside of the VPC.

CORRECT: "Create an S3 gateway endpoint. Configure the route table for the private subnet" is the correct answer.

INCORRECT: "Add a bucket policy to the S3 bucket permitting access from the IAM role" is incorrect. The question states that a role is assigned to the instances that has the correct permissions.

INCORRECT: "Update the route table of the private subnet with a route to the internet gateway" is incorrect. You cannot use an internet gateway with instances in private subnets as they do not have public IP addresses.

INCORRECT: "Create a NAT gateway in the private subnet and update the private subnet route table" is incorrect. When creating a NAT gateway for a private subnet the gateway must be deployed in a public subnet.

References:

https://docs.aws.amazon.com/vpc/latest/privatelink/vpce-gateway.html

Save time with our exam-specific cheat sheets:

https://digitalcloud.training/certification-training/aws-certified-sysops-administrator-associate/amazon-virtual-private-cloud-vpc/

QUESTION 46

An AWS Lambda function is used to process data received by a web application and store the processed data in an Amazon RDS database. The credentials for accessing the RDS database are stored in the Lambda function code.

A CloudOps Administrator needs to update the configuration so the database credentials are not stored in plaintext and the password is rotated every 30 days.

Which solution will meet these requirements in the MOST operationally efficient manner?

1. Use AWS Certificate Manager to create a public certificate that automatically rotates every 30 days. Update the RDS database to use certificate-based authentication and configure the Lambda function with the private key.
2. Use AWS Secrets Manager to store credentials for the database. Create a secret in Secrets Manager, select the RDS database, and configure and automatic rotation schedule. Update the Lambda function to use the credentials stored from Secrets Manager.

3. Use AWS Key Management Service (KMS) to create a key that can encrypt the database password. Create a custom Lambda function that rotates the password and uses the KMS key to encrypt it. Store the encrypted password in environment variables.
4. Use AWS Systems Manager Parameter Store to create a secure string to store credentials for the database. Create a custom Lambda function that rotates the password. Use Amazon EventBridge to schedule the custom function to run every 30 days. Update the Lambda function to use the credentials from Parameter Store.

Answer: 2

Explanation:

To help keep your secrets secure, Secrets Manager can automatically rotate them on a schedule. When it rotates a secret, Secrets Manager updates the credentials in both the secret and the database or service so that you don't have to manually change the credentials. Secrets Manager uses a Lambda rotation function to communicate with both Secrets Manager and the database or service. The rotation function:

- Calls the Secrets Manager API to retrieve and update secrets.
- Sends requests to the database or service to update the user password.

For Amazon RDS, Amazon DocumentDB, and Amazon Redshift secrets, you can turn on automatic rotation. This is the most operationally efficient solution as the functionality is built in and you do not need to write your own Lambda function code for rotation.

CORRECT: "Use AWS Secrets Manager to store credentials for the database. Create a secret in Secrets Manager, select the RDS database, and configure and automatic rotation schedule. Update the Lambda function to use the credentials stored from Secrets Manager" is the correct answer.

INCORRECT: "Use AWS Systems Manager Parameter Store to create a secure string to store credentials for the database. Create a custom Lambda function that rotates the password. Use Amazon EventBridge to schedule the custom function to run every 30 days.

Update the Lambda function to use the credentials from Parameter Store" is incorrect. This solution requires writing your own Lambda function code for rotation as parameter store cannot do automatic rotation. It is a less operationally efficient solution.

INCORRECT: "Use AWS Key Management Service (KMS) to create a key that can encrypt the database password. Create a custom Lambda function that rotates the password and uses the KMS key to encrypt it. Store the encrypted password in environment variables" is incorrect.

This solution does not mention how the key is rotated every 30 days as the question requires.

INCORRECT: "Use AWS Certificate Manager to create a public certificate that automatically rotates every 30 days. Update the RDS database to use certificate-based authentication and configure the Lambda function with the private key" is incorrect.

You cannot use ACM certificates, which are SSL/TLS certificates, for authentication between Lambda and Amazon RDS.

References:

https://docs.aws.amazon.com/secretsmanager/latest/userguide/rotating-secrets.html

https://aws.amazon.com/blogs/security/rotate-amazon-rds-database-credentials-automatically-with-aws-secrets-manager/

QUESTION 47

A Development account is being used to test a CPU-heavy application. To save costs, a CloudOps Administrator needs a solution to stop Amazon EC2 instances that are not in use in the account

Which solution will meet this requirement?

1. Use Amazon Athena to search AWS CloudTrail logs. Invoke a Lambda function to stop the EC2 instances when there is no API activity.
2. Create an Amazon CloudWatch metric to stop the EC2 instances when the VolumeIdleTime metric is >1800 seconds.

3. Use AWS Config to identify resource state changes and invoke an AWS Lambda function that stops the EC2 instances.
4. Create an Amazon CloudWatch alarm that monitors the CPUUtilization metric and stops the EC2 instances if the utilization is <5% for a 30-minute period.

Answer: 4

Explanation:

A CloudWatch alarm monitors and metric and when defined thresholds are met or exceeded it triggers an action. In this case we need to identify idle EC2 instances. This can be done by monitoring CPUUtilization metric and if the utilization is less than 5% for 30 minutes it will trigger an action to stop the instance.

CORRECT: "Create an Amazon CloudWatch alarm that monitors the CPUUtilization metric and stops the EC2 instances if the utilization is <5% for a 30-minute period" is the correct answer.

INCORRECT: "Create an Amazon CloudWatch metric to stop the EC2 instances when the VolumeIdleTime metric is >1800 seconds" is incorrect. This metric monitors the total number of seconds in a specified period of time when no read or write operations were submitted. It is unlikely that no activity will occur for an entire 30-minute period.

INCORRECT: "Use Amazon Athena to search AWS CloudTrail logs. Invoke a Lambda function to stop the EC2 instances when there is no API activity" is incorrect. A lack of API activity does not necessarily indicate the instance is idle, the CPU could still be processing data but not issuing API calls.

INCORRECT: "Use AWS Config to identify resource state changes and invoke an AWS Lambda function that stops the EC2 instances" is incorrect. This answer does not indicate which state changes it is monitoring and there is no good solution for monitoring state changes that indicate the instance is idle.

References:

https://docs.aws.amazon.com/AmazonCloudWatch/latest/monitoring/AlarmThatSendsEmail.html

Save time with our exam-specific cheat sheets:

https://digitalcloud.training/certification-training/aws-certified-sysops-administrator-associate/amazon-cloudwatch/

QUESTION 48

An Amazon RDS database is encrypted using a customer managed AWS KMS key. Snapshots of the database need to be shared with another AWS account owned by the same company. The database must always remain encrypted.

How can a CloudOps Administrator share the encrypted database snapshots?

1. Extract the data from the database snapshot using an AWS Lambda function and write it to an encrypted Amazon S3 bucket. Use a second AWS Lambda function in the target account that retrieves the data from bucket and creates an encrypted snapshot.
2. Add the second AWS account as a key user in the key policy of the customer managed KMS key that is used to encrypt the database. Copy and share the database snapshot with the target account using the KMS key.
3. Create an unencrypted copy of the database snapshot. Share the database snapshot with the target account and use a customer managed KMS key to encrypt the snapshot.
4. Create a copy of the database snapshot and encrypt it with the default AWS KMS encryption key. Add the second AWS account as a key user in the key policy of the KMS key. Copy and share the database snapshot with the target account.

Answer: 2

Explanation:

The process for sharing an encrypted Amazon RDS DB snapshot with another account is as follows:

1. Add the target account to a custom (non-default) KMS key.
2. Copy the snapshot using the customer managed key, and then share the snapshot with the target account.

3. Copy the shared DB snapshot from the target account.

The administrator will need to update the customer managed KMS key's policy to add a key user. The key user will be the account number of the target AWS account. This will give the target account the ability to use the KMS key to access the data.

CORRECT: "Add the second AWS account as a key user in the key policy of the customer managed KMS key that is used to encrypt the database. Copy and share the database snapshot with the target account using the KMS key" is the correct answer.

INCORRECT: "Create an unencrypted copy of the database snapshot. Share the database snapshot with the target account and use a customer managed KMS key to encrypt the snapshot" is incorrect. The data should be always encrypted as per the question.

INCORRECT: "Create a copy of the database snapshot and encrypt it with the default AWS KMS encryption key. Add the second AWS account as a key user in the key policy of the KMS key. Copy and share the database snapshot with the target account" is incorrect. You can't share a snapshot that's encrypted using the default AWS KMS encryption key.

INCORRECT: "Extract the data from the database snapshot using an AWS Lambda function and write it to an encrypted Amazon S3 bucket. Use a second AWS Lambda function in the target account that retrieves the data from bucket and creates an encrypted snapshot" is incorrect. Extracting data to an S3 bucket from a relational database and then putting it back into a snapshot that can be used to create a database would be extremely difficult as the format would be tricky to maintain.

References:

https://aws.amazon.com/premiumsupport/knowledge-center/share-encrypted-rds-snapshot-kms-key/

Save time with our exam-specific cheat sheets:

https://digitalcloud.training/certification-training/aws-certified-sysops-administrator-associate/amazon-rds/

QUESTION 49

A company uses Amazon S3 to store media content that is served through an Amazon CloudFront distribution. The media is consumed by global users but due to agreements in place in certain countries the content should not be viewable there.

What is the MOST cost effective solution to block access in specific countries?

1. Enable the geo restriction feature in the CloudFront distribution and create a blacklist of banned countries.
2. Update a Network ACL with a deny rule based on the IP addresses of the banned countries.
3. Create a secondary origin access identity (OAI). Configure the S3 bucket policy to prevent access from unauthorized countries.
4. Use Amazon Route 53 geolocation routing and route traffic from banned countries to an Amazon EC2 website that returns a 403 Forbidden HTTP response.

Answer: 1

Explanation:

You can use *geo restriction*, also known as *geo blocking*, to prevent users in specific geographic locations from accessing content that you're distributing through a CloudFront distribution.

When a user requests your content, CloudFront typically serves the requested content regardless of where the user is located. If you need to prevent users in specific countries from accessing your content, you can use the CloudFront geo restriction feature to do one of the following:

- Allow your users to access your content only if they're in one of the countries on a whitelist of approved countries.
- Prevent your users from accessing your content if they're in one of the countries on a blacklist of banned countries.

CORRECT: "Enable the geo restriction feature in the CloudFront distribution and create a blacklist of banned countries" is the correct answer.

INCORRECT: "Update a Network ACL with a deny rule based on the IP addresses of the banned countries" is incorrect. A Network ACL does not apply as the application does not use EC2 instances in subnets.

INCORRECT: "Create a secondary origin access identity (OAI). Configure the S3 bucket policy to prevent access from unauthorized countries" is incorrect.

You cannot have multiple OAIs for a single bucket and it would not be efficient to use a bucket policy do deny access from specific countries (you'd need a massive list of IPs that would change over time; and cached content may still be served).

INCORRECT: "Use Amazon Route 53 geolocation routing and route traffic from banned countries to an Amazon EC2 website that returns a 403 Forbidden HTTP response" is incorrect. It doesn't make much sense to run a website on EC2 just for this purpose and would not be cost-effective.

References:

https://docs.aws.amazon.com/AmazonCloudFront/latest/DeveloperGuide/georestrictions.html

Save time with our exam-specific cheat sheets:

https://digitalcloud.training/certification-training/aws-certified-sysops-administrator-associate/amazon-cloudfront/

QUESTION 50

A CloudOps Administrator us unable to connect to an Amazon EC2 instance which keeps returning a "request timed out" error message. The administrator is connecting from the public IP address of 200.10.11.12 and the instance's private IP address is 172.31.16.25. A VPC flow log has captured the following information:

2 0123456789992 eni-12345c7b2012345678 200.10.11.12 172.31.16.25 0 0 1 4 232 1357101112 1357101182 ACCEPT OK

2 0123456789992 eni-12345c7b2012345678 172.31.16.25 200.10.11.12 0 0 1 4 232 1357101112 1357101182 REJECT OK

What could be the cause of the problem?

1. Security group inbound deny rules.
2. Security group outbound deny rules.
3. Network ACL inbound rules.
4. Network ACL outbound rules.

Answer: 4

Explanation:

The information captured in the flow log shows that the inbound data was accepted but the outbound response data was rejected. The most likely cause of this issue is that a Network ACL is not configured correctly to allow the response traffic going outbound.

Network ACLs are not stateful and therefore require that a rule is configured for both inbound and outbound traffic, even if the outbound traffic is response traffic to a connection that was accepted inbound.

CORRECT: "Network ACL outbound rules" is the correct answer.

INCORRECT: "Network ACL inbound rules" is incorrect. The inbound traffic was accepted so this is not the issue.

INCORRECT: "Security group inbound deny rules" is incorrect. You cannot create deny rules with a security group.

INCORRECT: "Security group outbound deny rules" is incorrect. You cannot create deny rules with a security group.

References:

https://docs.aws.amazon.com/vpc/latest/userguide/vpc-network-acls.html

Save time with our exam-specific cheat sheets:

https://digitalcloud.training/certification-training/aws-certified-sysops-administrator-associate/amazon-virtual-private-cloud-vpc/

QUESTION 51

A stateful web applications runs on a fleet of Amazon EC2 instances behind an Application Load Balancer (ALB). The ALB is configured as the origin in an Amazon CloudFront distribution. Users who have recently signed in to the application have reported that they are sometimes asked to re-authenticate.

Which combination of actions should a CloudOps Administrator take to resolve this problem? (Select TWO.)

1. Configure the cache behavior to forward cookies.
2. Enable the slow start duration on the ALB target group.
3. Configure the cache behavior to forward headers.
4. Enable group-level stickiness on the ALB listener rule.
5. Enable sticky sessions on the ALB target group.

Answer: 1,5

Explanation:

The ALB uses load-balancer generated cookies that are stored on the client to bind a specific client to a specific EC2 instance. This is known as sticky sessions. When using a CloudFront distribution the default configuration is that cookies will not be forwarded to the origin. This means the user may be directed to another EC2 instance and will need to sign in again.

To resolve this issue the administrator should enable sticky sessions and then update the cache behavior for the CloudFront distribution so that it forwards cookies to the origin.

CORRECT: "Configure the cache behavior to forward cookies" is a correct answer.

CORRECT: "Enable sticky sessions on the ALB target group" is also a correct answer.

INCORRECT: "Enable the slow start duration on the ALB target group" is incorrect. This setting is used to define a duration within which a newly registered target receives an increasing share of requests, until it reaches its fair share.

INCORRECT: "Configure the cache behavior to forward headers" is incorrect. Sticky sessions uses cookies not headers.

INCORRECT: "Enable group-level stickiness on the ALB listener rule" is incorrect. If multiple target groups are configured in forwarding rule, group-level stickiness would ensure requests are routed to the same target group. This does not mean the same instance.

References:

https://docs.aws.amazon.com/AmazonCloudFront/latest/DeveloperGuide/Cookies.html

https://docs.aws.amazon.com/elasticloadbalancing/latest/application/sticky-sessions.html

Save time with our exam-specific cheat sheets:

https://digitalcloud.training/certification-training/aws-certified-sysops-administrator-associate/elastic-load-balancing/

QUESTION 52

An application vendor has reported that the latest version of their application is vulnerable to a cross-site scripting (XSS) attack. The CloudOps team has recently updated to the latest version, and it would be difficult to roll back.

Which AWS service can the CloudOps team use to mitigate this issue?

1. AWS Shield Standard
2. AWS Secrets Manager
3. AWS KMS
4. AWS WAF

Answer: 4

Explanation:

You can configure AWS WAF to block, allow, or monitor (count) requests based on Cross-Site Scripting (XSS) match conditions.

XSS attacks are those where the attacker uses vulnerabilities in a benign website as a vehicle to inject malicious client-site scripts (like JavaScript) into other legitimate user's web browsers.

This XSS match condition feature prevents these vulnerabilities in your web application by inspecting different elements of the incoming request.

CORRECT: "AWS WAF" is the correct answer.

INCORRECT: "AWS Shield Standard" is incorrect. This service is used for preventing Distributed Denial of Service (DDoS) attacks, not XSS attacks.

INCORRECT: "AWS KMS" is incorrect. KMS is used for creating and managing encryption keys.

INCORRECT: "AWS Secrets Manager" is incorrect. This service is used for storing secrets such as passwords.

References:

https://docs.aws.amazon.com/waf/latest/developerguide/classic-web-acl-xss-conditions.html

Save time with our exam-specific cheat sheets:

https://digitalcloud.training/certification-training/aws-certified-sysops-administrator-associate/aws-waf-and-shield/

QUESTION 53

A company uses Amazon ElastiCache Redis as the database for a web application. The database uses a single shard running on a large node which has 20% freeable memory. A CloudOps Administrator has been asked to resize the cluster and add high availability for the database.

Which actions should the administrator perform? (Select TWO.)

1. Add a read replica in a different Availability Zone.
2. Resize the cluster nodes to use extra-large nodes.
3. Add a shard in a different Availability Zone.
4. Enable multithreading and update the application.
5. Enable cluster mode and configure high availability.

Answer: 1,2

Explanation:

When using a single shard with cluster mode disabled you can create up to 5 replicas and the replicas can be in a separate AZ and this adds high availability with auto-failover.

The current database is showing 20% freeable memory which is relatively low so the administrator may wish to increase the size of the database node. In this case the extra-large node will provide more memory.

CORRECT: "Add a read replica in a different Availability Zone" is a correct answer.

CORRECT: "Resize the cluster nodes to use extra-large nodes" is also a correct answer.

INCORRECT: "Add a shard in a different Availability Zone" is incorrect. A shard is a data partition, so it won't add HA for the existing data that resides in a single AZ.

INCORRECT: "Enable multithreading and update the application" is incorrect. Multi-threading is not supported for Redis.

INCORRECT: "Enable cluster mode and configure high availability" is incorrect. Cluster mode allows the creation of additional shards of data, but the HA required in this question can be achieved through the deployment of a read replica in a separate AZ.

References:

https://docs.aws.amazon.com/AmazonElastiCache/latest/red-ug/Scaling.html

Save time with our exam-specific cheat sheets:

https://digitalcloud.training/certification-training/aws-certified-sysops-administrator-associate/amazonelasticache/

QUESTION 54

A company requires a solution for caching content globally and delivering it only to authorized users.
Which solution will meet these requirements?

1. Store the content in an Amazon S3 bucket with public access disabled. Create an Amazon CloudFront distribution that uses an origin access identity (OAI) to access the S3 bucket. Use CloudFront signed URLs to restrict access to the authorized users.
2. Store the content in an Amazon S3 bucket with public access disabled. Create an Amazon CloudFront distribution that uses an origin access identity (OAI) to access the S3 bucket. Use S3 presigned URLs to restrict access to the authorized users.
3. Store the content in an Amazon S3 bucket with public access disabled. Create an IAM role with permissions to the S3 bucket. Create an Amazon CloudFront distribution and assign the IAM role. Use CloudFront signed URLs to restrict access to the authorized users.
4. Store the content in an Amazon S3 bucket with public access enabled. Create an Amazon CloudFront distribution and enable field-level encryption. Use S3 presigned URLs to restrict access to the authorized users.

Answer: 1

Explanation:

To restrict access to the content whilst caching it globally CloudFront can be used with an OAI. The origin access identity (OAI) is a special user created in CloudFront that is allowed access to the bucket through bucket permissions. This ensures that it is not possible to access the content directly from the bucket (also need public access disabled).

The next step is to ensure that only the authorized users can access the CloudFront distribution. This can be achieved by using signed URLs that must be distributed through the application. Users can connect only using these URLs.

CORRECT: "Store the content in an Amazon S3 bucket with public access disabled. Create an Amazon CloudFront distribution that uses an origin access identity (OAI) to access the S3 bucket. Use CloudFront signed URLs to restrict access to the authorized users" is the correct answer.

INCORRECT: "Store the content in an Amazon S3 bucket with public access disabled. Create an Amazon CloudFront distribution that uses an origin access identity (OAI) to access the S3 bucket. Use S3 presigned URLs to restrict access to the authorized users" is incorrect.

S3 presigned URLs restrict access to S3 but this is already achieved through the public access settings and the OAI. A signed URL from CloudFront should be used instead.

INCORRECT: "Store the content in an Amazon S3 bucket with public access disabled. Create an IAM role with permissions to the S3 bucket. Create an Amazon CloudFront distribution and assign the IAM role. Use CloudFront signed URLs to restrict access to the authorized users" is incorrect.

A role is not used for accessing S3 using CloudFront. The access should be setup using the OAI and bucket permissions.

INCORRECT: "Store the content in an Amazon S3 bucket with public access enabled. Create an Amazon CloudFront distribution and enable field-level encryption. Use S3 presigned URLs to restrict access to the authorized users" is incorrect.

Everything is wrong with this answer! Public access should not be enabled on S3, field-level encryption will not assist, and a presigned URL is used with S3 not CloudFront.

References:

https://docs.aws.amazon.com/AmazonCloudFront/latest/DeveloperGuide/private-content-signed-urls.html

https://docs.aws.amazon.com/AmazonCloudFront/latest/DeveloperGuide/private-content-restricting-access-to-s3.html

Save time with our exam-specific cheat sheets:

https://digitalcloud.training/certification-training/aws-certified-sysops-administrator-associate/amazon-cloudfront/

QUESTION 55

A company manages several applications running across multiple AWS Regions. The applications use Amazon EC2 On-Demand instances and AWS Lambda functions. The CloudOps team must optimize the cost of running the workloads. The overall consumption of compute resources is stable.

Which approach should the CloudOps team use to optimize costs?

1. Purchase Compute Savings Plans based recommendations in Cost Explorer.
2. Purchase Convertible Reserved Instances based on CloudWatch metrics.
3. Purchase EC2 Instance Savings Plans based recommendations in Cost Explorer.
4. Purchase Standard Reserved Instances based on CloudWatch metrics.

Answer: 1

Explanation:

Savings Plans are a flexible pricing model that offer low prices on EC2, Lambda, and Fargate usage, in exchange for a commitment to a consistent amount of usage (measured in $/hour) for a 1 or 3 year term. Compute savings plans should be used when Lambda usage is required. You can get started with savings plans by following the recommendations in AWS Cost Explorer.

CORRECT: "Purchase Compute Savings Plans based recommendations in Cost Explorer" is the correct answer.

INCORRECT: "Purchase Convertible Reserved Instances based on CloudWatch metric" is incorrect. This will not provide any cost benefits for the AWS Lambda functions.

INCORRECT: "Purchase EC2 Instance Savings Plans based recommendations in Cost Explorer" is incorrect. This will not provide any cost benefits for the AWS Lambda functions.

INCORRECT: "Purchase Standard Reserved Instances based on CloudWatch metrics" is incorrect. This will not provide any cost benefits for the AWS Lambda functions.

References:

https://aws.amazon.com/savingsplans/

QUESTION 56

An application deployed on several Amazon EC2 instances in a VPC requires very low latency between nodes. A CloudOps Administrator has noticed unacceptable latency for inter-node communications and must find a solution to reduce latency.

Which approach should the administrator take?

1. Redeploy the application in a dedicated subnet.
2. Redeploy the application in a single Availability Zone.
3. Redeploy the application in a placement group.
4. Redeploy the application in an Auto Scaling group.

Answer: 3

Explanation:

Placement groups can be used to influence the placement of a group of *interdependent* instances to meet the needs of your workload. Depending on the type of workload, you can create a placement group using one of the following placement strategies:

- *Cluster* – packs instances close together inside an Availability Zone. This strategy enables workloads to achieve the low-latency network performance necessary for tightly-coupled node-to-node communication that is typical of HPC applications.
- *Partition* – spreads your instances across logical partitions such that groups of instances in one partition do not share the underlying hardware with groups of instances in different partitions.

This strategy is typically used by large distributed and replicated workloads, such as Hadoop, Cassandra, and Kafka.

- *Spread* – strictly places a small group of instances across distinct underlying hardware to reduce correlated failures.

For this application low latency inter-node communications are required so a cluster placement group would be the optimal solution.

CORRECT: "Redeploy the application in a placement group" is the correct answer.

INCORRECT: "Redeploy the application in a dedicated subnet" is incorrect. This would place the instances within a single AZ, but a cluster placement group would ensure they are close within the AZ.

INCORRECT: "Redeploy the application in a single Availability Zone" is incorrect. As per the previous answer.

INCORRECT: "Redeploy the application in an Auto Scaling group" is incorrect. This would not have a positive effect and may spread the instances across AZs.

References:

https://docs.aws.amazon.com/AWSEC2/latest/UserGuide/placement-groups.html

Save time with our exam-specific cheat sheets:

https://digitalcloud.training/certification-training/aws-certified-sysops-administrator-associate/amazon-ec2-placement-groups/

QUESTION 57

A company manages Amazon EC2 instances across several AWS Regions. A CloudOps Administrator has been tasked with ensuring that all instances are appropriately tagged.

What is the MOST operationally efficient way to identify tagged and untagged EC2 instances?

1. Create a tag-based resource group in AWS Resource Groups and choose a resource type of AWS::EC2::Instance.
2. Generate a cost and usage report in AWS Cost Explorer, choose a service type of EC2-Instances and filter by tag.
3. Use Cost Explorer. Choose a service type of EC2-Instances, and group by Resource.
4. Use Tag Editor in AWS Resource Groups. Select all Regions and choose a resource type of AWS::EC2::Instance.
5. Enable AWS Organizations and create a tag policy. Use Tag Policies in AWS Resource Groups to generate a compliance report.

Answer: 3

Explanation:

The most operationally efficient approach is to use tag editor to list the EC2 instances across all Regions. The output will show both tagged and untagged resources.

CORRECT: "Use Tag Editor in AWS Resource Groups. Select all Regions and choose a resource type of AWS::EC2::Instance" is the correct answer.

INCORRECT: "Enable AWS Organizations and create a tag policy. Use Tag Policies in AWS Resource Groups to generate a compliance report" is incorrect. This approach requires implementing a tag policy first which is overkill when the administrator simply needs to generate a status report.

INCORRECT: "Generate a cost and usage report in AWS Cost Explorer, choose a service type of EC2-Instances and filter by tag" is incorrect. This will not show tagged and untagged resources and will only display costs in the results.

INCORRECT: "Create a tag-based resource group in AWS Resource Groups and choose a resource type of AWS::EC2::Instance" is incorrect. This will simply group instances by tag.

References:

https://docs.aws.amazon.com/ARG/latest/userguide/find-resources-to-tag.html

QUESTION 58

A company is using AWS Organizations with multiple AWS accounts. The company has purchases Reserved Instances (RIs) and wants to ensure that each member account only receives discounts associated with RIs they own and not for RIs owned by other accounts.

Which solution will meet these requirements?

1. Purchase RIs in individual member accounts. Disable RI discount sharing in the management account.
2. Purchase RIs in individual member accounts. Disable RI discount sharing in the member accounts.
3. Purchase RIs in the management account. Disable RI discount sharing in the management account.
4. Purchase RIs in the management account. Disable RI discount sharing in the member accounts.

Answer: 1

Explanation:

For billing purposes, the consolidated billing feature of AWS Organizations treats all the accounts in the organization as one account. This means that all accounts in the organization can receive the hourly cost benefit of Reserved Instances that are purchased by any other account.

However, RIs can be purchased in individual member accounts and those accounts receive the discount first. To ensure that discounts are not shared with other accounts in the organization you can turn off Reserved Instance discount sharing on the **Preferences** page on the Billing and Cost Management console.

This means that RIs and Savings Plans discounts aren't shared between any accounts that have sharing turned off.

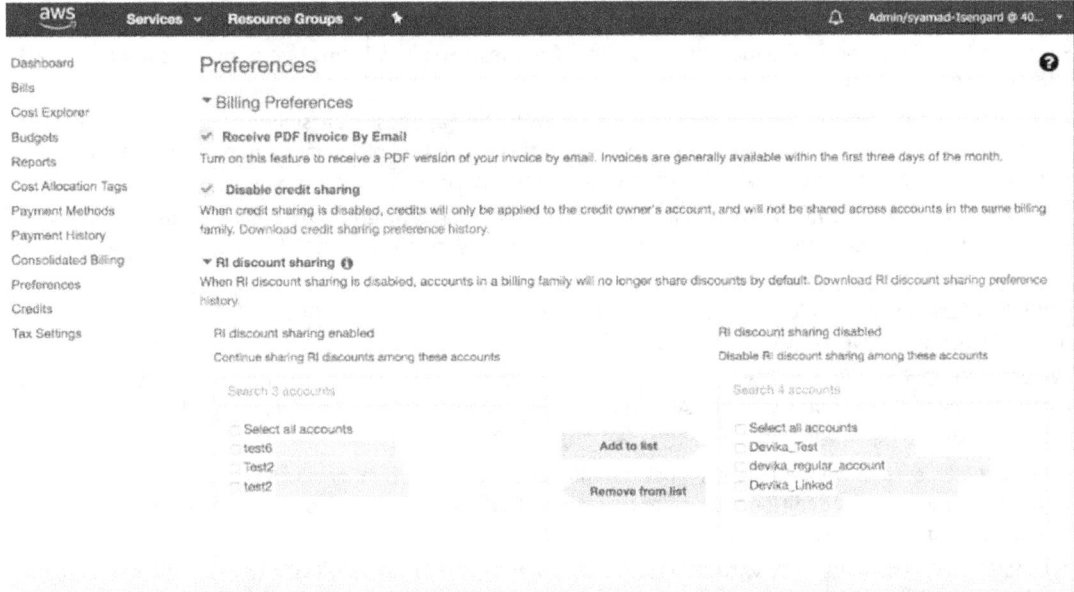

CORRECT: "Purchase RIs in individual member accounts. Disable RI discount sharing in the management account" is the correct answer.

INCORRECT: "Purchase RIs in individual member accounts. Disable RI discount sharing in the member accounts" is incorrect. Discount sharing is disabled in the management account.

INCORRECT: "Purchase RIs in the management account. Disable RI discount sharing in the management account" is incorrect. The RIs should be purchased in the member accounts otherwise they will not be accessible once discount sharing is disabled.

INCORRECT: "Purchase RIs in the management account. Disable RI discount sharing in the member accounts" is incorrect. As above, the purchase should be in member accounts and disabling sharing should be configured in the management account.

References:

https://docs.aws.amazon.com/awsaccountbilling/latest/aboutv2/ri-behavior.html

Save time with our exam-specific cheat sheets:

https://digitalcloud.training/certification-training/aws-certified-sysops-administrator-associate/aws-organizations/

QUESTION 59

A company has an application deployed behind an internet-facing Application Load Balancer (ALB). A CloudOps Administrator is concerned about DDoS attacks and wants to use AWS WAF to implement rate limiting for the ALB.

Which solution will meet these requirements?

1. Create a web ACL with a block default action. Create a rate-based rule to allow the matching traffic. Associate the web ACL with the ALB.
2. Create a web ACL with an allow default action. Create a rate-based rule to block the matching traffic. Associate the web ACL with the ALB.
3. Create a web ACL with a block default action. Create a regular rule to allow the matching traffic with an IP match condition. Associate the web ACL with the ALB.
4. Create a web ACL with an allow default action. Create a regular rule to block the matching traffic with an IP match condition. Associate the web ACL with the ALB.

Answer: 1

Explanation:

For a rate-based rule, enter the maximum number of requests to allow in any five-minute period from an IP address that matches the rule's conditions.

When an IP address reaches the rate limit threshold, AWS WAF applies the assigned action (block or count) as quickly as possible, usually within 30 seconds. Once the action is in place, if five minutes pass with no requests from the IP address, AWS WAF resets the counter to zero.

In this case the administrator wants to block the traffic if it exceeds a certain threshold. Therefore, the admin must use a block default action and then create an allow rule with a rate-limit. When the rate-limit is reached the block action happens.

CORRECT: "Create a web ACL with a block default action. Create a rate-based rule to allow the matching traffic. Associate the web ACL with the ALB" is the correct answer.

INCORRECT: "Create a web ACL with an allow default action. Create a rate-based rule to block the matching traffic. Associate the web ACL with the ALB" is incorrect. The default action should be block and the rate-based rule should be an allow rule.

INCORRECT: "Create a web ACL with a block default action. Create a regular rule to allow the matching traffic with an IP match condition. Associate the web ACL with the ALB" is incorrect. A rate-based rule should be used as explained above.

INCORRECT: "Create a web ACL with an allow default action. Create a regular rule to block the matching traffic with an IP match condition. Associate the web ACL with the ALB" is incorrect. A rate-based rule should be used as explained above.

References:

https://docs.aws.amazon.com/waf/latest/developerguide/classic-web-acl-rules-creating.html

Save time with our exam-specific cheat sheets:

https://digitalcloud.training/certification-training/aws-certified-sysops-administrator-associate/aws-waf-and-shield/

QUESTION 60

A CloudOps Administrator reviewed the performance of an Amazon CloudFront distribution and noticed the cache hit ratio was less than 20% causing excessive origin requests. The administrator needs to implement configuration changes to increase the cache hit ratio.

Which combination of changes should the administrator implement? (Select TWO.)

1. Modify the cache behavior settings to ensure only required cookies, query strings, and headers are forwarded.
2. Decrease the origin response timeout to cause more objects to be returned from the cache.
3. Change the viewer protocol policy to redirect HTTP to HTTPS to increase security.
4. Restrict allowed HTTP methods to GET and HEAD to limit the methods forwarded to the origin.
5. Use the Cache-Control max-age directive to increase the time objects remain in the cache.

Answer: 1,5

Explanation:

You can improve performance by increasing the proportion of your viewer requests that are served directly from the CloudFront cache instead of going to your origin servers for content. This is known as improving the cache hit ratio. There are several methods of achieving a higher cache hit ratio.

These include:

- Specifying how long CloudFront caches your objects
- Using Origin Shield
- Caching based on query string parameters
- Caching based on cookie values
- Caching based on request headers
- Remove Accept-Encoding header when compression is not needed
- Serving media content by using HTTP

Each of these methods is described in more detail in the AWS article linked below.

CORRECT: "Modify the cache behavior settings to ensure only required cookies, query strings, and headers are forwarded" is a correct answer.

CORRECT: "Use the Cache-Control max-age directive to increase the time objects remain in the cache" is also a correct answer.

INCORRECT: "Decrease the origin response timeout to cause more objects to be returned from the cache" is incorrect. This will not affect the cache hit ratio, it affects communications between CloudFront and the origin.

INCORRECT: "Change the viewer protocol policy to redirect HTTP to HTTPS to increase security" is incorrect. Improving security is not a requirement of the question.

INCORRECT: "Restrict allowed HTTP methods to GET and HEAD to limit the methods forwarded to the origin" is incorrect. This will affect the methods forwarded to the origin but will not affect the objects stored in the cache.

References:

https://docs.aws.amazon.com/AmazonCloudFront/latest/DeveloperGuide/cache-hit-ratio.html

Save time with our exam-specific cheat sheets:

https://digitalcloud.training/certification-training/aws-certified-sysops-administrator-associate/amazon-cloudfront/

QUESTION 61

A company uses third-party software to collect a large volume of application log files and store them in an Amazon S3 bucket. The company needs a fully managed service to search and analyze the log files and visualize the data using Kibana.

Which solution should the company use?

1. Create an Amazon Kinesis Data Firehose delivery stream to ingest data from the S3 bucket and stream it to the Elasticsearch domain.
2. Create an Amazon Elasticsearch cluster and use AWS Lambda to process the data from the S3 bucket and stream it to the Elasticsearch domain.
3. Create an Amazon DynamoDB table. Use an AWS Lambda function to load data from the S3 bucket to the table.
4. Create Elasticsearch cluster on Amazon EC2 instances and use AWS Lambda to process the data from the S3 bucket and stream it to the Elasticsearch domain.

Answer: 2

Explanation:

Amazon Elasticsearch Service is a fully managed service that makes it easy for you to deploy, secure, and run Elasticsearch cost effectively at scale.

You can load streaming data into your Amazon ES domain from many different sources. Some sources, like Amazon Kinesis Data Firehose and Amazon CloudWatch Logs, have built-in support for Amazon ES.

Others, like Amazon S3, Amazon Kinesis Data Streams, and Amazon DynamoDB, use AWS Lambda functions as event handlers. The Lambda functions respond to new data by processing it and streaming it to your domain.

CORRECT: "Create an Amazon Elasticsearch cluster and use AWS Lambda to process the data from the S3 bucket and stream it to the Elasticsearch domain" is the correct answer.

INCORRECT: "Create an Amazon Kinesis Data Firehose delivery stream to ingest data from the S3 bucket and stream it to the Elasticsearch domain" is incorrect. You cannot stream directly from an Amazon S3 bucket as it is not a supported source for Firehose.

INCORRECT: "Create Elasticsearch cluster on Amazon EC2 instances and use AWS Lambda to process the data from the S3 bucket and stream it to the Elasticsearch domain" is incorrect. This would not be a fully managed solution as you would need to build and manage the Elasticsearch cluster manually.

INCORRECT: "Create an Amazon DynamoDB table. Use an AWS Lambda function to load data from the S3 bucket to the table" is incorrect. DynamoDB is not suitable for this workload and does not support analysis of the data or using Kibana for data visualization.

References:

https://docs.aws.amazon.com/elasticsearch-service/latest/developerguide/es-aws-integrations.html#es-aws-integrations-s3-lambda-es

QUESTION 62

A CloudOps Administrator has deployed an application using an AWS CloudFormation stack set across multiple AWS accounts and Regions. The administrator plans to deploy and updated template and wants to test the update in subset of the accounts and Regions before rolling it out to the entire stack set.

How can the administrator implement the test update?

1. Create a nested stack to deploy the update.
2. Use a change set for the stack set to test the update.
3. Update the stack set and select a single account and Region.
4. Create a separate stack set to test the update.

Answer: 4

Explanation:

By default, updating a stack set updates all stack instances. If you have 20 accounts each in two regions, you will have 40 stack instances, and all will be updated when you update the stack set.

For stack sets with many stack instances, AWS recommends that to test the updated version of a template, you selectively update the stack instances in a few test accounts before updating all stack instances.

To get more granular control over updating individual stacks within your stack set, plan to create multiple stack sets.

CORRECT: "Create a separate stack set to test the update" is the correct answer.

INCORRECT: "Create a nested stack to deploy the update" is incorrect. A nested stack will not assist with deploying an updated template to a subset of accounts and Regions in a stack set.

INCORRECT: "Use a change set for the stack set to test the update" is incorrect. You can only preview changes with a change set, and you cannot select individual accounts and Regions within a stack set.

INCORRECT: "Update the stack set and select a single account and Region" is incorrect. As per the explanation above you can only deploy updates to the entire stack set.

References:

https://docs.aws.amazon.com/AWSCloudFormation/latest/UserGuide/stacksets-bestpractices.html

Save time with our exam-specific cheat sheets:

https://digitalcloud.training/certification-training/aws-certified-sysops-administrator-associate/aws-cloudformation/

QUESTION 63

A CloudOps Administrator has created an Amazon CloudFront distribution that uses an Amazon S3 bucket as the origin. The S3 static website endpoint is used as the origin domain name.

When testing access the administrator receives a 403 Access Denied message.

Which action should resolve this issue?

1. Remove the default bucket policy that denies read access to the bucket.
2. Ensure default encryption using the Amazon S3-managed keys.
3. Create a bucket policy that allows public read access for all objects in the bucket.
4. Create a bucket policy that allows public read access to the bucket.

Answer: 3

Explanation:

The most likely issue is that the administrator has not configured public access for the objects in the S3 bucket. A distribution using a website endpoint supports only publicly accessible content.

The administrator can grant public access to the object in one of the following ways:

- Create a bucket policy that allows public read access for all objects in the bucket.
- Use the Amazon S3 console to allow public read access for the object.

See the AWS article linked below for more information on possible issues.

CORRECT: "Create a bucket policy that allows public read access for all objects in the bucket" is the correct answer.

INCORRECT: "Create a bucket policy that allows public read access to the bucket" is incorrect. The objects rather than the bucket must have public access enabled.

INCORRECT: "Remove the default bucket policy that denies read access to the bucket" is incorrect. There is no default bucket policy denying read access. There is a configuration setting that disables public access but it's not a policy.

INCORRECT: "Ensure default encryption using the Amazon S3-managed keys" is incorrect. It's fine to use SSE-S3 for encrypting the objects (you can't use KMS keys in this scenario).

References:

https://aws.amazon.com/premiumsupport/knowledge-center/s3-website-cloudfront-error-403/

Save time with our exam-specific cheat sheets:

https://digitalcloud.training/certification-training/aws-certified-sysops-administrator-associate/amazon-cloudfront/

QUESTION 64

A company uses AWS Organizations with consolidated billing. A CloudOps Administrator would like to be alerted if the total billing for all accounts within the organization exceeds a specific threshold.

How can the administrator set this up?

1. Enable the Receive Billing Alerts preference in the payer account and setup a billing alarm in Amazon CloudWatch. Use SNS to send a notification based on the alarm.
2. Enable the Receive Billing Alerts preference in each member account and setup a billing alarm in Amazon CloudWatch in the payer account. Use SNS to send a notification based on the alarm.
3. Enable the Receive Billing Alerts preference in the payer account and setup a billing alarm in AWS Config. Use SNS to send a notification based on the alarm.
4. Enable the Receive Billing Alerts preference in each member account and setup a billing alarm in AWS Config in the payer account. Use SNS to send a notification based on the alarm.

Answer: 1

Explanation:

You can monitor your estimated AWS charges by using Amazon CloudWatch. When you enable the monitoring of estimated charges for your AWS account, the estimated charges are calculated and sent several times daily to CloudWatch as metric data.

In a consolidated billing account, member linked account metrics are captured only if the payer account enables the **Receive Billing Alerts** preference. You can then use an Amazon SNS topic to send a notification when the alarm is in ALARM state.

CORRECT: "Enable the Receive Billing Alerts preference in the payer account and setup a billing alarm in Amazon CloudWatch. Use SNS to send a notification based on the alarm" is the correct answer.

INCORRECT: "Enable the Receive Billing Alerts preference in each member account and setup a billing alarm in Amazon CloudWatch in the payer account. Use SNS to send a notification based on the alarm" is incorrect. Both configuration changes should be made in the payer account.

INCORRECT: "Enable the Receive Billing Alerts preference in the payer account and setup a billing alarm in AWS Config. Use SNS to send a notification based on the alarm" is incorrect. Amazon CloudWatch should be used for the billing alarm rather than AWS Config.

INCORRECT: "Enable the Receive Billing Alerts preference in each member account and setup a billing alarm in AWS Config in the payer account. Use SNS to send a notification based on the alarm" is incorrect. Amazon CloudWatch should be used for the billing alarm rather than AWS Config.

References:

https://docs.aws.amazon.com/AmazonCloudWatch/latest/monitoring/monitor_estimated_charges_with_cloudwatch.html

Save time with our exam-specific cheat sheets:

https://digitalcloud.training/certification-training/aws-certified-sysops-administrator-associate/amazon-cloudwatch/

QUESTION 65

A company wants to use an AWS IAM role with a SAML 2.0-compliant identity provider (IdP) and AWS to permit federated users to access the AWS Management Console. The workflow should open the AWS Management Console on behalf of the user.

Which of the following workflow steps should be included?

1. Configure the client to directly call the AssumeRoleWithSAML API.
2. Configure the client to post a SAML assertion and use an AWS SSO endpoint.
3. Configure the client to directly call the AssumeRoleWithWebIdentity API.
4. Configure the client to post a SAML assertion and use an Amazon Cognito endpoint.

Answer: 2

Explanation:
This workflow opens the AWS Management Console on behalf of the user. This requires the use of the AWS SSO endpoint instead of directly calling the AssumeRoleWithSAML API. The endpoint calls the API for the user and returns a URL that automatically redirects the user's browser to the AWS Management Console.

The full workflow is depicted below:

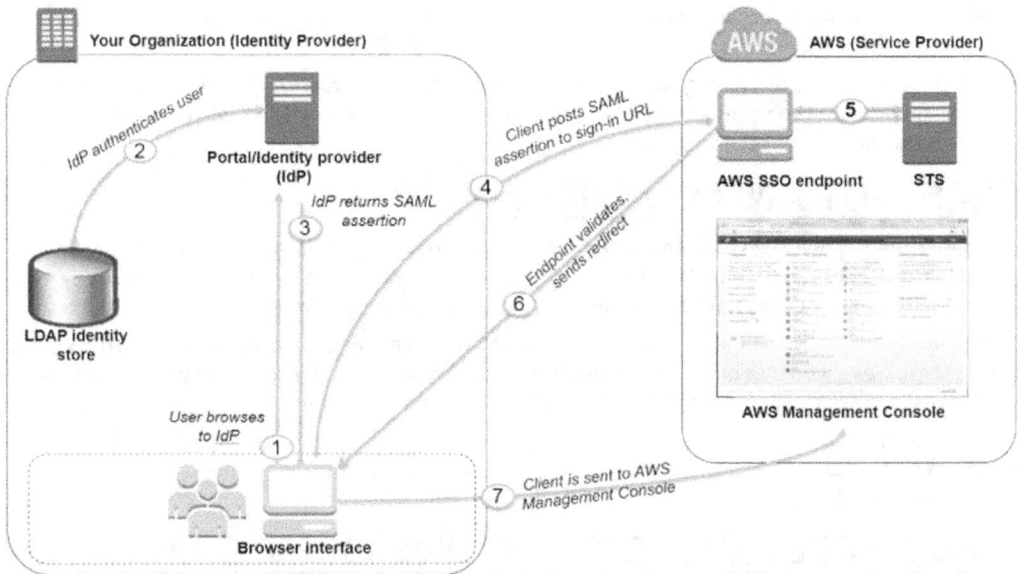

CORRECT: "Configure the client to post a SAML assertion and use an AWS SSO endpoint" is the correct answer.

INCORRECT: "Configure the client to directly call the AssumeRoleWithSAML API" is incorrect. Please refer to the explanation above.

INCORRECT: "Configure the client to directly call the AssumeRoleWithWebIdentity API" is incorrect. This would be used when the user has been authenticated in a mobile or web application with a web identity provider such as Amazon Cognito, Login with Amazon, Facebook, or Google.

INCORRECT: "Configure the client to post a SAML assertion and use an Amazon Cognito endpoint" is incorrect. AWS SSO should be used rather than Cognito which would be used with web identity federation.

References:

https://docs.aws.amazon.com/IAM/latest/UserGuide/id_roles_providers_enable-console-saml.html

Save time with our exam-specific cheat sheets:

https://digitalcloud.training/certification-training/aws-certified-sysops-administrator-associate/aws-iam/

CONCLUSION

Congratulations on completing these exam-style practice tests! We hope these high-quality questions, along with their detailed explanations, have equipped you with the knowledge and confidence to tackle the **AWS CloudOps Engineer Associate** exam.

The **SOA-C03** exam covers a broad set of technologies – so it's key to be fully prepared to handle any question that comes up in your exam.

To maximize your chances of success, we recommend reviewing these practice questions thoroughly and retaking these tests until you consistently achieve a score of 80% or higher - that's when you're ready to sit the exam and achieve a great score!

REACH OUT AND CONNECT

We're committed to providing you with a 5-star learning experience. If something isn't meeting your expectations, don't hesitate to email us at support@digitalcloud.training. We're here to address any questions or concerns you may have and ensure you get the most value from these training resources.

The AWS platform is evolving quickly, and the exam tracks these changes, typically with a 6-month delay. To stay up to date, we rely on feedback from students like you. If you encounter topics on your exam that weren't covered in our training materials, we'd greatly appreciate your input.

Please share your feedback using this form:https://digitalcloud.training/student-feedback/. Your feedback is invaluable in helping us continuously improve our AWS training resources. Thank you for helping us make these materials even better

BONUS: FREE ACCESS TO ONLINE EXAM SIMULATOR

We're excited to offer **FREE Access** to the **Exam Simulator** on the Digital Cloud Training website! This simulator randomly selects 65 questions from a pool of exam-style questions, mimicking the real AWS exam. The practice exam matches the format, style, time limit, and passing score of the official AWS exam.

To unlock FREE access to all 500 Practice Questions, simply send us a **screenshot of your review on Amazon** to info@digitalcloud.training with "**SYSOPSSIM**" in the subject line. You'll get free access to our Online Exam Simulator within 48 hours. If you experience any issues with your review, please don't hesitate to reach out - we're here to help!

Your reviews not only help us improve our courses but also guide fellow AWS students in making informed decisions. We value every honest review and deeply appreciate your support. You can leave a review anytime at amazon.com/ryp or your local Amazon store (e.g., amazon.co.uk/ryp).

Best wishes for your AWS certification journey!

LIVE BOOTCAMPS AND ON-DEMAND TRAINING

Digital Cloud Training offers a wide range of training options to help students prepare for AWS certification exams and build job-ready cloud skills. Below is an overview of the available learning options.

CLOUD MASTERY BOOTCAMP (VIRTUAL CLASSROOM)

The Cloud Mastery Bootcamp is Digital Cloud Training's flagship program, designed to help you build the in-demand cloud skills needed to excel in today's competitive cloud industry. This isn't just another training - it's a structured path toward securing a high-paying, future-proof career in cloud computing - guaranteed!

This hands-on program prepares learners to highly paid cloud roles, like Cloud Engineer, DevOps Engineer, or Solutions Architect. Whether you're just beginning your cloud journey or looking to deepen your expertise, the Cloud Mastery Bootcamp provides everything you need to succeed:

- **Customized Learning Path**: Upon enrollment, we'll create a personalized learning path tailored to your skills and career goals, helping you get the most from this 12-month program.
- **Gain Hands-On Experience:** Build practical, job-ready skills by working on real-world projects with direct access to expert instructors during live training sessions (via zoom).
- **Earn Recognized Certifications**: Prepare for in-demand cloud certifications like AWS Cloud Practitioner, AWS AI Practitioner, AWS Solutions Architect, AWS Developer, AWS CloudOps Engineer or Terraform Associate.
- **Comprehensive Support**: Benefit from personalized mentoring, career coaching, and ongoing guidance from our dedicated support team to help you stay motivated and on track.
- **Launch Your Cloud Career**: Leverage your new skills, experience, and certifications to secure a high-paying job in cloud computing.

With no specific prerequisites, this program is accessible to anyone ready to begin or advance their career in the cloud.

Secure your next-level cloud job with the Cloud Mastery Bootcamp: https://digitalcloud.training/cloud-mastery-bootcamp/

ON-DEMAND / SELF-PACED AWS TRAINING

Prepare for your next AWS certification with flexible, cost-effective, self-paced training. Our on-demand courses include video lessons, practice exams, and downloadable training notes for offline study.

A single subscription gives you unlimited access to our entire training library, along with early access to new content and updates. Whether you select a monthly plan for full flexibility or a 12-month option to maximize savings, you'll have everything you need to build your cloud expertise at your own pace.

Explore our full library of AWS training courses: https://digitalcloud.training/plans/

ABOUT THE AUTHOR

Neal Davis is the founder of Digital Cloud Training, an AWS Cloud Solutions Architect and a highly successful IT instructor. With over two decades of experience in the cloud computing industry, Neal is a recognized expert in solutions architecture.

In 2018, Neal launched Digital Cloud Training with the mission to bring the highest quality AWS learning resources to the market. His passion for teaching technology is matched by his commitment to helping learners achieve their cloud career goals.

Digital Cloud Training offers a range of top-quality training resources to help students build job-ready cloud skills – including live bootcamps and on-demand training courses.

By choosing Digital Cloud Training, you'll gain the skills, certifications, and real-world experience that will help you excel in the cloud industry and advance your career.

Join the growing AWS Community of more than 1,000,000 happy learners who have enrolled in Digital Cloud Training courses.

To learn more, visit: http://digitalcloud.training/

CONNECT WITH US ON SOCIAL MEDIA

Stay updated and engage with us on your favorite platforms.

All Links available on https://digitalcloud.training/about-neal-davis-and-digital-cloud-training/

 digitalcloud.training

 youtube.com/c/digitalcloudtraining

 facebook.com/digitalcloudtraining

 Twitter / X @digitalcloudt

 linkedin.com/company/digitalcloudtraining

 Instagram @digitalcloudtraining